AN INTRODUCTION TO THE ECONOMICS OF INFORMATION

Second Edition

AN INTRODUCTION TO THE ECONOMICS OF INFORMATION

INCENTIVES AND CONTRACTS

Second Edition

Inés Macho-Stadler

J. David Pérez-Castrillo

Translated by Richard Watt

OXFORD
UNIVERSITY PRESS

Great Clarendon Street, Oxford OX2 6DP

Oxford University Press is a department of the University of Oxford.
It furthers the University's objective of excellence in research, scholarship,
and education by publishing worldwide in

Oxford New York

Auckland Bangkok Buenos Aires Cape Town Chennai
Dar es Salaam Delhi Hong Kong Istanbul Karachi Kolkata
Kuala Lumpur Madrid Melbourne Mexico City Mumbai Nairobi
São Paulo Shanghai Taipei Tokyo Toronto

Oxford is a registered trade mark of Oxford University Press
in the UK and in certain other countries

Published in the United States
by Oxford University Press Inc., New York

First edition published 1997
Second edition published 2001

British Library Cataloguing in Publication Data

Data available

Library of Congress Cataloging in Publication Data

Data available

ISBN 0-19-924327-1 (hbk.)
ISBN 0-19-924325-5 (pbk.)

10 9 8 7 6 5

Printed in Great Britain
on acid-free paper by
Biddles Ltd., Guildford and King's Lynn

To our parents

PREFACE

The *economics of information* is possibly the area of economic theory that has evolved most over the past fifteen years. Developed in parallel with the new economics of Industrial Organization, its importance and applications have grown spectacularly. Its objective is to study the situations in which agents attempt to overcome their ignorance about some relevant information by taking decisions designed to acquire new information or to avoid some of the costs of their ignorance. When the information is asymmetrically distributed among agents, these decisions involve the designing of *contracts* intended to provide *incentives* and/or to induce the revelation of private information.

This book considers situations in which asymmetric information exists in a contractual relationship, that is to say, in which one participant knows something that another doesn't. We analyse three important themes: *moral hazard*, *adverse selection*, and *signalling*. The models in which these themes are studied allow us to explain a large number of economic situations, even though we do not analyse all the economic themes related to information. Our choice is based on the idea of looking at only a few themes but in enough depth for our readers to acquire a certain independence.

The book is organized in the following way. There are five chapters, the last three being dedicated to the above-mentioned themes. In Chapter 2 we present the symmetric information situation, the reference model, which serves as a necessary starting-point to understand the effects of each of the informational problems that follow. This chapter presents a base model in which the different problems are analysed. The homogeneous nature of this model has the advantage of allowing the results to be compared in a simple and natural way. The book begins with an introduction, in which the themes to be studied are presented together with several examples that show how the economics of information can be of interest.

Besides the examples contained in the principal text, each chapter has detailed applications of the models and their results. In these supplements, we present simple models with clear economic messages relating to interesting, and current themes (finance, insurance, technology transfer, firm regulation, public subsidies, etc.). Often, an application is a simplified version of an article published in a scientific journal and can be read quite independently from the main text of the chapter. This could be useful to those who prefer to begin each theme with a rigorously presented example.

Each chapter also contains exercises of varying difficulty, in order that the student can keep track of his level of learning, as well as serving as a complement to the text. Exercises of particular difficulty are marked with an asterisk. It is never easy to know if the best strategy from an instructor's point of view is to include the solutions to the exercises in the same text or not. Since the exercises are often non-conventional, we have decided to include the solutions at the end of the book. Finally, the more formal aspects of each chapter are relegated to complementary material sections.

The book is designed to be a one-semester undergraduate course, or to be a support text for a doctorate course on the subject. For this reason, we were unable to resist the temptation to include in the three central chapters sections on advanced themes. These sections do not present new models, but rather are designed to be a reading guide that we hope will be useful to the interested reader and that can be ignored for introductory courses.

With respect to the required background knowledge to be able to follow this introductory course on the Economics of Information, students who have done basic courses of maths and micro-economics should find no difficulties in following this book. The text is careful in its treatment of the solutions to constrained maximization problems, but to resolve any doubts on the theory of maximization we include a short appendix on the Kuhn–Tucker method.

ACKNOWLEDGMENTS

This text was born from the lecture notes used during several academic courses at the University of the Basque Country (Euskal Herriko Unibersitatea), and at the Autonomous University of Barcelona (Universitat Autònoma de Barcelona). The comments of the students who worked on preliminary versions of this book have contributed to its enrichment. Their interest in the themes analysed has been the driving force behind the project. The notes became *Introducción a la Economía de la Información*, published by *Ariel Economía* in 1994. *An Introduction to the Economics of Information* is basically the English translation of the Spanish version, with some minor revisions. We are gratetul to Ariel Economía and its editor Marcelo Covián for their help and support, and to Oxford University Press and its editor Andrew Schuller for advice and encouragement.

Many colleagues have collaborated in the improvement of the final version. We would like to thank Paul de Bijl, Fernando Branco, Antonio Cabrales, José

María Da Rocha, María Angeles de Frutos, Pau Olivella, Maite Pastor, Klaus Schmidt, and Joel Sobel. They read earlier versions of the chapters, and gave invaluable critiques and suggestions. We want to extend our acknowledgements to the people to whom we are academically indebted, from professors to co-authors with whom we have collaborated on different projects. Among the former, Salvador Barberà and Roger Guesnerie, deserve special mention.

We would like to acknowledge our debt to our colleague Richard Watt who was of enormous help during the preparation of the English material for this book. Finally, we thank the DGICYT no. PB 92–0590, and Human Capital and Mobility projects ERBCHRXCT no. 920055 and 930297 for financial aid.

Inés Macho-Stadler
David Pérez-Castrillo

Bellaterra, Barcelona
November 1995

CONTENTS

5. Signalling

1

INTRODUCTION

Summary

The economics of information is centred on a fundamental aspect of contractual relationships: the effect on the contractual format when one party has, or will have, an informational advantage over the other. Aside from this characteristic, the only interesting cases are when the participants have opposing objectives. In all our models, one of the participants, the principal, has all the bargaining power.

Different types of models appear when the informational asymmetry arises. We have a moral hazard problem when the informational asymmetry arises after the contract has been signed. There is an adverse selection problem when the agent has relevant private information before the contract is signed. Finally, a signalling situation occurs when the informed party is able to reveal private information via individual behaviour before the agreement is formalized.

1.1 Introduction

It has happened to us all at one time or another, while at a professional office you don't receive the service you expected. Sometimes there are long queues while the employees can be seen happily chatting away to each other, or talking on the phone to friends or relatives about their personal affairs. Often, in such a situation, someone will comment: 'it's obvious that their wages do no depend on how many clients they serve.' Behind these words is a criticism of the lack of incentives that is often present in certain contractual arrangements, such as bureaucratic labour contracts.

In some contracts, the central characteristic appears to be linked to the inclusion or exclusion of incentives. In other cases, the main feature is something else. In fact, the contracts that we can observe in everyday economic life are extremely varied, and hence a valid and interesting question to ask ourselves is exactly which type of contract should go with each particular circumstance.

One particular type of contract that we all may have been interested in at one time or another is that offered by automobile insurance companies. Motor car insurance is of two basic types. The client is generally offered a choice between a contract under which the insurance company pays the entire cost of any claim, and a much cheaper one, called a voluntary excess contract, under which the insurance company is liable only for that part of a claim over and above a stipulated amount. Different types of driver are interested in different types of coverage, and so the company offers various types of policy and lets each client choose the contract that he prefers.

In other cases the contract has other properties. An agreement is offered only to those who comply to certain characteristics, and the payment offered varies according to these characteristics. For example, it is usual to find in the situations vacant section of the newspaper adverts to the effect: 'Recent graduate required for new position in local firm', without actually specifying the degree type. It may seem strange that the employer is only interested in a graduate, rather than in what subject he qualified in, especially as going through the rituals of a university degree does not appear to prepare a person for any particular job.

The preceding situations are examples of those that will be studied in this book. We will be interested in the theory of *contracts under asymmetric information*, a theory that analyses the characteristics of optimal contracts and the variables that influence these characteristics, according to the behaviour and information of the parties to the contract. This will allow us to tackle questions such as: Should the employees of an office be paid a fixed amount, or should they receive some part of the profits of the firm? Or why does an insurance company offer several types of policy, one of which has a voluntary excess clause? Or what is the sense of a situations vacant advert in which the only relevant characteristic is being a graduate, without any reference to a specific subject? The answers to these, and many other questions, depend on the situation at hand. Our objective is to identify the characteristics of the relationship, especially those relevant to the distribution of information that may be important in answering these questions, and to analyse the contract format that should correspond to each particular situation.[1]

In this introduction we will attempt to clarify some of the most important concepts, and to present the type of situation that we intend to analyse. To this end, we begin by presenting the basic elements of the problem.

1.2 The Elements of the Problem

Assume a bilateral relationship in which one party contracts another to carry out some type of action or to take some type of decision. We will refer to the contractor as the *principal*, and the contractee as the *agent*.[2] Both principal and agent could be individuals, institutions, organizations, or decision centres. We could take, as an example, the relationship between the shareholders of a firm (the principal) and the firm's manager (the agent).

The objective of the contract is for the manager to carry out actions on behalf of the principal. In our previous example, the manager is contracted to run the principal's firm. The contract signed by both parties will specify the payments that the principal will pass on to the agent (later on we will consider what these payments will depend on). We shall assume that it is always the principal that designs the contract, and then offers it to the agent, who, after having studied the terms of the contract, must decide whether or not to sign it. The agent will accept the principal's contract whenever the utility obtained from it is greater than the utility that the agent would get from not signing. We

[1] Other books analysing asymmetric information situations, or including chapters on this theme, are e.g. Rasmusen (1987), Laffont (1989), Kreps (1990), Milgrom and Roberts (1992), and Mas-Colell, Whinston, and Green (1995).

[2] We could have used 'contractor' and 'contractee', 'leader' and 'follower', or 'master' and 'mastered', but we have preferred to maintain the terminology that the reader will habitually find in the literature. We also note that, in adherence to a historical custom, we refer to the principal with the feminine pronoun 'she' and to the agent with the masculine 'he'.

refer to this utility level as *reservation utility*. We do not permit that the agent makes a counter offer to the principal, a situation which is known as bilateral bargaining. Hence we are considering situations in which the principal has all the bargaining power. It is the principal who decides on the terms of the relationship, while the agent is limited to the decision of whether or not to take part. In effect, it is as if, when the principal offers a contract to an agent, it is with the comment: 'this is my proposal; take it or leave it.'[3]

If the agent decides not to sign the contract, the relationship does not take place, thus ending the problem. If, on the other hand, the agent does accept the offer, then according to the terms of the agreement, he must carry out the actions for which he has been contracted. In the example of the relationship between shareholders and manager, the latter must decide the firm's strategy, which implies a certain effort dedicated to different tasks and projects.

Up to now, the situation we are considering has the following features:

(i) The principal designs the contract, or set of contracts, that she will offer to the agent.

(ii) The agent accepts the contract if he so desires, that is if the contract guarantees him greater expected utility than the other opportunities available to him.

(iii) The agent carries out an action or effort on behalf of the principal.

From these elements, it can be seen that *the agent's objectives are in conflict with those of the principal.* A cost for one is revenue for the other: the wage paid is revenue for the agent and a cost for the principal, while the effort of the agent favours the principal but is costly for the agent. Soon we will consider the role of conflict in our models; it is, after all, one of the fundamental ingredients.

First, we will discuss exactly what is meant by a *contract*. A contract is a reliable promise by both parties, in which the obligations of each, for all possible contingencies, are specified. In particular, it includes the payment mechanism under which the agent will be compensated for his effort. It is a very important point that a contract can only be based on *verifiable variables*. In other words, the terms of the contract can only depend on variables that can be checked by an independent arbitrator, since this guarantees the fulfilment of the contract. The use of verifiable variables in the contract allows either of the parties to present a case before a court of law with proof of breach of contract in order to demand that the contract be fulfilled. How about contracts based on non-

[3] This, of course, does not mean that bargaining situations cannot be considered. There may be bargaining over the share that the agent receives, but we will be concerned exclusively with the design of the contract. The idea is that the participants have already arrived at an agreement (in some previous period, not studied here) and the principal has the authority to contract. Alternatively, the agent's payment may be determined by his reservation utility.

verifiable information? In this case it is difficult to rely on an independent arbitrator (for example, a court of law) to resolve any conflict that may arise, since the arbitrator will be unable to prove whether what the parties are alleging is true or not. Therefore, since all parties know that arbitration is impossible, they will have incentives to breach the terms of the contract. It is in anticipation of this situation that neither party will be prepared to sign such a contract, since it will not be respected and there will be no compensation for breach of contract.

So far, the very word that would appear to justify this book, *information*, has hardly been used at all. Information is related to the set of variables that are verifiable in a contractual relationship. In order to understand exactly how this new aspect is brought into play, let us return to the case of the shareholders in a firm and the manager that they contract. The relationship is established so that the manager, via his personal actions and decisions, defends the interests of the shareholders. Obviously the shareholders would prefer to contract the best manager, even if this is somewhat more expensive, in order to obtain the best possible results. However, clearly the shareholders are not in a good position to evaluate, or control, the decisions of the managers of their firms. This implies that it becomes impossible for the contract to be based on the manager's behaviour, since this is not a verifiable variable. On top of this, the shareholders do not have perfect information regarding the characteristics of the manager hired, either on an individual or group behaviour level. Hence it is also difficult to establish contractual terms that depend on certain competence or quality measures of the agents. Such informational advantages give the managers a certain leeway in order to enhance their own utility instead of that of the shareholders.

The objective of this book is to analyse situations in which a contract is contemplated under conditions of asymmetric information, that is, one party knows certain relevant things of which the other party is ignorant. We will analyse relationships between two individuals or institutions in which one of the participants has an informational advantage over the other, and the individual objectives are in conflict. The reason for mixing asymmetric information and conflict of interests is because if the contracting parties have common interests, then all relevant information will be automatically revealed, and so any asymmetry in information becomes irrelevant.

The theory is divided into three main themes: *moral hazard*, *adverse selection*,[4] and *signalling*. In moral hazard situations, the principal cannot observe the agent's behaviour (actions or decisions). In this case, the solution involves the internalizing of incentives, via the contract terms. An adverse selection

[4] The terms moral hazard and adverse selection come from the insurance literature.

situation appears when, previous to the signing of the contract, the agent is aware of some relevant information of which the principal is ignorant. The solution to this problem involves offering several alternative contracts, and the agent's choice between these alternatives reveals his private information. Finally, signalling models are related to situations in which one of the parties knows some important information, which is signalled to the other party via the informed participant's behaviour.

Returning to the examples presented earlier in the introduction to this chapter, even though it is somewhat premature to assume the reader is capable of dividing them into the correct informational category, we do point out that each one corresponds to one of the themes discussed in the previous paragraph (in the same order). In order better to understand the differences between these themes (aside from the identification of the participants), it is convenient to be a little more rigorous in the definitions, thereby establishing more exact structures.

1.3 The Intertemporal Development of the Relationship and Reference Framework

Most of the models to be analysed in this book can be presented in a common framework, which makes easier an understanding of their characteristics as well as a comparison of the conclusions reached.

The *reference* or *benchmark model* which we use assumes that both principal and agent have *the same information throughout the relationship*. That is, the principal and the agent share common information as to all relevant characteristics and variables, and the agent's effort is verifiable, so that it is possible for the principal to check that the agent fulfils his tasks. This 'control' situation, presented in Chapter 2, points out the way in which asymmetric information as to the form of the contract and other relevant characteristics affects the relationship.

In the reference situation, the principal and the agent are in no doubt as to who is signing the contract. The principal offers a different form of contract to each possible agent type (depending on abilities, knowledge, behaviour, etc.), and in the same way, each agent type will accept different contract formats, depending on which principal offers the contract, and the tasks for which he is being contracted. Since the agent's effort and the final result of the relationship are observable, it is possible to introduce these variables explicitly into the terms of the contract.

It is worth while pointing out that we do not assume that both parties to the contract are perfectly informed as to all aspects of the relationship (perfect and symmetric information), but rather that both are in the same informational position (symmetric, but possibly imperfect, information). Hence we do not exclude the possibility that there are random elements affecting the relationship. In order to represent the existence of a random variable, we shall say (following the classic game-theory terminology) that Nature is deciding something.

The order of moves of the benchmark game is summarized in Figure 1.1, where N represents Nature, P represents the principal, and A represents the agent.

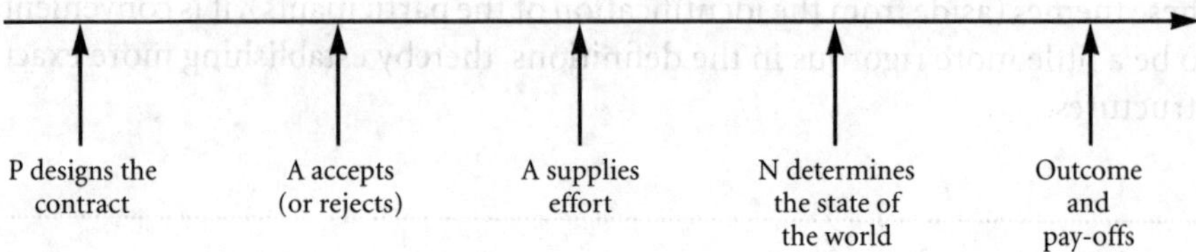
P designs the contract
A accepts (or rejects)
A supplies effort
N determines the state of the world
Outcome and pay-offs

Fig. 1.1

This representation of the game underlines the sequentiality of the decisions. Given this sequentiality, the solution concept that we apply is that of *subgame perfect equilibrium.*[5] This solution concept requires that at each point in time each player chooses an optimal strategy, given the situation which has been reached, and assuming that all other players will do likewise. In this way, the agent will offer the effort that maximizes his expected utility given that he has accepted the contract proposed by the principal; previous to this, and anticipating his own decision with regard to effort, the agent decides whether or not to accept the contract; the first to act is the principal, who, having calculated the future behaviour of the agent for each possible contract format, offers that format which maximizes her own expected utility.

In a game structure such as that shown in Figure 1.1, it is easy to see that in contractual relationships there are many reasons to expect that one of the parties may have more information than the other as to some relevant aspect of the relationship. However, different situations are characterized by different sources or forms of informational asymmetries. The correct classification of asymmetric information problems is important since it permits the identification of the influence of the nature of the distribution of information on the contract format, or on other aspects of the relationship.

[5] In situations in which there is incomplete information the appropriate solution concept is the perfect Bayesian equilibrium. The difference between them will be clear later. For a discussion on equilibrium concepts, see e.g. chap. 11 Tirole (1988*b*) and Fudenberg and Tirole (1991).

1.4 Types of Asymmetric Information Problems

We shall now present the different characteristics of the asymmetric information problems which we will be discussing throughout the book.

1.4.1 Moral hazard

A moral hazard problem exists when *the agent's action is not verifiable*, or when *the agent receives private information after the relationship has been initiated*. In moral hazard problems the participants have the same information when the relationship is established, and the informational asymmetry arises from the fact that, once the contract has been signed, the principal cannot observe (or cannot verify) the action (or the effort) of the agent, or at least, the principal cannot perfectly control the action.

The classic way of modelling this type of situation is to assume that the agent's effort, offered after the contract has been signed, is not verifiable, and so this variable cannot be explicitly included in the terms of the contract. Hence the agent's pay-off cannot depend on the effort that he offers, or that he has been contracted to offer. The time-schedule of the game corresponding to a situation of moral hazard in which the agent's effort is not verifiable is represented in Figure 1.2.

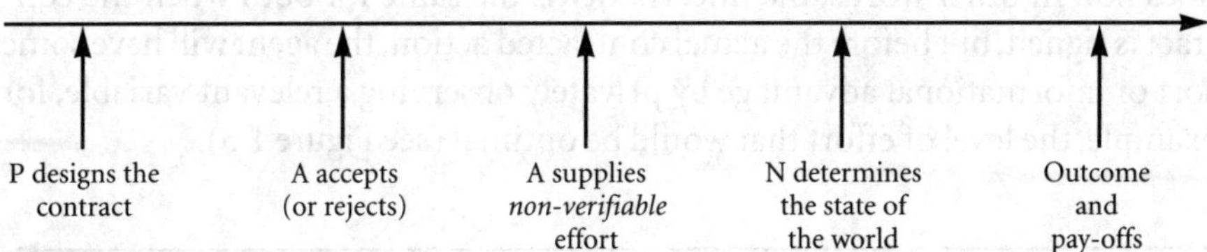
P designs the contract
A accepts (or rejects)
A supplies *non-verifiable* effort
N determines the state of the world
Outcome and pay-offs

Fig. 1.2

It is easy to imagine labour market situations in which, even though the worker's (the agent's) result is verifiable—for example, the number of units produced or sold—his effort is not verifiable for the principal. Consider a publishing firm that contracts a door-to-door salesman to sell encyclopaedias. The salesman will accept the contract offered if it guarantees him at least the same expected utility as the next best opportunity in the market. The result of the relationship, in this case, is the number of encyclopaedias sold. Although the number of orders that the salesman gets is obviously a verifiable variable, his effort is extremely difficult to measure. In fact, even the time dedicated to selling encyclopaedias is uncontrollable. Hence the publishing firm cannot link the salesman's wage directly to his effort.

This type of problem requires us to rethink the traditional framework in which labour (measured in hours) is exchanged for a fixed wage. Some labour markets, like the market for encyclopaedia salesmen, do not function in the traditional manner. Another example is that of a laboratory or research centre (the principal) who contracts a researcher to work on a certain project. It would appear that it is not optimal for the laboratory to pay a fixed wage in exchange for a certain number of hours on the job. It is difficult for the principal to distinguish between a researcher who is thinking about how to push the project through, and a researcher who is thinking about how to organize his weekend fishing trip! It is precisely this difficulty in controlling effort inputs, together with the inherent uncertainty in any research project, that generates a different type of labour market problem that the economics of information can tackle.

Traditional examples of moral hazard corresponding to Figure 1.2 come from the insurance sector. Insurance companies want the policyholder to try to avoid accidents: for example driving in a safe way or minimizing losses in case of a problem. However, once a person is insured he has an incentive to change his behaviour by taking less precautions than before.

Not all moral hazard problems correspond to the time-schedule in Figure 1.2. Some problems within this category are due to an informational asymmetry that arises when, before carrying out the effort for which he has been contracted, the agent observes the result of Nature's decision but the principal does not. In other words, the uncertainty is the same for both when the contract is signed, but before the actual contracted action, the agent will have some sort of informational advantage by privately observing a relevant variable, for example, the level of effort that would be optimal (see Figure 1.3).

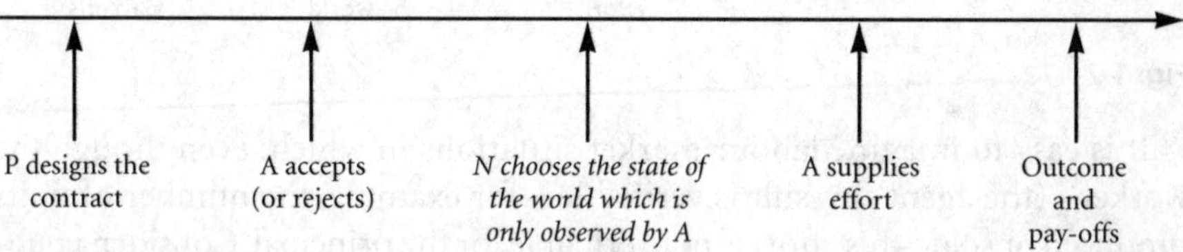
P designs the contract
A accepts (or rejects)
N chooses the state of the world which is only observed by A
A supplies effort
Outcome and pay-offs

Fig. 1.3

This time-schedule corresponds, for example, to a firm that hires an import-export agent to represent its product overseas. In some cases, the firm has little information on other existing products in the country, the state of the markets, etc. These things all are important for the determination of the best strategy to use to successfully introduce the new product. However, although the agent also doesn't know these things when he signs the contract, he can learn them once he begins to work on the introduction of the product. The principal may be able to observe the strategy adopted by the agent, but will not be able to evaluate whether or not the agent's actions with respect to the product were the most convenient, given the market characteristics.

There are many other economic situations in which a moral hazard problem is present. We will present the benchmark model of these problems in Chapter 3, analysing the situation of unobservable effort (that is to say, that situation represented in Figure 1.2), which is so often considered in the literature.[6]

1.4.2 Adverse selection

An adverse selection problem appears when *the agent holds private information before the relationship is begun.* In this case, the principal can verify the agent's behaviour, but the optimal decision, or the cost of this decision, depends on the agent's type, that is, on certain characteristics of the production process of which the agent is the only informed party. When the informational asymmetry concerns personal characteristics of the agent, then the principal knows that the agent could be any one of several different types between which she cannot distinguish. This situation can be modelled by assuming that Nature plays first, choosing the agent's type (see Figure 1.4). It is a game with asymmetric information previous to the signing of the contract.

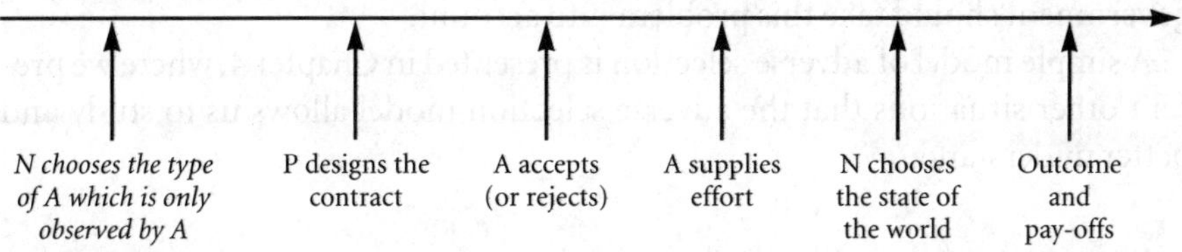
N chooses the type of A which is only observed by A
P designs the contract
A accepts (or rejects)
A supplies effort
N chooses the state of the world
Outcome and pay-offs

Fig. 1.4

It is difficult (or at least rather costly) for an insurance company to know a particular client's type when organizing coverage. In automobile insurance, the insurance company is not indifferent between a careful driver and a more reckless driver, who is much more likely to suffer an accident. This information would be most interesting to the company in order that different contracts be

[6] The pioneering work in moral hazard is due to Ross (1973). However, Ross does not include the action or effort in the agent's objective function. The first formal papers on this type of problem are those of Mirrlees (1974, 1975), Harris and Raviv (1978), Holmström (1979), and Shavell (1979). We also note that there exist some literature reviews, e.g. Rees (1987) and Hart and Holmström (1987).

offered to each type of driver, charging more per unit of coverage to the more reckless individual. However, when an individual contracts automobile insurance, the individual's habits or customs (whether or not he travels many hours without rest, whether or not he is a heavy drinker, or if he enjoys racing against his friends) are unknown to the company, and the individual's declarations will not be very believable. Hence we are up against a situation like that represented in Figure 1.4.

Adverse selection also crops up in more non-conventional contracts. The analysis of optimal regulation is a second area in which the theory that we shall study can be naturally applied. Classic regulation theory establishes simple recommendations to regulate public monopolies. Basically, economic efficiency requires that the price of the service be equal to its marginal cost, and that the regulator covers the firm's fixed costs with a subvention. If the regulator is restricted by some sort of budget constraint so that he cannot freely set the subvention, then the optimal policy is to fix price equal to average costs in the firm. It is very obvious that these policies are subject to important informational requirements. For example, they require that the regulator is as familiar with the production cost function as is the very firm. This is not a very realistic assumption. More convenient is the hypothesis that the firm is better informed than the regulator as to its cost structure. Now, we ask ourselves, in order to resolve the informational asymmetry, is it enough that the regulator asks the firm to reveal the required information in order to fix the adequate price (for which information on marginal cost is needed) and the corresponding subvention (fixed costs)? What would you do if you were the firm? It seems evident that we would attempt to take advantage of the situation. Therefore, the government should take this problem into account.

A simple model of adverse selection is presented in Chapter 4, where we present other situations that the adverse selection model allows us to study and better understand.[7]

1.4.3 Signalling

This situation is similar to adverse selection (asymmetric information). However, after learning his type, and before signing the contract, *the agent can send a signal that is observed by the principal* (see Figure 1.5). That is to say, before the principal offers the contract, the agent takes some sort of decision that may influence the principal's beliefs about the agent's identity.

[7] Early important contributions to adverse selection problems came from Akerlof (1970), Rothschild and Stiglitz (1976), Stiglitz and Weiss (1981), Myerson (1983), and Guesnerie and Laffont (1984).

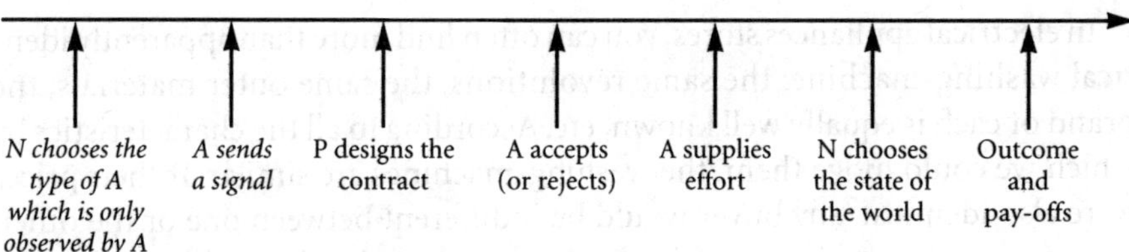
N chooses the type of A which is only observed by A
A sends a signal
P designs the contract
A accepts (or rejects)
A supplies effort
N chooses the state of the world
Outcome and pay-offs

Fig. 1.5

This could be the case of a worker whose abilities are difficult to measure when the principal is designing the contract, and so the worker tries to reveal his personal characteristics. It is likely that we have all asked ourselves at some time or another just how we can let it be known to our employer that we are hard workers or intelligent. Many people carry out certain activities for the sole purpose of proving that they are indeed hard-working or intelligent. For example, the fact that someone has been able to finish a university degree, even though its content may have absolutely nothing to do with the job at hand, is often considered to be a plus when a candidate is evaluated. We will consider the conditions that an activity must comply with in order that it may effectively be considered a signal of that characteristic that is desired to be made known.

Information is a very important part of financial markets. It is very difficult for investors to know the exact state of affairs of firms, the quality of their investments, the risks they have contracted, etc. Therefore, any decision made by the directors, for example, the debt level accumulated, is examined and valued in the market as a signal. The value of the shares is influenced by these decisions, even though classic micro-economic theory tells us that financial structure of a firm does not affect its value. The analysis of signalling models rationalizes this fact.

On occasions it is the principal rather than the agent who has private information that affects the well-being of the agent, and therefore it also affects the decision to accept or reject the contract. In such cases the principal may attempt to signal her private information via her behaviour. Since, at least in the models that we consider, the principal's only task is to design the contract, we are interested in how the very terms of the contract can be used to reveal relevant information (see Figure 1.6). This is also a signalling situation.

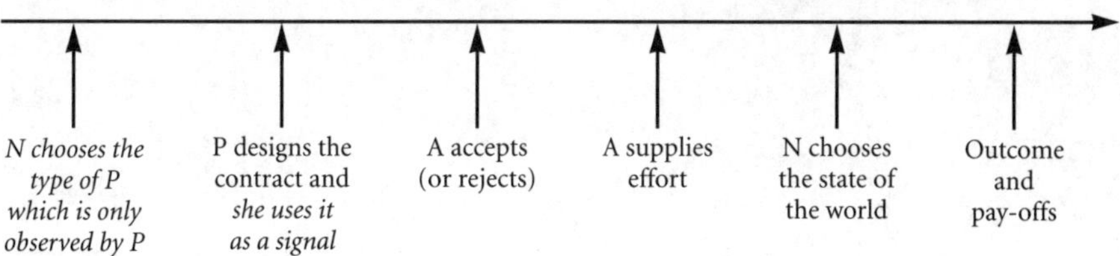
N chooses the type of P which is only observed by P
P designs the contract and she uses it as a signal
A accepts (or rejects)
A supplies effort
N chooses the state of the world
Outcome and pay-offs

Fig. 1.6

In electrical appliances stores, you can often find more than apparently identical washing-machine: the same revolutions, the same outer materials, the brand of each is equally well known, etc. According to all the characteristics by which we could judge them, the washing-machines are similar. If their prices were also identical, any buyer would be indifferent between one or the other. However, some washing-machines are more expensive than others. Often the most expensive brands include better guarantees (for example, three years instead of two). Signalling theory allows us to explain why two apparently identical products can sell at different prices.

In Chapter 5 we consider signalling models.[8] We shall see when an individual with private information is interested in revealing it what the conditions are under which a signalling decision is believable and several applications of this model.

[8] Spence (1973, 1974) was the first to consider signalling in economics. Other main contributions to this theory are Grossman (1981), Milgrom and Roberts (1982), and Cho and Kreps (1987). See also Kreps and Sobel (1994) for an overlook of the literature, and Gibbons (1992) for an introduction to signalling games.

2

THE BASE MODEL

Summary

In this chapter we analyse a reference situation that we will compare with the results of the following chapters in order properly to understand the consequences of the existence of asymmetric information. We consider a relationship between two individuals (or institutions) in which one works for the other, and in which a random result, depending in part on the effort supplied by the agent who is responsible for the activity in question, is obtained. Both participants have the same information, both before establishing the relationship and during it.

The main conclusion is that the agent's pay-off is determined by an optimal distribution of risk between the participants (principal and agent). If the principal is risk-neutral and the agent risk-averse, efficiency requires that the agent should receive a fixed wage for participating in the relationship. This wage will be independent of the result obtained, but will depend on the characteristics of the job to be done and on the effort demanded. When the agent is risk-neutral and the principal is risk-averse, then the optimal contract is a franchise, in which the agent pays a fixed amount to the principal and in return receives the result of the relationship. In the case in which both participants are risk-averse, the contract will establish the optimal distribution of risk between them according to their degree of risk-aversion.

2.1 Introduction

In this chapter we will present the basic framework that will be used as a comparison for the rest of the models to be analysed in this book. Since the final objective is to identify the consequences and costs that stem from the existence of asymmetric information, the natural reference framework is a situation in which all the participants have the same information. Hence Chapter 2 is dedicated to describing and analysing the optimal contract under symmetric information. This means that the information that both participants have could be incomplete, in the sense that there could exist random variables whose exact value is unknown, but all known information is common to both participants.

2.2 Description of the Model

The objective of this section is to present the participants, to discuss the characteristics of the relationship, and to analyse the legal union (the contract) between them.

We shall consider a bilateral relationship in which the participants could be individuals, institutions, or firms. The relationship is established through a contract. We shall refer to the participants as the principal and the agent, as is usual in the literature. The principal is responsible for designing and proposing the contract, while the agent, who is contracted to carry out some sort of task, decides if he is interested in signing or not. The relationship allows a certain *result* to be obtained, whose monetary value will be referred to as x. Let X denote the set of possible results. The final result obtained depends on the *effort* that the agent dedicates to the task, which will be denoted by e, and the value of a random variable for which both participants have the same prior distribution.

For example, think of the relationship between a tax inspector (the agent) and the tax authority (the principal). The result—the quantity of tax returns inspected and the amount of tax evasion detected—depends on the effort that the inspector dedicates to his job, but also on the difficulty of checking out certain facts, such as the degree of complexity of the tax forms under his control (the random variable). In the same way, the result of a shop assistant (the agent) depends on his effort (for example, the hours worked, his interest in selling, or his friendliness), but also on the amount of luck he has with respect to the number of customers entering the store, the general economic situation of the area in which the store is located, or even the climatic conditions (it may be a bathing-suit shop, or it may sell umbrellas).

Since the result depends not only on the agent's effort but also on a random component, the result is also a random variable. If the set of possible results is finite, then we can write the probability of result x_i conditional on effort e as:

$$\text{Prob}\,[x = x_i \mid e] = p_i(e)\,, \text{ for } i \in \{1, 2, \ldots, n\}.$$

Of course, if $X = \{x_1, \ldots, x_n\}$, it must be true that $\Sigma_{i=1}^{n} p_i(e) = 1$.[1] We shall assume that $p_i(e) > 0$ for all e, i. This means that we cannot rule out any result for any given effort level. The idea is that there are no results that are possible when the agent chooses certain effort levels, and not possible when he chooses others. If this were the case, the result obtained would be evidence of the agent's behaviour. Later (Chapter 3) we will discuss the consequences of this happening, and the reasons why we rule it out right from the start will become clearer.

Throughout this chapter we assume that the principal and the agent have the same information concerning the random component that affects the result. This means that they both have the same prior distribution over the set of possible states of nature. Hence the information they have when the relationship is established is the same for each.

Since uncertainty exists, we should consider how the participants react to risk. Risk preferences are expressed by their *utility functions.* We shall use the concept of expected utility, or, in other words, we assume that the utility functions of the participants are of the von Neumann–Morgenstern type.[2] Let's begin with the principal. She is the contractor, she receives the production (the result), and she must pay the agent for his part in the relationship. Using $B(.)$ as the utility function representing the principal's preferences, her objective is to obtain the greatest possible profit. Formally, the principal's behaviour depends on the function:

$$B(x - w)\,,$$

where w represents the pay-off made to the agent. We assume this function to be concave increasing: $B' > 0$, $B'' \leq 0$ (where the primes represent, respectively, the first and second derivatives). The concavity of the function $B(.)$ indicates that the principal is either risk-neutral or risk-averse. It is also worth noting that the profit function does not depend directly on the agent's effort (or on

[1] If the set X were a continuum, we would have a probability distribution conditional on the agent's effort and the associated density function. This case is proposed as an Exercise (see Exercise 1).

[2] Any classic micro-economics text, e.g. Malinvaud (1968) or Varian (1992), would be useful as an introduction to decision-taking under uncertainty.

the state of nature), but only on the result of the task for which the agent is contracted.

On the other hand, the agent receives a monetary pay-off for his participation in the relationship, and he supplies an effort which implies some cost to him. Formally, we assume that the agent's utility function is:

$$U(w, e) = u(w) - v(e),$$

additively separable in the components w (wage or pay-off) and e (effort). The assumption that the agent's preferences are described by an additively separable function implies that his risk-aversion does not vary with the effort he supplies. This is a restriction on the model we will use, but it does not represent an important loss of generality, and it does have the advantage of simplifying the analysis considerably.

The agent obtains utility from his wage and he may be either risk-neutral or risk-averse, which is to say the utility function that represents his preferences is concave in the pay-off. On the other hand, greater effort means greater disutility. We also assume that the marginal disutility of effort is not decreasing. Formally:

$$u'(w) > 0,\ u''(w) \leq 0,\ v'(e) > 0,\ v''(e) \geq 0.$$

From the objective functions of the principal and agent, it is easy to see that one of the basic ingredients of our model is the conflict of interests between them. This conflict is due to three elements. First, while the principal is interested in the result, the agent is not directly worried about this aspect. Secondly, the principal is not directly interested in effort, but the agent is since it is costly to him. Finally, there is the idea that greater effort makes better results more likely. Therefore, there is a conflict between the objectives of the participants, and the contract is the means by which they can be made compatible. In this way, the wage w that the principal pays the agent compensates him for the effort that the principal demands, thus a part of what the principal earns from the relationship ends up in the agent's pocket.

It should be pointed out that if there were no conflict of interests between the principal and the agent, they would agree on the 'best strategy' and, independently of whether or not the principal has more, less, or the same information as the agent, they would put this strategy into action (either by delegation, or by using the adequate communication mechanisms).[3]

[3] Of course, organizing a relationship between two individuals with the same information may not always be easy, even when they have the same objectives. Problems can turn up, for example, for reasons of bounded rationality (people normally have problems in carrying out complicated calculations), or it may be that the communication network between the principal and the agent is not perfect (and information is inevitably lost in transmission). However, the analysis of this type of problem is outside the scope of our models.

As we have said, in the game that we consider, it is the principal that offers the agent a contract, the terms of which are not subject to bargaining. The only alternatives open to the agent are to accept or to reject. Should he reject, he will have to fall back on the other opportunities that the market offers him. These other opportunities, by comparison, determine the limit for participation in the contract. The expected utility that external opportunities offer the agent is called his *reservation utility*, and it is denoted by $\underline{U}$.[4] So long as the contract allows the agent to earn expected utility not less than his reservation utility, he will accept it. In this case, the participants are linked together by this legal union until it expires.

If we reconsider the examples of a tax inspector and a shop assistant, the reservation utility represents the utility that they can obtain in other jobs (either contracted or self-employed.)

One of the most important objectives of the economics of information is to characterize the optimal contract between the principal and the agent. To do so, we should ponder on what exactly are contracts. A contract is a document that specifies the obligations of the participants, and the transfers that must be made under different contingencies. In order for a contract to be valid, both the contingencies and the terms in the contract must be verifiable. A variable is said to be verifiable when its value is observable and can be proved before a court of law. This means that any breach of the contract can be reported and judged by a court. Also, the contract may be different according to the characteristics of the agent and the task for which he is contracted. Therefore, this information, even if it cannot be specifically included in the contract, is important for its design.

In the example of the tax inspector, the contract that the tax authority offers him could be different according to certain characteristics of the individual or of the job. For example, it may depend on the inspector's educational level (for example, Ph.D, masters, or bachelor), or on the conditions in which he must work. With respect to the terms of the contract, they may include information such as the number of tax returns inspected, the fraud level detected, or the taxpayer claims accepted. In the same way, the contract for a store assistant may depend on his previous experience, his friendliness, etc. The wage paid may include a fixed part and a variable part that would depend for example on sales made, or the type of product. In both cases, assuming that the effort of the agent is verifiable, this can also be included in the contract.

4 Reservation utility as a concept has been lightly treated in agency models. In spite of its role in the literature, it has always been taken as being exogenous. However, some authors have indicated that it will depend on the interactions between the different principal–agent structures (interested readers can consult, for example, Ross (1973), one of the pioneers of the literature). This research direction, however, has not been exploited. Anyway, the lack of precision as to how the reservation utility is determined is not a serious impediment to knowing the characteristics of the optimal contract.

Finally, with respect to the duration of the contract, generally simple models refer to a static situation (a single period). All the models that we shall study will be relationships that are established only once ('one-shot' relationships). We will not be considering what differences would be incorporated if the relationship were repeated.[5]

2.3 Symmetric information contracts

We assume that all relevant information is verifiable. The principal's problem is to design a contract that the agent will accept in a situation in which both have the same information. Recall that the result of the relationship is a random variable, and that the contract can depend of all verifiable variables. In this framework, the principal must decide both the effort e that she demands of the agent, and the wages $\{w(x_i)\}_{i=1,\ldots,n}$ that will be paid according to the result. In order to do this, she must work out what contracts are acceptable by the agent, given the effort demanded, and then choose from the contracts that achieve this effort, the cheapest one. This situation is *efficient* and the central question is to determine the optimal risk sharing arrangement between the participants. Formally, the (Pareto) efficient solution is the solution to the following problem [P2.1]:

$$\text{[P2.1]} \quad \underset{[e,\{w(x_i)\}_{i=1,\ldots,n}]}{\text{Max}} \quad \sum_{i=1}^{n} p_i(e)\, B(x_i - w(x_i))$$

$$\text{s.t.} \quad \sum_{i=1}^{n} p_i(e)\, u(w(x_i)) - v(e) \geq \underline{U}.$$

This problem establishes that the principal maximizes the surplus that she obtains from the relationship, under the restriction that the agent is willing to accept the contract. This condition is known as the *participation condition.* In [P2.1] we are assuming that the principal can measure the agent's effort e since this is a verifiable variable. As we have already pointed out, the contract has two components: the effort (verifiable) and the pay-offs contingent on the result. Even though it has been established that the wage that the agent receives depends only on the result, $w(x_i)$, the contract includes a sufficiently large 'penalty' or 'fine' for the agent to decide to give the effort that was agreed upon.

5 In the corresponding chapters, among several extensions of the basic models, we shall give references so that the reader may study the consequences of the repetition of the relationship.

We could imagine that, in the case of a breach of contract, it would be a court of law that must inflict this punishment. For this reason, in what follows we shall bear in mind the fact that in the contract the principal can demand contracted effort from the agent, without having to worry about the 'punishment' that the agent will suffer should he decide to offer some other effort level. In any case, we assume that the fine that the court inflicts is sufficiently high to dissuade the agent from deviating from the contracted behaviour.

We point out that problem [P2.1] has good properties with respect to certain arguments and not so good with respect to others. More concretely, if we restrict ourselves to the analysis of the optimal contract, given an effort level (for example, given the optimal effort level), the problem is well behaved. Since $B(.)$ is a concave function, $B(x-w)$ will also be concave in wages. Besides, since the sum of concave functions is concave, we know that the objective function is concave. For the same reason, the restriction is also concave. Hence the Kuhn–Tucker conditions will be both necessary and sufficient for the global solution to the problem. However, we cannot be certain that the functions are concave (or quasi-concave) with respect to the effort variable, since the participants' objective functions are weighted by the probabilities of different results, and these depend on the effort. Therefore the expected functions are not necessarily concave in effort. Hence it is more difficult to obtain global conclusions with respect to this variable.

Let's consider the conclusions that we can extract from the solution of problem [P2.1] with respect to the optimal symmetric information contract. Let e^o denote the efficient effort level and let $\{w^o(x_i)_{i=1,\ldots,n}\}$ denote the associated pay-offs. Since we can use the Kuhn–Tucker theorem to calculate the optimal contract, the first-order conditions of problem [P2.1] with respect to the wages in the different contingencies are written as follows for all i:

$$\frac{\partial L}{\partial w(x_i)}(w^o(x_i), e^o, \lambda^o) = -p_i(e^o)\, B'(x_i - w^o(x_i)) + \lambda^o\, p_i(e^o)\, u'(w^o(x_i)) = 0,$$

from which,

$$\lambda^o = \frac{B'(x_i - w^o(x_i))}{u'(w^o(x_i))}, \text{ for all } i \in \{1, 2, ..., n\}. \qquad (2.1)$$

This expression requires that the multiplier associated with the participation condition, λ^o, be strictly positive: if it were zero, we would have either $B'(.) = 0$, or $u'(.) = +\infty$, which is impossible given our assumptions. Hence the participation condition binds. Intuitively, it is easy to understand why the solution to the problem saturates the agent's participation condition. Imagine that this were not so. Then the principal would be paying 'too much' to the agent. From problem [P2.1], the principal could reduce all the pay-offs $w(x_i)$ in such a way that the agent would still accept the new contract, and she would get greater utility (since she is paying less).

A second way to see that the participation condition must bind is the following. If the agent were to receive utility greater than $\underline{U}$ from the relationship, then he would be willing to pay to sign the contract. The principal could demand this payment from the agent, which is equivalent to reducing his wage by the same amount in all contingencies.

Two comments are interesting at this point. First, the above problem corresponds to a Pareto optimum in the most usual sense of the term. We are maximizing the utility of one participant under the restriction that the other participant receives at least a given level of utility. In this respect, using a utility function for the agent that is additively separable in the wage and effort is harmless (the analysis is easily extended to more general functions). Secondly, note that by varying $\underline{U}$ (that part of the surplus that the agent gets), we find the efficient allocation frontier. Therefore, the solution to this problem is conditional on the value of the parameter $\underline{U}$ and the validity of the method is general. Independently of how the level of $\underline{U}$ is fixed, problem [P2.1] gives us the characteristics of the optimal contract.

2.3.1 The optimal payments mechanism

We shall now turn to the characteristics of the optimal contract, found in [P2.1]. Equation (2.1) indicates that the optimal distribution of risk implies that the following equation is satisfied:

$$\frac{B'\,(x_i - w^O(x_i))}{u'\,(w^O(x_i))} = \text{constant} \tag{2.2}$$

or in other words, the ratio of marginal utilities of the principal and the agent should be constant whatever is the final result. This is the familiar condition equating marginal rates of substitution (tangency between indifference curves) that characterizes Pareto-efficient situations.

We can represent the problem graphically when there are only two possible results, x_1 and x_2, with $x_1 < x_2$, using the *Edgeworth Box* diagram.[6] The dimensions of the box are the results of the two contingencies, that is x_1 and x_2. In order to draw it, we denote $w(x_i) = w_i$ and we rewrite condition (2.2) for the case of two results in the following way:

[6] This representation is based on a paper by Ricketts (1986).

$$\frac{B'(x_2 - w_2)}{B'(x_1 - w_1)} = \frac{u'(w_2)}{u'(w_1)}. \tag{2.3}$$

Hence the point is determined by this condition and the participation condition binding:

$$\sum_{i=1}^{2} p_i(e)\, u(w_i) - v(e) = \underline{U}. \tag{2.4}$$

Graphically, in the Edgeworth box corresponding to the problem that we are considering, we draw the principal's indifference curves (they are increasing in the part of the result that goes to the principal, or in other words, towards the point O_A), and those of the agent (that increase towards O_P). The agent's participation condition translates into the fact that the only contracts that are acceptable to him are those located on or above the indifference curve corresponding to $\underline{U}$. The solution, given by the conditions (2.3) and (2.4), is at the tangency between the agent's reservation indifference curve and the indifference curve of the principal that is furthest from the origin O_P (see Figure 2.1). This optimal point is characterized by the contingent wage scheme that the principal offers the agent: w_1 if the result is x_1 and w_2 if it is x_2. Notice that w_1 is the vertical distance between O_A and the optimal point, while the vertical distance between this point and O_P is $x_1 - w_1$, which is the principal's profit when the result is x_1 (and similarly for w_2).

Note that the lines $[O_A A]$ and $[O_P P]$ represent sure things (the same payoff in both states of nature) for the principal and the agent respectively. As can be seen in Figure 2.1, the optimal solution requires the participants to share the

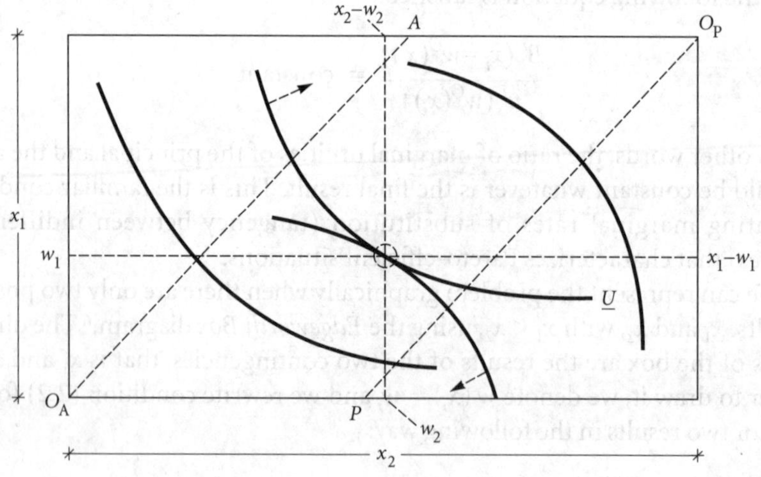

Fig. 2.1

risk if both are risk-averse since the optimal point is between the two certainty lines.

In order to better understand the implications of condition (2.2) in the general case with n possible results, we will consider several possibilities with respect to the objective functions of the participants.

i) If $B'(.) =$ constant, that is, the principal is risk-neutral, the efficiency condition (2.2) requires that $u'(w^o(x_i)) =$ constant for all i. If the agent is risk-averse, the only possible way in which the marginal utilities at two points can be the same is if the two points are the same. In other words, $u'(w^o(x_i)) = u'(w^o(x_j))$ requires that $w^o(x_i) = w^o(x_j)$. Therefore, at the optimal contract the agent receives a pay-off that is independent of the result: $w^o(x_1) = w^o(x_2) = \ldots = w^o(x_n)$.

The optimal distribution of risk when the principal is risk neutral is for her to accept all the risk, completely insuring the agent. The agent receives the wage w^o in all contingencies, and this wage will only depend on the effort demanded. In fact, we can calculate the exact wage payment:

$$w^o = u^{-1}(\underline{U} + v(e^o)), \tag{2.5}$$

since we know that the participation constraint binds.

The graphical representation of the two-result case when the principal is risk-neutral is given in Figure 2.2. The principal's indifference curves are straight lines in this case, and the result is that she completely insures the agent: $w_1 = w_2$.

ii) If the agent is risk-neutral, $u'(.) =$ constant, and the principal is risk-averse, $B''(.) < 0$, then we are in the opposite situation. The optimal contract

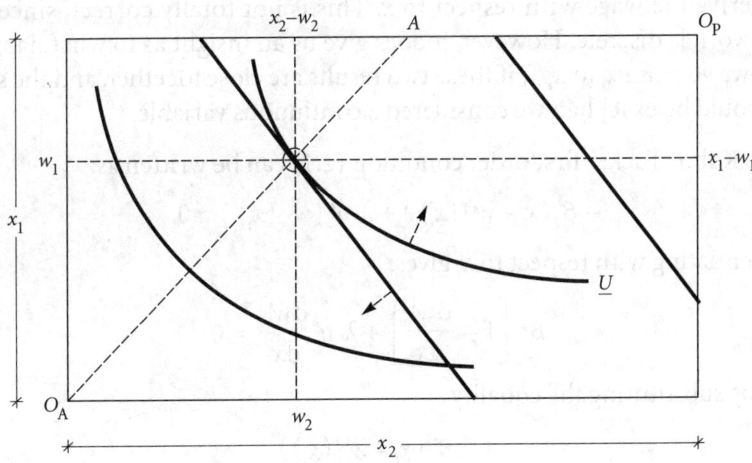

Fig. 2.2

will require that $B'(x_i - w^O(x_i)) =$ constant for all i. Using the same reasoning as above, it must be true that $x_1 - w^O(x_1) = x_2 - w^O(x_2) = \ldots = x_n - w^O(x_n)$. The principal's profit is now independent of the result. Consequently, the agent accepts all the risk, insuring the principal against variations in the result. The optimal contract is of the form:

$$w^O(x_i) = x_i - k. \tag{2.6}$$

We can interpret this as a 'franchise' contract: the agent keeps the result x and pays the principal a fixed amount k, independent of the result. In order that the participation constraint be saturated, the constant k must satisfy

$$\sum_{i=1}^{n} p_i(e^O)\,[x_i - k] = \underline{U} + v(e^O)$$

$$\Leftrightarrow \qquad k = \sum_{i=1}^{n} p_i(e^O)\,x_i - \underline{U} - v(e^O).$$

The amount that the principal sets as the price for the agent to keep the result is the difference between the expected profit from the activity and the amount required for the agent to accept the relationship. This contract can also be interpreted as the agent buying the activity (the firm) from the principal. The graphical representation is similar to Figure 2.2, but interchanging the roles of the principal and the agent.

iii) If both the principal and the agent are risk-averse, each one will need to accept a part of the variability of the result. Both participants receive a part of the risk of the relationship: exactly how much will depend on their degrees of risk-aversion. It is interesting to analyse how the degree of risk-aversion influences the distribution of the risk associated with the result. To do so we will derive the wage with respect to x. This is not totally correct, since our framework is discrete. However, it does give us an insight as to what happens when we go from x_i to x_{i+1} if these two results are close together, and the solution would be exact had we considered a continuous variable.

The Kuhn–Tucker first order condition (2.1) can be written as:

$$-B'(x_i - w^O(x_i)) + \lambda\, u'(w^O(x_i)) = 0.$$

Differentiating with respect to x_i gives:

$$-B''\left[1 - \frac{dw^O}{dx_i}\right] + \lambda\, u'' \frac{dw^O}{dx_i} = 0.$$

Now, by substituting the equality

$$\lambda = \frac{B'(x_i - w^O(x_i))}{u'(w^O(x_i))},$$

we can conclude that:

$$-\frac{B''}{B'}\left[1-\frac{\mathrm{d}w^{O}}{\mathrm{d}x_i}\right]+\frac{u''}{u'}\frac{\mathrm{d}w^{O}}{\mathrm{d}x_i}=0.$$

If we denote by $r_p = -B''/B'$ the principal's measure of absolute risk-aversion, and by $r_a = -u''/u'$ the agent's measure of absolute risk-aversion (recall that both will, in general, depend on the level of income or wealth), then the above equation can be written as:

$$\frac{\mathrm{d}w^{O}}{\mathrm{d}x_i}=\frac{r_p}{r_p+r_a}. \tag{2.7}$$

Equation (2.7) indicates how the agent's wage changes given an improvement in the result. Since $r_p/(r_p + r_a) \in (0,1)$ when both participants are risk-averse, the agent only receives a part of the increased result as increased wage. The more risk-averse is the agent, that is to say, the greater is r_a, the less the result influences his wage. On the other hand, the more risk-averse is the principal, greater r_p, changes in the result correspond to more important changes in the wage (since $r_p/(r_p + r_a)$ is decreasing in r_p). The two limit cases, when one of the participants is risk-neutral, $r_p = 0$ or $r_a = 0$, have been analysed in (i) and (ii).

As equation (2.7) shows, the optimal contracts can be very complicated. A rather attractive, for its simplicity, contract format is the set of *linear* contracts:

$$w^{O}(x_i) = c + b\,x_i.$$

We can ask the following question: when is a linear contract optimal? In order for such a contract to be optimal, it must occur that $\mathrm{d}w^{O}/\mathrm{d}x_i = b$, or in other words, the increase in the wage given an increase in the result must be constant; i.e. $r_p/(r_p + r_a) =$ constant. However, this condition is satisfied on very few occasions since, basically, it requires that the participants have constant risk-aversion. This, in turn, implies that the objective functions of the agent and the principal are, respectively,

$$u(w) = -k\exp(-r_a w) \quad \text{and} \quad B(x-w) = -k'\exp(-r_p[x-w]).$$

The above statement shows that, even when information is symmetric, optimal contracts are very rarely based on linear payments.

The nature of the results that we have presented so far in this section are well known, and they stipulate the optimal distribution of risk in a relationship. However, we must insist that in order that the allocation be Pareto-efficient it is necessary that the principal has the same information as the agent when the terms of the contract are established, and that breach of contract by the agent can be punished.

2.3.2 The optimal level of effort

Let's briefly consider what will be the effort level chosen by the agent. As we pointed out, the problem that appears when one attempts to solve [P2.1] is that it is not necessarily concave with respect to effort, even though the utility functions of the principal and the agent are well defined (concave). This is because the distribution of results also depends on the agent's effort. Therefore, unless we add new conditions related to the distribution function of the results conditional on effort, the expected utility functions may not be concave. In what follows, in order to attack this problem in the simplest possible way, we shall consider the first two cases discussed in the section on optimal contracts, since for these cases we can explicitly solve for the contract.

(i) First, assume that the principal is risk-neutral ($B'(.) =$ constant) and the agent is risk-averse. In this case we know, from (2.5), that the optimal contract is a wage that does not vary with the result, $w^o = u^{-1}(\underline{U} + v(e^o))$, but does depend on the effort demanded of the agent. Hence we can rewrite the principal's problem as:

$$\underset{e}{\text{Max}} \left[\sum_{i=1}^{n} p_i(e)\, x_i - u^{-1}(\underline{U} + v(e)) \right].$$

This problem is solved with an optimal effort of e^o. Since we are not sure that it is concave in the variable effort, we can only state that the first-order condition is a necessary condition for an interior maximum. In particular, if the optimal effort level e^o is interior, then it must be true that:

$$\sum_{i=1}^{n} p_i'(e^o)\, x_i = (u^{-1})'(\underline{U} + v(e^o))\, v'(e^o). \tag{2.8}$$

At the optimal effort level, the expected profits of an increase in effort, that is $\Sigma_{i=1}^{n} p_i'(e^o)\, x_i$, coincide with the marginal increase in the wage that the principal must pay the agent to compensate him for the increased disutility of effort, which is expressed by the right-hand side of (2.8). As was to be expected, the optimal effort depends on the values of the results, x_i, on the probabilities of getting each result in function of the efforts, $p_i(e)$, and the agent's utility function, $u(w)$ and $v(e)$.

In order to express condition (2.8) more simply, we shall use the inverse function theorem. This theorem says that the derivative of the inverse is equal to the inverse of the derivative (evaluated at the corresponding point). Recalling that $w^o = u^{-1}(\underline{U} + v(e^o))$, equation (2.8) can be written as:

$$\sum_{i=1}^{n} p_i'(e^o)\, x_i = \frac{v'(e^O)}{u'(w^O)}. \tag{2.9}$$

To calculate the second derivative of the above problem with respect to effort, we must bear in mind that

$$\frac{\mathrm{d}}{\mathrm{d}e}\left[-\frac{v'(e)}{u'(w)}\right] = -\frac{v''(e)}{u'(w)} + \frac{v'(e)\,u''(w)\,\dfrac{\mathrm{d}w}{\mathrm{d}e}}{[u'(w)]^2}.$$

And that, since $w = u^{-1}(\underline{U} + v(e))$, we have that:

$$\frac{\mathrm{d}w}{\mathrm{d}e} = (u^{-1})'(\underline{U} + v(e))\,v'(e) = \frac{v'(e)}{u'(w)}.$$

Therefore, the second-order condition, which is necessary in order that a point that satisfies (2.8) (or equivalently, (2.9)) is effectively a local maximum, is written as:

$$\sum_{i=1}^{n} p_i''(e^O)\,x_i + \frac{u''}{(u')^3}(w^O)\,v'(e^O)^2 - \frac{v''(e^O)}{u'(w^O)} \leq 0.$$

A sufficient condition for a local maximum is that this equation be satisfied with strict inequality. In fact, a sufficient condition for e^O to be a global maximum is that this inequality be satisfied for all effort levels. This is always the case if[7]

$$\sum_{i=1}^{n} p_i''(e)\,x_i \leq 0. \tag{2.10}$$

For the case in which the principal is risk-neutral, that is, there is only one wage for the agent since it is optimal to completely insure him, we can draw two different graphs of how the optimal effort (and, simultaneously, the wage) is determined, in the space (w, e). The first graph, shown in Figure 2.3, is to use

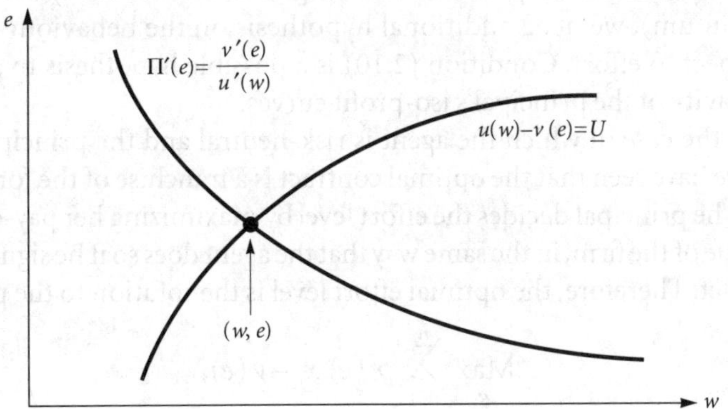

Fig. 2.3

[7] Exercise 3 of this chapter interprets this condition for the case in which only two results are possible.

equality (2.9) together with the participation condition (2.4). The optimal contract is found at the intersection of both curves.
In Figure 2.3, $\Pi(e)$ denotes the principal's gross profit, i.e.,

$$\Pi(e) = \sum_{i=1}^{n} p_i(e)\, x_i, \text{ hence } \Pi'(e) = \sum_{i=1}^{n} p_i'(e)\, x_i.$$

The other, somewhat more natural, way of graphing the optimal effort decision is to go back to problem [P2.1] and draw the participation constraint together with the principal's isoprofit curves (see Figure 2.4).

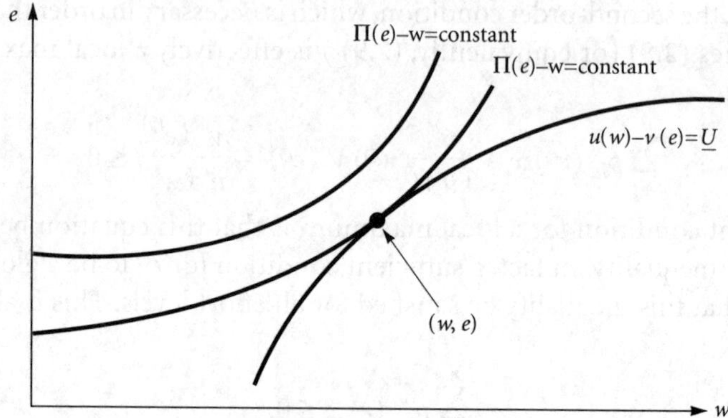

Fig. 2.4

This graph also illustrates the second-order condition problem: in order to draw, as we have done, the curves $\Pi(e)$ = constant as concave contours (which assures that when an iso-profit curve is tangent to the iso-utility curve, then it is a maximum), we need additional hypothesis on the behaviour of profits with respect to effort. Condition (2.10) is a possible hypothesis to guarantee the concavity of the principal's iso-profit curves.

(ii) In the case in which the agent is risk-neutral and the principal is risk-averse, we have seen that the optimal contract is a franchise of the form $w^o(x_i) = x_i - k$. The principal decides the effort level by maximizing her pay-off, which is the value of the firm, in the same way that the agent does so if he signs this type of contract. Therefore, the optimal effort level is the solution to the problem:

$$\underset{e}{\text{Max}} \sum_{i=1}^{n} p_i(e)\, x_i - v(e),$$

whose first-order condition is:

$$\sum_{i=1}^{n} p_i'(e^o)\, x_i = v'(e^o). \tag{2.11}$$

In words, the expected marginal pay-off should be equal to the marginal cost for effort to be optimal. In order for an effort level satisfying (2.11) to be a local maximum, we require that:

$$\sum_{i=1}^{n} p_i''(e^{o})\, x_i - v''(e^{o}) \leq 0. \tag{2.12}$$

In the same way as in (i), a sufficient condition for a global maximum is that the condition $\Sigma_{i=1}^{n} p_i''(e)\, x_i \leq 0$, be satisfied for all effort levels.

In general, the analysis of the optimal effort is more difficult than the analysis of the optimal payment scheme for a given effort level. In the following chapters, we will analyse the effects of the asymmetric information on the contract form and, on several occasions, we will also show the consequences on the effort required from the agent.

Exercises

Exercise 1. A principal contracts an agent to carry out a certain task. The agent, via the choice of effort, determines the distribution of the results, which are in the interval $X = [\underline{x}, \overline{x}]$ where $\underline{x}$ is the worst result and $\overline{x}$ is the best. The density function for the results conditional on the agents effort is $f(x; e)$. Assume that for all $x \in X$, for all e, $f(x, e) > 0$.

(*a*) Calculate the optimal wage function when the principal's objective function is $B(x - w)$ and the agent's objective function is $U(w, e) = u(w) - v(e)$.

(*b*) Calculate the optimal wage function if the principal is risk-neutral.

(*c*) Under the same assumption as (*b*), calculate the efforts satisfying the first-order condition and analyse when the second-order condition holds. What happens if the distribution is $f(x; e) = 1 + e[x - (1/2)]$, where $X = [0, 1]$, $e \in [0, 1]$?

Exercise 2. Consider an individual, or a firm, that has an initial wealth w and a property valued at L that is subject to a fire risk. In order to protect himself against the risk, the individual can buy an insurance policy from an insurance company. The company and the individual have the same prior as to the probability that a fire will occur. Denote this probability by p, assumed constant and independent of the individual's effort (alternatively, it depends on the individual's effort, but as there is symmetric information the insurance contract can demand that the individual exerts the correct effort, i.e. takes the adequate precautionary measures). The individual can insure the entire value of the property, or only a part of this value. Call the amount that he decides to insure the 'coverage', and denote it by q. The company demands a price for providing coverage of an indemnity of q should the property burn down. This price is known as the premium, and we denote it by ρ.

With respect to the objective functions of the participants, assume that the insurance company is risk-neutral and that the individual's preferences are described by the utility function $u(w)$.

(*a*) What is the individual's reservation utility in this case?

(*b*) What terms (verifiable variables) can be included in the insurance contract?

(*c*) If the insurance company chooses the premium and the coverage that it offers, calculate the optimal contract that would be offered to a risk-averse agent.

(*d*) What would happen if the individual were risk-neutral? Explain.

(*e*) Discuss the value that ρ would take if there were perfect competition between insurance companies in case (*c*).

(*f*) What would happen if both the insurance company and the individual were risk averse? Show that it would not be optimal for the company to completely insure the individual.

Exercise 3. Consider a special case of the model analysed in Chapter 2, in which there are only two possible results. Call them success (S) and failure (F), since $x_F < x_S$. Denote by $p_S(e)$ the probability of success when the agent uses effort e, so that the probability of failure is just $p_F(e) = 1 - p_S(e)$.

(*a*) Write the optimal contract and the necessary condition for the optimal effort level for the case when the principal is risk-neutral and the agent is risk-averse, and for the case when the agent is risk-neutral and the principal is risk-averse.

(*b*) Write the sufficient condition (2.10) for this special case, and interpret it.

Exercise 4. Consider a firm that has access to a group of N workers. Each worker can either work for the firm or remain unemployed, depending on the number of jobs offered. All workers are identical. The firm, which sells its product in a competitive market, has a production function $x = f(n, \varepsilon)$, where n is the number of workers contracted and ε is a random shock. The results belong to the set $\{x_1, \ldots, x_k\}$. Denote by $p_i(n)$ the probability of observing result x_i when n workers are employed. When the labour contract is signed, neither the workers nor the firm know the state of nature ε, but *ex post* everyone knows it (the information is symmetric).

The firm is risk-neutral, interested only in expected profits: $x - n\,w$, where the market price for output has been normalized to 1. The workers' utility function is of the form $u(w) - c\,e$, with $u'(\underline{w}) > 0$, $u''(\underline{w}) < 0$, and where e is the effort or input of the agent. Assume that $e \in \{0, 1\}$, where we interpret $e = 0$ as not working at all (only possible if he remains unemployed), and $e = 1$ as working a normal day. Intermediate effort levels are ruled out. We assume that work is a verifiable variable, and so if a worker receives an offer at wage w, he must choose between two possibilities: either work for the firm, which gives utility of $u(w) - c$; or remain unemployed, which gives utility of $u(s)$, where s is the unemployment benefit paid by the government. We can call $u(s) = \underline{U}$.

(*a*) Calculate the optimal contingent wage in function of the employment level.

(*b*) The theory of implicit contracts is a tool often used to analyse the labour market with the intention to try to explain observed wage rigidity and changes in employment levels. The theory is based on the idea that the labour market has particular characteristics that makes classical theory (equilibrium between supply and demand) inadequate. The idea is that firms and workers have contracts that are more or less durable, since there is more than just a purchase involved (pay a wage for a given labour input). A labor contract is also an insurance contract, in the sense that the results of the labour relationship are random, and firms generally insure their workers against such fluctuations in the results. In this way, the wage is not necessarily equal to the marginal productivity in each state. Comment on these ideas given the result of part (*a*).

(*c*) Calculate the optimal level of employment and analyse how it varies with the unemployment benefit s.

3

THE MORAL HAZARD PROBLEM

Summary

This chapter analyses the moral hazard model. The model studies those situations in which the agent's behaviour is not a verifiable variable in the relationship. Therefore, it cannot be included in the terms of the contract and so the systems of payment proposed by the symmetric information model are no longer adequate.

The analysis of the moral hazard model has two simple implications. First, our attention is directed to the fact that when a contract is offered, it is necessary to take into account the decisions (the effort) that the other party will take if he accepts the relationship. The fact that these decisions cannot be controlled implies an important efficiency loss and it also affects the type of contract that will be signed and the decisions that will be taken. Secondly, the analysis shows that the optimal contract is determined by the trade-off between two conflicting objectives: efficiency (in the optimal distribution of risk between the participants) and the incentives of the agent (additional risk).

We show that for the contract to influence the behaviour of the accepting party, then it must pay him more when the results are a good 'signal' (they 'inform') that his decision was the required one. The incentives of the agent must be linked to just how informative the result is that the decision taken (the effort exerted) was that which the principal wanted.

3.1 Introduction

In Chapter 2 we studied a simple relationship between two participants, based on one, the principal, contracting the other, the agent, to exert an effort, or to take some sort of decision, in exchange for a monetary payment. We analysed the reference situation in which both participants have the same information, with respect to the variables and functions determining the relationship (such as the production function, or the distribution of the random variable), and with respect to identities (both know the utility function of the other) and behaviour (the relevant decisions of the participants are observable). However, it is easy to think of situations in which the information of the parties to a contract is not symmetric. It is also easy to imagine that the party who has an informational advantage will try to use it to his benefit.

In this chapter we will concentrate on a certain type of informational asymmetry, having to do with the behaviour of the agent during the relationship. As of now, we shall assume that the *agent's behaviour* is not observable by the principal, or, if it is observable by the principal, it is *not verifiable* (for a court of law). This asymmetric information problem is known as *moral hazard.* We shall continue to assume that all other ingredients of the problem are symmetric information. That effort is not verifiable means that it *cannot be included in the terms of the contract*, since if it were, in case of breach of contract, no court of law could know if the contract had really been breached or not.

Let us consider a few examples that describe the type of situation that we want to analyse. In labour contracts, it is common that the effort (or a part of the effort) of the workers is not a verifiable variable. In these cases the contract cannot include clauses of the type: 'if I see that you have exerted a lot of effort then your wage will be greater than if you slack', since it is very difficult, if not impossible, for the firm to prove that the worker has indeed slacked. In the same way, the level of investment of firms in a specific project is a very difficult variable to quantify, and so a government that regulates these firms will, on many occasions, not be able to use this information when it establishes the optimal regulation policy. It is also very difficult for an insurance company to observe just how careful a client has been in order to avoid accidents, and so neither the coverage nor the premium can depend on this information.

Even though the agent's effort is not verifiable, and so cannot be used as a contracted variable, we assume that the result of this effort is verifiable at the end of the period. Consequently, the result obtained will be included in the contract that stipulates the agent's pay-off. In the above examples this means that a worker's wage will depend on the sales or the production achieved, that the amount the government pays a regulated firm could depend on its sales or its profits, or the terms of an insurance contract may depend on the number and importance of the accidents that the client suffers.

The general scheme of the game that we will be analysing is shown in Figure 3.1. Chronologically, in the first place, the principal decides what contract to offer the agent. Then the agent decides whether or not to accept the relationship, according to the terms of the contract established by the principal. Finally, if the contract has been accepted, the agent must decide the effort level that he most desires, given the contract that he has signed. This is a free decision by the agent since effort is not a contracted variable. Hence, when she designs the contract that defines the relationship, the principal must bear in mind that, after signing the contract, the agent will choose the effort level that is the best for him personally.

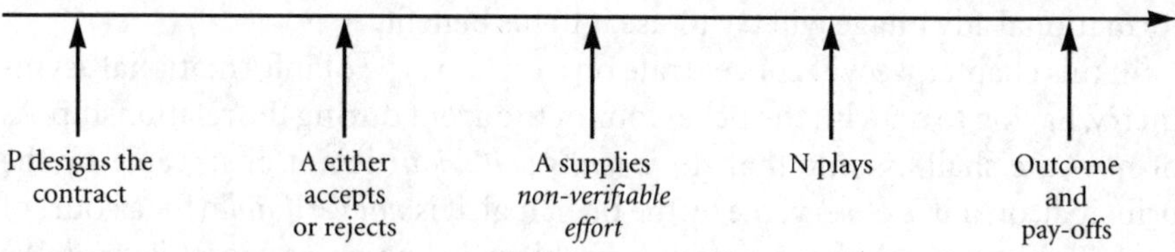
P designs the contract
A either accepts or rejects
A supplies *non-verifiable effort*
N plays
Outcome and pay-offs

Fig. 3.1

In order to understand the nature of the problem facing the principal, consider what would happen if she proposes the efficient contract (the solution found in Chapter 2) when the agent's effort is not a contracted variable. Consider the case of a risk-neutral principal and a risk-averse agent. Recall that in this case, the symmetric information optimal contract is for the principal to completely insure the agent. However, if the agent's effort is not observable, once he has signed the contract he will exert the effort level that is most beneficial for himself. Since the wage is independent of the result, the agent is in a situation in which his wage does not depend on his effort, and so he will use the lowest possible effort. Consequently, the principal will obtain a lower expected profit than that corresponding to the symmetric information situation since the agent's effort is different (less than) the efficient level.

With a contract based on a fixed wage, the agent's behaviour will always be the same: he will choose the smallest possible effort. The principal will anticipate this reaction, and so if she proposes a contract based on a fixed pay-off, she will choose the wage that exactly compensates the agent for the effort he uses. Therefore the wage will be w^{MIN}, as defined by

$$w^{MIN} = u^{-1}\left(\underline{U} + v\left(e^{MIN}\right)\right),$$

where e^{MIN} is the smallest possible effort.[1]

Is it impossible to achieve greater effort than e^{MIN} under contracts that completely insure the agent. However, the principal can make the agent 'interested' in the consequences of his behaviour, by making his pay-off depend on the result obtained. In order to understand how this works, consider the following: in spite of the principal's risk-neutrality and the agent's risk-aversion, a franchise-type contract is signed under which the agent buys the production from the principal. In this case the principal receives a fixed payment and the participant who accepts all the risk is the agent. Obviously, the agent is now interested in the result. However, given the differences in the objective functions, he is not interested in the result in the same way as the principal. Besides, the franchise contract was also a possibility in the symmetric information case. If the principal did not use this contract format, it was because the agent does not enjoy taking risks and he is not prepared to pay too much to accept the risks involved. This is why the franchise is not efficient. A franchise gives the agent incentives (although perhaps not the best ones), but at a very high cost.

Even if a franchise does not appear to be the best solution to our current problem, it does make one of the characteristics of moral hazard models rather evident: the *trade-off* between *efficiency*, in the sense of the optimal distribution of risk, and *incentives.* This trade-off is what is defined by the optimal contract in this type of situation. Throughout this chapter we will be interested in studying the characteristics of this optimal contract.

3.2 The Moral Hazard Problem

In order to study the *optimal contract* under conditions of asymmetric information with respect to effort, we need to formally define the problem. We will use the model of Chapter 2, but always bearing in mind that since effort is now not a verifiable variable the principal cannot include the effort level in the terms of the contract. In other words, the principal can 'propose' a certain effort, but she must make sure that this is precisely the level that the agent wants

[1] We can always assume that there is a minimum effort level for the agent that may be $e^{MIN} = 0$, which is doing nothing, or e^{MIN} = 'go to work' (not going is easily verifiable). A second way of interpreting the effort level e^{MIN} is to consider that the principal and the agent do not have completely conflicting objectives. It is possible that the agent gets some utility from his work, but only up to a certain effort level. We assume that the level that the agent is willing to spontaneously offer is e^{MIN}. The agency problem turns up in this case since the principal would like the agent to offer an effort greater than his spontaneous level.

to exert. The idea is to solve the game shown in Figure 3.1. The natural solution concept is subgame perfect equilibrium. The final stage of the game—and this is the fundamental point of the moral hazard problem—is that in which the agent chooses the effort he will exert. This choice can be written as:

$$e \in \arg \underset{\hat{e}}{\text{Max}} \left\{ \sum_{i=1}^{n} p_i(\hat{e})\, u(w(x_i)) - v(\hat{e}) \right\}. \tag{3.1}$$

This condition is what we shall call the *incentive restriction*, or the *incentive compatibility constraint*. This restriction reflects the moral hazard problem: once the contract has been accepted and since effort is not verifiable (it is not included in the terms of the contract), the agent will choose that level of effort that maximizes his objective function.

In the second stage of the game, given the effort that he will exert and the contract terms, the agent decides whether or not to accept the contract that the principal is proposing. Formally,

$$\sum_{i=1}^{n} p_i(e)\, u(w(x_i)) - v(e) \geq \underline{U}. \tag{3.2}$$

We shall refer to this restriction as the participation constraint, or the individual rationality condition, and it was present in the symmetric information framework. Equation (3.2) reflects the fact that the agent can always reject the contract if what he gets by signing it is not at least equal to what he can obtain from the alternatives in the market.

In the first stage of the game, the principal designs the contract, anticipating the agent's behaviour. Formally, the contract that the principal proposes is the solution to the following problem:

$$\underset{[e,\{w(x_i)\}_{i=1,\ldots,n}]}{\text{Max}} \quad \sum_{i=1}^{n} p_i(e)\, B(x_i - w(x_i))$$

[P3.1]

$$\text{s.t.} \quad \sum_{i=1}^{n} p_i(e)\, u(w(x_i)) - v(e) \geq \underline{U} \tag{3.2}$$

$$e \in \arg \underset{\hat{e}}{\text{Max}} \left\{ \sum_{i=1}^{n} p_i(\hat{e})\, u(w(x_i)) - v(\hat{e}) \right\} \tag{3.1}$$

where the first restriction is the participation constraint (3.2) and the second is the incentive compatibility constraint (3.1).

When the agent can choose between a finite, but large, number of effort levels, or when effort is a continuous variable, this problem is difficult to analyse and poses solution problems. We will consider these problems later on. First, we look at the conclusions we get in a simpler framework that is easier to analyse.

3.3 The Agent Chooses between Two Effort Levels

Many of the conclusions of more general models can be obtained by studying the problem in which the agent can choose between only two possible effort levels, high (H) and low (L). This case is easy to analyse. We shall also assume that the principal is risk-neutral. This hypothesis simplifies the analysis and, above all, allows us to determine the effect that the asymmetric information has on the form of the optimal contract since under symmetric information the optimal contract is a fixed payment to the agent. Any deviation from this contractual form is due to the existence of the moral hazard problem.

The other case that is easy to solve is that in which the agent is risk-neutral. However, this situation is not interesting since a franchise, that is to say, the same contract as in symmetric information, solves the problem. This case does not allow us to see how information influences the optimal contract, since the asymmetry in this situation is inoffensive.[2] Consequently, we concentrate on a relationship involving a risk-averse agent.

We assume that effort can only take two possible values: $e \in \{e^H, e^L\}$. The level e^H represents the situation in which the agent works hard, while exerting e^L, means that he is being lazy or slacking. Naturally, the disutility of effort is greater when the agent works hard than for a lazy agent: $v(e^H) > v(e^L)$. In the interests of simplicity, we order the set of results X from worst to best: $x_1 < x_2 < \ldots < x_n$. Let $p_i^H = p_i(e^H)$ be the probability that the result will be x_i when the agent offers high effort, for all $i \in \{1, 2, \ldots, n\}$. In the same way, we denote by $p_i^L = p_i(e^L)$ the probability that the result will be x_i when the agent offers low effort. We assume that, for all results, these probabilities are greater than zero. Finally, the principal prefers high effort to low. One case in which productivity is greater given high effort than given low effort is when p^H first order stochastically dominates p^L,[3] that is,

$$\sum_{i=1}^{k} p_i^H < \sum_{i=1}^{k} p_i^L, \quad \text{for all } k = 1, \ldots, n-1.$$

This inequality represents this fact that bad results are more likely when the agent is lazy than when he works hard. Or, in other words, it is easier that the result is greater than x_k (for any $k < n$) when effort is high than when it is low. It is obviously true that $\Sigma_{i=1}^{n} p_i^H = \Sigma_{i=1}^{n} p_i^L = 1$.

[2] See Harris and Raviv (1978) and Shavell (1979). See also Complement 3.

[3] In the two-effort case, e^L and e^H, if the set of results is continuous, it is said that $f^H(x)$ dominates $f^L(x)$ following the first-order dominance criterium if $F^H(x) < F^L(x)$.

It is easy to understand that, if the principal demands low effort, then no true moral hazard problem exits. It is enough to pay the agent a fixed amount, the same that he would be paid under symmetric information in order to guarantee him his reservation utility level, and the agent will choose e^L. To see this, note that given a fixed pay-off, the agent will always choose the minimum effort level, since this will maximize his utility (it minimizes his disutility of effort). Therefore, the optimal contract under symmetric information for e^L, which was to offer the agent the fixed wage $w^L = u^{-1}(\underline{U} + v(e^L))$, satisfies the incentive compatibility constraint only if the principal indeed demands the effort level e^L:

$$u(w^L) - v(e^L) \geq u(w^L) - v(e^H).$$

The symmetric information contract continues to be optimal in this case.

The problem becomes interesting if the principal demands e^H (which will be the case when the good results are very attractive, or in other words, when x_i is large for large i). As we have pointed out earlier, any fixed payment (even that which is optimal under symmetric information for e^H) will only get the agent to choose e^L. In order that the agent chooses e^H we need to search for a contract under which his pay-off depends on the final result achieved. In this case, the incentive compatibility constraint is written as follows:

$$\sum_{i=1}^{n} p_i^H u(w(x_i)) - v(e^H) \geq \sum_{i=1}^{n} p_i^L u(w(x_i)) - v(e^L),$$

which can be written as,

$$\sum_{i=1}^{n} [p_i^H - p_i^L] u(w(x_i)) \geq v(e^H) - v(e^L). \qquad (3.3)$$

Condition (3.3) has a very intuitive interpretation. The agent will choose effort level e^H if the expected utility gain associated with this effort is greater than the implied increase in cost (disutility).

In order to calculate the optimal contract under which the agent chooses high effort, the principal must solve the following problem:

$$\max_{\{w(x_i)\}_{i=1,\ldots,n}} \sum_{i=1}^{n} p_i^H [x_i - w(x_i)]$$

[P3.2]

$$\text{s.t.} \sum_{i=1}^{n} p_i^H u(w(x_i)) - v(e^H) \geq \underline{U} \qquad (3.4)$$

$$\sum_{i=1}^{n} [p_i^H - p_i^L] u(w(x_i)) \geq v(e^H) - v(e^L). \qquad (3.3)$$

We now search for the contracts that are candidates for the solution to problem [P3.2], that is those points that satisfy the Kuhn–Tucker conditions of the problem. The Lagrangean of the system is:

$$L(\{w(x_i)\},\lambda,\mu) = \sum_{i=1}^{n} p_i^H [x_i - w(x_i)] + \lambda \left[\sum_{i=1}^{n} p_i^H u(w(x_i)) - v(e^H) - \underline{U}\right]$$
$$+ \mu \left[\sum_{i=1}^{n} [p_i^H - p_i^L]\, u(w(x_i)) - v(e^H) + v(e^L)\right].$$

Differentiate the Lagrangean with respect to the wage $w(x_i)$, for all $i = 1,\ldots, n$. The first-order conditions are:

$$-p_i^H + \lambda p_i^H u'(w(x_i)) + \mu [p_i^H - p_i^L]\, u'(w(x_i)) = 0, \quad \text{for all } i = 1,\ldots,n,$$

which reduces to,

$$\frac{p_i^H}{u'(w(x_i))} = \lambda p_i^H + \mu [p_i^H - p_i^L], \quad \text{for all } i = 1,\ldots,n. \tag{3.5}$$

Summing equation (3.5) from $i = 1$ up to $i = n$, and bearing in mind that $\Sigma_{i=1}^{n} p_i^H = \Sigma_{i=1}^{n} p_i^L = 1$, we get:

$$\lambda = \sum_{i=1}^{n} \frac{p_i^H}{u'(w(x_i))} > 0 \tag{3.6}$$

(we should point out that, in spite of the incentive constraint not being a concave function in wages, the solution of the first-order conditions is a maximum).[4] Therefore, the Kuhn–Tucker condition with respect to the

[4] To show that the solution of the first-order conditions is a local maximum, we can write the Lagrangean as:

$$\sum_{i=1}^{n} p_i^H [x_i - w(x_i)] + \sum_{i=1}^{n} [\lambda p_i^H + \mu (p_i^H - p_i^L)]\, u(w(x_i)) - \lambda v(e^H) - \mu v(e^H)$$
$$+ \mu v(e^L) - \lambda \underline{U}.$$

The second derivative of this Lagrangean with respect to $w(x_i)$ is:

$$[\lambda p_i^H + \mu (p_i^H - p_i^L)]\, u''(w(x_i)),$$

which is always negative at the points that satisfy the Kuhn–Tucker conditions, since at these points equation (3.5) gives $\lambda p_i^H + \mu (p_i^H - p_i^L) > 0$. Also, the crossed second derivative is always zero. Hence the Hessian of the Lagrangean at a point that satisfies the Kuhn–Tucker conditions is always definite negative. This guarantees a local maximum.

In fact, using a trick provided by Grossmann and Hart (1983), we can even show that the first-order conditions characterize a global maximum of [P3.2]. In order to prove it, the programme should be transformed before it is analysed. Let denote $u_i \equiv u(w(x_i))$ and then $w(x_i) = u^{-1}(u_i)$. Note that $u^{-1}(.)$ is convex. Substituting these expressions in [P3.2], we have a concave programme with linear constraints. For this programme, the Kuhn–Tucker conditions are necessary and sufficient for a maximum. Therefore, the first-order conditions on u_i characterize the global maximum, and note that they correspond to (3.5) once we substitute back u_i by $u(w(x_i))$.

participation constraint multiplier (that requires that $\lambda \geq 0$) is satisfied, and we have shown that the *participation constraint binds* (it holds with equality).[5]

The properties of the optimal contract can be more easily deduced if we rewrite the first-order conditions (3.5) in the following way:

$$\frac{1}{u'(w(x_i))} = \lambda + \mu \left[1 - \frac{p_i^L}{p_i^H}\right] \quad \text{for all } i = 1, \ldots, n.^{6} \qquad (3.7)$$

Note that from this equation it is easy to see that $\mu \neq 0$. This is because if $\mu = 0$, then (3.7) indicates that $w(x_i)$ would have to be constant, as for the symmetric information case. However, if this happens, the incentive compatibility constraint cannot be satisfied: the left-hand side is equal to zero, while the right-hand side is strictly positive. Besides, as we have repeatedly pointed out, a constant wage will only buy the lowest possible effort level.

The Kuhn–Tucker conditions impose that the multiplier μ associated with the incentive compatibility constraint must be non-negative. Therefore, μ is strictly positive. The fact that $\mu > 0$ (the shadow price of the restriction is strictly positive) means that the existence of the moral hazard problem implies a strictly positive cost to the principal. The principal's profits are strictly greater when information on effort is symmetric than when she faces a moral hazard situation.

Since $\mu > 0$, the agent's wage varies according to the result obtained. In particular, the wage will be greater the smaller is the ratio p_i^L/p_i^H. The greater is this quotient the smaller will be the right-hand side of the condition (3.7). If the left-hand side becomes smaller, the denominator must increase, which in turn requires that $w(x_i)$ increase since u' is decreasing. The ratio p_i^L/p_i^H is called the *likelihood ratio*. It indicates the precision with which the result x_i signals that the effort level was e^H. The smaller is the likelihood quotient, the greater is p_i^H with respect to p_i^L, and so the signal that the effort used was e^H is stronger. In other words, a reduction in the likelihood ratio is an increase in the probability that the effort was e^H when the result x_i is observed. Therefore, the wage must be greater if we want the agent to exert high effort. Think, for example, of a situation in which (within the set of results) the probabilities

[5] We note that this property, which is easy to establish for the class of utility functions of the agent that we are considering, is not necessarily satisfied in other contexts (although such contexts are rare). When the agent's utility function is additively separable in pay-off and effort, as is the case of the model we are using, the agent's risk-aversion is independent of the level of effort that he exerts in the relationship. Therefore, if the participation constraint were not binding, the principal could reduce all the wages, respecting the distances between the utilities that the agent gets in the different contingencies, and the incentive constraint would continue to be satisfied. When the agent's utility is not separable in wage and effort, this last statement need not be true, and we cannot initially be sure that the agent's participation constraint will bind.

[6] If we had assumed the principal to be risk-averse, the equation would be unchanged except for the left-hand side which would become $B'(w(x_i))/u'(w(x_i))$ instead of $1/u'(w(x_i))$.

depending on the effort of result x_j are $p_j^H = 0.9$ and $p_j^L = 0.01$, while result x_k has the following probabilities $p_k^H = 0.001$ and $p_k^L = 0.8$. Common sense indicates that if the principal wants to induce the agent to exert effort e^H she must associate a premium with the observation of x_j, and a punishment with the observation of x_k.

If the principal, being risk-neutral, pays the agent according to the result, it is only to give him incentives. Hence she must consider finding an equilibrium between the benefits from insuring the agent, as in the efficient solution, and those available from him having the correct incentives. To satisfy this objective, in the contract she uses the only verifiable variable as a source of information on the agent's behaviour. The principal uses the result in this case with a similar objective to that of statistical inference. The benefit of introducing the result in the contract is the information that it provides on the agent's effort.[7]

An example may help to clarify this point. Assume that no variables relevant to the agent's behaviour are observable and able to be included in the contract. The weather is verifiable, but the agent cannot affect it through his effort, and it has no influence on the agent's performance. The principal could make the agent's wage contingent on the result of the random variable 'weather'. Is she interested in doing this? No. By doing so the only effect is to make the agent's wage variable, but it varies according to something that the agent, or his behaviour, cannot influence. Therefore, this variable has no value as a means of giving the agent incentives, but rather only introduces more risk into the relationship. This increased risk means that the agent will require a higher wage in order to participate, and it has no effect whatsoever on his incentives.

This conclusion is altered when the result is a verifiable variable and the weather has some influence over it (as is the case of agricultural produce). In spite of the fact that the agent's effort does not influence the weather, it does provide information on the result, and so should be taken into account in the optimal contract. A good harvest is generally a much stronger signal of high effort if the weather has been bad than when the weather has been ideal. The optimal payment to an agricultural worker who obtains a good harvest should be greater for bad weather than for good weather.

A fundamental aspect of the optimal scheme is that the wage should not depend at all on the value that the principal places on the result. This is due to the fact that this valuation is independent of the effort exerted, and therefore is not informative as to effort, and does not serve as an incentive for the agent. On the

[7] This is the only value of the result in a moral hazard situation in which the principal is risk-neutral and the agent is risk-averse. In Chapter 2 we have shown that when both participants are risk-averse, the result enters into the optimal symmetric information contract, the objective being the optimal risk-sharing arrangement between them. If we have a moral hazard situation in which both participants are risk-averse, the result will form a part of the contract for two reasons: to achieve the optimal distribution of risk and to provide incentives.

other hand, the result is valuable as an informative device as to the agent's behaviour. The pay-offs are related to this information and will increase in the result so long as a greater result is associated with greater effort. Is it always optimal that the wage be increasing in the result? No. For example, situations exist in which the principal wants the agent to choose an effort whose possible consequences are a huge success or a dismal failure, both with significant probability, and with no intermediate results being very likely. In this case the optimal contract should pay more for low results than for intermediate ones. The contract's objective is not the optimal risk-sharing arrangement, but rather it is a device to give incentives.

The necessary condition for a better result to give a better wage is that p_i^L/p_i^H be decreasing in i. In statistics, this is called the *monotonous likelihood quotient property*. It should be pointed out that it is a strong condition. The hypothesis of first-order stochastic dominance, $\Sigma_{i=1}^{n} p_i^H < \Sigma_{i=1}^{n} p_i^L$, for all $k = 1, \ldots, n-1$, does not guarantee the monotonous likelihood property. However, if this property is satisfied then $w(x_i)$ increases with i. Formally, from condition (3.7) we obtain:

$$u'(w(x_i)) = \frac{1}{\lambda + \mu\left[1 - \dfrac{p_i^L}{p_i^H}\right]},$$

which can be rearranged to get

$$w(x_i) = (u')^{-1}\left(\frac{1}{\lambda + \mu\left[1 - \dfrac{p_i^L}{p_i^H}\right]}\right).$$

In this equation it is easy to see that for those results x_i such that $p_i^L = p_i^H$, $w(x_i) = (u')^{-1}(1/\lambda) = \bar{w}$. We can take this value as a reference. For the x_i such that $p_i^L/p_i^H > 1$, we have $w(x_i) < \bar{w}$ (remember that u' is decreasing), and for those x_i such that $p_i^L/p_i^H < 1$ (indicating that it is more probable that $e = e^H$), we have $w(x_i) > \bar{w}$.

Before continuing with the discussion on the characteristics of the solution to moral hazard, we note with respect to the above arguments that the principal in fact does not carry out statistical inference since it is she who effectively chooses the agent's effort by solving problem [P3.2]. Hence she will know with certainty how the agent will behave. If the agent's wages depend on the result it is because this is the only way to influence his effort, not because the effort choice that the agent makes once the contract has been signed is not predictable.

3.4 Solution Using the First-Order Approach

We have seen the characteristics of the optimal contract given a moral hazard problem when there are only two possible effort variables. As we have noted, taking the agent's effort as a continuous variable, for example $e \in [0, 1]$, is not easy. Problem [$P^{3.1}$] would imply a double maximization, which causes many technical difficulties since one of the restrictions of [$P^{3.1}$] is a second maximization problem: equation (3.1). This incentive compatibility constraint appears in an unmanageable form. In the first studies on moral hazard models, this problem was overcome by substituting the maximization problem of the agent by its first-order condition (Holmström, 1979). This procedure is called the *first-order approach*. The idea is to substitute restriction (3.1) in problem [$P^{3.1}$] for the equation:

$$\sum_{i=1}^{n} p_i'(e)\, u(w(x_i)) - v'(e) = 0. \tag{3.8}$$

The problem posed by this method of solving for the optimal contract is that (3.8) is not always equivalent to the agent's maximization problem (3.1). The reason is that it is only the necessary condition. In general there are more efforts that satisfy (3.8) than those that satisfy (3.1), since it need not be a concave problem. This is a serious setback since we are not discussing the properties of the solution, but rather we are introducing this equation as a restriction in a constrained maximization problem. Therefore, we are allowing ourselves to consider too many points, and we could end up choosing one that is not optimal (for more details, see complementary material 2).

When the first-order approach is correct, the maximization problem of the principal is:

$$\max_{[e,\{w(x_i)\}_{i=1,\dots,n}]} \sum_{i=1}^{n} p_i(e)\,(x_i - w(x_i))$$

[$P^{3.3}$]

$$\text{s.t.} \sum_{i=1}^{n} p_i(e)\, u(w(x_i)) - v(e) \geq \underline{U} \tag{3.2}$$

$$\sum_{i=1}^{n} p_i'(e)\, u(w(x_i)) - v'(e) = 0. \tag{3.8}$$

Letting λ be the multiplier for the participation constraint and μ be that of the incentive compatibility constraint, the first-order condition of the Lagrangean with respect to the wages $w(x_i)$ tells us that:

$$-p_i(e) + \lambda p_i(e) u'(w(x_i)) + \mu p_i'(e) u'(w(x_i)) = 0.$$

This is the necessary condition that the optimal contract must satisfy. We also know that this condition is sufficient for a local maximum since the Hessian at a point that satisfies this condition is negative definite (the reason why is similar to that developed in note 4 of this chapter). Rewriting the first-order condition, we obtain the equality

$$\frac{1}{u'(w(x_i))} = \lambda + \mu \frac{p_i'(e)}{p_i(e)}. \tag{3.9}$$

Equation (3.9) implies that, when $\mu > 0$,[8] that is when there is a real moral hazard problem, the condition of optimal risk-sharing associated with the case of symmetric information is not satisfied. That is, the wages will depend on the result obtained. The dependence of the wages on the result in turn depends on the form of the function $p_i'(e)/p_i(e)$.

Assume that $p_i'(e)/p_i(e)$ is increasing with i, $i = 1, \ldots, n$. In this case, the right-hand side of (3.9) also increases with i, and so the same must happen to the left-hand side. Given the characteristics of the utility function, this implies that $w(x_i)$ is increasing in i. The condition that the likelihood quotient is increasing means that a good result is a signal that, with high probability, good effort was exerted. Or, in other words, it is more likely that when effort is high, the result is good. The conclusion is the same as that for the two possible efforts case.

Finally, a comment on the effort that the principal demands of the agent under the optimal contract. In spite of the fact that problem [P3.3] is generally not concave in effort, we know that a necessary condition that the optimal effort must satisfy is the first-order condition of the Lagrangean with respect to e. This condition is written as:

$$\sum_{i=1}^{n} p_i'(e)(x_i - w(x_i)) + \mu \left[\sum_{i=1}^{n} p_i''(e) u(w(x_i)) - v''(e) \right] = 0,$$

which can be expressed as,

$$\sum_{i=1}^{n} p_i'(e) x_i = \sum_{i=1}^{n} p_i'(e) w(x_i) - \mu \left[\sum_{i=1}^{n} p_i''(e) u(w(x_i)) - v''(e) \right] \tag{3.10}$$

(we have used the fact that when we derive the participation constraint with respect to effort, the same expression appears as for the incentive compatibility constraint, which we know to be zero). What is interesting about (3.10) is that it shows the trade-off between profits (the term on the left-hand side of

[8] We will not prove that $\mu > 0$, which is very intuitive but requires some calculations. Holmström (1979) proves that $\mu > 0$ so long as the sum $\Sigma_{i=1}^{k} p_i(e)$ is increasing in e for $k = 1, \ldots, n-1$, or in other words the condition of first-order stochastic dominance is satisfied.

the equality) and costs (the right-hand side). The costs are associated with how an agent's expected wage changes for given changes in effort and the incentive compatibility constraint, whose shadow price is given by the multiplier μ.

Let's go back for a moment to the symmetric information framework. Equation (2.9) is, in this case, the necessary condition of problem [P2.1] that the optimal effort must satisfy. In fact, had we obtained the necessary condition directly from the Lagrangean, the expression would have been:

$$\sum_{i=1}^{n} p_i'(e)\, x_i = \sum_{i=1}^{n} p_i'(e)\, w(x_i) - \lambda^o \left[\sum_{i=1}^{n} p_i'(e)\, u(w(x_i)) - v'(e)\right] \quad (3.11)$$

(it is easy to show that this equation is identical to (2.9)). Comparing (3.10) and (3.11) shows that, while under symmetric information the participation constraint determines the optimal effort level, when there is a moral hazard problem it is the cost implied by the incentive compatibility constraint that becomes the most important element in determining the effort to be demanded of the agent.

We have already mentioned that the first-order approach is not always valid. In complementary material 2 we illustrate graphically the problems that this method can pose. The way to avoid these problems is either to work with models in which the initial hypotheses guarantee that the problem is well defined (in the sense that it is possible to apply the first-order method without errors), or to find some other way to solve the problem. The first method consists of introducing restrictions on the distribution function for the results conditional on effort. In the following section we analyse a simple framework in which sufficient conditions for the correct use of the first-order approach are satisfied. The second method is what is known as a two-stage process, and it was proposed by Grossman and Hart (1983). They showed that it is possible to analyse the characteristics of the optimal contract independently of being able to identify the optimal effort or not. We will not enter into their model, although their ideas have been implicitly included in the analysis that we have developed up to now.

3.5 A Simple Case with Continuous Effort

In this section we shall describe a situation with a continuum of possible efforts, but which is in fact only a simple extension of the model with only two efforts that we have already worked with. Assume that the probability function for the agent's effort takes the following form:

$$p_i(e) = e\,p_i^H + (1-e)\,p_i^L,$$

for $e \in [0,1]$. Hart and Holmström (1987) call this form the *condition of linearity of the distribution function.* It is as if the agent could play a (random) mixed strategy in the case of two efforts. The greater is the effort e that the agent exerts, the closer is the probability to those of the discrete case for e^H. In any case, it is only meant to be an illustrative example.

In this model the first-order approach is valid. To see this, note that the agent's expected utility in function of effort is:

$$\begin{aligned} \mathrm{E}U(e) &= \sum_{i=1}^{n} [e\,p_i^H + (1-e)\,p_i^L]\; u(w(x_i)) - v(e) \\ &= \sum_{i=1}^{n} p_i^L\, u(w(x_i)) + e \sum_{i=1}^{n} [p_i^H - p_i^L]\; u(w(x_i)) - v(e). \end{aligned}$$

Given that we have assumed $v''(e) \geq 0$, this expression is concave in effort since $\mathrm{E}U''(e) = -v''(e) \leq 0$. If we also assume that the solution is interior, for example if $v'(0) = 0$ and $v'(1) = +\infty$, then an effort level satisfies the incentive compatibility constraint if and only if it satisfies the first-order condition:

$$\sum_{i=1}^{n} [p_i^H - p_i^L]\; u(w(x_i)) = v'(e).$$

Therefore, for the probability function that we are considering, problems [P3.1] and [P3.3] are equivalent, and we can be sure that the conclusions of the previous section are valid. The problem that the principal must solve to design the contract is:

$$\max_{[e,\{w(x_i)\}_{i=1,\dots n}]} \sum_{i=1}^{n} [e\,p_i^H + (1-e)\,p_i^L]\,(x_i - w(x_i))$$

[P3.4]

$$\text{s.t.} \sum_{i=1}^{n} [e\,p_i^H + (1-e)\,p_i^L]\; u(w(x_i)) - v(e) \geq \underline{U} \qquad (3.12)$$

$$\sum_{i=1}^{n} [p_i^H - p_i^L]\; u(w(x_i)) - v'(e) = 0. \qquad (3.13)$$

Calling λ and μ the multipliers of the participation and incentive compatibility constraints respectively, we can rewrite equation (3.9), that gave us the wage in function of the result, in the following way:

$$\frac{1}{u'(w(x_i))} = \lambda + \mu \frac{[p_i^H - p_i^L]}{[e\,p_i^H + (1-e)p_i^L]}. \qquad (3.14)$$

If the function

$$\frac{[p_i^H - p_i^L]}{[e\,p_i^H + (1-e)p_i^L]}$$

increases in the results, that is, if it increases with i, then (3.14) indicates that the pay-off associated with the contingencies increases with the results (recall that we have ordered the set of results from smallest to biggest). It is easy to see that this expression would increase in the results if p_i^L/p_i^H decreases in i. Hence the condition is the same as was needed in the two possible efforts model analysed in Section 3 of this chapter.

In the simple model that we are studying in this section, we can also think about how to calculate the optimal effort level that the principal will demand of the agent. Note that in problem [P3.4] the objective function is linear in e, the participation constraint (3.12) is concave in effort, and the necessary and sufficient condition for the incentive compatibility constraint to be concave in e is $v'''(e) \geq 0$. For simplicity, we shall assume this in order to have a problem that is concave in effort. In this case, we can be sure that the necessary and sufficient condition for an effort level to be optimal is that it satisfies the first-order condition of the Lagrangean with respect to effort. That is:

$$\sum_{i=1}^{n} [p_i^H - p_i^L]\ (x_i - w(x_i)) - \mu\, v''(e) = 0\,. \tag{3.15}$$

The continuous effort model that we have presented in this section is very simple, but it does have the advantage of allowing us to discuss the same aspects as more general models, in which the first-order approach is applied. In applications and exercises, we shall see that the simple conclusions we derive from this model have important consequences in numerous relevant economic situations.

3.6 Moral Hazard with Hidden Information

Up to now we have been considering a moral hazard problem in situations in which the principal has no direct control over the agent's effort. However, a second form of moral hazard exists, to which the literature has paid scant attention, but which deserves to be looked at here. We have defined a moral hazard situation as one in which the agent's behaviour is his private information. This can be so in two ways: either because it is not observable, or because even if it is observable, it is impossible for the principal to know if it is the best-effort decision. In this other type of moral hazard problem, once the relationship is established, the agent obtains information on the environment that will determine which effort level is the most adequate, and this information is not observable or not verifiable by the principal (see Figure 3.2).

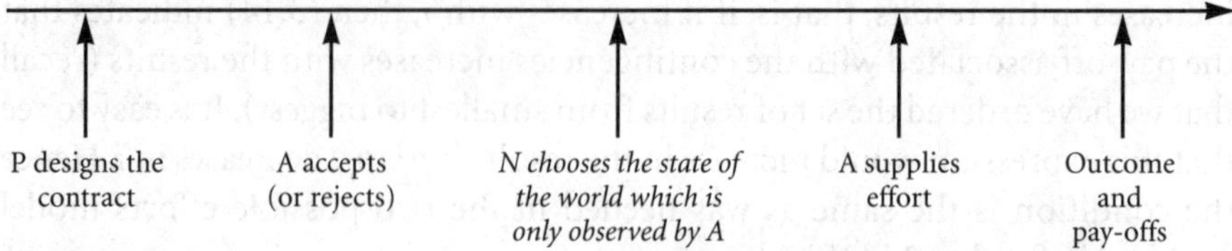
P designs the contract
A accepts (or rejects)
N chooses the state of the world which is only observed by A
A supplies effort
Outcome and pay-offs

Fig. 3.2

For example, we could consider an import-export agent who works for a firm. The agent does not know how well the product will fare in foreign markets until he begins to work there, but according to this information he must choose the best strategy for the firm in the foreign market. The firm (the principal) observes the agent's decision as to the strategy, but since she doesn't observe the conditions under which this decision was taken, she cannot know if it is optimal or not. As a second example in which this type of asymmetric information is present, consider the case of an individual who gives money to a financial intermediary to be invested. The investment decision is observable to the investor since he knows which shares have been bought with his money. However, the investor cannot know if this is the best decision given the information that the intermediary has on the current stock-market conditions.

In this section we briefly present the results of this type of model, without solving it properly. Given the similarity between these problems and those of adverse selection, we present a problem of this type as complementary material to Chapter 4, and we leave a second example as an exercise for that chapter.

Before beginning, we should make a comment and a distinction. At the moment of the signing of the contract, the agent does not know the conditions under which he will carry out his tasks, but he does know these conditions before exerting any effort. Therefore, the agent learns if he has had good luck (the conditions are favourable) or bad luck (unfavourable conditions) before taking any effort decisions. Given that he will normally get less utility in the second case than in the first, and since the principal cannot observe the conditions under which he works, it is possible that when he obtains the information, he may repent having accepted the job in the first place (his expected utility may be less than his reservation utility). Depending on the institutional conditions under which the contract was signed, it is possible that if the agent has bad news with respect to the conditions, he may break off the relationship. For this reason there are two types of model: those that include an *ex ante* participation constraint (that is, given the expected utility at the moment at which the contract is signed, if the agent accepts he cannot break off the contract at a later date), as has been the case up to now, and a second class of model that includes *ex post* participation constraints (one for each contingency) so that the agent gets an expected utility never less than his reservation utility in all contingencies.

Let us describe a model that reflects the type of situation that we want to analyse. Assume that after having signed the contract the agent learns, for example, whether the job is easy or arduous, or whether the market conditions are good or bad. We denote the market conditions by the variable θ. A high level of θ ($\theta = \theta^G$) indicates a favourable situation, while any effort decision will be more costly to the agent if the value of θ is low ($\theta = \theta^B$, where $\theta^B < \theta^G$). In order that the model be simple, we assume that the agent exerts a total effort of E, but that this effort is more costly under unfavorable market conditions. In particular, $E = \theta + e$, where the decision on e implies a disutility to the agent, but the θ part doesn't. The agent chooses the costly part of effort, e, contingent on the information he learns on θ. It is only after the contract has been signed that the agent (and not the principal) learns the true value of θ , θ^B, or θ^G. The principal observes the total decision E, but since she is unable to distinguish the market conditions, she does not know if the agent has exerted high or low effort. For example, in the case of the import-export agent, the firm knows how many clients the agent has achieved and what was the transaction price, but does not know if the agent had to work hard to get this result, or if it was very easy (in which case the agent should have been able to get more clients since the conditions were favourable).

In symmetric information, that is, when the principal observes the state of nature θ and the total effort E, she knows the costly effort: $e = E - \theta$. Let's assume that the principal's profits are just the total effort $E = \theta + e$. In this case, in the optimum the marginal product should equal the marginal cost (see the complementary material of Chapter 4 for more details). The marginal product of e is 1, while the marginal cost depends on the disutility of effort and the form in which the wage affects the agent's utility (but it does not depend on θ). The optimal effort is therefore independent of θ ; $e^*(\theta^B) = e^*(\theta^G) = e^*$. Besides this, since the agent is risk-averse, the optimal contract requires that in both contingencies he receives the same wage w^*. It is easy to show that the optimal contract (e^*, w^*) must satisfy the efficiency condition: $u'(w^*) = v'(e^*)$. Note that this contract leads to two different total efforts, $E^B = \theta^B + e^* < \theta^G + e^* = E^G$. Now, if the principal observes the agent's effort decision E, but not the conditions under which this decision was taken, we have a moral hazard problem. If the principal offers a fixed wage, whenever the agent observes θ^G he will be interested in exerting an effort e less than the optimum, and then telling the principal that the market conditions were unfavourable ($\theta = \theta^B$), and so his decision was E^B. This is true because if the agent takes the total decision E^B when the conditions are θ^G, the cost is determined by $e = E^B - \theta^G < E^B - \theta^B = e^*$, from which the disutility of effort will be less than had he exerted, e^*, thus giving him greater than reservation utility.

When the moral hazard problem appears (whether under the *ex ante* or the *ex post* incentive constraint), the contract has the following characteristics. The principal demands a different effort e according to the information the agent has. In particular, when the agent learns that the conditions are good, the contract will lead him to exert an effort of e^G such that the efficiency condition is satisfied, $u'(w^G) = v'(e^G)$, where w^G is the wage that the principal pays him in this situation. On the other hand, a distortion is introduced with respect to the effort demanded when the market is bad, since $v'(e^B) < u'(w^B)$. The objective of this distortion is to make this contract less attractive to the agent when the market situation is good.

When the participation constraint is to be satisfied *ex ante*, that is, when the agent cannot break off the relationship once the contract has been signed, the utility that he gets under good market conditions is greater than his utility under bad market conditions. However, on average, the utility will be equal to the reservation level. In the case in which the agent can break off the relationship, that is, if the participation constraint is to be satisfied *ex post*, the agent gets expected utility greater than the reservation level. He will get $\underline{U}$ when the market situation is bad, but his utility will be greater than $\underline{U}$ if the situation is favourable. This case brings us close to the conclusions of adverse selection models, as will become clear in the next chapter.

The existence of a moral hazard problem with hidden information introduces important inefficiencies into the contract that the principal offers the agent. On the one hand, the principal distorts the contract when the market conditions are bad, thereby provoking an inefficient effort in this case. On the other hand, the agent obtains utilities that differ according to the state of the market. As we know, this is also inefficient when the agent is risk-averse and the principal is risk-neutral.

3.7 Some Comments on Simple Moral Hazard Models

The conclusions of the models analysed in this chapter are very simple, but they do give a good general idea as to many aspects of the relationships and they do explain many of the characteristics of the optimal contract. Here we briefly discuss a few of these characteristics.

3.7.1 The value of information

The moral hazard problem implies a cost to the relationship, since it leads to a worse situation than that obtained under symmetric information. In order to alleviate this problem as far as possible, the principal is interested in any signals that reveal new information on the agent's effort (Holmström, 1979). This means that the contract can be contingent on many things, not only the result of the relationship. Any information related to the state of nature is useful, since it allows better estimations of the agent's effort thus reducing the risk inherent in the relationship. This result is known as the *sufficient statistic result*, and it is perhaps the most important conclusion in the moral hazard literature. Its empirical content is the following. A contract should exploit all available information in order to filter out risk optimally. (Not in order to better infer the agent's effort, since the principal knows the agent's effort with certainty in equilibrium.) The sufficient statistic result has as a consequence, for example, when a principal enters into a relationship with more than one agent, she may take into account the results of all of them when paying each one. This is the case when the result of one agent provides information on the state of nature affecting another agent.

All information on the effort of the agent is valuable since it allows the cost of the contract to be reduced. Therefore the principal is willing to pay to get this information. Control activities that do not affect the result may be useful (even if they are costly) so long as they act as signals on the effort exerted by the agent. The usefulness of the control system will depend on the degree of information that it gives on the behaviour of the participants. Of course, the intensity of the control chosen by the principal will depend on the trade-off between the associated costs of the control and the benefits of the information obtained on the agent's effort.

3.7.2 Mechanisms based on severe punishments

Sometimes contracts include very severe punishments when certain results are obtained. This occurs when these results are a perfect signal that the effort is not that demanded (Harris and Raviv, 1979). For example, even if it is difficult to prove that a worker has worked hard or has slacked, it is easy to know if he has appeared on the job. If the worker has not even gone to work, then the principal can conclude that without doubt his effort has been low (or zero). Therefore, contracts can stipulate that not coming to work will result in being fired (a very severe punishment). Notice, however, that severe punishments are not intended to be implemented: they work as a threat. We could say that only a bad coachman has actually to use his whip, for a good coachman the threat is sufficient.

If the principal has access to a perfect signal on the agent's effort, she will be able to reach the first best using enough severe threats, so there is no moral hazard 'problem'. It is for this reason (to avoid perfect signals) that we have assumed that all results have a strictly positive probability under any effort level.

In many relationships, a perfect signal on the agent's behaviour is only obtainable through the use of a control system. In this case, we should find a trade-off between the frequency with which the control is used and the punishment. The more often the control is used, the less interested will the agent be in offering low effort, and so the punishments required so that he will not deviate are small. However, if the control is carried out infrequently, then the punishments required will have to be very severe in order that the agent is dissuaded from slacking on the job.

3.7.3 The strategic effects of contracts

In the study that we have carried out on optimal contracts for the agency relationship, we have not taken into account the possible effects that the decisions and actions of the participants may have on third parties. For example, in applying the analysis to contracts between shareholders and managers, we did not take into account how the contracts would affect the production decisions of the firm's competitors. This is not important for two types of situations. The first is when the relationships do not affect, and are not affected by, third-party decisions. For example, in a monopoly firm, the manager's contract searches only for internal efficiency, i.e. to solve in the best possible way the incentive aspects. The second type of situation for which third parties are irrelevant is when there exist conditions close to perfect competition. That is, when the size of the relationship under consideration is very small compared to external interrelationships, then the internal aspects will be more important than the strategic ones.

However, the strategic aspects become much more relevant in those cases in which the decisions of others (normally rivals) is affected by the contract signed by the principal and the agent. In such a situation a contract is not only an incentive device, but also is an attempt to influence the behaviour of third parties. Vickers (1985), in a symmetric information framework, analysed the strategic value of contracts. He showed that shareholders are interested in paying their managers according to the results obtained with the objective of making their competitors produce less, or set higher prices. Also Salas Fumás (1992) and Faulí (1995) explicitly introduce both ingredients into their model.

Their fundamental goal is to analyse how strategic interests influence the optimal incentive contracts between shareholders and managers.

Hence we should take into account the fact that the conclusions arrived at in this chapter may well be affected if the strategic aspects of the contracts are important.

3.7.4 What happens when it is the agent who offers the contract?

In this chapter, as is usual in the literature, we have always assumed that it is the principal (the owner of the relationship) who offers the contract, and that the agent can only accept or reject it. However, in certain real-life situations the opposite occurs: the person who will carry out the job is the one who offers the contract to the owner of the relationship. In this case, the principal still gets the result of the relationship, but can only accept or reject the agent's proposition. The conclusions obtained in this framework are exactly the same as in the models presented in this chapter (in the same way in which in the definition of a Pareto-efficient situation it doesn't matter if one maximizes the utility of one individual under the restriction that the other gets a certain utility level, or vice versa). When the agent designs the contract, he must take into account the fact that the principal will only accept believable contracts, that is, those contracts under which the agent will effectively offer that effort that he announces in the contract. In other words, the same trade-off between incentives and efficiency appears, and the characteristics of the optimal contract are the similar. The only difference is that it is the principal (instead of the agent) who is put at her reservation utility level.

3A Complementary Material

3A.1 A geometric illustration of the moral hazard problem[9]

In order to graphically present the moral hazard problem, we consider a relationship between a principal and an agent with only two possible results: one high, x_2, and the other low x_1, with $x_2 > x_1$. The probability with which they each occur depends on the agent's effort, e, and a random state variable. We

[9] In the same way as for Ch. 2, this graphical representation is based on the article by Ricketts (1986).

assume that the agent can only choose between two possible effort levels, e^H and e^L. We denote Prob $[x = x_2 \mid e^H] = p^H$ and Prob $[x = x_1 \mid e^H] = 1 - p^H$. In the same way, Prob $[x = x_2 \mid e^L] = p^L$ and Prob $[x = x_1 \mid e^L] = 1 - p^L$, and we assume that $p^H > p^L$. The agent's utility is of the form $U(w, e) = u(w) - v(e)$, with the same assumptions as in Chapters 2 and 3, and with $v(e^H) > v(e^L)$. The principal is risk-neutral.

In Chapter 2, we showed the optimal symmetric information contracts in the *Edgeworth Box.* Now we shall draw the optimal choice for the moral hazard problem. When the agent's effort is not public information, the problem that defines the optimal contract when the principal wants the agent to exert an effort of e^H is written:

$$\max_{[w_2, w_1, e]} \quad p^H (x_2 - w_2) + (1 - p^H)(x_1 - w_1)$$

$$[\text{P}] \qquad \text{s.t.} \quad p^H u(w_2) + (1 - p^H) u(w_1) - v(e^H) \geq \underline{U}$$

$$p^H u(w_2) + (1 - p^H) u(w_1) - v(e^H) \geq p^L u(w_2) + (1 - p^L) u(w_1) - v(e^L).$$

Let $f(w_2, w_1)$ be the set of contingent contracts (w_2, w_1) such that the incentive compatibility constraint binds. That is, $(w_2, w_1) \in f(w_2, w_1)$ if the following restriction is satisfied:

$$p^H u(w_2) + (1 - p^H) u(w_1) - v(e^H) = p^L u(w_2) + (1 - p^L) u(w_1) - v(e^L). \qquad (3.C1)$$

For the contracts that belong to $f(w_2, w_1)$ the agent is indifferent between offering effort level e^H or effort level e^L. It is easy to show that if, for a contract in the set $f(w_2, w_1)$, the wage w_2 is increased (an increase in the pay-off associated with the result x_2) while w_1 remains unchanged, the first term of the above expression will be greater than the second, while if it is w_1 that increases and w_2 that remains unchanged, then the second term will be greater than the first. This can also be expressed by rewriting the above condition for the contracts in $f(w_2, w_1)$ as:

$$u(w_2) = u(w_1) + \frac{v(e^H) - v(e^L)}{p^H - p^L}. \qquad (3.C2)$$

Condition (3.C2) is shown in Figure 3.3 (we draw the set $f(w_2, w_1)$ as a straight line for simplicity, but there is no reason to assume that it will not be curved). In order to see how the incentives of the agent work, think about what would be his optimal decision for a contract that is above the line $f(w_2, w_1)$. These contracts, for the same pay-off for good results (w_2), pay more for bad results (w_1). Therefore, for these contracts the agent does not have much incentive to work hard. To see this, you only need to check that the two effort levels give the same utility only on the set $f(w_2, w_1)$. Consequently, the effort that gives the agent greatest utility if he signs a contract located above the line is e^L, while below the line he will choose the effort e^H.

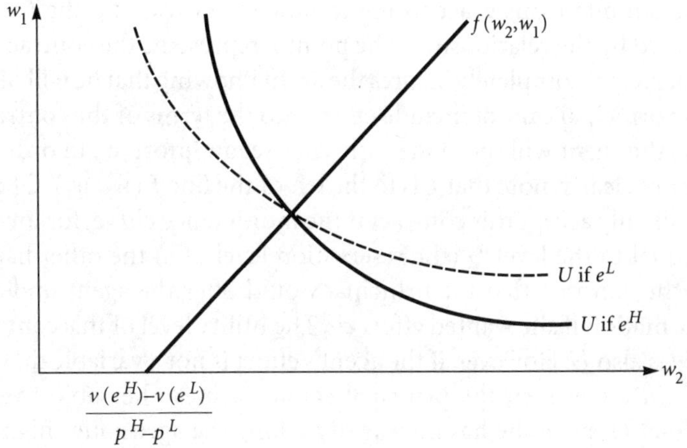

Fig. 3.3

Concerning the principal, it is easy to show that the points at which her expected profit is the same independent of the agent's effort choice are those that satisfy the following equality:

$$p^H(x_2 - w_2) + (1 - p^H)(x_1 - w_1) = p^L(x_2 - w_2) + (1 - p^L)(x_1 - w_1).$$

This equation defines the 45° line in the space $(x_2 - w_2), (x_1 - w_1)$. This allows us to draw the graph of Figure 3.4 (where B will always be used to refer to the principal's profits). The principal is only indifferent between both effort levels

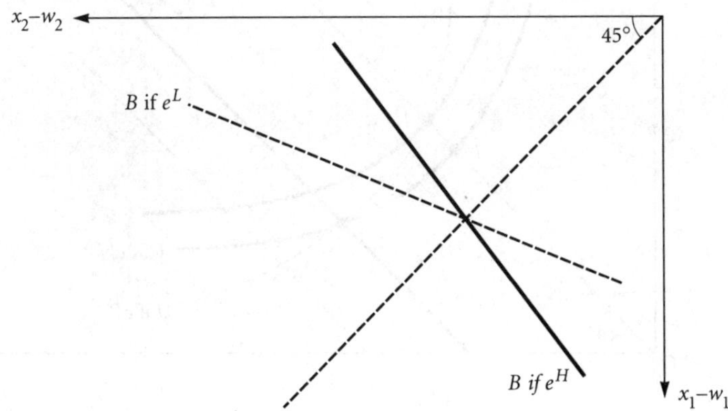

Fig. 3.4

when the contract she offers the agent is such that $x_2 - w_2 = x_1 - w_1$, and so she prefers high effort to the left of the 45º line (when the surplus from a bad result $(x_1 - w_1)$ is less than the surplus from a good result $(x_2 - w_2)$) and low effort to the right.

Now put both Figures together. Figure 3.5 shows the level contours of both participants simultaneously, according to how they divide up the (random) surplus created by the relationship. The point L represents the contract under which the principal completely insures the agent knowing that he will offer low effort. If the principal cannot include effort into the terms of the contract and she offers L, the agent will spontaneously choose low effort, e^L. In order to see this even more clearly, note that L is to the left of the line $f\,(w_2, w_1)$. Of course, the agent will only accept this contract if the indifference curve, for low effort, is at least equal to the level $\underline{U}$ (the reservation level). On the other hand, the point H is the contract that the principal would offer the agent under symmetric information if she wanted effort e^H. The utility level of this contract for the effort e^H is also $\underline{U}$. However, if the agent's effort is not a variable that can be allowed for in a contract, the principal cannot achieve her objective if she offers contract H, since she has no way of making the agent offer high effort, and the agent will spontaneously choose low effort since H is to the left of the line $f\,(w_2, w_1)$. Contract H will lead the agent to offer the effort level e^L since this is the strategy that maximizes his utility (see Figure 3.5). However, this would result in the principal getting less profits than she expected.

What contract should the principal offer in order to get the agent to exert the effort level e^H? It must be a contract such that the agent will agree to sign, and then once the relationship has been established, he must spontaneously choose to exert e^H. This implies that the principal should offer the contract H'

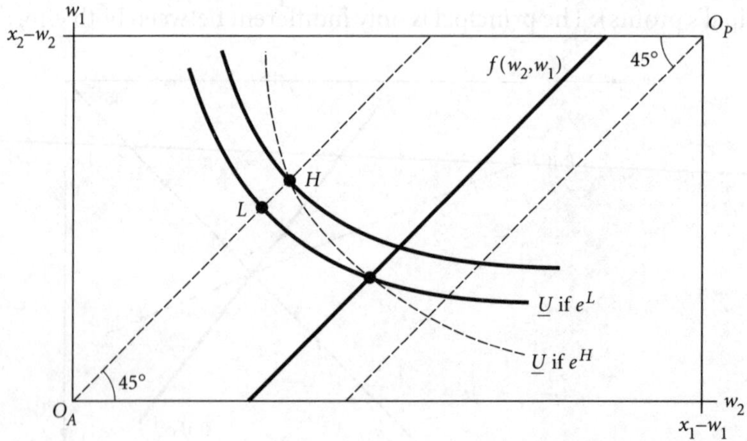

Fig. 3.5

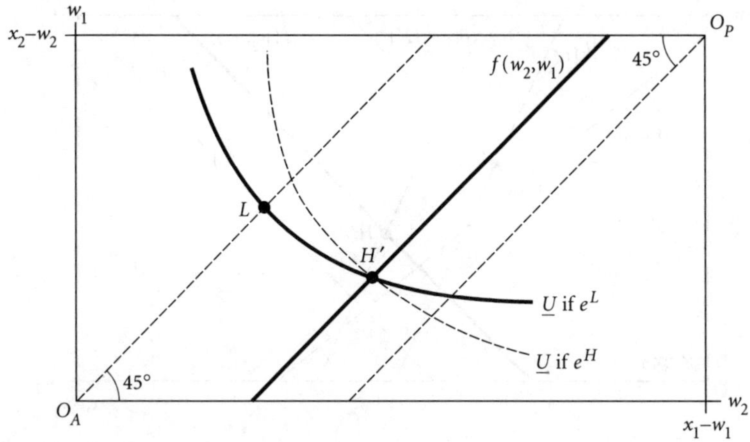

Fig. 3.6

(see Figure 3.6) since it is the least-cost way of satisfying the incentive compatibility constraint (it is on or to the right of the line $f(w_2, w_1)$) and the participation constraint (it is on or above the indifference curve with expected utility of $\underline{U}$, assuming effort level e^H).

Formally, H' is the solution of problem [P] set out above, and is expressed by the equations:

$$u(w_2) = \underline{U} + v(e^H) + (1 - p^H)\,\frac{v(e^H) - v(e^L)}{p^H - p^L}$$

$$u(w_1) = \underline{U} + v(e^H) - p^H\,\frac{v(e^H) - v(e^L)}{p^H - p^L}.$$

Now we know which is the optimal pay-off system when the principal wants the agent to exert low effort (point L), and which is the optimal contract should she require high effort (point H'). The important question that remains is just which effort level does the principal prefer that the agent exerts. In order to decide, we only need to compare the expected profits of each alternative and then choose the best one. In Figure 3.7 (where, in the interests of simplicity, we have eliminated the indifference contours of the agent) we have drawn a situation in which, even though in symmetric information the principal would choose high effort, under asymmetric information she contracts the agent to exert low effort (the continuous line that passes through L crosses the 45° line through origin O_P below where the discontinuous line that passes through H' does so).

In other cases, like that shown in Figure 3.8 for example, the principal will continue to contract the agent to exert high effort, but she will obtain a lower

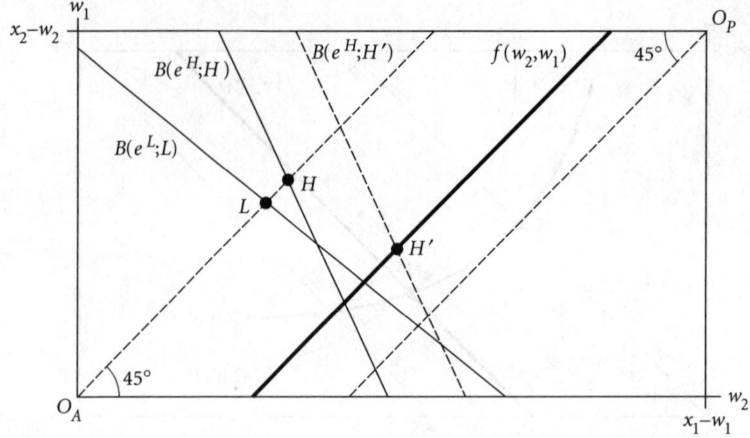

Fig. 3.7

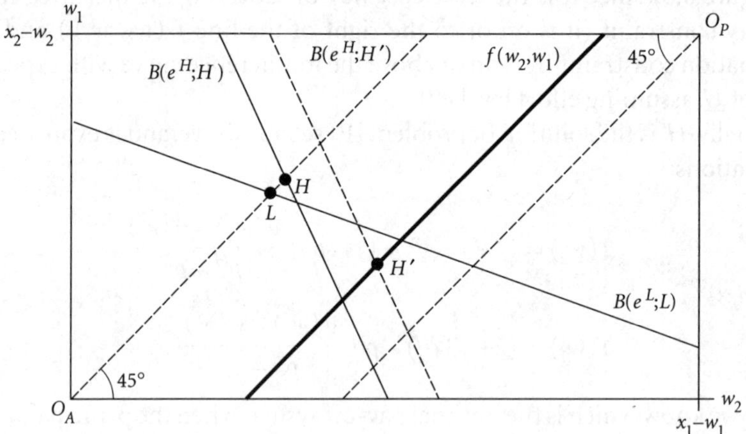

Fig. 3.8

expected profit than when she could observe the agent's effort (note where the different iso-expected profit curves cross the 45° line through origin O_P).

In spite of the difficulty of analysing most moral hazard problems graphically, the graphs of this section are useful for at least two reasons. First, since the reference point for asymmetric information models is a Pareto-efficient allocation, and since this allocation is so often represented in an Edgeworth Box diagram, the analysis that we have carried out allows us to see graphically the distortions generated by the informational asymmetries. Secondly, for those readers who are graphically minded, this section should be helpful in clarifying the results obtained mathematically.

3A.2 The problem that may be found when applying the first-order approach

The first-order approach that allows us to study the characteristics of the optimal contract under moral hazard is not always correct, as was pointed out by Mirrlees (1975). The problem that can occur is the following. Even though the habitual hypothesis on the utility function guarantee that it is concave in effort, the expected utility function

$$\mathrm{E}U(e) = \sum_{i=1}^{n} p_i(e)\, u(w(x_i)) - v(e),$$

in which effort also influences the distribution of results, will only be concave in e under additional restrictions. It is only under these restrictions that the first-order condition is sufficient and thus adequately resumes the agent's behaviour. In any other case, the first-order condition is necessary for a maximum, but it is not sufficient. This means that, when we use the first-order condition, we are considering too many points as candidates to satisfy the incentive compatibility constraint. In fact, some of them are not optimal, that is, in reality they do not satisfy this constraint (they do not maximize the agent's utility, but rather are minima or saddle points).

The difficulty of applying the first-order approach indiscriminately can be shown graphically (see Figures 3.9 and 3.10).[10] We use the space defined by effort and wage (using the wage as a representation of the multidimensional payment scheme). In this space we draw the set of points that satisfy the first-order condition of the agent's maximization problem. That is, EE' is the set of

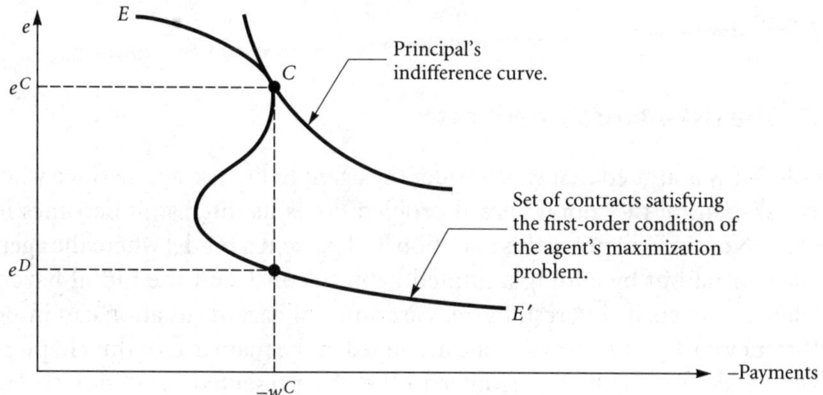

Fig. 3.9

[10] This graphical illustration was proposed by Andreu Mass-Colell.

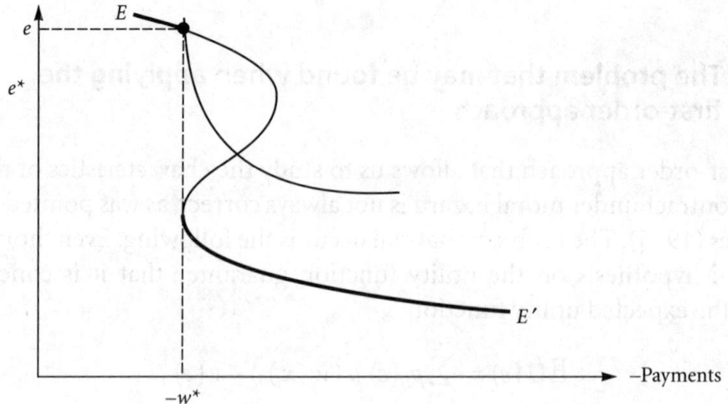

Fig. 3.10

points that satisfies equation (3.7). If the principal chooses from this set that contract that maximizes her objective function, she will propose contract *C* to the agent.

However, *EE*′ does not reflect optimal behaviour on behalf of the agent (shown in bold print in Figure 3.10), and if the principal proposes contract *C*, the agent will respond with effort e^D instead of e^C (the wages are the same, and effort e^D is lower than effort e^C). Hence, in fact contract *C* will not be the solution to the principal's problem. The solution is shown in Figure 3.10, where only the true optimal choices of the agent are taken into account. This is due to the fact that, since the agent's preferences are decreasing in $(e, -w)$, only the bold parts of *EE*′ are compatible with maximizing behaviour. The consequence is that, applying the first-order approach without being sure that the problem behind the incentive constraint is well defined can lead to incorrect solutions.[11]

3A.3 The risk-neutral agent case

In note 3 it was argued that we consider the agent to be risk-averse since when he is risk-neutral the moral hazard problem loses its interest; it becomes irrelevant. Now we will prove this assertion and present a model where the agent is risk-neutral but by adding a limited liability constraint the moral hazard problems recovers its interest. In this case a moral hazard situation can imply inefficiency costs (similar to the one discussed in the main text of this chapter).

The model we use here is similar to the one presented in Section 3. The effort can only take two possible values: $e \in \{e^H, e^L\}$, with $e^H > e^L$. The set of

[11] Rogerson (1985*a*) obtains sufficient conditions for this problem to disappear.

results is $X = \{x_1, x_2, \ldots, x_n\}$, where results are ordered from worst to best. Let p_i^H be the probability that the result will be x_i when the agent offers e^H, while p_i^L denotes the probability that the result will be x_i when the agent offers e^L, for all $i \in \{1, 2, \ldots, n\}$.

Both the principal and the agent are assumed to be risk-neutral. In this case the optimal contract under which the agent chooses high effort is the solution to:

$$\max_{\{w(x_i)\}_{i=1,\ldots,n}} \sum_{i=1}^{n} p_i^H [x_i - w(x_i)]$$

$$\text{s.t.} \quad \sum_{i=1}^{n} p_i^H w(x_i) - v(e^H) \geq \underline{U}$$

$$\sum_{i=1}^{n} [p_i^H - p_i^L]\, w(x_i) \geq v(e^H) - v(e^L)\,.$$

Let us denote by λ the Lagrange multiplier associated to the participation constraint and μ the one associated to the incentive compatibility constraint. From the first order conditions with respect to the wage $w(x_i)$ (for all $i \in \{1, 2, \ldots, n\}$) it is easy to prove that (and that relies on the risk-neutrality of the agent) $\lambda = 1$ and $\mu = 0$. The result $\lambda = 1$ means that if we increase in one (expected) monetary unit the agent's utility, the principal's welfare will decrease (in expectation) exactly in this amount. The condition $\mu = 0$ means that the incentive compatibility constraint is not binding, which in turn says that the solution to the previous programme is in fact the first-best solution. The intuition behind this result is simple. Given that the agent is risk-neutral, the principal does not face the trade-off between incentive provision and risk-sharing, since the agent can bear all the risk at no cost.

Imagine now that there is some legal precept forbidding payments under some threshold, say w^{MIN}. That is, a limited liability constraint must be taken into account. The programme defining the optimal contract will now include the extra set of constraints:

$$w(x_i) \geq w^{MIN} \quad \text{for all } i \in \{1, 2, \ldots, n\}$$

When none of these constraints is binding, we return to the previous framework. But it may be the case that the principal would need to set some payment under w^{MIN} in order to reach the first-best solution. In this case, the limited liability constraint makes it no longer possible to reach this solution. In order to induce the agent to offer e^H, which requires certain separation between the different payments, the principal is forced to give the agent an expected utility greater than $\underline{U} + v(e^H)$, since payments are binding from below.

Let us clarify the discussion by an example. Imagine that the set of results includes only the two items, that we will refer to as failure and success. Let w_F denote the payment associated with failure, and w_S the one associated with success. Assume that $v(e^H) = 7$, $v(e^L) = 0$, $p_S^H = 0.9$, $p_F^H = 0.1$, $p_S^L = 0.2$ and $p_F^L = 0.8$. Let $\underline{U} = 1$. In this example the incentive compatibility and participation constraints can be written as:

$$0.1\ w_F + 0.9\ w_S - 7 \geq 1$$

$$(0.1 - 0.8)\ w_F + (0.9 - 0.2)\ w_S \geq 7 \leftrightarrow \quad w_S - w_F \geq \frac{7}{0.7} = 10.$$

The incentive compatibility constraint just says that the difference between both payments must be, at least, 10 monetary units. If there is no limited liability constraint, the principal can set $w_S = 9$ and $w_F = -1$ and induce the agent to offer high effort paying him in expectation just 8, as in the first-best solution. However, if there is some regulation stating that the minimum payment an agent can receive is $w^{MIN} = 0$, then $w_S = 10$ and $w_F = 0$ is the least costly contract inducing the agent to choose e^H. But this contract costs 9 to the principal, so it is not first best (note, however, that it is still Pareto-optimal).

This kind of model has been often used since it is easy to deal with it; it allows to calculation of the optimal contract, and integration of the moral hazard problem in more sophisticated games with low complexity cost.

3B Applications

3B.1 Incentives for managers

In many limited liability firms, the managers do not receive a fixed payment for their work, but rather they are paid according to the results (such as profits or sales). A possible explanation for this phenomenon is the existence of a moral hazard problem with respect to the manager's behaviour once he has been contracted.

We analyse the problem in the case of a limited liability firm that acts in a competitive market. The objective of the shareholders is to obtain the greatest possible profit, and this depends on how the firm is managed. However, they need to contract a manager to run the firm since the shareholders are not qualified to do it themselves. The problem is that the shareholders cannot control the effort of the manager that they hire. The manager's effort is not a verifiable variable. If the manager is risk-averse and the set of shareholders is risk-neutral, then it is efficient for the manager to receive a fixed wage for his work. However, when the manager's effort is not verifiable, this type of contract will not give him incentives to make as much profit as he can for the shareholders. Consequently, in this moral hazard situation, the manager should be paid according to some other criteria (at least partially).

Assume that the manager's utility function is of the form:

$$U(w, e) = u(w) - v(e),$$

where w represents the wage he receives and e ($e \geq 0$) is the effort that he dedicates to his work (analysis of market conditions, the search for the best conditions from suppliers, investment strategy of the firm, etc.). We assume that $u' > 0$, $u'' < 0$, $v' > 0$, $v'' > 0$, $v(0) = 0$ and $v'(0) = 0$ (this warrants that the effort level will reach an interior solution). In order to give the agent incentives, the shareholders can include the result of the manager's effort in his pay-off. This could be the firm's profits or sales. Which variable is used depends on which variable is verifiable. We assume that the profits or the true value of the firm are difficult to control and that, on the other hand, sales are verifiable.

The shareholder's profits take the form,

$$B(x, w) = p\,x - c\,x - w,$$

where p is the price of the product fixed in the market, $x \in X$ represents the sales (we will denote by X the interval of possible sales), and c is the marginal cost, which is assumed to be constant. Sales depend on the agent's effort and a random variable. This implies that sales are also a random variable conditional on effort. Assume that the density of the distribution of variable sales is $f(x; e)$.

The problem of the shareholders in the case of symmetric information is,

$$\begin{aligned} &\underset{w(x)}{\text{Max}} \quad \int_X [p\,x - c\,x - w(x)]\, f(x; e)\, dx \\ &\text{s.t.} \quad \int_X u(w(x))\, f(x; e)\, dx - v(e) \geq \underline{U}. \end{aligned}$$

The first-order condition of the Lagrangean with respect to the salary, having denoted by λ the participation constraint multiplier, is:

$$-f(x; e) + \lambda\, u'(w(x))\, f(x; e) = 0,$$

from which $w(x)$ is constant. From the participation constraint, we can calculate the optimal wage as $w = u^{-1}(\underline{U} + v(e))$ for all x.

Using this result, we can rewrite the shareholder's problem as

$$\text{Max} \quad \int_X [p\,x - c\,x]\, f(x; e)\, dx - u^{-1}(\underline{U} + v(e)).$$

Consequently the optimal effort satisfies:

$$\int_X [px - cx] f_e(x; e)\, dx - \frac{v'(e)}{u'(u^{-1}\underline{U} + v(e))} = 0,$$

which just says that expected marginal revenue from effort is equal to marginal cost of effort.

In the case in which the manager's effort is not a verifiable variable, we need to add the incentive constraint. The shareholder's problem becomes:

$$\text{Max} \int_X [px - cx - w(x)]\, f(x; e)\, dx$$

$$\text{s.t.} \int_X u(w(x))\, f(x; e)\, dx - v'(e) \geq \underline{U}$$

$$\int_X u(w(x))\, f_e'(x; e)\, dx - v'(e) = 0,$$

where we have applied the first-order approach, assuming that it is valid. If we use λ to denote the participation constraint multiplier and μ for the incentive constraint multiplier, then the first-order condition for optimal wages is:

$$-f(x; e) + \lambda\, u'(w(x))\, f(x; e) + \mu\, u'(w(x))\, f_e'(x; e) = 0$$

from which,

$$\frac{1}{u'(w(x))} = \lambda + \mu \frac{f'_e(x; e)}{f(x; e)}.$$

Assuming that the incentive compatibility constraint binds (see complementary material 3 of this chapter), we have the manager's wage depending on sales x. When $f_e'(x; e)/f(x; e)$ is increasing in x, for given effort, then the manager's wage will also be increasing in x, or in other words, he receives a bonus (possibly variable) according to sales. Recall that the likelihood quotient measures ability to infer from sales if the agent's behaviour has or has not been as expected. That it is increasing in x indicates that greater sales in general signal greater effort. This property is satisfied, for example, if sales take the form $x = e + \varepsilon$, where ε is normally distributed.

3B.2 Fishing contracts between countries[12]

The theory of contracts has many applications in the area of the environment and natural resources. The objective of this application is to use the general analysis in a model that reflects some of the basic characteristics of optimal contract design for a fishery problem. This choice is justified since fishing

[12] This application is based on work by Gallastegui, Iñarra, and Macho-Stadler (1993).

contracts between countries have experienced increasing importance since the Third United Nations Conference on the Law of the Sea in 1982. The conference proposed the establishment of a system of property rights over fishery resources, defining Exclusive Economic Zones as having an extension of 200 miles. In this way, 90 per cent of the world's fishery resources became controlled by coastal countries. Some coastal states (which we shall refer to as CS as of now) have limited fishing traditions and out-of-date fishing technology, while other fishing states (FS) that fish in waters far from their own coasts have the adequate technologies to properly exploit the resource. Consequently, after the conference there was a substantial increase in the number of fishing contracts between countries.

We shall analyse the relationship between a CS and a FS. The assumed (simplified) situation will be the following:

(i) The CS does not process the appropriate technology or fleet to exploit its resources by itself (to exclusively exploit the resources). On the other hand, the FS, while having an appropriate technology (fleet), cannot carry out any fishing activity since it has no resources in its exclusive territorial waters (or it has insufficient resources).

(ii) The CS cannot directly observe the effort that the FS exerts on the resources, which implies that the contracts should be designed taking into account the imperfect information of the CS as to the actions of the FS.

(iii) The FS does not take into account the fact that the stock of fish is a renewable resource the exploitation of which can generate revenues during different time-periods. The CS should optimally administer its resources ensuring their conservation, demanding the most appropriate fishing techniques.

A fishing contract is normally of short duration (one year) and it establishes an amount to be paid in order to have the right to fish, and the amount to be paid according to the catch (the levy or tax). We shall consider the form that fishing contracts should take.

Let us assume that fishing technology implies a relationship between effort exerted in the activity (e), the stock of fish available (X), and the final catch (x). The stock is a renewable resource subject to its own particular laws of growth and reproduction. Effort is an indication of the labour and capital used in the activity, measuring such factors as the capacity of the boat, the size of the nets used, the number of trips made, etc. This effort is not observable by the CS, although the catch can be costlessly observed (for example, the fish must be unloaded and weighed at some particular predetermined port).

Define $\{e^1, e^2, \ldots, e^m\}$ as the set of possible efforts, where e^i is a particular effort level. The set of possible catches is $\{x_1, x_2, \ldots, x_n\}$, where x_j is one particular catch level. Given that different environmental conditions (climate, location of the stock, etc.) also influence the catch, uncertainty will be modelled by assuming that nature randomly modifies the result that can be obtained by any particular effort level. Let $P_j(e) = \text{Prob}(x_j \mid e)$ be the probability of result x_j conditional on effort e, where we assume $P_j(e) > 0$ for all j, e, and $\Sigma_{j=1}^{n} P_j(e) = 1$.

The decrease in the stock generated by fishing is a loss to the CS. We assume that the CS (the principal) assigns a shadow price $\beta(x)$ to a catch of x tons. If the CS is risk-neutral, its objective function can be represented by $\mathrm{E}\{T(x(e)) - \beta(x(e))\}$, where $T(.)$ is the revenue obtained from the contract, and $\beta(.)$ is the cost to the CS of the decrease in the stock.

The FS obtains the catch by exerting an effort whose cost is represented by the function $v(e)$, and must pay an amount $T(x)$ that depends on the final catch, x. The objective function of the FS is

$$U(x, e) = u(px - T(x)) - v(e),$$

where p is the exogenous market price for each unit of the catch and where $u' > 0$, $u'' < 0$, $v' > 0$, $v'' \geq 0$. The reservation utility $\underline{U}$ indicates the possibility of not fishing, or of fishing in other waters.

The FS is not worried about preserving the stock level, and given that effort is not verifiable, there is a tendency in the relationship to fish too much, as far as the CS is concerned.[13] Hence the CS will attempt, via the contract, to limit the damage done to the stock, by inducing the FS to choose an effort level that is lower than that which would be spontaneously chosen. Let e^* be the effort level that the CS would like the FS to exert. The contract will maximize the profits of the CS under the usual participation and incentive compatibility conditions.

$$\max_{\{T(x_j)\}_{j=1,\ldots,n}} \quad \sum_{j=1}^{n} P_j(e^*)\,[T(x) - \beta(x_j)]$$

$$\text{s.t.} \; \sum_{j=1}^{n} P_j(e^*)\, u(px_j - T(x_j)) - v(e^*) \geq \underline{U}$$

$$\sum_{j=1}^{n} P_j(e^*)\, u(px_j - T(x_j)) - v(e^*) \geq \sum_{j=1}^{n} P_j(e^i)\, u(px_j - T(x_j)) - v(e^i)$$

$$\text{for all } e^i \neq e^*.$$

We note that the important incentive constraints are those that correspond to effort levels greater than the optimum, $e^i > e^*$, since this is the FS's tendency (in

13 In this application, it is the principal who prefers low effort while the agent prefers high effort. The moral hazard problem is just as important in this case as in that in which the opposite was true.

the same way as in the classic moral hazard model, the agent has a tendency to use less effort).

If we use λ and μ^i (for effort levels greater than e^*, or in other words, those that are indexed by $i = *+1, \ldots, m$) to denote the Lagrange multipliers, after some simple calculations similar to those already done on several occasions, we arrive at the following expression:

$$\frac{1}{u'(p\,x_j - T(x_j))} = \lambda + \sum_{i=*+1}^{m} \mu^i \frac{P_j(e^*) - P_j(e^i)}{P_j(e^*)} \quad \text{for all } j = 1, \ldots, n \tag{3.A1}$$

In order to analyse the properties of fishing contracts it is, as always, convenient to use the symmetric information situation as a base of comparison. It is easy to see that if we solve the above problem, without taking into account the incentive compatibility constraints, that is, if we solve the problem under symmetric information, using λ' for the participation constraint Lagrange multiplier, we get:

$$\frac{1}{u'(p\,x_j - T(x_j))} = \lambda' \quad \text{for all } j = 1, \ldots, n. \tag{3.A2}$$

Equation (3.A2) implies that $p\,x_j - T(x_j)$ must be constant, for all j, which is to say, $T(x_j) = p\,x_j - k$. Note that the solution to the problem is for the unitary tax to be equal to the market price of fish p, and for the licence k to be negative. That is to say, the CS makes a constant payment k to the FS, and receives the outcome. Notice that the particular form of the contract relies on the CS (the country with resources) being risk-neutral, while the FS (the fisherman) is risk-averse.

Under the moral hazard problem, what the FS receives depends on the catch. To see the form of the contract, imagine two possible results, a small catch, x_1, and a large one, x_2, with $x_2 > x_1$. The greater is the effort exerted, the easier it is to get a large catch, and so $P_2(e^*) - P_2(e^i)$ is negative for all effort levels $e^i > e^*$, while $P_1(e^*) - P_1(e^i)$ is positive. Using equation (3.A1), and given that the multipliers μ^i are positive, we know that

$$\frac{1}{u'(p\,x_1 - T(x_1))} > \frac{1}{u'(p\,x_2 - T(x_2))},$$

which is to say, $p\,x_1 - T(x_1) > p\,x_2 - T(x_2)$, or:

$$T(x_2) - T(x_1) > p\,x_2 - p\,x_1. \tag{3.A3}$$

Expression (3.A3) indicates that, at the optimal contract, it must be true that when the catch is large, the FS should pay the CS more than what it earns in the market for having a large catch (the increase in the payment due is greater than the increase in revenue).

This is a clear example of the incentive problem leading to a paradoxical situation. The above contract is very strange and not very believable: if the FS gets too many fish, it would prefer to throw the excess back into the sea instead of taking it to port, since that would lead to an increase in the tax that is greater than the market worth of the excess. Therefore, in fact the CS really cannot observe the result, it only observes what the FS brings to port, which could be less than what was really caught. This analysis allows us to gain some insight as to why fishing contracts generally specify (besides the payment) maximum catch levels; the optimal payment associated with larger catches would be greater than the market value, and so it makes no sense even to propose it.

3B.3 Moral hazard and rationing in the credit market[14]

This model explains the existence of rationing in the credit market as a consequence of a moral hazard problem. We say that a firm's credit is rationed if it cannot obtain all the money it wants even though it is prepared to pay the current market rate of interest.

Consider a businessman who can choose between two investment projects, which we shall denote by a and b. Both projects require an investment of I to be carried out. The result $\tilde{X}_i$, for $i = a, b$, is risky for both projects:

$$\tilde{X}_i = \begin{cases} X_i & \text{with probability } P_i \\ 0 & \text{with probability } 1 - P_i \end{cases}$$

We assume that project a is less risky and more profitable in expected value, although project b's pay-off is greater when it is successful:

$$p_a X_a > p_b X_b > I, \quad 1 > p_a > p_b > 0, \quad \text{and} \quad X_b > X_a.$$

The firm must borrow to pay the amount I. The gross interest payment, denoted by R, will be paid only if the project is successful, i.e. the bank cannot get payments out of a bankrupt firm.

The expected pay-off of the businessman when project i ($i = a, b$) is started is:

$$U(R, i) = p_i (X_i - R),$$

while the bank's expected profit is:

$$\Pi (R, i) = p_i R - I.$$

In other words, we are assuming that all participants are risk neutral.

[14] We follow the model developed by Bester and Helwig (1987).

We should point out that under symmetric information the optimal contract from the bank's point of view is to ask for $R = X_a$ and to contractually require that only project *a* be carried out. In this case $U(X_a, a) = 0$, and so no businessman earns strictly less without credit than with credit. Hence there would be no credit rationing.

Now assume that there is a moral hazard problem in this market, in that the debt contract cannot be made contingent on the project chosen (the choice of project is the agent's effort). Once the gross interest payment *R* has been fixed, the firm will choose that project that gives the greatest profits. Given *R*, the businessman will invest in project *a* if and only if:

$$p_a(X_a - R) \geq p_b(X_b - R) \Leftrightarrow R \leq \frac{p_a X_a - p_b X_b}{p_a - p_b}.$$

If we denote $\hat{R}$ by

$$\hat{R} = \frac{p_a X_a - p_b X_b}{p_a - p_b},$$

then the businessman will choose project *a* if $R \leq \hat{R}$, and will prefer *b* if $R > \hat{R}$ (for $R = \hat{R}$ the businessman is indifferent, and, for simplicity, we assume he chooses project *a*).

Given that the choice of project is dependent on *R*, the bank's profits are given by:

$$\Pi^*(R) = \begin{cases} p_a R - I & \text{if } 0 \leq R \leq \hat{R} \\ p_b R - I & \text{if } \hat{R} < R \leq X_b \end{cases}$$

(X_b is the greatest amount that the businessman is willing to pay when he undertakes project *b*.) The form of the function $\Pi^*(R)$ is shown in Figure 3.11:

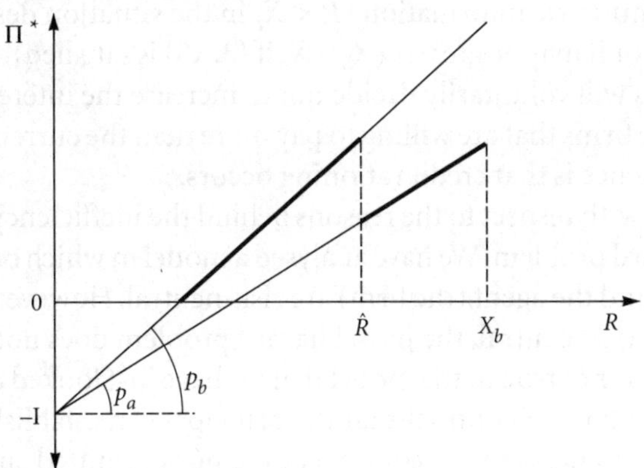

Fig. 3.11

We assume that we are in a monopoly situation, and that as always the bank chooses R to maximize its profits. Therefore, the bank compares the two maximums of the function $\Pi^*(R)$: $\hat{R}$ and X_b. It will set $R = \hat{R}$ if

$$p_a \hat{R} > p_b X_b, \tag{3A.4}$$

since $\Pi^*(\hat{R}) > \Pi^*(X_b)$. On the other hand, if

$$p_a \hat{R} < p_b X_b, \tag{3A.5}$$

then the optimal interest rate is $R = X_b$.

To analyse the credit-rationing problem, let's assume that the total amount of money that the bank can lend is fixed and equal to L, where $I \leq L < NI$. Here N represents the number of firms. Consider firstly the situation described by equation (3.A5), in which the optimal interest rate is $R = X_b$. In this case, the firm's profits are:

$$U(X_b, b) = p_b(X_b - X_b) = 0,$$

or in other words, at this interest rate firms are indifferent between loaning money or not. Hence, there is no credit rationing.

However, in the situation described in (3.A4), when the optimal interest rate is $R = \hat{R}$, the profits of a firm that obtains a loan are:

$$U(\hat{R}, a) = p_a(X_a - \hat{R}) > 0.$$

This means that all the firms will ask for a loan (they can earn strictly positive profits if they get the loan), and so the demand for loanable funds is NI, whilst the offer is $L < NI$. There will be some firms that want a loan, and that are willing to pay the market interest rate, but that will not get a loan.

There are two consequences of the moral hazard problem. On the one hand, the market interest rate will change. It may be either less than that which would exist under symmetric information ($\hat{R} < X_a$ in the situation described by equation (3.A4)), or it may be greater ($X_b > X_a$ if (3.A5) is satisfied). On the other hand, the banks will voluntarily decide not to increase the interest rate, even though there are firms that are willing to pay more than the current market rate. The consequence is that credit rationing occurs.

One last comment with respect to the reasons behind the inefficiency result due to the moral hazard problem. We have analysed a model in which both the principal (the bank) and the agent (the firm) are risk-neutral. However, when both participants are risk-neutral, the moral hazard problem does not imply inefficiency. Why is this not true in the model that we have just looked at? The reason is that here the type of contract that the principal can establish is restricted. In particular, franchise-type contracts were not permitted since the principal cannot establish any form of payment when the result is bad (the case of bankruptcy), and so the linear contract that makes the moral hazard problem disappear cannot be used. In exercise 10 of this chapter, we analyse what would happen if this restriction is removed.

3B.4 Introduction of know-how in technology transfer contracts[15]

Analysing technology-licensing contracts, we see the following: when the contracts imply the transmission of know-how, rather than fixed payments, they are more often based on pay-offs according to the sales achieved by the firm that adopts the new technology. This application gives a possible explanation for this concept, from the point of view of the theory of contracts under asymmetric information.

There is an important difference between patents and know-how. Patents include a sufficiently precise legal description of the new technology. In this way, the firm that buys the right to use a patent has good information as to exactly what it is buying, and the contract can perfectly specify what will be transacted. On the other hand, know-how is very difficult to verify and measure, and is not easy to describe in a contract. Therefore, it is possible that the party that cedes the technology has incentives not to transmit all of its know-how once the contract has been signed.

Consider a market served exclusively by the firm that buys the technology (so this firm is a monopolist). The inverse demand function in the market is:

$$p = a - Q,$$

where p represents the price, Q the quantity sold, and a is a positive parameter representing the size of the market. There exists a research laboratory (the principal) in possession of a technology T that can be ceded to the monopolist (the agent).[16] This technology is verifiable, which means that it can be specified in the contract, and it allows the monopolist to produce at a lower cost. At the same time as the technology is transacted, the principal can also transmit her know-how, but this is very difficult to measure, and so cannot be included in the contract. The transmission of know-how can only take two values $K \in \{0, k\}$. The case $K = 0$ is interpreted as the know-how not being transmitted and $K = k$ means it is transmitted in a quantity (or quality) of k.

As to the agent's cost function, $C(0, 0)$ represents the (constant) marginal cost of the agent when no technology is received. The case $C(T, 0)$ corresponds

[15] This application is based on Macho-Stadler, Martínez-Giralt, and Pérez-Castrillo (1996).

[16] In this application the principal, the technology-ceding firm, which is the one that proposes the terms of the licensing contract, is also the one who has a non-verifiable component in her behaviour, and so is the one who generates the moral hazard problem.

to the marginal cost when the verifiable part of the technology is transmitted but not the know-how. Finally, $C(T, k)$ is the marginal cost when both the technology and the know-how are transmitted. We assume that the cost function is such that:

$$\frac{\partial C}{\partial k} < 0, \ C(T, 0) > C(T, k).$$

A technology transmission contract is a pair (F^K, V^K), where F^K represents the fixed payment of the technology-licensing contract and V^K is the variable part, known as the royalty on sales. Denote by (F^0, V^0) the contract that includes no know-how, while (F^k, V^k) denotes the contract under which the principal, the technology-ceding firm, commits herself in a believable manner, having effective incentives to transmit her know-how.

The objective function of the receiving firm is his profit function:

$$\Pi(Q, T, K) = (a - Q)Q - \left[C(T, K) + V^K\right]Q - F^K,$$

while the objective function of the technology ceding firm is:

$$B(Q, T, K) = F^K + V^K Q - d(K),$$

where $d(K)$ is the disutility (or cost) of transmitting know-how K. We assume that $d(0) = 0$ and $d(k) = d > 0$.

In order to calculate the subgame perfect equilibrium we begin by looking at how the agent firm will produce given the new technology available:

$$\hat{Q}(T, K, V) = \arg\max_{Q} \Pi(Q, T, K).$$

The optimal production decision is:

$$\hat{Q}(T, K, V) = \frac{a - C(T, K) - V^K}{2}. \quad (3.A6)$$

Given the influence of the technology and the know-how on the firm's production, the principal must decide exactly what know-how to transmit. The contract (F^k, V^k) would effectively lead the ceding firm to communicate all non-patent knowledge if and only if

$$F^k + V^k\hat{Q}\left(T, k, V^k\right) - d \geq F^k + V^k\hat{Q}\left(T, 0, V^k\right), \quad (3.A7)$$

i.e. if she is guaranteed a greater profit from this strategy. Using (3.A6) and (3.A7), we arrive at the following condition:

$$V^k \geq \frac{2d}{C(T, 0) - C(T, k)}. \quad (3.A8)$$

In the same way, as can be expected, the contract (F^0, V^0) leads the ceding firm to not transmit know-how if:

$$V^0 \leq \frac{2d}{C(T,0) - C(T,k)}. \tag{3.A9}$$

In the second stage of the game, the technology-receiving firm must decide whether or not to accept the proposed licensing contract. The agent's reservation utility ($\underline{U}$) is the profit obtainable if the contract is rejected, or in other words, without adopting the new technology. Formally, the participation constraint is $\Pi\ (Q, T, k) \geq \Pi\ (Q, 0, 0)$, when the contract is designed to transmit know-how. Using (3.A6), this condition can be written as:

$$F^k \leq \left[\frac{a - C(T,k) - V^k}{2}\right]^2 - \left[\frac{a - C(0,0)}{2}\right]^2. \tag{3.A10}$$

Similarly, if the ceding firm offers a contract under which know-how is not transferred, then the receiving firm will accept if $\Pi\ (Q, T, 0) \geq \Pi\ (Q, 0, 0)$, which is to say,

$$F^0 \leq \left[\frac{a - C(T,0) - V^0}{2}\right]^2 - \left[\frac{a - C(0,0)}{2}\right]^2. \tag{3.A11}$$

Finally, in the first stage of the game, the principal must design the contract. First, she will determine what is the optimal contract if know-how is to be transmitted along with the technology, and then the optimal contract if only the technology is to be transmitted.

To choose the best contract for the case in which know-how is not ceded, (F^0, V^0), the principal must solve:

$$\begin{array}{ll} \text{Max} & F^0 + V^0 q(T, 0, V^0) \\ \text{s.t.} & (3.A6), (3.A9), \text{ and } (3.A11). \end{array}$$

which is just maximizing her profits under the restrictions that the quantity that the monopolist produces be optimal for him (3.A6), that the contract will effectively lead the principal to transmit zero know-how (3.A9), and that the agent is interested in accepting the contract (3.A11). Given that (3.A11) binds in the optimum (it is easy to see that its multiplier is strictly positive), substituting this restriction together with (3.A6) into the objective function, we get that V^0 is the solution to

$$\begin{array}{ll} \text{Max} & \left[\frac{a - C(T,0) - V^0}{2}\right]^2 - \left[\frac{a - C(0,0)}{2}\right]^2 + V^0 \frac{a - C(T,0) - V^0}{2}. \\ \text{s.t.} & (3.A9) \end{array}$$

If we derive the ceding firm's profit function with respect to V^0, ignoring for the time being the restriction (3.A9), we get

$$-\left[\frac{a-C(T,0)-V^0}{2}\right]+\left[\frac{a-C(T,0)-V^0}{2}\right]-\frac{V^0}{2}=-\frac{V^0}{2}<0, \text{ for all } V^0.$$

The unrestricted maximum is $V^0 = 0$. But this maximum also satisfies (3.A9). Therefore, the solution to the constrained problem will also be $V^0 = 0$. The fact that the ceding firm's profit decreases in royalties when there is no non-verifiable ingredient in the contract was predictable. The principal is not interested in distorting the production costs of the agent since the latter gets greater profits if the costs are low, and the former takes her part using the fixed term of the licensing contract, which is

$$F^0=\left[\frac{a-C(T,0)}{2}\right]^2-\left[\frac{a-C(0,0)}{2}\right]^2. \tag{3.A12}$$

For the contract (F^k, V^k) the ceding firm must solve the problem:

$$\begin{array}{ll}\text{Max} & F^k+V^k q(T,k,V^k)-d \\ \text{s.t.} & \text{(3.A6), (3.A8) and (3.A10).}\end{array}$$

Solving this problem in a similar fashion to the previous one, we find that restriction (3.A8) binds, and the optimal contract is

$$V^k=\frac{2d}{C(T,0)-C(T,k)} \tag{3.A13}$$

$$F^k=\left[\frac{a-C(T,k)-V^k}{2}\right]^2-\left[\frac{a-C(0,0)}{2}\right]^2 \tag{3.A14}$$

Therefore, if the ceding firm decides to transmit her know-how together with the verifiable part of the technology, then the licensing contract should include a royalty payment. This royalty is an increasing function of the cost of transferring know-how (d) and decreasing in the value of the know-how (k). This can be proved by differentiating V^k, which, according to equation (3.A13), is strictly positive. Unambiguously we have:

$$\frac{\partial V^k}{\partial d}>0 \quad \text{and} \quad \frac{\partial V^k}{\partial k}<0$$

This result tells us that in order for the ceding firm to effectively transfer her knowledge once the contract has been signed, we must have $V^k > 0$. The intuition behind this is the following. When the contract only includes a fixed payment, the ceding firm has no incentive to go ahead and transmit her know-how, since doing so is costly and, in this case, gives no extra profit. In order for there to be an incentive to transmit knowledge, we require that doing so be profitable. Hence, the payment that the ceding firm receives must depend on how the technology is used, or in other words, how well the agent produces and sells. For this reason the royalties are included in the contract.

We have just seen an example of the application of the techniques used in this chapter to patent licensing contracts. This example has several particularities. First, it is the principal or the ceding firm, who has unverifiable behaviour, and yet who proposes the contract. Secondly, the trade-off between incentives and efficiency in this case does not imply a distortion in the optimal distribution of risk. The reason why is obvious: in this application there was no uncertainty. The trade-off is between the efficiency in production, which requires that marginal costs not be distorted, and incentives. This leads us to set a royalty for the case of high effort (transmit know-how), which is a consequence of the moral hazard problem, and a measure of the cost of the problem. Finally, we will return to this application of technology transmission contracts in the two following chapters. This will allow us to illustrate the effects of each type of asymmetric information and how a single economic phenomenon can be analysed using one or another type of model according to its characteristics. In this case, we have concentrated our attention on the consequences of including or not know-how together with the other technological ingredients in licensing contracts.

Exercises

Exercise 1. In 1995 the Ukrainian pole vaulter Sergei Bubka received $30,000 every time he broke the world pole vault record. The experts all agreed that he was able to break the record by close to 10 centimetres. However, up to September 1995, he had broken his own record 35 times, each time by one centimetre. Comment on this incentive system from the point of view of the world record achieved. Reason out the objectives that could justify offering this type of prize to an athlete.

Exercise 2. A worker can exert two effort levels, good or bad, which induce a production error with probability 0.25 and 0.75 respectively. His utility function is $U(w, e) = 100 - (10/w) - v$, where w is the wage received and v takes the value 2 if effort is good and 0 if effort is bad. Production errors are observable and so can be introduced into the worker's contract, but effort cannot. The product obtained is worth 20 if there are no errors and 0 otherwise. The principal is risk-neutral. Assume that the worker has reservation utility equal to $\underline{U} = 0$. Calculate the optimal contract and the effort that the principal desires, both under conditions of symmetric information and asymmetric information on the agent's behaviour.

Exercise 3. Consider an agency relationship in which the principal contracts the agent, whose effort determines the result. Assume that the uncertainty present is represented by three states of nature. The agent can choose between two effort levels. The results are shown in Table 3.E1.

		states of Nature		
		ε_1	ε_2	ε_3
Efforts	$e = 6$	60,000	60,000	30,000
	$e = 4$	30,000	60,000	30,000

Table 3.E1

The principal and the agent both believe that the probability of each state is one third. The objective functions of the principal and the agent are, respectively:

$$B(x, w) = x - w$$

$$U(w, e) = \sqrt{w} - e^2,$$

where $x = x(e, \varepsilon)$ is the monetary result of the relationship and $w = w(x)$ is the monetary pay-off that the agent receives. Assume that the agent will only accept the contract if he obtains an expected utility level of at least 114 (his reservation utility level).

(*a*) What can be deduced from the participants' objective functions?

(*b*) What would be the effort and the wage in a situation of symmetric information? What would happen if the principal were not risk-neutral?

(*c*) What happens in a situation of asymmetric information? What pay-off scheme allows an effort level of $e = 4$ to be obtained? What pay-off scheme allows the effort level of $e = 6$ to be obtained? Which effort level does the principal prefer? Discuss the result.

Exercise 4. Research and Development (R&D) subsidies can also be studied in a moral hazard framework. There are many reasons for the government to intervene in the private R&D activities of firms. It is often argued that R&D is a risky activity and that it generates enormous externalities. This means that, in general, the private gains from carrying out R&D are less than the social ones, or in other words, too little research is undertaken. This is why it is often necessary for the government to subsidize firms that are involved in R&D processes. The objective of the subsidies is to give the firms incentives to undertake R&D

to a greater degree than they would without public intervention. Now, it is also well known that R&D is a very difficult process to control, that is, it is very difficult for the government to know exactly how much money a given firm is dedicating to this activity.

A subsidy is a contract between the government (the principal) and a firm (the agent), for the firm to exert an effort (dedicate money to R&D) greater than that which it would spontaneously exert (without a subsidy). The government obtains utility from the result (the final technology level), since a better technology is useful for other firms, is beneficial to consumers since it induces lower prices, etc. The technological advances achieved are the result of an investment of effort and random components.

(*a*) Where does the moral hazard problem appear in this context? In which case would there be no moral hazard problem?

(*b*) Consider a subsidy that consists of giving money to a firm independently of the final result of the research. In other words, the government gives a sum of money to the firm before the research project is begun. Comment on this contract. What would be the effect on the firm's decision?

(*c*) The concession of patents is often taken as a sign of research success. Imagine that the government gives a subsidy that consists of giving more money to the firm if it gets its idea patented. Comment on this technology policy. Is it better or worse than the previous one?

(*d*) Can you think of any other forms of subsidies that might induce the firm to invest in R&D a greater amount than what it would do without the subsidy?

Exercise 5. Drivers who have consumed a certain amount of alcohol suffer a reduction in ability to react, and a change in behaviour. Thus there are more automobile accidents when drivers consume alcohol. The social cost of these accidents is very high. The principal, the social authorities, would like to prevent these accidents by trying to get drivers to avoid consuming large amounts of alcohol.

Denote by e^N the action 'drink little or "No" alcohol' and by e^B the action 'drink too much "Booze" ', and let $P(e^N)$ and $P(e^B)$, $P(e^N) < P(e^B)$, be the probabilities of having an accident conditional on the driver's action. Given the objectives of the principal, discuss which of the following two policies would be most adequate from the point of view of incentives:

(*a*) Setting up random controls to test drivers, alcohol level, and fining those whose test gives an index of alcohol in the blood that is too high.

(*b*) Testing the alcohol/blood index for drivers involved in accidents, and fining those that have an index that is too high at the time of the accident.

In order to discuss these policies, design a simple model that allows them to be compared.

(*c*) Now assume that when an accident occurs, other people may or may not be injured, but that this does not depend on whether the driver causing the crash is drunk or not. A political party has proposed that the fines should be greater when someone is injured than the fine to be paid by a drunk driver who causes an accident in which no one is injured. Comment on the effectiveness of this policy.

(*d*) The same political party has proposed that smaller fines should also be applied to sober drivers who cause an accident. Comment on the properties of this new proposition.

(*e*) What conclusions can we obtain from incentive mechanisms in general?

Exercise 6. Consider a relationship between a principal and an agent in which only two results, valued at 50,000 and 25,000, are possible. The agent must choose between three possible efforts. The probability of each of the results contingent on the efforts is given in table 3.E2.

		Results	
		25,000	50,000
Efforts	e^1	0.25	0.75
	e^2	0.50	0.50
	e^3	0.75	0.25

Table 3.E2

Assume that the principal is risk-neutral and that the agent is risk-averse, with their respective preferences described by the following functions:

$$B(x, w) = x - w \quad \text{and} \quad U(w, e) = \sqrt{w} - v(e)$$

with $v(e^1) = 40$, $v(e^2) = 20$, and $v(e^3) = 5$. The reservation utility level of the agent is $\underline{U} = 120$.

(*a*) Write down the optimal contracts under symmetric information for each effort level and the profits obtained by the principal in each case. What effort level does the principal prefer?

(*b*) Write down the optimal contracts when there exists a moral hazard problem. What is the optimal effort level and the contract chosen by the principal? Where does the moral hazard problem have its influence?

Exercise 7. Consider a relationship between a principal and an agent in which the agent's effort influences the result but is not observable. The principal is risk-neutral, and the agent is risk-averse, having a utility function $U(w, e) = \sqrt{w} - e^2$, where w represents the wage and e represents the effort. The agent can choose between low effort $e = 0$, or high effort $e = 3$. His reservation utility is 21. The production technology is such that only three results x are possible, where x represents the value of the result to the principal $x \in \{0, 1{,}000, 2{,}500\}$. The probabilities conditional on effort are: Prob $(x = 0 \mid e = 0) = 0.4$; Prob $(x = 1{,}000 \mid e = 0) = 0.4$; Prob $(x = 2{,}500 \mid e = 0) = 0.2$; Prob $(x = 0 \mid e = 3) = 0.2$; Prob $(x = 1{,}000 \mid e = 3) = 0.4$; Prob $(x = 2{,}500 \mid e = 3) = 0.4$.

(*a*) What are the optimal symmetric information contracts? What effort will the principal demand from the agent?

(*b*) What is the optimal contract under which the agent will exert an effort of $e = 0$ if the only verifiable variable in the relationship is the result x?

(*c*) Given a moral hazard problem, what is the constrained maximization problem that determines the optimal contract if the principal wants the agent to exert an effort of $e = 3$? (Kuhn–Tucker may be useful.)

(*d*) Which contract will the principal offer the agent under a moral hazard problem?

(*e*) Discuss the optimal contract if the agent were risk-neutral.

Exercise 8. Fred has just finished his law degree and has begun to work in a local law firm. The first job that is assigned to him requires him to spend all his time working on a case for which the firm and the client have agreed that the firm will receive $8,000 at the end of the year should they win the case, and nothing otherwise.

(*a*) From past experiences, Fred's boss knows that there is a 50 per cent chance that they will win the case. Would it be logical to pay Fred $8,000 this year if they win the case and nothing otherwise?

(*b*) Assume that Fred would prefer $3,000 to the expected wage of $4,000 that corresponds to the deal proposed in (*a*). In light of this new information, reconsider the wage deal for Fred proposed in (*a*).

(*c*) Now assume that the result of the case depends on the effort that Fred exerts on it. He will have less incentives to work hard if his annual income does not depend on winning the case. Comment on the consequences of this and discuss the use of bonus payments and promotions to stimulate effort.

Exercise 9. Consider a relationship between a principal and an agent in which there are only two possible results, one high, x_2, and the other low, x_1. The frequency with which each result occurs depends on the agent's effort, $e \in [0, 1]$, and a random state variable. Assume that Prob $[x = x_2 \mid e] = e$, so that Prob $[x = x_1 \mid e] = 1 - e$.

The agent's utility is of the form $U(w, e) = u(w) - v(e)$, with the same assumptions as in Chapters 2 and 3. The principal's objective function is $B(x - w)$, which is increasing and concave (that is, she could be risk-averse).

(*a*) Write down the constrained maximization problem of the principal, and find the conditions that determine the optimal contract.

(*b*) Now we assume that the agent's effort is not publicly known. Write down the constrained maximization problem that defines the optimal contract in this case. Is the first-order approach valid in this example? Describe the relationship between the optimal contract's wages and the differences in this contract compared to (*a*) above.

Exercise 10. Consider the situation analysed in Application 3. Assume now that the firm that applies for credit has funds that cannot be invested in the project (and so the firm still needs a loan of I from the bank), but that will become available once the project is finished. Hence the bank can get the firm to pay the interest due both if the project is successful and if it is not. What is the optimal contract in this case?

Exercise 11. A risk-neutral businessman, whose profits are $x - w$, contracts a risk-averse worker, whose utility function is $u(w) - v(e)$, where w is the wage paid, e is the worker's effort, and x is the result of the relationship. The worker's effort can only take two possible values, $e \in \{e^L, e^H\}$, with $v(e^L) < v(e^H)$, and this effort determines the probabilities, $p^L(x_i)$ and $p^H(x_i)$, of getting a given result x_i. The worker's reservation utility is $\underline{U}$.

(*a*) Assume that there are only three possible results, x_1, x_2, and x_3, with $x_1 < x_2 < x_3$. The probability of getting each result is given in Table 3.E3. If the businessman would like the worker to exert the effort level e^H, is it possible that the worker will be paid a lower wage for getting result x_2 than for getting result x_1? (Write down the businessman's constrained maximization problem and the first-order conditions.)

	x_1	x_2	x_3
$p^L(x)$	0.25	0.5	0.25
$p^H(x)$	0.25	0.25	0.5

Table 3.E3

(*b*) Now assume that probabilities are given by Table 3.E4. Would it be possible to pay $w(x_2) = w(x_3) = v(e^H)$ and still get the worker to exert e^H? How must $w(x_1)$ be? (This is a thinking, rather than a calculation, problem.)

	x_1	x_2	x_3
$p^L(x)$	0.25	0.5	0.25
$p^H(x)$	0	0.5	0.5

Table 3.E4

Exercise 12. The owner of a firm puts a manager in charge of a project. The project can give rise to two different results, measured in terms of the owner's profits: π_1 and π_2, where $\pi_1 < \pi_2$. The probability of each result depends on the manager's effort.

Now assume that there are only two possible effort levels; high effort, e^H and low effort $e^L = 0$. Under high effort the probability of getting the good result π_2 is p, and so the probability of getting result π_1 is $(1 - p)$. On the other hand, under low effort the result is always π_1. Exerting high effort implies a disutility to the manager of v, while low effort has no disutility.

The manager's utility function is $U(w, e^H) = \sqrt{w} - v$, or $U(w, 0) = \sqrt{w}$, depending on whether he exerts high or low effort. If the manager decides not to work on the project, he is guaranteed a reservation utility of $\underline{U} = \sqrt{\underline{w}}$, where $\underline{w}$ is his reservation wage.

(*a*) Assume that the manager's effort is observable and verifiable. Describe the optimal contract for the firm's owner if he prefers low effort and if he prefers high effort. When will the owner demand each effort level?

(*b*) Now assume that the manager's effort is not verifiable, and so the only variable that can appear in the contract is the final result obtained. What is the optimal contract that the owner offers when he would like the manager to exert effort $e = 0$? If he would like the manager to exert high effort, what is the constrained maximization problem that the owner must solve to calculate the optimal contract? Describe the optimal contract in this case.

(*c*) What are the owner's profits for each effort level? Describe what the owner must compare in order to decide which effort level to demand.

(*d*) Now assume that $\underline{w} = 4$, $v = 2$ and $p = 1/2$. Analyse the owner's decision as to the effort level to demand both when effort is verifiable and when it is not, for the following three situations:

$$\text{(d1) } \pi_1 = 50 \text{ and } \pi_2 = 100,$$
$$\text{(d2) } \pi_1 = 50 \text{ and } \pi_2 = 80,$$
$$\text{(d3) } \pi_1 = 50 \text{ and } \pi_2 = 60.$$

Comment on the results.

Exercise 13. We now pose a problem with several agents in order to gain an insight this situation in an example. After analysing some statistics, the professor of the 'Introduction to the Economics of Information' course has realized that, on average, half of the class pass the final exam. He has already prepared the exam, and he is considering the relative benefits of offering the students a system under which the top half pass independently of whether the last passing student has a passing grade or not. In other words, he proposes to the students that they decide between the following two forms of examination: either only those students that achieve a passing grade will get the course credit (which, on average, is half of the class), or the top half of the class will get the course credit, independently of their final grade (so that it is possible that students will pass the course with a D, and it is also possible to fail the course with a B).

(*a*) Comment on the advantages and disadvantages of each system from the point of view of individual incentives.

(*b*) Sometimes students prepare for an exam together, helping each other out with difficulties. Which system is best to encourage such collaboration?

(*c*) On other occasions, there is a problem of students having a tendency to copy during the exam. If this problem is severe, which system is best to avoid it?

Exercise 14.* Let e stand for the agent's effort and $x = e + \varepsilon$ the production level observed by the principal. ε is a random variable which is normally distributed with mean zero and variance σ^2. Assume that the principal chooses a linear incentive system,

$$w(x) = A + Bx = A + Be + B\varepsilon,$$

where A and B are the parameters to be determined. Since the principal is risk-neutral, her utility is

$$\mathrm{E}\,(x - w(x)) = \mathrm{E}\,(e + \varepsilon - A - Bx - B\varepsilon) = (1 - B)\,e - A.$$

Assume that the agent's utility function has the form

$$U(w, e) = \mathrm{E}\,(w) - r\frac{\sigma_w^2}{2} - v(e),$$

where r represents his index of absolute risk-aversion, $\mathrm{E}\,(w)$ is the expected wage, and σ_w^2 is the variance of the wage.

(*a*) Calculate the optimal contract when the principal can verify the agent's effort.

(*b*) Calculate the optimal contract when the agent's effort is not verifiable. Discuss the characteristics of the optimal contract as a function of the exogenous variables (to do so, express the parameters of the wage equation in function of the parameters of the exercise).

Exercise 15.* Consider a simple agency relationship in which the principal contracts an agent whose effort is not verifiable. The principal is risk-neutral and thus values the result of the relationship, which can take either of two values, $\overline{x}$ or $\underline{x}$. The probability of getting these results depends on a random variable and the agent's effort. We shall also assume that the agent's effort can take four possible values: $e \in \{e_1, e_2, e_3, e_4\}$. Therefore, we can write:

$$\text{Prob}\,\{x = \overline{x} \mid e = e_i\} = p_i \quad \text{for all } i = 1, 2, 3, 4.$$

Assume that the probabilities satisfy the following relationship $p_1 < p_2 < p_3 < p_4$ and that the monetary value of result $\overline{x}$ is X while that of result $\underline{x}$ is zero.

The agent's utility function is

$$u(w) - v(e_i) = w^{1/n} - v_i,$$

where w represents the wage he receives, $1/n$ is his index of relative risk-aversion, and v_i measures the cost or disutility of effort e_i. Naturally, we assume that greater effort implies greater disutility; $0 = v_1 < v_2 < v_3 < v_4$. Let $\underline{U} = s^{1/n}$ be the agent's reservation utility, where s is, for example, the unemployment subsidy.

(*a*) Show how the principal calculates the optimal contract under symmetric information.

(*b*) Show how the principal calculates the optimal contract under asymmetric information.

(*c*) Discuss the differences between the above two cases.

3C Advanced Themes

In this section we shall briefly present some extensions to the moral hazard model, paying most attention to the aspects that are analysed and mentioned in relevant articles in each line of research.

3C.1 Optimal payment mechanisms in situations of moral hazard with several agents

There exist many examples of relationships in which it is best to apply a model with several agents instead of the simple moral hazard model. To take a concrete example, consider a firm that contracts a group of salesmen. The organization of sales, the technical characteristics of the process, and the behaviour of the salesmen among themselves all influence the results obtained by the firm.

The time-line of the relationship between a principal and several agents is similar to the simple framework. First, the principal decides the contracts and she simultaneously proposes them to the agents that she wants to contract. Secondly, each agent accepts and signs the contract (if the contract is rejected, the game is over). If the agents all accept their contracts, in the third stage they decide on their action or effort. Finally, the results are observed and the payoffs stipulated in the contracts are made.

In the multi-agent relationships, the crucial stage is the third one. This stage, which is translated into the incentive compatibility constraint of the agency problem, depends on the *game among the agents*, since the interaction among them is relevant to the feasible situations that are to be considered. With respect to this game, it is natural to assume that each agent attempts to maximize his own utility, so the agents are playing a non-cooperative game (or the strategies that they choose should form a Nash equilibrium). However, this does not mean that they will never co-operate. Even in a non-co-operative game, if there exist mechanisms that allow the agents to arrive at co-operative agreements, and to take advantage of them, these mechanisms may well be used. A second possibility is to analyse what happens when the agents use co-operative behaviour anyway. All these considerations influence the third stage of the game, the incentives stage, and so by backward induction they also influence the optimal contract.

The participation stage is similar to that of the simple models, as is the contract design stage. We should always bear in mind that the contract intended for a particular agent may include all the verifiable variables of the entire relationship, those directly referring to the agent at hand as well as those referring to the other agents.

In the literature on optimal contracts with several agents there exist different groups of models according to the aspect analysed. The *personalized information models* (whose basic references are Holmström (1979) and Mookherjee (1984)) analyse contracts designed for each agent using not only the personalized information, but also the information on the results obtained by the other agents. The principal will be interested in paying each agent according to his own production and that of the other agents if these other results can inform on the actions of the agent at hand. If the results of the other agents do not add information, or in other words, if an agent's result is a *sufficient statistic* for his effort, then he will be paid according to his own result only.

Let us consider a simple example to illustrate the above message. A department store contracts two salesmen, one for the book department, and the other for the umbrella department. Sales depend on the effort of the salesmen and on a random variable, but the random variable that affects each department is different. In this case, it is optimal for each agent to be paid only according to the sales of his own department; the book salesman will be paid according to the number of books that are sold, the umbrella salesman according to the number of umbrellas. The reason is that the effort of the book salesman does not affect the sales of umbrellas, and these sales do not reveal anything on the book salesman's effort, since the events that make the sales of umbrellas high are different from those that affect the book market. Consequently, including the sales of umbrellas as one of the variables that determines the bookseller's wage can only make the salesman suffer additional risk without motivating him further. Now imagine what would happen if both salesmen were working in the same department, for example, both sell umbrellas. In this case we can safely assume that the randomness that affects sales is the same for both agents. Hence if the efforts were the same, it is likely that the results would be also similar, but if the efforts were different, it is likely that the results would be different. For example, the fact that it rains is common to the results of both salesmen. Since the outcome of the random weather variable is the same for both, if one salesman sells a lot and the other doesn't sell many umbrellas, it is difficult for the one who has the worst result to argue that it was due to bad luck. Instead, it is a signal that he exerted less effort. This leads us to a situation in which the optimal contract for each agent should take into account the results of both of them. The department store should pay more to a salesman the less his workmates have sold. However, it is possible for the contract to include this information in the opposite direction. For example, it seems reasonable that we should place a higher value on the sales of an umbrella salesman the greater the sales of bathing-suits have been (high sales of this item is a signal that the weather has been hot, which is an adverse condition for the umbrella salesman).

In general optimal contracts can become very complicated. Sometimes, however, we observe a very particular type of contract. Think of businesses that pay a bonus to the salesman who sells the most (the employee of the month). This type of pay-off, for which the only important factor is the order in which the agents place themselves, is known as a *tournament* contract. Under this type of contract an agent's pay-off depends only on the ranking of his result in the ordering of the results of the other agents. Sports competitions are the clearest example of this type of contract. However, tournaments are only efficient in very particular cases, since for the optimal contract to depend only on the order of the results, it is necessary that all the relevant information be summarized in this ranking.

Lazear and Rosen (1981), Green and Stokey (1983), and Malcomson (1986) analyse the advantages and disadvantages of the most simple payment mechanisms, those that depend only on the individual result, and those that depend only on the final ordering of the results. As we have seen, in spite of the fact that these contracts are optimal only under rather restrictive conditions, they are the most used in practice, which justifies studying them. A basic conclusion is that contracts based only on individual results are better when the common noise (the randomness that simultaneously affects all results) is small, while tournaments are better when the common noise is important. Introducing a lack of commitment or a non-stationary environment can also provide circumstances where tournaments are optimal. Malcomson (1984) considers the case in which the performance is observable by the principal but not verifiable to the courts. Now the principal has an incentive to renege on the promised bonus. However, she may be able to commit to a tournament where the prize has to be paid anyway. Nalebuff and Stiglitz (1983) argue that an advantage of tournaments is that they provide 'flexible' incentives, in the sense that they change automatically with changes in the environment, while the optimal contract must be recalculated each time.

The literature has also considered what are known as *joint production models*, in which the final result depends on teamwork. This is the case of a group of agents whose individual efforts combine to produce a single good. Examples of this type of situation are research teams that develop a given product, a group of firms that carry out a common project, or a football team trying to win a championship.

When the final production is the only verifiable variable, and it depends on the vector of (non-observable) efforts, from the perspective of the idea of an optimal contract we cannot obtain conclusions that are very different from those that correspond to models with only one agent. The fundamental difference is that group relationships are closer to the traditional problem of public goods, and so the problem that arises is one of *free-riding* since the effect of any reduction in effort exerted is shared between all the agents. We need each agent to feel responsible for all the product in order to provide the right incentives for him. That is why Alchian and Demsetz (1972) and Holmström (1982) suggest that situations of joint production (in which it is impossible to identify the individual contributions) cannot be efficient when all the income is distributed amongst the agents. In other words, if the budget constraint always binds, it is not possible to achieve efficiency. This means that, in certain cases, another agent should be contracted to control the productive agents. On top of this, the external participant (the principal) can be in charge of making sure that *the agreements that do not balance the budget* (i.e. that do not distribute the outcome in any contingency among the agents) *are fulfilled*. The pressure of control and the role of residual claimant can provoke efficiency gains and thus justify the presence of a principal.

Until now we have always assumed that the agents play non-co-operatively. If they can co-ordinate, then *coalitions* form, which can be *harmful* for the relationship.[17] Consider, for example, a principal who contracts two agents; one is in charge of the productive tasks (we call him the agent), and the other is in charge of supervision and control (the foreman). In this case, it is not unreal

[17] References on the effect of coalitions on an organization's form of co-operation are e.g. Tirole (1986, 1992), Laffont (1988, 1990), Holmström and Milgrom (1990), Macho-Stadler and Pérez-Castrillo (1991*b*), and Itoh (1993).

nor infrequent for the agent to say to his foreman 'if something goes wrong, and you don't let on that it was my fault, then I'll pay you for it', or for the foreman to go to see the agent and to tell him 'listen, if something goes wrong, if you like we can come to an arrangement for me to protect you'. If this type of coalition is formed, then the foreman's objective is to protect the agent when the results are adverse, covering up the evidence and announcing to the principal that the control did not give any conclusive results. Therefore, the only information that the principal would have is that which favours the agent.

The consequence of this is that, when the principal designs the pay-off mechanism, she will anticipate that her workers may have incentives to collude and will try not to leave any margin for coalitions to be profitable to their participants. This brings us to an important thought for the theory of organizations. If coalitions are possible, the principal cannot let the agent's punishment (or prize) depend totally on the supervisor. If the objective is to reduce the establishment of agreements between the agents and their supervisors, she will have to apply rules that are impersonal, uniform (that eliminate the consequences of personal and repeated contracts), and do not use all the information (the source of the distortions) as is done in bureaucratic rules. The message is that when the individuals in an organization have enough leeway, we can find an argument in favour of the technical superiority of bureaucracy over other forms of organization. This superiority is based on its precision, continuity, and the uniformity of its norms, which saves on costs and frictions, and avoids the formation of income-seeking coalitions. However, in the same way, the possibility that coalitions may exist unambiguously implies that there is an efficiency loss in the operation of the organization.

A relatively widespread result is that the more leeway the agents have, or the more complex the situation under consideration, then the rules that are imposed tend to be simpler. The application of bureaucratic rules is, however, not the only solution. A second possible solution to the problem of efficiency losses due to coalition formation between supervisors and agents is to systematically use the services of external auditors or supervisors (see Kofman and Lawarrée, 1993). This system is costly, since the external supervisor must be paid, but it allows the establishment of a control and punishment mechanism that dissuades the participants in the hierarchy from adopting collusive behaviour.

The conclusion of the models that we have just considered is rather pessimistic. However, it is easy to think of examples in which co-ordination can improve the input of a group of agents, and in which the advantages of bureaucracy are only available when it is important to achieve a frictionless combination of numerous activities directed at a single foreseeable and invariant end. In every organization, the success of its operation depends on the co-operation of all its members, but the commitments are not foreseeable in the long run, nor are they invariant or uniform. In this type of organization, there cannot be any precise delimitation of responsibility and it is more convenient to use methods that strengthen group work. Articles in which the advantages of co-operation and its consequences on optimal contracts are analysed are: Holmström and Milgrom (1990), Itoh (1990, 1993), Macho-Stadler and Pérez-Castrillo (1991*a*, 1993), and Ramakrishnan and Thakor (1991).

3C.2 Organizational design in relationships with several agents

Apart from the design of contracts, the principal also decides the organization with which she will relate. This includes such fundamental decisions as how many agents to contract and how should they be structured. One aspect studied in the literature concerns the advantages of *delegation* of tasks, which analyses the question of when it is better for the principal to delegate some task to an agent instead of doing it herself.

Consider a principal who contracts an agent to carry out some productive task. In order to obtain evidence about the production, it is necessary to use a supervisory and control mechanism. The probability of observing the result depends on the effort exerted by the supervisor. We want to know if it is useful for the principal to delegate the task of supervision to an agent (called the supervisor), or if it is better for her to do it herself. It is evident that for the introduction of a new member in the hierarchy (in the relationship) to be profitable, it is necessary for him to be able to perform some task that the principal is incapable of doing. This is the case when the principal has less technical abilities than the supervisor to carry out the task, or if the cost of doing it herself is higher. In these cases the principal should delegate supervision to a more efficient agent. It is also possible that the principal is just as able to carry out the supervision task as the supervisor, but that there are commitment problems.

Think of a someone doing a data collection survey. In order to motivate him to exert effort, the wage of a data collector is normally based on how many questionnaires have been correctly filled in. In order to know that the questionnaires have been correctly filled in or not, the supervisor could visit a few of the households that the agent says he has visited, in order to check out the authenticity of the answers, to see if the agent was sufficiently persuasive, etc. But the probability that the supervisor learns that the surveys are properly or improperly done depends on the effort he dedicates to his job. The problem of lack of commitment is posed in the following way; it is one thing for the supervisor to say what he is going to do, and another is what he really ends up doing. We must bear in mind that the task of supervision is not useful once the productive effort has been carried out, since the objective of supervision is precisely to motivate this effort. Hence, once the initial job has been done, the incentives to supervise it are minimal.

We need to compare the two possible situations: that in which the principal takes care of the supervision task personally, and that in which she contracts a supervisor to do it. If the principal and the potential supervisor are identical, the choice is easy. When the principal supervises, given that she cannot commit to her control strategy (that is to say, to the effort that she will use and the report that she will send), the contract with the agent will simultaneously determine the control level that she will be interested in maintaining. Besides, she will only report her findings if by doing so she reduces the pay-off that she must give to the agent (if the pay-off when quality is not observed is less than when high quality is observed, the principal will never report high quality even if it is observed). If the principal contracts a supervisor, she will design the contract in order for him to be interested in exerting the adequate level of effort, and honestly to announce what he observes. Comparing both situations, we conclude that delegation of the supervisory task leads to a strictly better solution than not delegating, when the principal cannot commit to a control strategy or to the honesty of her report. Does this mean that delegating the control tasks is always beneficial when the principal has problems to make her behaviour believable? The answer is no. The example we have presented is very simplified. To get a more profound vision of the advantages and disadvantages of delegation, see Demski and Sappington (1986), Melumad and Reichelstein (1987), Riordan and Sappington (1987), Macho-Stadler and Pérez-Castrillo (1991*b*), and Olivella (1995).

A second aspect considered in the literature is the comparison between *centralized* and *decentralized* structures as far as contracting goes. The central question is, what type of organizational structure is the best, one centralized on the principal proposing all the contracts, or a decentralized one? Are the two ever equivalent? In order that the comparison be simple, consider a relationship between a principal and two agents. A centralized organization is, in this case, one in which the principal contracts both agents. On the other hand, a decentralized organization is one in which the principal establishes a contract with one agent, who then contracts the other (see Macho-Stadler and Pérez-Castrillo, 1998).

First, remember that coalitions between agents are always harmful to the efficiency of the relationship. Second, it can be proved that a decentralized situation is equivalent to a centralized one in which the agents can establish coalitions between themselves. Therefore, decentralization of contracting is harmful since by allowing the agents to enter into contractual relationships between themselves, the trade-off between insurance and incentives is not the most adequate for the relationship. Finally, if a centralized organization signs the contracts sequentially, i.e. the principal first establishes the contract with one agent (let's say agent 1) and then with the other (agent 2), then we need to rethink our conclusions. A sequential centralized organization is equivalent to a centralized one in which the contracts are formed simultaneously, but in which the principal can establish collusive agreements with agent 2. If the contracts are formed sequentially, the question of whether it is better to use a centralized structure or a decentralized one no longer has a clear answer.

The conclusion is that centralization is superior when contracts can be signed simultaneously. When this is not true, however, the result may be reversed. With sequential contracting, either centralizing or decentralizing will be optimal depending on the characteristics of the participants, and on the particular environment in which the relationship takes place. Centralized structures are more efficient the more separated the tasks are, the more random the environment is, and the more risk-averse the agents are (i.e. circumstances under which coalitions between agents are really harmful, while principal-agent coalitions are not). Conversely, we would expect to find decentralized structures when different divisions of a hierarchy undertake strongly interdependent tasks, in economic environments which are not very risky, or when agents are not very risk-averse.

3C.3 Moral hazard with several tasks

Until now we have only considered moral hazard problems in agency relationships in which each agent exerts an effort on a single task. Holmström and Milgrom (1991) analyse a situation in which the agent carries out several tasks, each one of which gives rise to a different result, considering only linear contracts.

An important aspect is the relationship between the tasks from the agent's point of view. Assume that the agent only carries out two tasks. We say that the tasks are *complements* when, having exerted an effort for task 1, the effort cost of task 2 is reduced. On the other hand, the tasks are *substitutes* when exerting more effort on one increases the cost of the other. When tasks 1 and 2 are complementary in the agent's cost of effort function, the principal is interested in motivating task 1, since in this way she simultaneously motivates the agent to work on task 2. On the other hand, if the two tasks are substitutes, then giving incentives for one task can be achieved in two ways: either through the pay-offs related to the result of the particular task, or by reducing the opportunity cost through reductions in the incentives of the other tasks that the agent must do.

Assume that there is no available signal as to the second task. That is, it is only possible to obtain information on the agent's effort from the first task. If the principal wants the agent to exert effort in the second activity as well, then she must consider the relationship between the two tasks. In this way, if the tasks are substitutes, then the principal must think about the trade-off between paying high wages, which gives the agent incentives to exert high effort on the first task and to slack on the second, or to set low wages for good results on the first task, which will lead the agent to exert low effort on this activity, but not to abandon task 2 so much. It is even possible for the optimal contract to establish that the most convenient solution is not to give incentives at all. This is another argument in favour of bureaucratic systems; they could be optimal when, amongst the activities that the agent must carry out, some are impossible to control.

In fact, surprisingly, many contracts do not include pay-off schemes that give incentives to the agent. For example, in general it is not convenient to include explicit incentives to satisfy finishing dates in home construction contracts. This is so in spite of the fact that delays in this business are normal, and it would be easy to include this type of clause in the contract. Whether or not clauses concerning the finishing-date are included in the contract depends on the capacity of the buyer (the principal) to control other aspects of the agent's activity. For example, the quality of construction is a very difficult variable to verify. By including explicit finishing-date incentives, the buyer pushes the constructor towards dedicating most of his energy to finishing the job on time, while the quality of his work will be further from his mind. Since the quality of the building is also important, it may turn out that it is better not to include incentives to satisfy some specific time-limit.[18]

A second important aspect is whether the agent is prohibited or not from doing external jobs. Casual observation shows that in some relationships this type of prohibition is normal, while in others it is not. In particular, it is usual for individuals with heavy responsibilities to be able to use their position to extract private benefits, while those in jobs with less responsibility do not have this possibility. The reason is that in some cases it is easier for the principal to prohibit or to impede such activities than to simply control them, limiting the degree to which the agents may take advantage of them.

Assume that the agent can carry out a set of potential tasks that the principal can only control by exclusion. The private use that the agent makes of these tasks are entirely for his own benefit. The principal can control the private business of the agent by allowing him to be involved in a subset of tasks. The

[18] Schmidt and Schnitzer (1995) consider a repeated moral hazard model where some of the actions of the agent cannot be allowed for in a contract. They show that the set of actions that can be implemented may increase or decrease if it becomes possible to govern some of the agent's actions by an explicit contract.

agent exerts an effort for the principal and other efforts on tasks that are entirely his own private affairs. In this case it is necessary to consider the cost to the agent of the total effort exerted, and the earnings that he can obtain from his external business.

The principal's profit depends only on the effort that the agent exerts for her, and the information available concerns only this task. If the agent is allowed to take part in external affairs, then he will have less time to dedicate to the internal tasks. However, this practice can also have some advantages. The main benefit is that, by allowing the agent to obtain income from external activities, he can be paid less in the relationship. Therefore, in order to discuss whether or not it is convenient to allow him to engage in external business, we need to compare this benefit with the opportunity cost of the agent dedicating this time to the external task and not the internal one. In this way the optimal set of tasks that the agent can work on privately while under a contractual relationship with the principal, is determined; they are all those tasks in which the benefit (the wage savings) is greater than the opportunity cost (the reduction in effort in the relationship). In other words, we need to consider whether the agent's effort is more profitable in the task he performs for the principal, or in the task he performs for his own private gain.[19]

The analysis of Holmström and Milgrom (1991) supports the common idea that responsibility and authority should go hand in hand. It is efficient to give agents greater liberty to involve themselves in private business the more responsible they are with respect to their productivity in the principal's firm. On the other hand, the exclusion of this type of activity should be greater when it is more difficult to motivate the agent for the task that he must perform for the principal. The analysis also predicts that there will be more restrictions on carrying out external tasks in those cases with weak incentives, due to problems in the measurement of the results. Rigid pay-off schemes and the limitation of activities are common in bureaucracies and other organizations in which production estimations are difficult to achieve. External tasks for private gain that it is convenient to prohibit could be, for example, collusion with other participants (see Tirole, 1986), an activity that was discussed in the above sections, and any activities intended to accumulate influence (Milgrom, 1988).

[19] Related to this discussion on the advantages of delegation of responsibility is the paper by De Bijl (1995). He studies whether a principal who does not design pecuniary incentives schemes is still able in some cases to motivate the agent by appealing to his private benefits (e.g. job satisfaction). In his model, the principal can do so by giving the agent responsibility to select a project among a predetermined number of them. If the agent has enough discretion, he finds it worth while to find out about this private benefits of the possible projects, and recommend his preferred one. Delegation of responsibility may benefit the principal because the agent will work hard if he is allowed to implement his preferred project.

3C.4 Repeated moral hazard

Certain relationships in which a moral hazard problem is posed do not take place only once, but rather are repeated over time (for example, work relationships, insurance, seller–client relationships, etc.). In other words, the participants are united by the relationship during a given number of periods or years. It is important to consider what happens in these cases, since the duration aspect (the repetition) of the relationship gives rise to new elements that are absent in static models.

As is usual in game theory, the consequences of repetition depend on whether there are a finite or infinite number of periods. Infinitely repeated relationships are analysed in, for example, Radner (1981) and Rubinstein and Yaari (1983). These authors apply the theory of supergames to a model without a discount rate, and with a risk neutral principal. Intuitively, frequent repetition of the relationship allows us to converge towards the efficient solution. This result is based on the idea that, in this framework, incentives are not determined by the pay-off scheme contingent on the result of each period, but rather on average effort, and the information available on this is very precise when the number of periods is large. A sufficiently threatening punishment that would be applied when the principal believes that the agent, on average, does not fulfil his tasks, is sufficient to dissuade him from slacking (or at least not to slack very often).

The other group of studies which we shall analyse in what follows consider relationships that are repeated a finite number of times. In order to see the results that are obtained from this repetition, we shall consider a framework of pure moral hazard, i.e. throughout the relationship, both in the initial period and in any intermediate one, both participants have the same information. In other words, we put aside any element that may give an informational advantage (of the adverse selection type) to the agent before signing the contract in the second period.

The contracts or agreements that can be reached depend on whether the participants can sign long-term agreements or whether, even though they will be in contact in several periods, they can only sign contracts for one period at time. Agreements that are limited to the current period only are called *short-term* contracts. At the other extreme are the bilateral agreements that cover the entire duration of the relationship. These are called *long-term* contracts, and they require that the participants can achieve this type of commitment in a believable manner.

A part of the literature is dedicated to the analysis of whether or not the long-term contract in general has a memory (i.e. the pay-offs in any single period will depend on the results of all previous periods in such a way that the files of the relationships are crucial).[20] The answer is positive since the long-term contract internalizes the agent's consumption over time, which depends on the sequence of payments received (as a function of the past contingencies). The theme of another important part of the literature is the analysis of when the optimal long-term contract can be implemented through the sequence of optimal short-term contracts. To 'implement' in this sense means that the subgame perfect equilibrium of short-term contracts leads to efforts and consumptions that coincide with those obtained under the long-term contract.[21] In order for the sequence of optimal short-term contracts to admit the same solution as the long-term contract (so that they are equivalent), two conditions must be met (see Chiappori, Macho-Stadler, Rey, and Salanié, 1994):

(i) First, the long-term contract internalizes the agent's consumption over time, which depends on the past history. Therefore the optimal sequence of single-period contracts should have a memory. But when the reservation utility is invariant (as it is the case in a stationary context), the optimal sequence of short-term contracts will not replicate the long-term optimum unless there exist means of smoothing consumption, that is, the agent has access to credit markets.

(ii) Secondly, since the optimal short-term contract sequence is a subgame perfect equilibrium of the game between the agents, the long-term contract must be renegotiation-proof. A contract is said to be renegotiation-proof if at the beginning of any intermediate period, no new contract or renegotiation is possible that would be preferred by all participants. This means that there is not the possibility that, at a certain moment of time, both participants are interested in sitting down and changing the clauses of the contract.[22]

Let us explain the forces at work through the examination of two cases (for more details, see Chiappori, Macho-Stadler, Rey, and Salanié, 1994). First, when the agent has no access to credit markets, the optimal long-term contract will be renegotiation-proof. However, short-term contracting prevents consumption-smoothing: the optimal sequence of short-term contracts is just the repetition of the static optimal contract. Thus short-term implementation will not obtain. The long-term contract has an indisputable advantage over the single-period contract sequence; it can distribute the agent's consumption over time better, and it can never be inferior since it is always possible to

20 Such as Lambert (1983), Rogerson (1985*b*), and Chiappori and Macho-Stadler (1990).

21 See Malcomson and Spinnewyn (1988), Fudenberg, Holmström, and Milgrom (1990), and Rey and Salanié (1990).

22 Dewatripont (1989) shows that when the possibility of renegotiation is anticipated by principal and agent in the initial contract design (i.e. when the contract is made renegotiation-proof) the set of admissible contracts is reduced and that induces a loss of efficiency (*ex ante*).

propose the optimal sequence of short-term contracts as a possible long-term arrangement.

Second, if the agent has free access to the credit market and there is no wealth effect in the agent preferences (i.e. the agent is risk-neutral, or has preferences exhibiting constant absolute risk-aversion), then the savings decision does not determine any contract. Thus, even if the agent's savings are not observable, the optimal long-term contract is renegotiation-proof and can be implemented through short-term contracts.

3C.5 Relationships between several principals and one agent

There are situations in which one agent works for (is contracted by) several principals simultaneously (*common agency* situation). This multiple principal structure can be delegated if the agent is voluntarily put in charge of a task by several principals, or intrinsic if the agent's natural decisions affect several principals. Examples of delegated structures are representatives who work with more than one product, travel agencies who represent several transport companies and hotels, supermarkets that sell the products of different manufacturers, etc. Examples of relationships with several intrinsic principals are agents whose decisions are of interest to more than one regulator, as is the case of the central government and provincial authorities.

In the single agent–multiple principal structure it is evident that, in general, the principals are better off if they co-operate. Anything that they can do in a non-co-operative way can be done in a co-operative game. Under co-operative behaviour, the game is similar to the simple moral hazard model, since in that model the principal could be either an individual or a group of individuals acting co-operatively. However, it is not always possible for the principals to be able to achieve the co-ordination and commitment necessary to act as a single individual. We are interested in the framework of situations in which the principals behave non-co-operatively (see Bernheim and Whinston, 1986). This is important when the principals do not value the results in the same way, and so they each demand different efforts from the agent.

Consider that the agent's decision depends on the total pay-off he receives, independently of which principal has paid which part of this payment. When the principals act non-co-operatively, in general it is not possible to achieve the same situation as when they can reach an agreement. Intuitively, in this case the free-rider problem appears, since none of them gets the entire result of the relationship. Thus, no single principal is able to exclusively profit from the incentives she provides, even though the cost of these incentives must be fully borne by this principal. In general, the effort that the principals receive when they do not co-operate is less than the effort that would maximize their collective profits. However, even in the non-co-operative case, the final contract that is offered to the agent has an efficiency property with respect to its costs; independently of the effort attained in equilibrium, the aggregate incentive scheme minimizes the cost of getting the agent to choose this effort.

One way of solving the problem of co-ordination between the principals is to use the same type of mechanism as that proposed by Holmström (1982) for the case of a team of agents. The two principals could appoint a 'principals' principal' who would supersede them both in the organization but who would not deal directly with the agent. This 'principal' would offer contingent payoffs to the two original principals, and they would then offer contingent payoffs to the agent. A second idea to restore efficiency is to contract a risk-neutral intermediary. The principals would contract this intermediary, paying him according to the result, and he would be responsible for offering a contingent contract to the agent (from which the original principals no longer have the right to establish the relationship with the agent).

Spiller and Urbiztondo (1991) have applied this type of model to the analysis of the relationships between interest groups (the agent) and the US Congress and the President (the principals). They show that the use of interest groups to control regulated activities can be more efficient than contracting independent regulators, since the incentives to collude with one of the principals is less for the interest groups than for the independent regulator.

4

THE ADVERSE SELECTION PROBLEM

Summary

In this chapter we study the adverse selection problem, which is present when, before the signing of a contract, the party that establishes the conditions of the contract (the principal) has less information than the other party (the agent) on some important characteristics affecting the value of the contract.

In a simple adverse selection framework, with one principal and one agent, the fundamental conclusions obtained from the analysis are the following. First, it is optimal for the principal to offer a self-selecting 'menu' of contracts, i.e. the principal will prepare a contract format for each possible agent type, establishing terms such that each agent type will choose to sign that contract that was designed for his type. Secondly, within the optimal contract menu, the worst agent (that agent who, given his private characteristics is not interested in passing himself off as some other type), will obtain exactly his reservation utility, while all other agent types will achieve an informational rent. Finally, the only efficient contract will be that designed for, and signed by, the best agent (that agent type for which no other agent types wish to pass themselves off), since the other contracts will be distorted in order to limit the informational rent.

In situations in which there is competition between principals, the best agents lose out under private information, since the equilibrium contract offered to them will be distorted in order to avoid bad agents choosing it. The bad agents' contract is efficient, but the good agents' one is not.

4.1 Introduction

Very often, the most serious problem that appears in contractual relationships (agency relationships) is that the parties to the contract do not have all the relevant information about each other. For example, consider a person who hires a carpenter for home renovations. Even though the actual task to be done may be well defined, the worker's ability, cleanliness, and manners are not. In terms of agency theory, we would say that, before the signing of the contract, the agent has more information than the principal concerning certain aspects regarding his personal characteristics. With respect to the example above, the homeowner doesn't have all the relevant information concerning the carpenter.

There are many examples in which the informational structure is similar to that in the case of the carpenter. A lawyer is usually better informed than his client with respect to his personal characteristics (for example, if he is interested in the job or not, or if his attitude and capabilities are the most adequate for the case at hand). A driver knows more than his insurance company about his driving habits (if he uses motorways or local roads, or the number of daily hours spent behind the wheel). A firm has more information than the government about the costs of carrying out a certain project. This type of situation is known as an *adverse selection* problem.

Adverse selection is present not only when the agent's informational advantage concerns his own personal characteristics, but also when there is asymmetric information regarding any variable relevant to the contractual relationship. Take the example of a firm negotiating a licence agreement for the acquisition of a technology. In general, it has more information than the patent-holder about the profitability of the market in which it is going to use the technology. In the example of the homeowner who hires a carpenter, the former may not be aware of the job's difficulty, or of the cost of the required materials, or, indeed, any other aspect of the job. A lawyer not only has more information than his client about his own capability, but also about the legal history concerning similar cases, which influences the probability of winning the case. A final example of the many possibilities in which the agent is better informed than the principal as to particular aspects concerning the relationship is the case of a regulated firm that knows more than the government about the market in which it operates.

When the agent has more information than the principal concerning certain important aspects of the relationship, this information will only be revealed if it is in the interests of the agent to do so. The idea that the holders of private information may be interested in keeping it private is briefly and clearly pointed out in the following statement, made in 1914 by N. P. A. Alifas, spokesman for the International Association of Machinists:[1]

> The only way in which the workman has been able to retain time enough in which to do the work with the speed with which he thinks he ought to do it, has been to keep the employer somewhat in ignorance of exactly the time needed.... Most people walk to work in the morning, if it isn't too far. If somebody should discover they could run to work in one-third of the time, they might have no objection to have that fact ascertained, but if the man who ascertained it has the power to make them run, they might object to having him find it out.

If the agent tries to profit from information by keeping it private, the principal's problem is to find a way to reduce her informational disadvantage. Since this implies manipulation and departure from the first-best agreement, the existence of asymmetric information between the various participants in a market can result in modifications (read inefficiencies) in the market equilibrium, or even in some cases, non-existence of equilibrium. In order to see some of the consequences of an adverse selection problem, consider the market for second-hand cars analysed in the original article by Akerlof (1970), who pioneered this literature. It is refered as the *lemons* model. As we all know, in this market it is possible to find vehicles of many different qualities. Some cars are placed on the market because their owners simply want a bigger or better one, while others are on sale after being involved in a major accident or after having been used as hire cars or driving-school vehicles. Anyone who has ever been a buyer in the second-hand car market will know that it is very difficult to distinguish the respective qualities of the cars, or to learn something of their past history. Since the sellers know the origin of their cars, or at least they have had more time to try the car out, it is clear that they possess much more information regarding the car's quality than does any particular buyer. Hence we are faced with an asymmetric information problem of the type we have called adverse selection (since it is previous to the signing of a contract).

Consider the following simple model in which we represent the quality of a second-hand car by a real number. Let this parameter, which we shall call k, be distributed uniformly on the interval $[0, 1]$. Cars of quality 0 are the worst and those of quality 1 are the best. That we assume all quality levels to have the same probability is only for simplicity. We shall also assume that both the seller and the buyer are risk-neutral. A seller is willing to sell a car of quality k for a price $p_0\, k$. On the other hand, a buyer values a car of quality k at $p_1\, k$. In order for a market to exist it is necessary that $p_1 > p_0$. Let's simplify even more by assuming $p_1 = (3/2)\, p_0$.

[1] Taken from Trevor I. Williams (1982), *A Short History of Twentieth-Century Technology c. 1900–c.1950*, Oxford, Clarendon Press; New York, Oxford University Press.

What would happen if the information were symmetric? In this case all cars would be sold. A car of quality k would sell in the market at a price between $p_0 k$ and $p_1 k$, the exact selling price depending on the relative bargaining powers of the buyer and the seller. For example, if the buyer had all the bargaining power, the selling price of the car would be $P = p_0 k$.

However, when the seller knows the quality of the car and the buyer doesn't, the above contracts do not comprise an equilibrium. The buyer, upon seeing a price, does not know what quality he is being sold. A Bayesian consumer would calculate the average quality of the products being offered, knowing that this depends on the selling price, and would base his decision to buy or not on that average. Let's consider how the buyer reasons and what occurs in this market.

Assume that the price at which a car is being offered is P. If this were the market price of second-hand cars, the sellers would only offer to sell cars that, in their eyes, are worth at most P, that is, the only quality levels on sale would be such that $P \geq p_0 k$. In other words, it would only be possible to find qualities $k \leq P/p_0$. Given the assumed a priori distribution of quality, the average quality in the market at price P is $K = P/(2\, p_0)$. Now, since the average quality is $K = P/(2\, p_0)$, the consumers that buy at this price receive an average utility of $p_1 K = (p_1/(2\, p_0))\, P = (3/4)\, P$. This means that the consumers are not willing to buy, since the price P is greater than the average utility of consuming $(3/4)\, P$. Therefore, no transactions will take place. In fact, the only price at which consumers would be willing to buy in our example is $P = 0$, since then they are sure that the car they buy is of the worst possible quality. The informational problems presented are sufficient to cause the disappearance of the market for second-hand cars.

In the above example, it was assumed that there is no way that the seller can convince the buyer that a certain car is of high quality, thus the asymmetric information results in not only an important inefficiency, but even the *disappearance of the market* (except, perhaps, the market for 'lemons'). This is not always the case. Even though the asymmetric information implies a cost, as we shall see, *sometimes it is possible to discriminate.*

In order to understand how the principal can discriminate, that is, how the agent can be motivated to reveal private information, imagine you are the buyer of a used car (the principal). What type of agreement between you and the seller (the agent) would convince you that the vehicle you are buying is of good quality? One possibility is to only buy if the seller is ready to accept a sufficiently long guarantee period. Since low-quality cars are likely to break down soon after the transaction, the seller of a lemon would be reluctant to accept a contract including a guarantee, since doing so may well cost him more than what he gets by selling his lemon for the price of a 'peach' (a good-quality car). On the other hand, a seller of a peach would accept a contract with a guarantee, at least at a reasonable price. Hence, it may be possible to discriminate between cars according to the clauses of the transaction contract.[2]

This chapter will consider optimal discriminating contracts when the agent has private information. We will study the characteristics of these contracts both when the relationship is between one principal and an agent, and when there are many principals in the market, all interested in signing with the agent.

4.2 A Model of Adverse Selection

In the following we present the consequences of the appearance of an adverse selection problem[3] in the framework of Chapter 2. Hence we will consider a risk-neutral principal who contracts an agent (who could be risk-neutral or risk-averse) to carry out some effort on her behalf. We assume that the exertion of effort e is associated with an expected payment to the principal of $\Pi(e)$. Since here the agent's effort will be assumed to be verifiable and the principal is risk-neutral, we will simplify the notation by dropping the (effort dependent) probabilities of each outcome. Therefore, $\Pi(e) = \Sigma_{i=1}^{n} p_i(e)\, x_i$. In order that the objective function be concave, we assume for simplicity $\Pi'(e) > 0$ and $\Pi''(e) < 0$.

The agent could be either of *two types*, between which the principal cannot distinguish. The two types differ only with respect to the disutility of effort function, which is $v(e)$ for type 1, and $k\,v(e)$, with $k > 1$ for type 2. Hence the disutility of any particular effort is greater for an agent of type 2. We shall refer to the first as a 'good' type (denoted by G) and the second as 'bad' (denoted by B), since for the same effort, the principal will have to pay more to the second type than to the first. Given this notation, the agents' utilities are (respectively) $U^G(w, e) = u(w) - v(e)$ and $U^B(w, e) = u(w) - k\,v(e)$.

The game is represented in Figure 4.1.

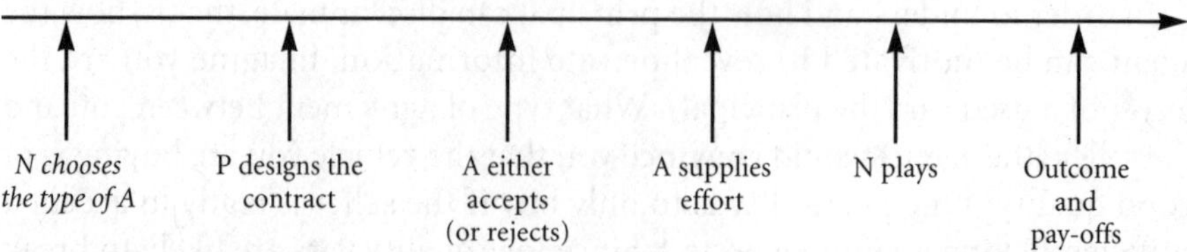
N chooses the type of A
P designs the contract
A either accepts (or rejects)
A supplies effort
N plays
Outcome and pay-offs

Fig. 4.1

[2] In Ch. 5 we will analyse the situation in which it is the seller (the informed party) who offers the contract. Then the contract can *signal* the quality of the car.

[3] Some important papers in these topics are Mirrlees (1971), Spence (1974), Mussa and Rosen (1978), Baron and Myerson (1982), and Guesnerie and Laffont (1984).

If there was no adverse selection problem, and the principal was contracting with a type-G agent, she would then solve the following problem:

$$\begin{aligned}&\underset{[e,w]}{\text{Max}} \quad \Pi(e) - w \\ &\text{s.t.} \quad u(w) - v(e) \geq \underline{U},\end{aligned}$$

which, given the initial assumptions, is concave in (e, w). The optimal contract for a type-G agent (e^{G*}, w^{G*}) is characterized by the following equations:

$$u(w^{G*}) - v(e^{G*}) = \underline{U}.$$

$$\Pi'(e^{G*}) = \frac{v'(e^{G*})}{u'(w^{G*})}.$$

The first of these two equations is the *participation constraint*, and the second is the *efficiency condition* which demands that the marginal rates of substitution of effort and wages be the same for the type-G agent and the principal.

If the agent were of type B, then the optimal contract (e^{B*}, w^{B*}) would be given by:

$$u(w^{B*}) - k\,v(e^{B*}) = \underline{U}$$

$$\Pi'(e^{B*}) = \frac{k\,v'(e^{B*})}{u'(w^{B*})}.$$

In order to make clear the relationship between the two contracts, the conditions that define them are depicted in Figure 4.2.[4] It is easy to see, both in Figure 4.2 and from the equations, that it is optimal for the principal to demand more effort from the agent to whom effort is less costly, which is to say $e^{G*} > e^{B*}$. However, we cannot be sure about the relationship between the

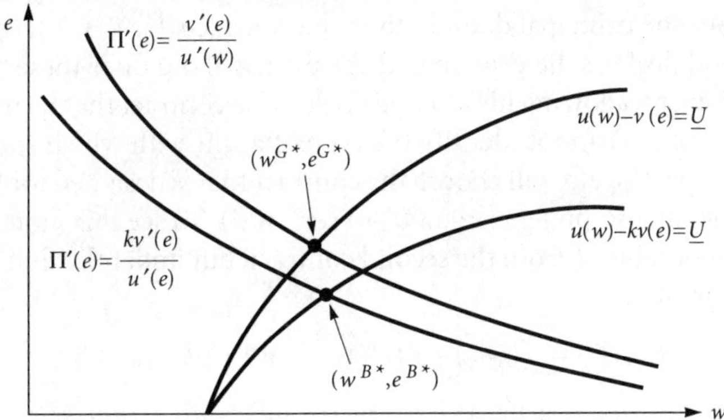

Fig. 4.2

[4] The curve $u(w) - k\,v(e) = \underline{U}$ is beneath $u(w) - v(e) = \underline{U}$ since $k > 1$, while $\Pi''(e) < 0$, $v''(e) > 0$ and $u''(w) \leq 0$ imply that the curve $\Pi'(e) = k\,v'(e)/u'(w)$ is beneath $\Pi'(e) = v'(e)/u'(w)$.

wages, since there are two effects of opposite sign. On the one hand, any particular effort level is more costly to B than to G, and so for a given effort level, B requires a greater wage than G in order to participate. But, on the other hand, the principal demands less effort from B than from G, and so the latter should receive a greater wage, at equal effort costs.

Figure 4.3 shows a second form of seeing graphically how the optimal contracts are calculated. In Figure 4.3, the highest isoprofit curves that the principal can obtain, given the combinations of (e, w) for which the agent obtains exactly his reservation utility are shown. Once again, it can be seen that, under symmetric information, the efforts are ordered, but exactly which agent type receives the greater wage will depend on the particular problem at hand.

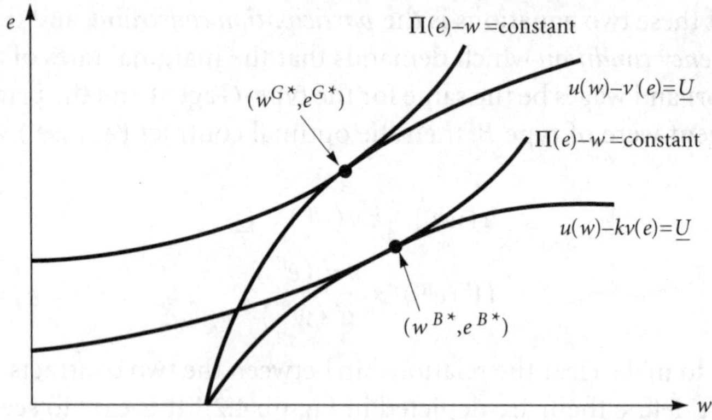

Fig. 4.3

If there is an asymmetric information problem in which the agents know their type, but the principal doesn't, then the contracts $\{(e^{G*}, w^{G*}), (e^{B*}, w^{B*})\}$ are not a good deal for the principal. If the principal did offer these two contracts to any agent, allowing him to freely select the contract that he most likes (since the principal cannot identify the type of agent with which she is dealing), then a type-B agent will choose the contract that is designed for him, but the type-G agent also prefers (e^{B*}, w^{B*}) to (e^{G*}, w^{G*}). To see this, note that the type-G agent obtains $\underline{U}$, from the second contract, but under the first contract his utility is greater:

$$U^G(w^{B*}, e^{B*}) = u(w^{B*}) - v(e^{B*}) > u(w^{B*}) - k\,v(e^{B*}) = \underline{U}.$$

As with the case of moral hazard, *symmetric information contracts are not optimal under asymmetric information.* This can also be seen graphically in Figure 4.2, given the position of both contracts in (e, w) space and the fact that utility increases with increases in w or decreases in e.

In order to calculate the best contracts that the principal can offer in this situation, we must first describe the problem that she faces. To do so, assume that the principal considers that the probability of an agent being type G is q, where $0 < q < 1$.

What form will the contract that the principal offers an agent take? Perhaps we could think that the best is to design a contract (e, w) that takes into account the probability of an agent being of one type or the other, and that is acceptable to either type of agent. However, as will become clear in what follows, the principal can, in general, do better. She can design a *menu of contracts* $\{(e^G, w^G), (e^B, w^B)\}$, where (e^G, w^G) is directed towards the most efficient type of agent, while (e^B, w^B) is intended for the least efficient type. That is to say, it is as if the principal offered a contract saying: 'I have these wage schedules, one for each of the possible types you can be. So, tell me which is your type, and I'll give you your corresponding contract.' In fact, the case in which the principal offers a single contract to both agent types is a special case of this contract menu in which both contracts coincide. Thanks to the separation of the two contracts the principal can, in general, obtain greater expected profits than if only one contract were offered. Note, however, that for the menu of contracts to be correctly designed, the type-G agent must select that contract designed for him, and the type-B agent must select the contract intended for him. Hence *the scheme must be self-selective.* Since agent type is not observable by the principal, the menu of contracts must be such that each agent obtains greater utility by truthfully revealing his type than by deceiving the principal.

Menus of contracts are not as unusual as they may seem. On many occasions an employee will offer different contract possibilities to a worker in order that the latter chooses the one which most suits his own personal work habits. Similarly, insurance companies offer several possible insurance contracts and each client may freely choose the one he most prefers. In both cases, these are menus of contracts, in which each contract is designed with a particular type of worker or client in mind.

The design of the optimal contract could have a more complicated structure than offering a choice of two contracts, or receiving signals that belong exclusively to the characteristic space (in the case at hand, announce type G or B). However, offering three different contracts would be unnecessary since each type of agent will prefer only one of the three, hence at least one will never be chosen, and so it may as well be eliminated from the menu, thus leaving only two contracts. The same can be said of complex mechanisms in which the agents must send more sophisticated signals. This discussion is the foundation of the *revelation principle.* This principle asserts that, in the search for the optimal contract, the principal may restrict the menu of contracts to those that provide each type of agent with the incentive to truthfully reveal his characteristic. These mechanisms are normally referred to as *revealing* or *direct.*[5] The intuition for this principle is the following. Assume that the principal is concerned about a certain agent's information that the agent can manipulate, say his income. She can ask the agent a variety of indirect questions, for example, how he shares his expenditure among the different goods, his political preferences, his hobbies. These messages will be used by the principal to deduce the agent's income through a certain rule, rule that the agent also knows. Consequently, the agent has the same incentives to manipulate the set of answers that will be used to deduce his income, as he would have to manipulate the information concerning his income. Hence one gets the same result by straightforwardly asking the agent's income, that is, using a direct mechanism.

The principal's problem, therefore, is to maximize her expected profits subject to the restrictions that, after considering the contracts offered, the agent decides to sign with the principal, choosing that contract designed for his particular agent type:

$$\max_{[(e^G, w^G), (e^B, w^B)]} \quad q\,[\Pi(e^G) - w^G] + (1-q)\,[\Pi(e^B) - w^B]$$

$$[P^{4.1}] \quad \text{s.t.} \quad \begin{aligned} & u(w^G) - v(e^G) \geq \underline{U} && (4.1)\\ & u(w^B) - k\,v(e^B) \geq \underline{U} && (4.2)\\ & u(w^G) - v(e^G) \geq u(w^B) - v(e^B) && (4.3)\\ & u(w^B) - k\,v(e^B) \geq u(w^G) - k\,v(e^G). && (4.4) \end{aligned}$$

The first two restrictions ensure that the two agent types will accept their respective contracts (participation constraints), while the last two are the conditions that ensure that each agent type is personally interested in accepting the contract designed for his type rather than the one designed for the other type of agent. These are known as *self-selection* or *incentive compatibility constraints.*

Before solving the problem, note that (4.1) is implied by (4.2) and (4.3):

$$u(w^G) - v(e^G) \geq u(w^B) - v(e^B) \geq u(w^B) - k\,v(e^B) \geq \underline{U},$$

and so we can exclude restriction (4.1). In fact, this is a feature of adverse selection problems. *The only participation constraint that the principal need to be concerned with is that corresponding to the least efficient agent.* This is because the most efficient agent's incentive compatibility constraint says that he will

[5] More precisely, the revelation principle guarantees that any Bayesian equilibrium resulting from a mechanism (M, g) proposed by the principal, where M is the agent's set of messages and g is the result of the game, can also be found as the Bayesian equilibrium of a direct mechanism in which she asks the agent about his type and the agent tells the truth. Discussions on this topic can be found (for example) in Kreps (1990) and Fudenberg and Tirole (1991). Gibbard (1973), Green and Laffont (1977), and Myerson (1979) were the founders of this principle.

not want to pass himself off as some other type, and these other types, given their own participation constraints, are guaranteed at least the reservation utility, even with greater disutility associated with the contracted effort. Hence the most efficient agent type must also be guaranteed at least the reservation utility.

Note also that, in order that the restrictions are satisfied, the optimal contracts must be such that *greater effort is demanded of the most efficient agent*, that is, $e^G \geq e^B$, since (4.3) and (4.4) imply:

$$v(e^G) - v(e^B) \leq u(w^G) - u(w^B) \leq k\,[v(e^G) - v(e^B)], \tag{4.5}$$

which, since $k > 1$, implies that $v(e^G) \geq v(e^B)$.

Result 4.1 characterizes the optimal menu $\{(e^G, w^G), (e^B, w^B)\}$.

Result 4.1. The menu of contracts $\{(e^G, w^G), (e^B, w^B)\}$ which solves problem $[P^{4.1}]$ is defined by the following equations:

$$u(w^G) - v(e^G) = \underline{U} + (k-1)\,v(e^B)$$

$$u(w^B) - k\,v(e^B) = \underline{U}$$

$$\Pi'(e^G) = \frac{v'(e^G)}{u'(w^G)}$$

$$\Pi'(e^B) = \frac{k\,v'(e^B)}{u'(w^B)} + \frac{q\,(k-1)}{(1-q)}\,\frac{v'(e^B)}{u'(w^G)}.$$

Proof. Let λ, μ, and δ be the Lagrange multipliers associated with (4.2), (4.3), and (4.4) respectively. The Lagrangean first-order conditions are:

$$-q + \mu\,u'(w^G) - \delta\,u'(w^G) = 0 \Leftrightarrow \mu - \delta = \frac{q}{u'(w^G)} \tag{4.6}$$

$$-(1-q) + \lambda\,u'(w^B) - \mu\,u'(w^B) + \delta\,u'(w^B) = 0 \Leftrightarrow \lambda - \mu + \delta = \frac{1-q}{u'(w^B)} \tag{4.7}$$

$$q\,\Pi'(e^G) - \mu\,v'(e^G) + \delta\,k\,v'(e^G) = 0 \Leftrightarrow \mu - \delta\,k = \frac{q\,\Pi'(e^G)}{v'(e^G)} \tag{4.8}$$

$$(1-q)\,\Pi'(e^B) - \lambda\,k\,v'(e^B) + \mu\,v'(e^B) - \delta\,k\,v'(e^B) = 0$$

$$\Leftrightarrow \lambda\,k - \mu + \delta\,k = \frac{(1-q)\,\Pi'(e^B)}{v'(e^B)} \tag{4.9}$$

Equations (4.6) and (4.7), and (4.8) and (4.9), in particular imply (respectively):

$$\lambda = \frac{q}{u'(w^G)} + \frac{1-q}{u'(w^B)} > 0 \tag{4.10}$$

$$\lambda\, k = \frac{q\,\Pi'(e^G)}{v'(e^G)} + \frac{(1-q)\,\Pi'(e^B)}{v'(e^B)} \tag{4.11}$$

by which the participation constraint of agent B, (4.2), binds. Moreover, $\mu > 0$ because (Kuhn–Tucker conditions require the Lagragean multipliers to be non-negative) $\mu = 0$ would, by equation (4.6), imply $\delta < 0$ which is impossible.

Before presenting the characteristics of the optimal contract, we will prove that it cannot be optimal to offer a contract that demands the same effort from both agent types. Note that if $e^G = e^B$, then it must also be true that $w^G = w^B$ (since equation (4.5) implies that $u(w^G) - u(w^B) = 0$). On the other hand, (4.10) and (4.11) in this case imply that:

$$\lambda = \frac{1}{u'(w)} = \frac{\Pi'(e)}{k\, v'(e)},$$

for values of e and w common to both agent types. Finally, equations (4.6) and (4.8) in this case imply that:

$$\mu = \frac{q}{u'(w)} + \delta = q\lambda + \delta$$

$$\mu = \frac{q\,\Pi'(e)}{v'(e)} + k\delta = q\,k\lambda + k\delta = k(q\lambda + \delta),$$

which is impossible since μ cannot be equal to $k\,\mu$, with $k > 1$ and $\mu > 0$. Consequently, the optimal menu will really include two different contracts for the agent.

Since $e^G > e^B$, it is not possible for both self-selection conditions (4.3) and (4.4) to bind simultaneously, since $k > 1$ implies that one of the two inequalities of expression (4.5) must be strict. Equation (4.3) binds since $\mu > 0$. Therefore, (4.4) does not bind, which implies $\delta = 0$. Equation (4.3) can be rewritten as:

$$\begin{aligned} u(w^G) - v(e^G) = u(w^B) - v(e^B) &= u(w^B) - k\,v(e^B) + (k-1)\,v(e^B) \\ &= \underline{U} + (k-1)\,v(e^B), \end{aligned}$$

that is, the contract designed for the most efficient agent is such that he will obtain welfare strictly greater than his reservation utility.

Since $\delta = 0$, equations (4.6) and (4.8) imply:

$$\frac{1}{u'(w^G)} = \frac{\Pi'(e^G)}{v'(e^G)},$$

which is the familiar efficiency condition that the contract (e^{G*}, w^{G*}) fulfils. Finally, given that (4.7) is equivalent to:

$$-\mu = \frac{1-q}{u'(w^B)} - \lambda$$

equation (4.9) can (using (4.10)) be written as:

$$\frac{(1-q)k}{u'(w^B)} + \frac{q(k-1)}{u'(w^G)} = \frac{(1-q)\,\Pi'(e^B)}{v'(e^B)},$$

that is,

$$\frac{q(k-1)}{(1-q)}\frac{v'(e^B)}{u'(w^G)} + \frac{k\,v'(e^B)}{u'(w^B)} = \Pi'(e^B),$$

which is the fourth equation defining the optimal contract menu. *Q.E..D.*

The optimal contract menu $\{(e^G, w^G), (e^B, w^B)\}$ has the following characteristics. First, the participation condition only binds for the agent with the highest costs, while the other agent receives an *informational rent* of $(k-1)\,v(e^B)$. That is, *the most efficient agent receives utility greater than his reservation level due to his private information.* This is a characteristic feature of contracts under adverse selection. The only restriction about which the principal need be worried is that corresponding to the least efficient agent.

Secondly, the incentive condition for high-efficiency agents binds in the solution, while that corresponding to low-efficiency agents does not.

Thirdly, the efficiency condition binds for the good agent. This property is known as '*non distortion at the top*' and indicates that, given an adverse selection problem, the only efficient contract is that designed for the agent with the 'best' characteristic (in other words, the contract designed for the agent for whom no one else wants to pass themselves off, is not distorted). It should be noted that if the agent is risk-neutral, then the efficiency condition $1/u'(w^G) = \Pi'(e^G)/v'(e^G)$ does not depend on w^G, since $u'(w^G)$ is a constant. This implies $e^G = e^{G*}$. If the agent is risk-averse, then the efficiency condition depends on w^G. The optimal salary w^G in an adverse selection situation is different from w^{G*}, and this implies that e^G is different from e^{G*}. However, the contract proposed to type G agent is efficient in both cases.

Finally, a distortion is introduced into the efficiency condition of the least efficient (type-B) agents. The intuition behind this distortion is to make the contract (e^B, w^B) less attractive to type-G agents. By distorting, the principal loses efficiency with respect to type-B agents, but she pays less informational rent to the type-G's. The trade-off between these two effects is favourable to the distortion. Starting from agent B's efficient effort level, a marginal change only induces a second order effect on the welfare the principal extracts from agent B (the first order effect of a change at the optimal level is zero) while it causes a first order effect on agent G's informational rent.

Before commenting these conditions, we will consider the relationship between the wages and the efforts offered given the presence of an adverse selection problem, and those resulting from maximization under symmetric information. For agent type G the efficiency condition is the same in both situations, although the participation condition binds under symmetric information but does not under asymmetric information. Graphically, the situation is presented in Figure 4.4, where we denote $A=(k-1)\,v(e^B)$. It is easy to check that $e^G \leq e^{G*}$ and $w^G > w^{G*}$ holds true.

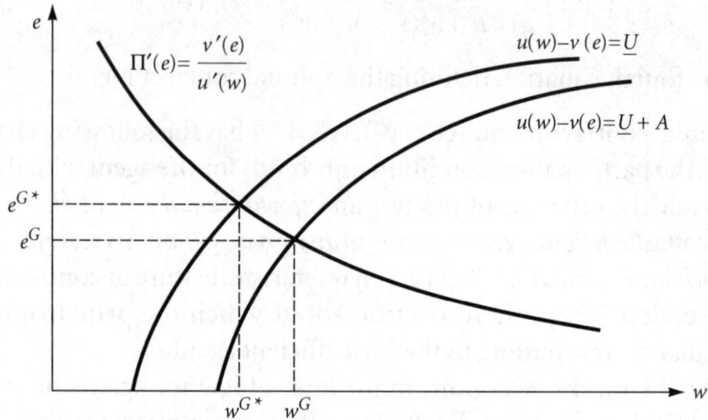

Fig. 4.4

On the other hand, for agent type B we have Figure 4.5, where

$$C=\frac{q\,(k-1)}{(1-q)}\frac{v'\,(e^B)}{u'\,(w^G)}.$$

For this contract $e^B < e^{B*}$ and $w^B < w^{B*}$.[6] Bear in mind that it is also true that $e^G > e^B$ and, as is easy to see, $w^G > w^B$ (no agent will choose a contract that demands more effort if less is paid for it).

What is the form that the optimal contracts under adverse selection take due to? Assume that we begin with a symmetric information contract and that we wish to see how we can improve it. The problem with the symmetric information optimal contract menu $\{(e^{G*}, w^{G*}), (e^{B*}, w^{B*})\}$ is that it is not self-selecting

6 The shapes of the graphs are due to the following properties. For the curve $u\,(w)-v\,(e)=\underline{U}+A$ $\partial e/\partial w>0$ and $\partial e/\partial A<0$, while the curve $C+(v'\,(e^G)/u'\,(w^G))=\Pi'(e^G)$ satisfies $\partial e/\partial w<0$ and $\partial e/\partial C<0$. On the other hand, the isoutility curve must be concave, although the concavity of the curve $C+(v'\,(e^G)/u'\,(w^G))=\Pi'\,(e^G)$ is indeterminate.

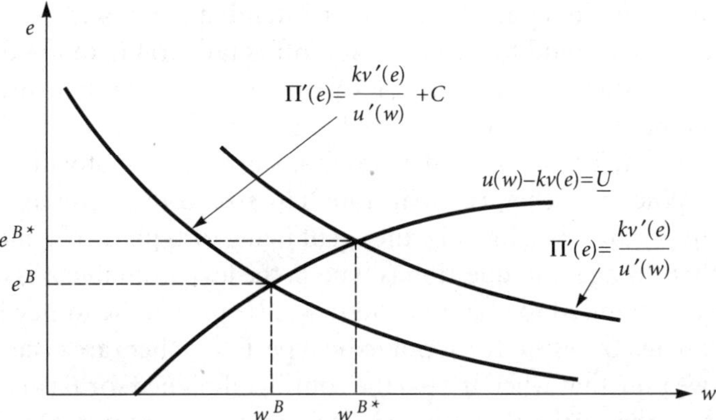

Fig. 4.5

when the principal cannot identify the agent types. If this menu is offered, agent type G will prefer to sign the contract designed for agent type B, rather than his own. Therefore, to begin with, we have only one contract, (e^{B*}, w^{B*}). How can we change this contract, such that the new one is at least as attractive to G and that it gives greater expected profits to the principal?

The difference between the agents is that one type suffers more disutility of effort than the other. Hence the wage that the principal must pay to compensate an increase in effort demanded is greater if it is demanded from B than if it is demanded from G. In other words, if the principal wanted to, she could offer a menu of contracts $\{(e^G, w^G), (e^{B*}, w^{B*})\}$ such that $e^G > e^{B*}$, $w^G > w^{B*}$ so that it is self-selecting: $U^G(w^G, e^G) = U^G(w^{B*}, e^{B*})$ and $U^B(w^{B*}, e^{B*}) > U^B(w^G, e^G)$. Anyway, the principal has greater interest in demanding more effort from G than from B, as can be seen by the fact that e^{G*} is greater than e^{B*}. Therefore, one way of improving the original contract is to demand greater effort from the most efficient agent, duly compensating him with a higher wage (only just sufficient for him not to choose the contract intended for the least efficient agent). For example, the efficient effort level could be demanded, while paying a wage higher than that paid under symmetric information.

However, trying to improve the situation by changing only G's contract, leaving B's contract unaltered is not the best solution for the principal. The contract designed for B is G's 'temptation'. Hence under adverse selection the contract intended for B is also modified: $e^B < e^{B*}$ and $w^B < w^{B*}$. The reason for this modification is that through a distortion (and thus an efficiency loss) in the contract offered to B, this contract becomes less interesting to agent G, and the informational rent that is necessary to pay him (the difference between the wage paid now and the wage that would be paid for the same effort under symmetric information) is, therefore, lower. Thus there is a *trade-off* between creating an inefficiency in the contract intended for B and reducing the informational rent paid to G. This trade-off is favourable to the distortion since the modification of B's effort level only induces a second-order effect in the principal's welfare, while the reduction of G's informational rent is a first-order effect. This argument states that starting the distortion is always profitable. When will the principal stop? The size of the optimal distortion will depend on the probability of the agent being of type G. The more probable it is that the agent in question is type B, the less profitable it is to change the contract intended for type B, and it will be preferable to pay informational rent when the agent turns out to be type-G, a rather rare occurrence. At the limit, we note that when $q \to 0$ the contract designed for B (in result 4.1) converges to the optimal symmetric information contract. On the other hand, if the agents are almost all type-G, the principal will prefer to design a contract menu that introduces a large distortion in the least efficient agent's contract (they are scarce) but that gives a low informational rent to the most efficient agents. Hence, if $q \to 1$ then the distortion in the contract is maximized.

Finally, two comments are in order. First, we should point out that adverse selection problems turn up independently of the agent's risk-aversion. Even if the agent is risk-neutral, the problem has the same basic characteristics, and it is solved in the same way. The reason for this (as opposed to problems of moral hazard) is that there is no insurance incentive problem, but rather the principal is unsure to whom she is offering a contract.

Secondly, we have analysed the optimal contract menu when the principal is interested in contracting the agent independently of his type. The other option the principal has is to offer a contract that will only be accepted by low-effort cost individuals, leaving the position vacant should the agent be of type B. This case is equivalent to a situation of symmetric information with only one agent type, but the contract only takes place with probability q. In this case, the expected profits will be $q\,[\Pi\,(e^{G^*}) - w^{G^*}]$. In order to see which is the best strategy (only hire agents of type G, or offer a self-selecting contract menu, thus never leaving the position vacant) it is necessary to compare the expected profits in each case. The principal will offer the optimal menu $\{(e^G, w^G), (e^B, w^B)\}$ characterized in result 4.1 when:

$$q\,[\,\Pi\,(e^G) - w^G] + (1-q)\,[\,\Pi\,(e^B) - w^B] \geq q\,[\Pi\,(e^{G^*}) - w^{G^*}].$$

Otherwise, she will propose (e^{G^*}, w^{G^*}), a contract that will be accepted only if the agent is of type G. In the latter case, the adverse selection problem does not cause any distortion in the contract (only efficient contracts are proposed), but it does imply that, with probability $1 - q$, the transaction will not take place.

4.3 When Principals Compete for Agents

The conclusions of the above adverse selection models are different if we consider situations in which several principals compete in order to attract agents, rather than the case of one principal who designs a menu of contracts that maximizes her expected profits. The effect of this type of competition is that each principal will have to offer the agent greater than reservation utility so that her offer will be accepted above the offers of the other principals. In this case it is possible that we may find ourselves in situations in which no equilibrium exists (as was shown by Rothschild and Stiglitz (1976) for the insurance market, an example that we will consider in the applications). We shall also see that when we observe pay-offs functionally related to the results of the relationship, these pay-offs are not necessarily due to the existence of a moral hazard problem, but rather they could be motivated by the principal's ignorance of the agent's type. Finally, we will see which agent types win and which lose, given the asymmetric information.

Let's consider a simple case in which there are two possible agent types, as in Section 2. We shall continue to call them good (G) and bad (B). However the two types are now not different with respect to their effort disutility, but rather one (G) is more productive than the other. In particular, we assume that G is more careful than B, in the sense that he commits fewer errors. In other words, his average result is better.[7]

In modelling this situation, we will assume that the productive process is not deterministic, but that the final result depends on luck (that is, it depends on a random variable). In order to simplify the problem, we assume that effort is not a choice variable, but rather it is unique and observable. Therefore the principal cannot separate the two agent types by demanding greater effort from one of them. When the agent exerts effort, the result could be either a success (S) or a failure (F). The probability that it is successful is p^G when the agent is type G and p^B when he is type B, where $p^G > p^B$. The principal values a successful result at x_S, and a failure at x_F. The result is observable, and so the principal can pay the agent according to the result should she so desire. Call w_S the agent's pay-off (wage) if S is observed, and w_F the pay-off if the result is F.

There are several competitive principals trying to contract with the agents. Principals are risk-neutral. Consequently, if the probability of success is p, and the pay-offs offered to agents are (w_S, w_F), a principal's expected profits are

7 In this section we deal with a model something different from the model used in the previous section. To understand the reason for this, see exercise 16.

$$E\Pi = p\, x_S + (1-p)\, x_F - p\, w_S - (1-p)\, w_F.$$

Agents are risk-averse. Their expected utility function, when offered pay-off scheme (w_S, w_F) is

$$EU^G = p^G\, u(w_S) + (1-p^G)\, u(w_F) \quad \text{or} \quad EU^B = p^B\, u(w_S) + (1-p^B)\, u(w_F),$$

depending on whether his type is G or B.

Since only one effort is possible and since effort implies the same disutility to each agent type, we can effectively forget about effort, assuming that it is taken account of in reservation utility. That is, an agent will only accept a contract that guarantees him the same expected utility as not signing plus the disutility that the contract implies, a value that we will call the agent's reservation utility.

The fact that there are now many principals in the market implies that we no longer consider the contract that a principal would offer to an agent, but rather we are interested in the set of equilibrium contracts in the game played by principals competing to attract agents. Since there are many principals, in order for a pay-off scheme to be an equilibrium it must hold that no other principal can offer a different contract that would be preferred by all or some of the agents, and that gives the principal greater expected profits. Note that, since there are two agent types, the equilibrium pay-off scheme must indicate which is the wage to be offered to type-G agents, and which is the wage to be offered to the type Bs. Therefore, a payment scheme will take the form $\{(w_S^G, w_F^G), (w_S^B, w_F^B)\}$. It is possible that the pay-offs to each agent type could coincide, depending on the problem at hand.

4.3.1 The benchmark: Symmetric information

Before attacking the asymmetric information problem, we will analyse the situation under symmetric information. When all principals can perfectly distinguish agent types, the problem of equilibrium determination can be broken into two independent analysis: what contract forms an equilibrium for type-G agents, and what contract forms an equilibrium for the type Bs.

Consider a representative agent type, T ($T = G, B$ in our model), and denote the probability that the result is successful for this agent by p^T. There are two conditions that determine this agent's equilibrium contract $C^T \equiv (w_S^T, w_F^T)$:

(i) *The expected profits of the principals must be zero.* This is true since if the expected profits of a principal who offers (w_S^T, w_F^T) were $\Pi > 0$, then some other principal could offer the contract $(w_S^T + \lambda\Pi, w_F^T + \lambda\Pi)$, $0 < \lambda < 1$, which is strictly preferred by type-T agents, and yet still offers an expected profit of

$(1-\lambda)\,\Pi$ for each agent hired. Hence, a situation in which the contract offers positive expected profits cannot support an equilibrium.

(ii) *The contract C^T must be efficient.* This requires that the contract must be Pareto optimal in the sense that no other contract exists that would be preferred by both principal and agent. This must be true since, if such a contract did exist, some other principal would have sufficient incentives to offer it since it gives positive expected profits, and the agent would have sufficient incentives to accept it since it gives him greater expected utility than C^T. This efficiency condition implies that the contract $C^T \equiv (w_S^T, w_F^T)$ is the solution to the following problem:

$$\underset{(w_S,\, w_F)}{\text{Max}} \quad p^T x_S + (1-p^T)\, x_F - p^T w_S - (1-p^T)\, w_F$$

$$\text{s.t.} \quad p^T u(w_S) + (1-p^T)\, u(w_F) \geq \mathrm{E}U^{T*}$$

where $\mathrm{E}U^{T*}$ is the reservation utility of the agent, as defined above. The above problem demands that the contract be Pareto optimal. If some other principal wants to attract the agent, she must offer expected utility of at least $\mathrm{E}U^{T*}$, and so the new principal will receive expected profits strictly less than those obtained through the above problem (which will be zero in equilibrium). It is easy to see that the problem is concave, and that the Kuhn-Tucker conditions require:

$$w_S^T = w_F^T$$

This is a predictable result. From Chapter 2 we know that the optimal risk share will require that the risk-neutral principal fully insures the agent.

The wage will be given by the zero expected profit condition:

$$w_S^T = w_F^T = p^T x_S + (1-p^T)\, x_F.$$

Hence the optimal contracts for type G and B agents are determined by the conditions:

$$w_S^G = w_F^G = p^G x_S + (1-p^G)\, x_F$$

$$w_S^B = w_F^B = p^B x_S + (1-p^B)\, x_F.$$

In Figure 4.6 the symmetric information equilibrium contracts C^{G*} and C^{B*} are shown.

In Figure 4.6 we observe that the indifference curves of each agent type are such that for any given contract the indifference curve of G is steeper than that of B. This fact can be proved analytically using the probability distributions associated with each agent type:

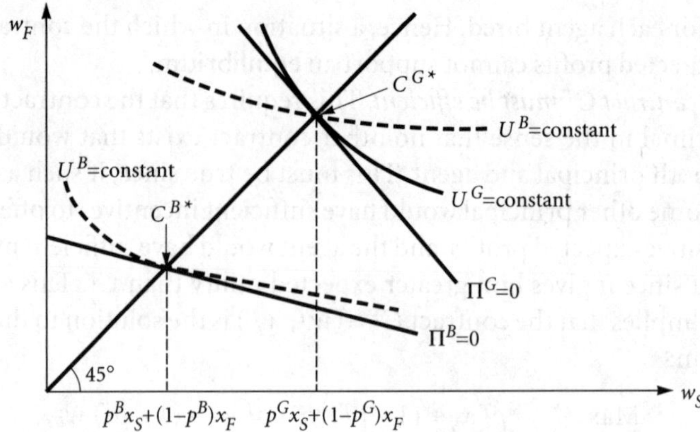

Fig. 4.6

$$\left.\frac{dw_F}{dw_S}\right|_{EU^G=\text{constant}} = -\frac{p^G u'(w_S)}{(1-p^G)\,u'(w_F)} < -\frac{p^B u'(w_S)}{(1-p^B)\,u'(w_F)}$$
$$= \left.\frac{dw_F}{dw_S}\right|_{EU^B=\text{constant}}.$$

The principal's iso-expected profit curves are also such that those corresponding to contracting a good agent are steeper than those corresponding to contracting a bad agent. Formally, the slopes of the iso-expected profit curves are, respectively, $-p^G/(1-p^G)$ and $-p^B/(1-p^B)$.

At the optimal contracts, the slopes of the indifference curves coincide with the slopes of the corresponding iso-expected profit curves. Also, the contracts are on the 45° line since the principal fully insures the agent. Finally, we have used the notation $\Pi^G = p^G x_S + (1-p^G)\, x_F - p^G w_S - (1-p^G)\, w_F$, and similarly for Π^B.

In the same figure, it is easy to see that $\{C^{G*}, C^{B*}\}$ would not be an information-revealing equilibrium if there were asymmetric information concerning agent type. In order to see this, note that if both C^{G*} and C^{B*} coexisted in the market, even though the former is intended for type-*G* agents, and the latter is intended for type-*B* agents, all type-*B*s have an obvious incentive to pass themselves off as type-*G* (higher indifference curves give greater expected utility). Of course, since all principals anticipate this behaviour, C^{G*} will not be offered as it is consistent with negative expected profits if signed by both agent types. Here it is the bad agents that have incentives to pass themselves off as something they are not.

4.3.2 Principals cannot distinguish agent type

When the principals cannot observe the type of agent accepting a particular contract (and hence discrimination is not possible), the problem is no longer separable into two independent problems, one for each type. When a principal offers a contract intended for good agents, she must make sure that, given the rest of the contracts on offer, type-G agents are effectively interested in signing the contract, and type-B agents are not. The same reasoning is applied to a principal who wants to offer a contract intended for both agent types (a contract that 'pools' all agents).

An equilibrium situation is defined by a contract pair which we denote by $\{C^G, C^B\} \equiv \{(w_S^G, w_F^G), (w_S^B, w_F^B)\}$, which may turn out to be equal, each intended for a particular type of agent. The equilibrium contract pair must satisfy three conditions:

Condition 1: no contract, $C \equiv (w_S, w_F)$, can exist that is preferred to C^G by good agents, that is not preferred to C^B by bad agents, and that gives strictly positive expected profits to the principal offering it, given that only type-G agents will agree to sign it.

Condition 2: no contract C can exist that is preferred to C^B by bad agents, that is not preferred to C^G by good agents, and that gives strictly positive expected profits to the principal offering it, given that only type-B agents will agree to sign it.

Condition 3: no contract C can exist that is preferred to C^G by good agents, that is preferred to C^B by bad agents, and that gives strictly positive profits to the principal offering it, given that both types of agent will agree to sign it.

These three conditions can be summarized as follows: an equilibrium contract pair $\{C^G, C^B\}$ must satisfy the condition that no principal can add a contract (w_S, w_F) that would give positive expected profits from the agents that prefer this new contract to C^G and C^B. In particular, this condition assures that any equilibrium contract set will give zero expected profits (otherwise there would be a principal who would be prepared to reduce her expected profits per agent, but take on all the agents in the market by offering a slightly more attractive contract).

If the two equilibrium contracts for the two agent types turn out to be the same, that is, there is only one contract that is accepted by both agent types, then the equilibrium is said to be *pooling*. On the other hand, when there is a different equilibrium contract for each agent type, then we have a *separating* equilibrium. In what follows, we shall see that the first class of equilibria do not exist in the market under consideration.

The non-existence of pooling equilibria

Given the equilibrium conditions, in order for there to be a pooling equilibrium it must be consistent with zero expected profits for the principals offering the pooling contract. Therefore, the contract must be on the line:

$$\Pi^I = p^I x_S + (1 - p^I)\, x_F - p^I w_S - (1 - p^I)\, w_F = 0,$$

where $p^I = q\, p^G + (1 - q)\, p^B$ is the probability that the result will be successful when the principal does not know which type her agent is. (This property is implied by condition 3.) Figure 4.7 shows a pooling contract C^I situated on the line $\Pi^I = 0$.

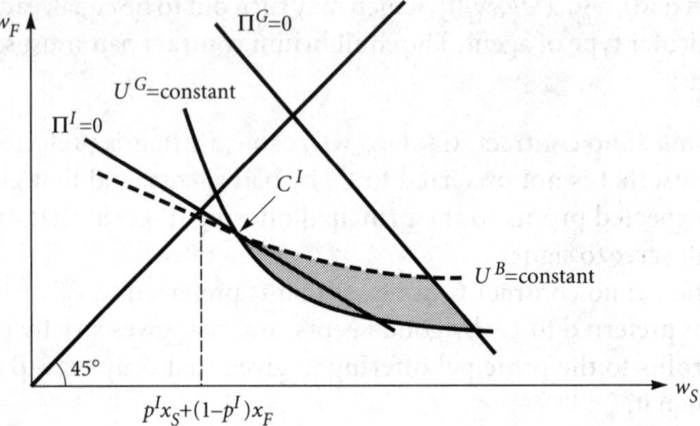

Fig. 4.7

Now, we must check if conditions 1 and 2 are satisfied. At C^I, as at any other contract, a type-G agent's indifference curve is steeper than that corresponding to a type-B agent. This leaves a non-empty zone (the shaded area) between both indifference curves, which are contracts that pay more for a success but less for a failure. That this area exists is sufficient for the pooling contract not to be an equilibrium. If a principal offers a contract in the shaded area, the new contract will be preferred to C^I by good agents but not by bad agents (it is above the indifference curve of the good agents but below the indifference curve of the bad agents). Note that, since only good agents will accept the new contract, the principal who offers it will earn strictly positive expected profits since the new contract is below the line $\Pi^G = 0$. C^I therefore cannot be an equilibrium situation.

The above logic shows that, for the situation at hand, pooling equilibria do not exist. If an equilibrium does exist, it must be such that each type of agent is offered a different contract.

Finding the separating equilibrium.

Remember that the problem is that the bad agents wish to pass themselves off as type G, but not vice versa. For this reason, for any contract $\{C^G, C^B\}$ that is candidate as an equilibrium, it must hold that C^B is equal to the contract C^{B*}, the symmetric equilibrium contract for type-B agents. This must be true since the contract C^B must be on the zero expected profits line ($\Pi^B = 0$) in order for it to be an equilibrium contract. Besides, any contract on the zero expected profits line that is not C^{B*} is strictly worse for the agent, and therefore it would be possible for a principal to Pareto-improve it (consequently, condition 2 is not satisfied). Figure 4.8 presents this argument. Let $C^{B'}$ be a candidate contract to form a part of the equilibrium menu. The graph shows that the contracts within the shaded zone are strictly preferred, by both the principal and agent, to $C^{B'}$.

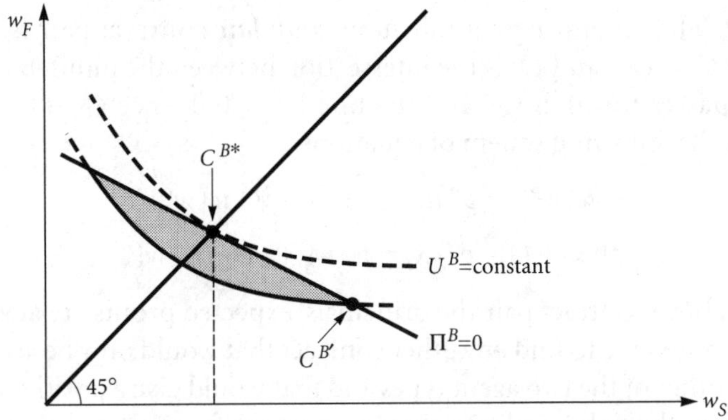

Fig. 4.8

Once the separating equilibrium candidate contract, $C^B = C^{B*}$, has been found it is not difficult to determine what contract to offer type-G agents, C^G. Figure 4.9 locates this contract graphically.

The contract C^G is found at the intersection of B's indifference curve (passing through C^{B*}) and the line $\Pi^G = 0$. First, C^G must be on the line $\Pi^G = 0$ in order to form a part of an equilibrium (as has been pointed out several times). Also, it must be below (or on) the indifference curve of B that passes through C^{B*} so that a type-B agent still prefers C^{B*} to the contract offered to type-G agents. Finally, any contract on the line $\Pi^G = 0$ below C^G is strictly dominated (for the agent) by C^G, and so we will always be able to find a principal that can offer a contract that improves both her own and the agent's position, while maintaining a point below (or on) B's indifference curve (condition 1).[8] We have, therefore, proved the following:

[8] We are assuming that, when presented with two different contracts between which he is

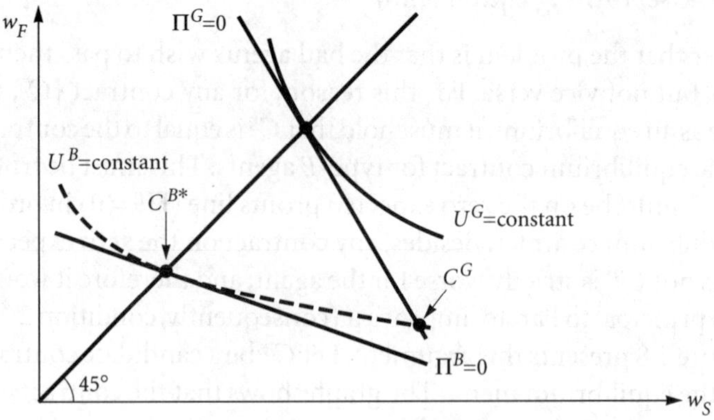

Fig. 4.9

Result 4.2. The separating equilibrium *candidate* contract pair is $\{C^G, C^B\}$ defined as $C^B = C^{B*}$, and C^G is the intersection between the indifference curve of B that passes through C^{B*} and the line $\Pi^G = 0$. Hence $C^G \equiv (w_S^G, w_F^G)$ is defined by the following system of equations:

$$u\,(w^{B*}) = p^B\,u\,(w_S^G) + (1 - p^B)\,u\,(w_F^G)$$

$$p^G\,x_S + (1 - p^G)\,x_F = p^G\,w_S^G + (1 - p^G)\,w_F^G.$$

For the above contract pair the principals' expected profits are always zero. Also, it is impossible to find any other contract that would only be accepted by one or the other of the two agent types and that would give a positive expected profit. Hence, the only condition that we must verify is that no other contract exists that is preferred by *both* agent types to their own contract, and that would give positive expected profits to the principal proposing it (condition 3). Graphically, in order for such a contract to exist, it must be located beneath the line $\Pi^I = 0$ (see Figure 4.7), since the principal's expected profits are greater for contracts closer to the origin, and above the indifference curves of both G and B passing through the points C^G and C^B respectively. Although we won't carry out the formal proof, graphically it is easy to see that such a contract may or may not exist, depending on the parameter values. Figure 4.10 shows a situation in which $\{C^G, C^B\}$ does constitute a separating equilibrium, while a second situation, in which $\{C^G, C^B\}$ is not an equilibrium situation, is presented in Figure 4.11. This situation is not an equilibrium since there exists a zone of contracts that are preferred by both agent types to their own contract, and that give positive expected profits (the shaded area of Figure 4.11).

indifferent, the type-B agent will chose that contract that the principal wants him to, that is, he will truthfully reveal his identity.

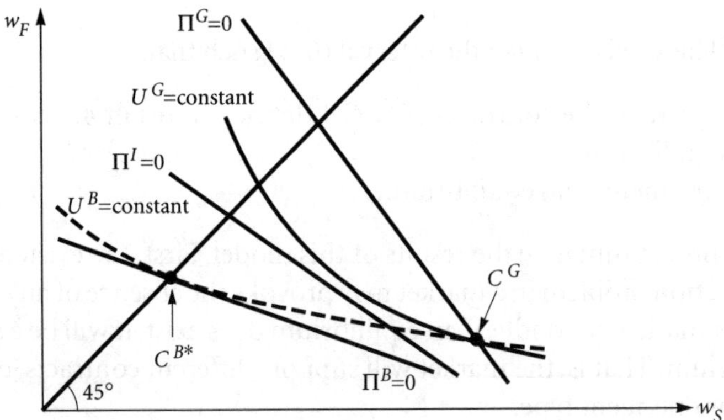

Fig. 4.10

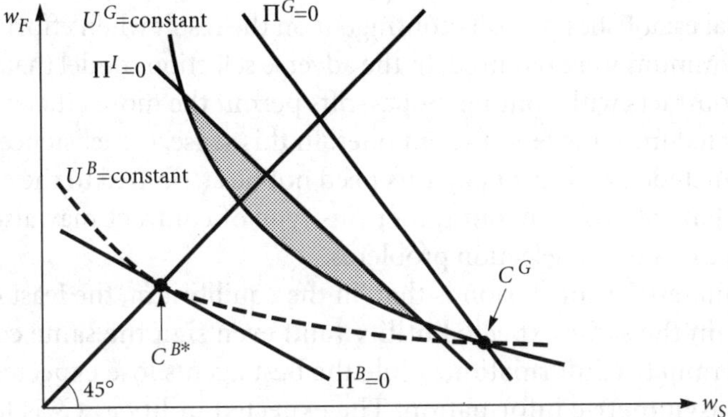

Fig. 4.11

Figures 4.10 and 4.11 clearly illustrate the conditions under which we would expect a separating equilibrium to exist or not. When the probability that the agent is good is rather low, that is, q is small, then the line $\Pi^I = 0$ will be relatively close to the line $\Pi^B = 0$, making it more likely that the separating equilibrium exists. On the other hand, when q is close to 1, which is to say that there is a high probability that the agent is of type G, then it is less likely that the separating equilibrium exists. Note that, if the separating equilibrium does not exist, then *the market has no equilibrium.* The reason for the difference between the two situations is that, when q is large the incentive to attract all the agents increases, even though there is a risk that the agent will turn out to be bad (this is a low-probability event). Separating the agent types is difficult in both cases, since there are efficiency losses, but offering a contract that both agent types accept is more profitable the greater is q.

Result 4.3. There exists a q^O in the interval (0, 1) such that:

(i) if $q \leq q^O$, then the contracts $\{C^G, C^B\}$ defined in result 4.2 constitute a separating equilibrium.
(ii) if $q > q^O$, there is no equilibrium.

We shall now summarize the results of this model. First, the existence of an adverse selection problem in a market may provoke the absence of any equilibrium in that market. Secondly, if an equilibrium does exist, it will be a separating equilibrium. That is, the market will support different contracts, each one intended for one agent type.

Thirdly, in spite of the differences in the type of asymmetric information and in the method of solving, the equilibrium that results in this market is similar to the conclusions of the moral hazard model. In the moral hazard model, the principal establishes pay-offs contingent on the result when efforts greater than the minimum were required. In the adverse selection model that we have analysed, contracts with contingent pay-offs permit the more efficient agents to be separated from the less efficient ones. In this sense, the existence of contracts that include contingent pay-offs need not be attributed to the existence of a moral hazard problem, but rather this type of contract may also be the consequence of adverse selection problems.

A final interesting conclusion is that, in the equilibrium, the least efficient agents obtain the same expected utility (and even sign the same contract) as under symmetric information, while the best agents lose expected utility due to the asymmetric information. The expected utility at C^G is less than that at C^{G*}. The agent's expected pay-off is the same under both contracts since:

$$p^G x_S + (1 - p^G)\, x_F = p^G w_S^G + (1 - p^G)\, w_F^G.$$

However, while at C^{G*} the agent always receives the same pay-off, at C^G he earns more in some states and less in others. The reason why these agents must lose expected utility is that in order to be sure that only type-G agents sign the contract, it is necessary to sacrifice efficiency, distorting the terms of the contract so that type-B agents do not prefer it to their own contract. Thus, the good agents (those that are successful more often) prefer to reveal their characteristic to the principals, while this information has no value for bad agents. In this situation, the 'non-distortion at the top' property holds for the type-B agents, because in adverse selection problems the 'top' agents are those for whom no one else wants to pass themselves off (and not necessarily the most efficient ones).

4.4 Adverse Selection with a Continuum of Possible Types[9]

The assumption of the previous sections that there are only two types of agent is rather unrealistic, but does simplify considerably the analysis, allowing the use of graphical intuition. On the other hand, however, it is useful to know what happens in more general models, above all since it is interesting to recognize which hypothesis are relevant to the solution of an adverse selection problem (in other words, when the solution to these problems is similar to that under the assumption of two agent types). The objective of this section is to present the solution method for the case of many possible agent types. Solving for a discrete number (greater than two) of agent types is very tedious. It is easier, and on many occasions more natural, to assume that the set of possible agent types is a continuous space. Hence we shall now solve the mechanism design problem for a continuum of agent types.

The classic framework for adverse selection problems is that which we considered in Section 2. Hence we shall reuse this framework for the present section. We consider a risk-neutral principal, with profit function $\Pi\,(e)$, and a risk-averse (or neutral) agent, whose utility is given by the function $U(w, e; k) = u\,(w) - k\,v\,(e)$. k is a parameter that measures the disutility of effort of the agent, and we assume that it belongs to a compact support $\mathrm{K} \equiv [k', k'']$. Only the agent knows the exact value of this parameter. The principal has initial (*ex ante*) beliefs as to the distribution of the agent's type. These beliefs are represented by a distribution function $F(k)$, with $F(k') = 0$ and $F(k'') = 1$. The associated density function will be denoted by $f(k)$, and we will assume that $f(k) > 0$ for all $k \in \mathrm{K}$.

In the same way as in the case of two agent types, the principal designs a contract menu, where each contract is intended for one agent type. Hence, the contract menu will be a set of two functions $\{(e\,(k), w\,(k)\,) \mid k \in \mathrm{K}\}$, and should be interpreted as the principal offering the wage $w\,(k)$ to a type-k agent, in exchange for an effort of $e\,(k)$. In order for the contract menu to make sense, the principal must be sure that a type-k agent will really be interested in choosing the contract $(e\,(k), w\,(k)\,)$, rather than (untruthfully) declaring himself to be some other type, k^O, in order to sign the contract $(e\,(k^O), w\,(k^O)\,)$. In the current framework, this incentive compatibility condition is written:

[9] The analytical content of this section is slightly more difficult than that of the previous sections. It is, however, the most classic form of treating the adverse selection problem, and for that reason it is included in the main body of the text of this chapter. The conclusions that we will arrive at are similar to, although more complete than, those presented in Sect. 2. Some readers might want to skip this section as it is not necessary to follow the rest of the book.

$$u(w(k)) - k\,v(e(k)) \geq u(w(k^O)) - k\,v(e(k^O)),\ \text{for all}\ k, k^O \in \mathbf{K},$$

which is the equivalent to (4.3) and (4.4) in the discrete set-up. This condition can also be written as:

$$k \in \arg\max_{k^O}\, u(w(k^O)) - k\,v(e(k^O)) \quad \text{for all}\ k \in \mathbf{K}.$$

In order for the agent to accept the offer, he must receive at least his reservation utility from the contract. Thus the principal's problem can be written:

$$\underset{\{(e(k), w(k))\}}{\text{Max}} \int_{\mathbf{K}} [\Pi(e(k)) - w(k)] f(k)\, dk$$

$$[\text{P4.2}] \quad \text{s.t.} \quad u(w(k)) - k\,v(e(k)) \geq \underline{U} \qquad \text{for all}\ k \in \mathbf{K} \qquad (4.12)$$

$$k \in \arg\max_{k^o}\, u(w(k^o)) - k\,v(e(k^O)) \quad \text{for all}\ k \in \mathbf{K}. \qquad (4.13)$$

The above problem has some special characteristics. The following properties are important for the solution.

(*a*) **Definition.** The agent's preferences $U(w, e; k)$ satisfy the *Spence–Mirrlees condition* (C.S.$^+$) if

$$\frac{\partial}{\partial k}\left(\frac{\partial U/\partial e}{\partial U/\partial w}\right) > 0,$$

while they verify the (C.S.$^-$) condition if

$$\frac{\partial}{\partial k}\left(\frac{\partial U/\partial e}{\partial U/\partial w}\right) < 0.$$

For any particular utility function, the ratio $(\partial U/\partial e)/(\partial U/\partial w)$ is the marginal rate of substitution between effort and the wage. Therefore, the condition (C.S.$^-$) indicates that the lower is an agent's k parameter (the more efficient is the agent), the lower is the wage required to induce a given effort level. Hence it is possible to associate each effort level with a wage that allows the agent types to be separated. The condition that the marginal rate of substitution between effort and the wage is always decreasing (or increasing) in the agent's type guarantees that the agents' indifference curves only cross once, and it is for this reason that it is often referred to in the literature as the *single-crossing condition.* It is also known as the *sorting,* or *constant-sign* (C.S.) *condition.*

The agent's preferences, $U(w, e; k) = u(w) - k\,v(e)$, satisfy the Spence–Mirrlees condition (C.S.$^-$). In order to check that the preferences we are assuming do effectively satisfy (C.S.$^-$), observe that, for our assumptions,

$$\frac{\partial}{\partial k}\left(\frac{\partial U/\partial e}{\partial U/\partial w}\right) = -v'(e)/u'(w) < 0.$$

Of course, not all utility functions satisfy the conditions (C.S.$^-$) or (C.S.$^+$). The assumed separability in wage and effort simplifies the analysis notably.

(*b*) We can divide the principal's problem into two stages. First, for each function $e(k)$ that she may want the agent to use, the principal must find the wage function $w(k)$ that ensures that each agent type will effectively choose that contract $(e(k), w(k))$ that was designed for him. Secondly, between all the functions $e(k)$ for which a wage function $w(k)$ can be found (that is, those effort functions that are *implementable*), the principal must choose that which maximizes her expected welfare.

Now, since the agent's expected utility function satisfies the condition (C.S.$^-$), that is to say, for a given effort, agents with a lower k will accept contracts with lower wages, the only way in which the principal can implement a particular effort function $e(k)$ is if the function satisfies the condition $de/dk \le 0$, for all $k \in \mathbf{K}$. In other words, *we can restrict our attention to those effort functions that are increasing in agent efficiency*. The proof of this important result (for a general utility function) is presented as complement 1 to this chapter.

(*c*) In the same way as in the two agent type model, there is no need to worry about the participation constraint (4.12) for all possible agent types. In the current framework, the incentive compatibility condition for any particular $k \in \mathbf{K}$, together with the participation constraint for k'' (the agent with greatest disutility of effort), ensure that condition (4.12) is satisfied for the rest of the agent types. All that is needed is to note that, for all k,

$$\begin{aligned} u(w(k)) - k\,v(e(k)) &\ge u(w(k'')) - k\,v(e(k'')) \\ &\ge u(w(k'')) - k''\,v(e(k'')) \ge \underline{U} \end{aligned}$$

Therefore, in the problem [P4.2], *it is sufficient to introduce only the participation condition of the type-k'' agent.*

(*d*) The incentive compatibility constraint (4.13) can be transformed using the agent's indirect utility function, which we shall denote by $I(k)$:

$$I(k) \equiv \max_{k^O} u(w(k^O)) - k\,v(e(k^O)) = u(w(k)) - k\,v(e(k)).$$

The function $I(k)$ measures the utility that a type-k agent obtains from the contract. Given the definition of $I(k)$, the envelope theorem ensures that we can take the derivative of $I(k)$ without taking into account the influence of k into $w(k)$ and $e(k)$. That is:

$$\frac{dI}{dk}(k) = -v(e(k)).$$

Thus, $I(k)$ can be written as the integral of $dI/dx\,(x)$ from k'' to k as follows:

$$I(k) = I(k'') + \int_{k''}^{k} \frac{dI}{dx}(x)\,dx = I(k'') + \int_{k}^{k''} v(e(x))\,dx.$$

Given this equation, it is easy to understand why the participation condition must be saturated for k'': $I(k'') = \underline{U}$. Note that if the condition were not saturated, then the principal could reduce the wage $w(k'')$ for this agent until it is saturated, which would also have positive effects on the utility level $I(k)$ that the principal must guarantee to the other agents (and so their wage could also be reduced). Therefore we have:

$$I(k) = u(w(k)) - k\,v(e(k)) = \underline{U} + \int_{k}^{k''} v(e(x))\,dx,$$

from which the informational rent of a type-k agent is equal to:

$$\int_{k}^{k''} v(e(x))\,dx.$$

The above equation determines how type-k agents must be paid in order for their incentive compatibility constraint to hold for a given effort function $e(k)$:

$$u(w(k)) = k\,v(e(k)) + \int_{k}^{k''} v(e(x))\,dx + \underline{U}. \tag{4.14}$$

We have shown that if $e(k)$ is implementable, then we can be sure that the wages will behave in the manner described by equation (4.14). Also, in complement 1 we prove that $e(k)$ is implementable if and only if it is not increasing in k. Hence, condition (4.13) is equivalent to (4.14) with $e(k)$ non-increasing. We can also state that the participation condition (4.12), which is only active for $k = k''$, is implied by (4.14), i.e. for $k = k''$, (4.14) ensures that $u(w(k'')) = k''\,v(e(k'')) + \underline{U}$.

Given the above comments (*a*) - (*d*), we can write the principal's problem [P4.2] as:

$$\max_{\{(e(k),\, w(k))\}} \int_{K} [\Pi(e(k)) - w(k)]\, f(k)\,dk$$

[P4.3] s.t. $$u(w(k)) = k\,v(e(k)) + \int_{k}^{k''} v(e(x))\,dx + \underline{U}$$

$$\frac{de}{dk}(k) \leq 0.$$

We should point out that some important conclusions are implicit in this form of the problem. First, the more efficient is the agent (the lower is the disutility of effort parameter k), the greater is the effort that the principal demands of him. Secondly, since the wage $w(k)$ must compensate at least the reservation utility plus the disutility of effort, it must be true that the wage will be greater the more efficient is the agent. Aside from this, greater efficiency also corresponds to greater informational rent, measured by:

$$\int_{k}^{k''} v(e(x))\,dx.$$

This expression is greater the lower is k.

In order to accumulate even more results, assume a simple situation in which the agent is risk-neutral, $u(w) = w$. By substituting the expression for $w(k)$ into the objective function, the problem is written as:

$$\underset{\{e(k)\}}{\text{Max}} \int_{\mathbf{K}} \left(\Pi(e(k)) - k\,v(e(k)) - \int_{k}^{k''} v(e(x))\,dx \right) f(k)dk$$

[P4.4] s.t. $\frac{de}{dk}(k) \leq 0$.

We have not introduced $\underline{U}$ into the principal's objective function, since it takes the form

$$\int_{\mathbf{K}} -\underline{U} f(k)\,dk = -\underline{U} \int_{\mathbf{K}} f(k)\,dk = -\underline{U},$$

i.e. it is constant.

Ignore, for the moment, the requirement that effort must be decreasing in the characteristic, and denote by [P4.5] problem [P4.4] where this restriction has been removed. If the solution to [P4.5] satisfies the restriction, then it will also be the solution to [P4.4]. Only if the restriction is not satisfied in the solution do we need to take it into account. To solve [P4.5], integrate by parts to arrive at:

$$\int_{\mathbf{K}} \int_{k}^{k''} v(e(x))\,dx f(k)\,dk = \left(F(k) \int_{k}^{k''} v(e(x))\,dx \right) \Bigg|_{k'}^{k''} - \int_{\mathbf{K}} v(e(k))\,F(k)\,dk =$$

$$= -\int_{\mathbf{K}} v(e(k)) \frac{F(k)}{f(k)} f(k)\,dk,$$

since $F(k') = 0$ and $\int_{k'}^{k''} v(e(k))\,dk = 0$. Therefore, problem [P4.5] is written as:

[P4.5] $$\underset{\{e(k)\}}{\text{Max}} \int_{\mathbf{K}} \left[\Pi(e(k)) - \left(k + \frac{F(k)}{f(k)} \right) v(e(k)) \right] f(k)\,dk.$$

The first-order conditions of [P4.5] are:

$$\Pi'(e(k)) - \left(k + \frac{F(k)}{f(k)}\right) v'(e(k)) = 0 \Leftrightarrow v'(e(k)) = \frac{\Pi'(e(k))}{k + \dfrac{F(k)}{f(k)}}. \quad (4.15)$$

In order to understand this equation, it must be understood that[10] the solution to the problem under symmetric information is given by $e^*(k)$ such that

$$v'(e^*(k)) = \frac{\Pi'(e^*(k))}{k}. \quad (4.16)$$

Therefore, as with the discrete case, the action of the most efficient agent, $k = k'$, does not distort (since $F(k') = 0$, and therefore the solutions to (4.15) and (4.16) coincide for k'), and so the effort that the principal demands of him is the same under adverse selection as under symmetric information. This property is known as '*no distortion at the top*'. However, *from all other agents, the principal demands less effort under adverse selection*, that is, $F(k)/f(k) > 0$ implies $e(k) < e^*(k)$. The reason for this is that by distorting the effort of a type-k agent, the informational rents of all agents $k^o < k$ are reduced. The principal must balance out the costs and benefits of demanding an efficient effort level from a type-k agent (equation (4.16)), and reducing the informational rents of all agents more efficient than k (equation (4.14) shows that by reducing $e(x)$ the rents of all types $k < x$ are reduced). The result of this trade-off is equation (4.15).[11]

When may we be certain that the solution to equation (4.15), $e(k)$, satisfies the monotonicity property, $\mathrm{d}e/\mathrm{d}k \leq 0$, required by problem [P4.4]? Differentiating the first-order condition (4.15), we have:

$$\left[\Pi''(e(k)) - \left(k + \frac{F(k)}{f(k)}\right) v''(e(k))\right] \mathrm{d}e - \left(1 + \frac{\mathrm{d}}{\mathrm{d}k}\left(\frac{F(k)}{f(k)}\right)\right) v'(e(k))\,\mathrm{d}k = 0.$$

Since we are analysing a maximum, the second-order condition must hold, and so the expression accompanying $\mathrm{d}e$ must be negative (in particular, this is true if $v'' > 0$ and $\Pi'' < 0$). Therefore,

$$\frac{\mathrm{d}e}{\mathrm{d}k} \leq 0 \Leftrightarrow \frac{\mathrm{d}}{\mathrm{d}k}\left(\frac{F(k)}{f(k)}\right) \geq -1.$$

[10] See exercise 12 in this chapter.

[11] Lewis and Sappington (1993) study the case in which the agent may or may not have more information than the principal before the contract, and the principal is ignorant of whether or not the agent has this informational advantage. They show that, in these circumstances, a pooling contract appears, that production is discontinuous, and that there is a significant distortion in the contract designed for the highest ks. Analytically, this situation is similar to one in which the distribution of the ks is not continuous, but rather there exists a mass point of k with strictly positive probability.

To guarantee the monotonicity property in our framework (and in fact, in several others), it is sufficient that the *hypothesis of monotonicity of the risk ratio* holds:

$$\frac{\mathrm{d}}{\mathrm{d}k}\left(\frac{F(k)}{f(k)}\right) \geq 0.$$

The above hypothesis is satisfied by distributions such as the uniform, the normal, the exponential, the logistic, and the Laplace, among others. One particular case for which the hypothesis holds is for distributions characterized by $f(k)$ decreasing, since $F(k)$ is always increasing.

Finally, we will consider a graphical treatment of what happens if, for some set of points, the solution to [P4.5] does not satisfy the restriction that $e(k)$ is non-increasing.[12] Consider the function $e(k)$, solution to [P4.5], as presented in Figure 4.12. A 'problematic zone' appears (between e_1 and e_2), since in this zone effort is first decreasing, then increasing, and finally decreasing again.

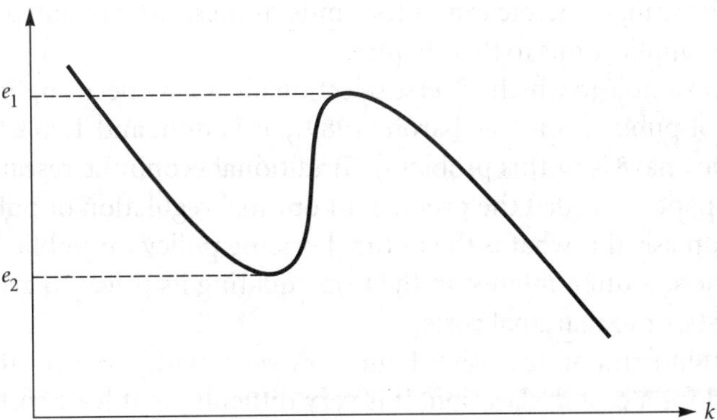

Fig. 4.12

The solution to [P4.4] represents a compromise to solve the problem of the zone between e_1 and e_2. There will exist a number $\hat{e} \in (e_1, e_2)$ such that the solution to [P4.4] follows the first decreasing segment of the solution to [P4.5], then, between the k corresponding to $\hat{e}$ and that level at which the solution rejoins the second negatively sloped portion, the solution to [P4.4] will be constant (see Figure 4.13).

12 For a rigorous analysis of this situation, see Guesnerie and Laffont (1984), or Fudenberg and Tirole (1991).

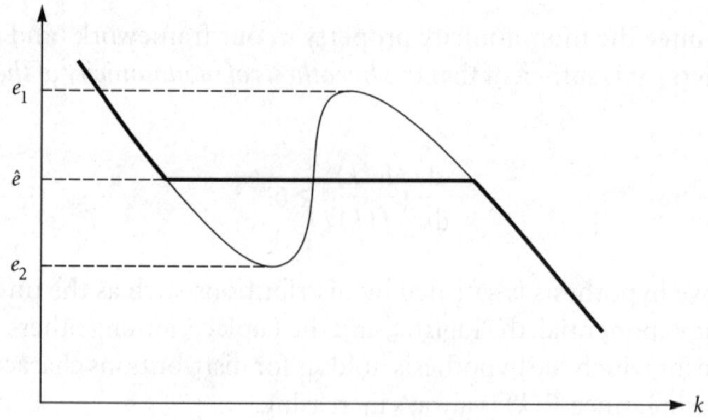

Fig. 4.13

4.5 Comments

In conclusion, it is worth while briefly to discuss the interpretation of the above results using concrete examples. Some of these are presented in greater depth in the applications to this chapter.

A classic example in which adverse selection ideas have been applied is in the regulation of public firms (see Baron (1989), or Laffont and Tirole (1993) for an extensive analysis of this problem). Traditional economic research has, in numerous papers, tackled the problem of optimal regulation of public firms. The question asked is what is the optimal pricing policy for public firms. For example, there is often interest in the firm equating its prices to average production costs, or to marginal costs.

A regulated firm, on the other hand, can work with a significant margin when asked for a cost declaration. It is very difficult, or at least costly, for the government to verify that the costs declared by the firm correspond to the true costs, or if the firm is exaggerating the costs in order to achieve greater profits. In this case, the optimal policy for the government (the principal) is to offer a range of prices and production levels (the contracts), each one designed for a firm (an agent) with a particular cost function (the private information, or agent type). The above simple adverse selection results tell us that in the regulation problem, the optimal solution has the following characteristics:

(*a*) The greater are the costs declared by the firm, the greater will be the price that the government will set in the market, but the less will be the quantity that the firm will be allowed to produce.

(*b*) The regulated firm will obtain strictly positive expected profits, except for the case in which its costs are the highest possible. The lower are the costs, the greater will be the expected profits (which could result in higher wages, better working conditions, etc.).

(*c*) The production level that the government demands from the firm is inefficient (from an *ex post* point of view, i.e. given the declared costs), except for the firm with the lowest possible costs.

A second situation in which an adverse selection problem is present is a monopolist that sells her product to different consumers, differentiated by the value that they place on the product. The conclusions of this model are also very useful. The monopolist would like to discriminate perfectly between the consumers in order to maximize profits. However, the values the consumers place on the product is private information, and so they will misrepresent it to the monopolist if it is in their interests to do so. The monopolist can only discriminate by offering different quantities at different prices. That is, the unitary price need not be constant. In this case, the results are:

(*a*) The consumers that most value the product will pay a lower average price for each unit bought. Therefore, quantity discounts is an optimal discrimination policy.

(*b*) All consumers will receive positive utility by consuming, except for the consumer that has the lowest private valuation for the product, since the monopolist manages to take all the surplus from him.

The competition between insurance companies for clients was the analytical framework in which situations of many principals was originally studied (Rothschild and Stiglitz, 1976). In this case, the companies (insurers) are the principals, and the clients (insured) are the agents. The insured can be different, according to the a priori probability of the insured event. The companies, which are assumed to be risk-neutral since they insure many clients, are willing to offer up to full coverage, but the price charged for each unit of coverage must depend on the probability of the insured event, which is different for different clients. As applied to the insurance market, the adverse selection results in this chapter can be read as follows:

(*a*) If there is a high proportion of 'good risk' (clients with a low probability of the insured event) to 'bad risk' in the market, then no equilibrium will exist.

(*b*) Aside from the situation in (*a*), the equilibrium will be separating. By this, we mean that the insurance companies will place different coverage-price packages on the market, and the clients will choose that which they most prefer according to their probability of the insured event. The 'bad-risks' will be fully insured, at a high price, while 'good-risks' will be insured at a cheaper rate, but the contract will include an 'excess clause' under which the client must pay a part of any claim. The result implies that the 'bad-risk' contracts are efficient, but that the 'good-risk' contracts are not.

4A Complementary Material

4A.1 Implementable mechanisms

In this first complementary section we analyse the characteristics that the decision function, $e(k)$, must satisfy in order that it be implementable, that is, it is possible to find a second function, $w(k)$, such that the contract menu $\{(e(k), w(k)) \mid k \in K\}$ is autoselective.[13] In what follows we will assume a more general form for the agent's utility function than that which we have used up to now, specifically, the agent's utility is described by $U(w, e; k)$.

Definition. A function $e: K \to \mathbb{R}$ is *implementable* if there exists a payment function $w(k)$ such that the allocation $\{(e(k), w(k)) \mid k \in K\}$ satisfies the incentive constraint;

$$U(w(k), e(k); k) \geq U(w(k^O), e(k^O); k) \qquad \text{for all } k, k^O \in K.$$

We shall restrict our attention to continually differentiable decision functions, i.e. $e(k)$ is C^1. The following properties analyse the implementability of this type of function.

Result (*necessary condition*). A decision function $e(k)$ is implementable only if

$$\frac{\partial U}{\partial w}\frac{\mathrm{d}e}{\mathrm{d}k}\frac{\partial}{\partial k}\left(\frac{\partial U/\partial e}{\partial U/\partial w}\right) \geq 0.$$

Proof. A type-k agent will choose the allocation that corresponds to his type if

$$k \in \arg\max_{k^O \in K} \; U(w(k^O), e(k^O); k).$$

The first- and second-order conditions of this problem are:

$$\frac{\partial U(w(k^O), e(k^O); k)}{\partial k^O}\Big|_{k^O = k} = 0$$

$$\frac{\partial^2 U(w(k^O), e(k^O); k)}{\partial k^{O2}}\Big|_{k^O = k} \leq 0$$

These conditions must be satisfied for all k, at each point $k^O = k$. Differentiating the first-order condition with respect to k gives:

[13] The formulation presented is a simplification of the general analysis of Guesnerie and Laffont (1984).

$$\frac{\partial^2 U(w(k^O), e(k^O); k)}{\partial k^{O2}}\Big|_{k^O=k} + \frac{\partial^2 U(w(k^O), e(k^O); k)}{\partial k^O \partial k}\Big|_{k^O=k} = 0,$$

from which the second-order condition can be written as:

$$\frac{\partial^2 U(w(k^O), e(k^O); k)}{\partial k^O \partial k}\Big|_{k^O=k} \geq 0.$$

Rewriting the derivatives of the function $U(.)$, the above equation can be written as:

$$\frac{\partial}{\partial k}\left(\frac{\partial U(k;k)}{\partial e}\right)\frac{\mathrm{d}e}{\mathrm{d}k}(k) + \frac{\partial}{\partial k}\left(\frac{\partial U(k;k)}{\partial w}\right)\frac{\mathrm{d}w}{\mathrm{d}k}(k) \geq 0,$$

where we have simplified the notation by introducing $U(k';k) = U(w(k'), e(k');k)$. Since, from the first-order condition, we know that

$$\left(\frac{\partial U(k;k)}{\partial e}\right)\frac{\mathrm{d}e}{\mathrm{d}k}(k) + \left(\frac{\partial U(k;k)}{\partial w}\right)\frac{\mathrm{d}w}{\mathrm{d}k}(k) = 0,$$

which can be written as

$$\frac{\partial w}{\partial k}(k) = -\frac{\partial U(k;k)/\partial e}{\partial U(k;k)/\partial w}\frac{\mathrm{d}e}{\mathrm{d}k}(k),$$

the second-order condition can be shown to be

$$\frac{\partial}{\partial k}\left(\frac{\partial U(k;k)}{\partial e}\right)\frac{\mathrm{d}e}{\mathrm{d}k}(k) - \frac{\partial}{\partial k}\left(\frac{\partial U(k;k)}{\partial w}\right)\frac{\partial U(k;k)/\partial e}{\partial U(k;k)/\partial w}\frac{\mathrm{d}e}{\mathrm{d}k}(k) \geq 0$$

$$\Leftrightarrow \frac{\partial U}{\partial w}\frac{\mathrm{d}e}{\mathrm{d}k}\left[\frac{\frac{\partial U}{\partial w}\frac{\partial}{\partial k}\left(\frac{\partial U}{\partial e}\right) - \frac{\partial U}{\partial e}\frac{\partial}{\partial k}\left(\frac{\partial U}{\partial w}\right)}{(\partial U/\partial w)^2}\right] \geq 0 \Leftrightarrow \frac{\partial U}{\partial w}\frac{\mathrm{d}e}{\mathrm{d}k}\frac{\partial}{\partial k}\left(\frac{\partial U/\partial e}{\partial U/\partial w}\right) \geq 0.$$

Q.E.D.

Bearing in mind that the utility function is increasing in the wage, $\partial U/\partial w \geq 0$, and given the definition, given earlier, of the *Spence-Mirrlees condition*, the following theorem is a direct corollary of the above result.

Result (*monotonicity*). If the agent's preferences satisfy (C.S.$^-$) (or (C.S.$^+$), respectively), then a necessary condition for a decision function $e(k)$ to be implementable is that $e(k)$ be non-increasing, i.e. $e(k) \geq e(k^O)$ for all $k \leq k^O$ (or non-decreasing, respectively, i.e. $e(k) \leq e(k^O)$ for all $k \leq k^O$).

When an agent's preferences satisfy the Spence–Mirrlees condition, the monotonicity of the effort decision function, $e(k)$, is a necessary condition for its implementability. The following theorem assures that this condition is also sufficient for global implementability.

Result (*sufficient condition*). If the agent's preferences satisfy (C.S.$^-$) (respectively (C.S.$^+$)), then a decision function $e(k)$ is implementable if it is monotone non-increasing (respectively non-decreasing).

Proof. As shown in the proof for the result concerning the necessary condition, the payment function that locally implements the decision function $e(k)$ must satisfy:

$$\frac{\mathrm{d}w}{\mathrm{d}k}(k) = \frac{\partial U(k;k)/\partial e}{\partial U(k;k)/\partial w}\frac{\mathrm{d}e}{\mathrm{d}k}(k).$$

In order to prove that the allocation $\{e(k), w(k)) \mid k \in \mathbf{K}\}$ is globally implementable, we must show that, for all $k \in \mathbf{K}$,

$$U(k;k) \geq U(k^o;k) \qquad \text{for all } k^o \in \mathbf{K}.$$

To see that this is so, assume that the result does not hold, and so there exists some $k^o \neq k$ such that:

$$U(k;k) - U(k^o;k) < 0.$$

But this is the same as requiring that:

$$\int_k^{k^o} \frac{\mathrm{d}U}{\mathrm{d}x}(x;k)\,dx > 0.$$

Since we can write:

$$\frac{\partial U}{\partial e}(x;k) = \frac{\partial U}{\partial w}(x;k)\left(\frac{\partial U/\partial e}{\partial U/\partial w}(x;k)\right),$$

it must be true that:

$$\frac{\mathrm{d}U}{\mathrm{d}x}(x;k) = \frac{\partial U}{\partial w}(x;k)\left(\frac{\partial U/\partial e}{\partial U/\partial w}(x;k)\right)\frac{\mathrm{d}e}{\mathrm{d}x}(x) + \frac{\partial U}{\partial w}(x;k)\frac{\mathrm{d}w}{\mathrm{d}x}(x),$$

and from the equation for $\mathrm{d}w/\mathrm{d}x$, it can be shown that:

$$\int_k^{k^o} \frac{\partial U}{\partial w}(x;k)\,[\Gamma(x) - \Gamma(k)]\,\frac{\mathrm{d}e}{\mathrm{d}x}(x)\,dx > 0,$$

where

$$\Gamma(x) = \frac{\partial U/\partial e}{\partial U/\partial w}(x; k) \qquad \text{and} \qquad \Gamma(k) = \frac{\partial U/\partial e}{\partial U/\partial w}(k; k).$$

Assume $k^O > k$. Hence, if (C.S.$^+$) is satisfied then we have $\Gamma(x) - \Gamma(k) > 0$ since $x > k$, which implies that the integral is not positive when $e(x)$ is non-increasing. On the other hand, if (C.S.$^-$) is satisfied, then $\Gamma(x) - \Gamma(k) < 0$ for $x > k$, from which $e(x)$ non-decreasing implies that the integral is, once again, non-positive. The same reasoning applied to the case of k^O less than k, in which case the function inside the integral is non-negative, gives the result that the integral is non-positive (since it is an integral from a large value to a small one). *Q.E.D.*

4A.2 Moral hazard with private information (*ex ante* contract acceptance)

In Section 5 of Chapter 3 we briefly introduced a second type of moral hazard problem: the principal observes the agent's decision, but is unsure if it was the best decision or not, since she doesn't have as much information concerning the economic environment as the agent. That is, after signing the contract, the agent receives information relevant to his decision. He will attempt to take advantage of this information, which is not known by the principal, in order to supply the least possible effort. Here we shall consider the case in which, once the contract has been signed, the agent cannot breach it, even when he observes that the final situation is not good.[14]

The model to be considered is constructed as follows. After signing the contract, the agent learns the value of some parameter, θ, that indicates the current market conditions. This parameter can take two possible values: θ^G means that the market conditions are good, while θ^B means that they are bad, where $\theta^G > \theta^B$. The probability of θ^G is q. The result of the relationship depends on the agent's decision, E, while the state of nature, θ, determines the cost to the agent of his decision, since the effort that he must exert is assumed to be $e = E - \theta$. The principal observes the decision E, but not the state of nature, θ, and so cannot judge if the decision was the most adequate, given the market conditions. For example, if the decision is observed to be E^*, the principal is unsure if the agent has supplied high effort in adverse conditions, $e = E^* - \theta^B$, or low effort in good conditions $e = E^* - \theta^G$.

14 Milgrom (1987*a*) relates classical moral hazard (called moral hazard with hidden actions) and moral hazard with private information (also called moral hazard with hidden information), showing that the conclusions of both types of model are more similar than what one might expect at first glance.

When the principal designs the contract, she must take into account the possibility that the agent may try to mislead her. Hence, in the expected profit maximization problem, there will be two incentive compatibility constraints: one that says the agent won't have incentives to make believe the market conditions are bad when they are good, and another that avoids the opposite. As for the adverse selection problem, the principal will offer a contract menu $\{(e^G, w^G), (e^B, w^B)\}$, such that the agent chooses (e^G, w^G) when market conditions are θ^G, and (e^B, w^B) when they are θ^B. We should point out that, when the agent signs the contract, he accepts the entire menu, without yet knowing which of the two situations he will be confronted with.

The principal's problem is:

$$\max_{(e^G, w^G, e^B, w^B)} \{q(\theta^G + e^G - w^G) + (1-q)(\theta^B + e^B - w^B)\}$$

$$\text{s.t.} \quad q[u(w^G) - v(e^G)] + (1-q)[u(w^B) - v(e^B)] \geq \underline{U} \quad (\lambda)$$

$$u(w^G) - v(e^G) \geq u(w^B) - v(e^B + \theta^B - \theta^G) \quad (\mu)$$

$$u(w^B) - v(e^B) \geq u(w^G) - v(e^G + \theta^G - \theta^B), \quad (\gamma)$$

(where we have labelled the equations according to the corresponding Lagrange multiplier). Notice that $v(e^B + \theta^B - \theta^G)$ is the effort disutility of an agent whose decision is $e^B + \theta^B$, while the state of nature is θ^G, and similarly for $v(e^G + \theta^G - \theta^B)$. The first-order conditions with respect to e^G, e^B, w^G, and w^B respectively are:

$$q - \lambda q v'(e^G) - \mu v'(e^G) + \gamma v'(\theta^G - \theta^B + e^G) = 0 \quad (4.C1)$$

$$(1-q) - \lambda(1-q) v'(e^B) + \mu v'(\theta^B - \theta^G + e^B) - \gamma v'(e^B) = 0 \quad (4.C2)$$

$$-q + \lambda q u'(w^G) + \mu u'(w^G) - \gamma u'(w^G) = 0 \quad (4.C3)$$

$$-(1-q) + \lambda(1-q) u'(w^B) - \mu u'(w^B) + \gamma u'(w^B) = 0. \quad (4.C4)$$

Equations (4.C3) and (4.C4) imply:

$$\lambda q = \frac{q}{u'(w^G)} - (\mu - \gamma) \quad \text{and} \quad \lambda(1-q) = \frac{1-q}{u'(w^B)} + (\mu - \gamma),$$

from which:

$$\lambda = \frac{q}{u'(w^G)} + \frac{1-q}{u'(w^B)} > 0 \quad (4.C5)$$

$$\frac{1}{u'(w^G)} = \frac{1}{u'(w^B)} + \frac{\mu - \gamma}{q(1-q)}. \quad (4.C6)$$

These expressions will allow us to characterize both the optimal contract under symmetric information, and the optimal contract menu for the moral hazard situation.

(i) We shall first consider the efficient solution, in other words, that in which the incentive compatibility constraints (μ) and (γ) are not binding. In the above problem, this results in the same first-order conditions, but with $\mu = \gamma = 0$. Aside from this, the efficient solution will allow us to show that for any situation in which $\mu = \gamma = 0$, the Kuhn–Tucker conditions cannot be satisfied when incentive compatibility constraints appear.

When $\mu = \gamma = 0$, conditions (4.C1) and (4.C2) imply that $e^G = e^B$. If we denote this value by e^*, (4.C1) and (4.C2) imply that $\lambda = 1/v'(e^*)$. On the other hand, note that (4.C3) and (4.C4) imply that $w^G = w^B$ so long as $u'' < 0$. We denote this wage by w^*. Hence, from (4.C5), it is also true that $\lambda = 1/u'(w^*)$. Therefore we have the result that $u'(w^*) = v'(e^*)$, which, together with the participation constraint, defines the optimal symmetric information contract (e^*, w^*).

At the point (e^*, w^*), the restriction (μ) is not satisfied since it requires that $u(w^*) - v(e^*) \geq u(w^*) - v(e^* + \theta^B - \theta^G)$, which is impossible when $\theta^B - \theta^G < 0$.

(ii) Note that the incentive compatibility constraints (μ) and (γ) imply that:

$$v(e^G + \theta^G - \theta^B) - v(e^G) \geq v(e^B) - v(e^B + \theta^B - \theta^G).$$

If we define the function $f(e) = v(e + \theta^G - \theta^B) - v(e)$, it will be true that $f'(e) > 0$ (since $v'' > 0$ and $\theta^G - \theta^B > 0$). On the other hand, $f(e^G) = v(e^G + \theta^G - \theta^B) - v(e^G)$, while $f(e^B + \theta^B - \theta^G) = v(e^B) - v(e^B + \theta^B - \theta^G)$. Therefore, it must always be true that $e^G + \theta^G - \theta^B \geq e^B$, and so, given ($\mu$), we have $u(w^G) - u(w^B) \geq v(e^G) - v(e^B + \theta^B - \theta^G) \geq 0$, from which $w^G \geq w^B$. Hence, from (4.C6), we conclude that $\mu \geq \gamma$. This analysis is always valid. In particular, it allows us to reject that Kuhn–Tucker will be satisfied in a situation in which $\mu = 0$ and $\gamma > 0$.

(iii) We shall now show that the Kuhn–Tucker conditions are also never satisfied when $\mu > 0$ and $\gamma > 0$. These two conditions imply that the two incentive compatibility constraints (μ) and (γ) must bind. Hence $v(e^G + \theta^G - \theta^B) - v(e^G) = v(e^B) - v(e^B + \theta^B - \theta^G)$. A similar argument to that in paragraph (ii) above ensures us that $e^G + \theta^G - \theta^B = e^B$. Aside from this, it must also be true that $u(w^G) - u(w^B) = 0$, i.e. $w^G = w^B$ (a wage we shall denote w). Given that the wages are equal, condition (4.C5) becomes $\lambda = 1/u'(w)$, while (4.C6) implies that $\mu = \gamma$. Using these expressions, we can write equations (4.C1) and (4.C2) as follows:

$$1 - \frac{v'(e^G)}{u'(w)} + \frac{\mu}{q}\,[v'(e^G + \theta^G - \theta^B) - v'(e^G)] = 0$$

$$1 - \frac{v'(e^B)}{u'(w)} - \frac{\mu}{1-q}[v'(e^B) - v'(e^B + \theta^B - \theta^G)] = 0.$$

Since $v'(e^G + \theta^G - \theta^B) - v'(e^G) > 0$, and $v'(e^B) - v'(e^B + \theta^B - \theta^G) > 0$, we must have $v'(e^G) > u'(w)$ and $v'(e^B) < u'(w)$, and hence $e^G > e^B$. However, this is incompatible with the condition, obtained previously, that $e^G + \theta^G - \theta^B = e^B$.

(iv) Therefore the optimal contract satisfies $\mu > 0$ and $\gamma = 0$. In order to analyse the characteristics of this contract, we point out that equations (4.C5) and (4.C6) determine the values of the multipliers, functionally related to the wages. In particular, simple calculations reveal that $q\lambda + \mu = q/u'(w^G)$ and $\lambda(1-q) - \mu = (1-q)/u'(w^B)$. Using these two equations, we can rewrite (4.C1) and (4.C2) as:

$$q - q\frac{v'(e^G)}{u'(w^B)} = 0 \quad \Leftrightarrow \quad v'(e^G) = u'(w^G) \tag{4.C7}$$

$$(1-q) - (1-q)\frac{v'(e^B)}{u'(w^B)} + \mu[v'(e^B + \theta^B - \theta^G) - v'(e^B)] = 0. \tag{4.C8}$$

(Equation (4.C8) implies that $v'(e^B) < u'(w^B)$). The optimal contract (e^G, w^G, e^B, w^B) is therefore characterized by equations (4.C7) and (4.C8) plus the two equations that state that the participation constraint (λ) and the incentive compatibility constraint for the good state of nature (μ) both bind.

The *characteristics of the optimal contract* are the following. The effort level demanded of the agent in the good state is efficient with respect to the wage, as shown by equation (4.C7). However, a distortion is introduced in the effort level demanded should the agent observe θ^B, since $v'(e^B) < u'(w^B)$ indicates that less than the efficient effort level is demanded. On the other hand, even though the agent obtains (in expected value terms) his reservation utility ((λ) binds), he obtains greater utility in the good state of nature than in the bad state. This is easy to see if we write (μ) as:

$$u(w^G) - v(e^G) = u(w^B) - v(e^B) + [v(e^B) - v(e^B + \theta^B - \theta^G)] > u(w^B) - v(e^B).$$

4B Applications

4B.1 Competition between insurance companies[15]

We will now consider the case of a group of insurance companies that compete in order to attract clients who want to insure themselves against some risk. We

[15] Based on Rothschild and Stiglitz (1976).

shall assume that there are two types of client (agent), characterized by their probability of suffering an accident. We shall call those agents with a low probability of accident 'good' risks, while those with a high probability of accident will be called 'bad' risks. Let π^G and π^B be the respective probabilities of accident, with $\pi^G < \pi^B$. If no accident occurs, the agents have wealth w, while an accident is defined as a loss of L, leaving a net wealth of $w - L$ in the accident state of nature. All agents are risk-averse, and we shall denote their utility function by u (.). On the other hand, all insurance companies are assumed to be risk-neutral.

To begin with, assume that there is only one insurance company, and that it offers coverage at a constant price p per unit, letting each client choose his optimal coverage amount. Thus if an agent pays pz to the principal, he will receive the amount z should an accident occur. A type-G agent must solve the following problem:

$$\underset{z}{\text{Max}} \ \{\pi^G u\,(w - L - p\,z + z) + (1 - \pi^G)\ u\,(w - p\,z)\}.$$

The optimal coverage for the type-G agent, z^G, is given by the first-order condition:

$$\frac{u'\ (w - L - p\,z^G + z^G)}{u'\ (w - p\,z^G)} = \frac{(1 - \pi^G)\ p}{\pi^G\,(1 - p)}.$$

On the other hand, the condition that determines the optimal coverage for a type-B agent is:

$$\frac{u'\ (w - L - p\,z^B + z^B)}{u'\ (w - p\,z^B)} = \frac{(1 - \pi^B)\ p}{\pi^B\,(1 - p)}.$$

Since $(1 - \pi^G)/\pi^G > (1 - \pi^B)/\pi^B$, these first-order conditions require that $z^G < z^B$. The situation is represented graphically in Figure 4.14. The straight lines are the insurance company's iso-expected profit lines (their slope depends on the relative prices of the two contingencies), while the indifference curves drawn as a continuous curve are those corresponding to a good-risk individual, and those drawn discontinuously correspond to a bad-risk agent. The point labelled O represents the autarky, or no insurance point. The point I^B represents an insurance contract with full coverage at an actuarially fair price for a type-B agent, $p = \pi^B$, which guarantees zero expected profits for the principal so long as it is a type-B agent who signs this contract. The point I^G represents the same idea, but corresponding to a type-G agent. Finally, the points E^B and E^G are the optimal choices of the agents when the price that they are offered by the principal is the same for both, with $\pi^B > p > \pi^G$. If the price is the same for both, the bad-risk individual will overinsure (the price is strictly less than π^B, the price at which he would fully insure), while the good-risk individual will

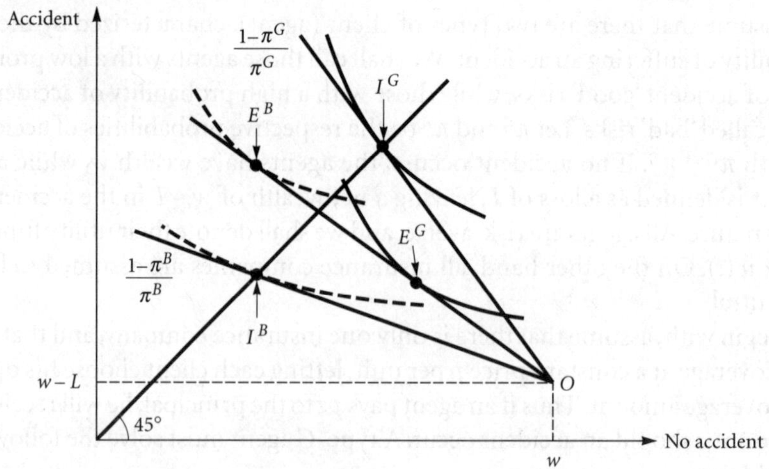

Fig. 4.14

underinsure. In this case the company will make expected losses with the first type of agent, and positive expected profits with the second. In order to see this, note that the iso-expected profit lines of the company indicate greater expected profits the closer they are to the origin, and bear in mind the position of the zero expected profit lines corresponding to each agent type.

The previous situation raises the following problem: we may find that the principal always makes losses, independently of the contract she offers. For example, consider a contract under which an insurance company offers a 'fair premium' $p = q\pi^G + (1-q)\pi^B$, where q is the proportion of good-risks. In this case, since the bad-risks always choose greater coverage than the good-risks, the company will make (expected) losses. In order to compensate these losses, it will have to charge a greater price. But then the good-risks will elect even less coverage, and the bad-risks will want even more. This process can take us to the point in which no contract that allows the company to earn non-negative profits exists.

A second possibility is that there is an equilibrium at which only the bad-risks buy insurance. This is the case if the indifference curves of the agents take the form shown in Figure 4.15. As we can see, in this case at the corresponding price $p = \pi^B$, the bad-risk individuals will buy full coverage, with the insurance company earning zero expected profits with them, while the good-risk types prefer not to insure since the point I^G is not offered, and at the price $p = \pi^B$ the point preferred by the good-risk types is O. Hence self-selection occurs: in equilibrium only high risks are insured. This situation is similar to that studied by Akerlof (1970), in which only bad-quality second-hand cars (lemons) are exchanged in the market.

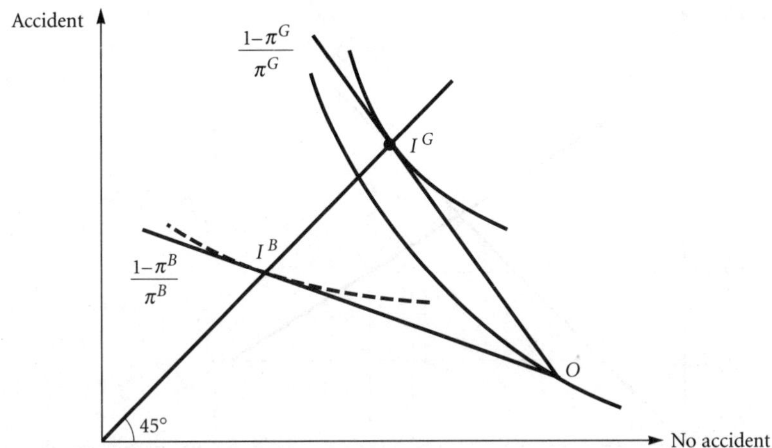

Fig. 4.15

The above analysis is based on the idea that the insurance companies can determine the price per unit of coverage, and that the clients can choose the coverage that they desire. Since they cannot discriminate among different types of clients, in the previous model insurance companies only use an instrument, the price, in the contract. In fact insurance companies have greater leeway; they can propose contracts that are specific price/coverage packages, between which the clients may freely choose. In other words, when the client chooses a price, he simultaneously chooses a coverage amount. Graphically this means that the company only offers points in the contract space (rather than the contract menu lines offered up to now).

Figure 4.16 shows the situation in which only contract *A* and contract *O* are offered. The point α_1 represents the premium and α_2 is the net compensation in case of accident. This is equivalent to offering a price of $\alpha_1/(\alpha_1 + \alpha_2)$ for a coverage of $z = \alpha_1 + \alpha_2$. We could consider that the case in which the company offers both the price and the coverage is a special case of the previous one in which only the price was given and each agent chooses the coverage desired at that price.

We shall now consider how the competition between the firms determines the equilibrium contracts, assuming that each one can offer one or more contracts. Since there are two types of agent, there can be two types of contract:

- pooling contracts, (α_1, α_2) intended for all agent types,
- separating contracts, $((\alpha_1^B, \alpha_2^B), (\alpha_1^G, \alpha_2^G))$ that lead to self-selection.

The first thing to look at is which contracts are likely to be proposed, that is, which are robust to competition. First, it can be seen that a pooling contract is not robust to competition. Note that for a pooling contract to be robust to

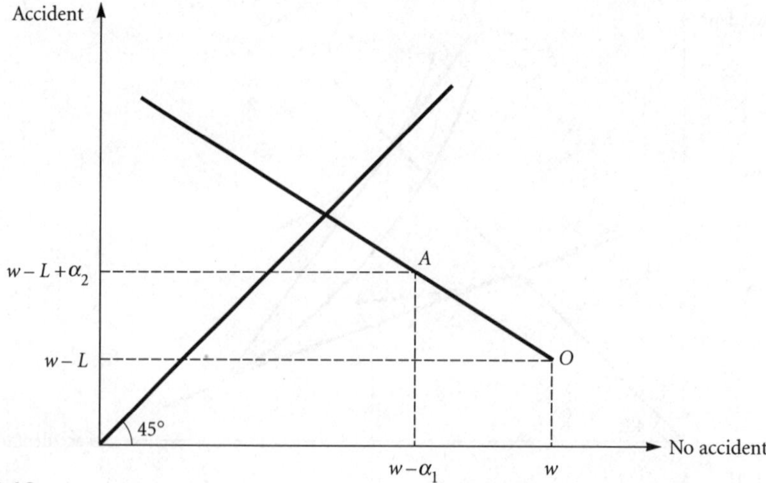

Fig. 4.16

competition, it must imply zero expected profits (since if this were not the case, there would always be a firm that would offer slightly lower prices and still obtain positive expected profits). Hence any pooling contract candidate to be robust to competition must be on the line corresponding to the price $\rho = q\pi^G + (1 - q)\pi^B$, where q is the proportion of low probability of accident agents.

Choose any particular contract C along the line defined by the price ρ. The indifference curves of the two types of agent must cross, as is shown in Figure 4.17. In order to see that contract C is not robust to competition, assume that a rebel firm offers a contract in the shaded area. This contract will only attract low probability of accident individuals (those with the steepest indifference

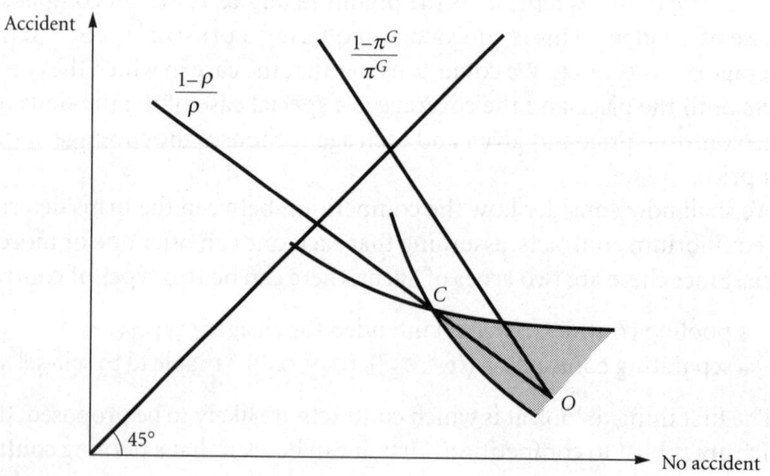

Fig. 4.17

curves), since only these clients prefer the new contract to C (the high-risk types still prefer C to the new contract). However, if a company offers a contract beneath the fair price line for type-G agents (that line with slope $-(1-\pi^G)/\pi^G$), and it is a type-G agent that signs it, expected profits will be strictly positive. Therefore, we can expect some company to offer this contract, leaving negative expected profits at contract C, since only the bad-risk types are left to sign this contract, whose price less than π^B.

We now go on to consider if a separating equilibrium (two contracts such that the agents self-select themselves) exists. For similar reasons to those considered in the pooling contract case, the only candidate solution pair is C^G and C^B (see Figure 4.18).

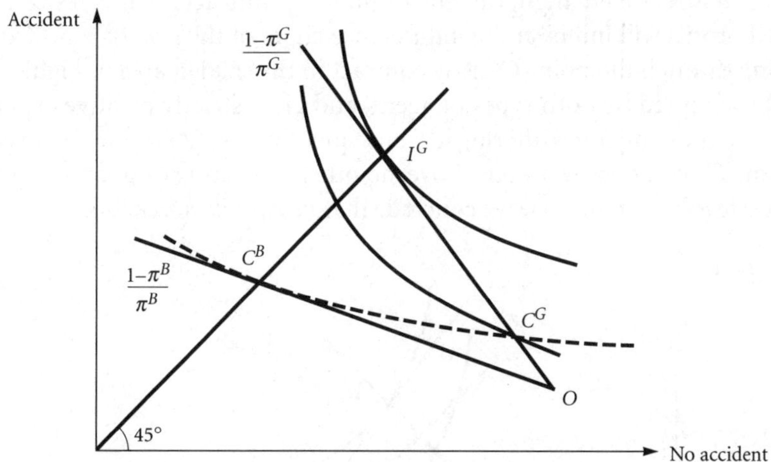

Fig. 4.18

The candidate contract pair must be those indicated because:

(i) C^G must be on the iso-expected profit line with slope $-(1-\pi^G)/\pi^G$ in order that the expected profits from this contract, given that only good-risk types will sign it, are zero (otherwise there will always be some other company prepared to offer a rebel contract at a slightly lower price in order to take the customers). For the same reason, C^B must be on the line with slope $-(1-\pi^B)/\pi^B$.

(ii) Beginning with the contract C^B on the appropriate iso-expected profit line, C^G must be located at the point where agent B's indifference curve intersects the iso-expected profit line corresponding to the price π^G. This is because if it were any higher (geometrically), the bad-risk agent would prefer it to the contract C^B, while if it were any lower, then a rebel company could offer the type-G agents a better (for them) contract, which would be separating, and which would offer positive expected profits (this is due to the fact that any contract strictly lower than C^G is dominated by C^G and so offers some margin for offering contracts that are more favourable to both the firm and the client).

(iii) C^B must be on the 45° line, since otherwise there would exist other contracts closer to the 45° line under which the type-B agents are better off. Hence, $C^B = I^B$.

We have shown that the contract pair that is our candidate to be the separating equilibrium is such that the high-risk individuals choose C^B and thus receive full insurance, while the low-risk individuals only get partial coverage. However, we still need to check that this separating contract is not dominated by some pooling contract. In order to do so, we need to distinguish two cases, depending on the value of q, the proportion of good-risk individuals:

(i) If q is relatively high, the line of pooling contracts that gives zero expected profits will intersect the indifference curve of the low-risk individuals passing through the point C^G. Any contract in the shaded area of Figure 4.19 will be accepted by both types of agent, and gives strictly positive expected profits to the companies offering it. Consequently, $\{C^G, C^B\}$ cannot be an equilibrium. Since, as we have seen above, no other separating or pooling equilibrium is feasible, in this case we conclude that *no equilibrium exists.*

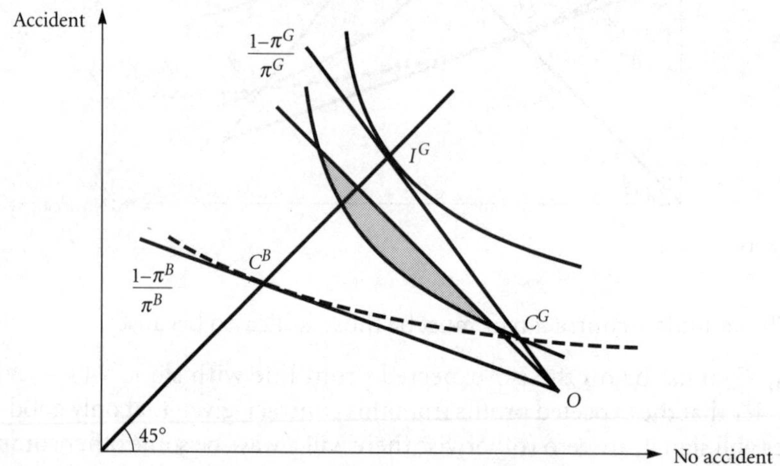

Fig. 4.19

(ii) Now assume that q is relatively small. In this case the line of zero expected profit pooling contracts will be everywhere below that indifference curve of the type-G agents passing through the point C^G. Now the pair $\{C^G, C^B\}$ is a separating equilibrium (see figure 4.20). The explanation of this result is that, if there are relatively few good-risk individuals in the population, the incentive for a firm to offer a contract that all agents will sign is low. This contract should attract every agent, so the price should be low enough. However, most

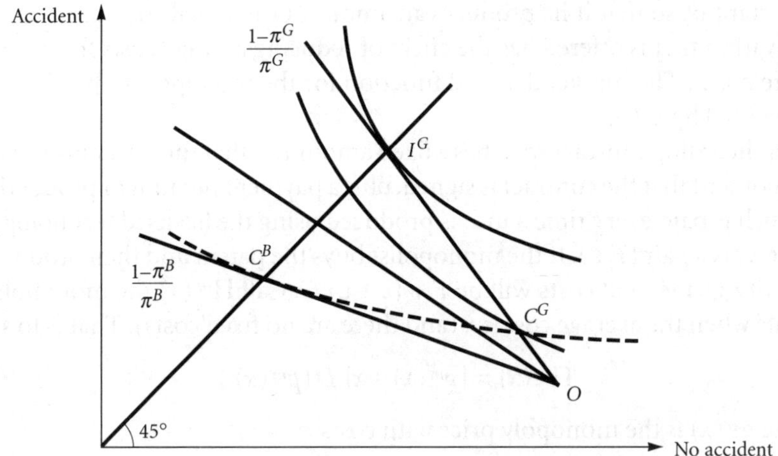

Fig. 4.20

of the clients that will sign the contract will be bad-risk types, with which the company will suffer expected losses that will not be compensated by the positive profits expected from the few good-risk types.

If the equilibrium exists, comparing it with the optimal symmetric information contract menu $\{I^G, I^B\}$, we can point out the following properties. The high-risk agents receive the same allocation in both situations. On the other hand, the low-risk agents must pay the consequences of the informational asymmetry (which does not allow them to be identified as such), since even though the insurance price is fair, they are not permitted to fully cover their risk. These are the agents who are interested in identifying themselves as being low risk, signalling this characteristic (in a believable manner) by accepting the partial coverage contract.

4B.2 An analysis of optimal licensing contracts[16]

In this section we will analyse the optimal manner in which a technology-licensing contract can be established between the owner of a patent (the seller) and the firm that wants to use the patent (the buyer). We begin with optimal contracts under symmetric information and then we will go on to see what happens if there is some sort of informational asymmetry.

We shall assume the simplest possible case: the seller is a research laboratory that owns a patent from which it cannot obtain any profit except through a licensing contract. The buyer is a monopolist. His average production costs are

[16] This application is based on Macho-Stadler and Pérez-Castrillo (1991*c*).

a constant c^0, so that if he produces an amount Q, his total costs are $c^0 Q$. The innovation that is offered has the effect of reducing average costs from c^0 to c, where $c < c^0$. The market demand function for the monopolist's product will be denoted by $D(p)$.

The licensing contract specifies a fixed amount, F, that the buyer must pay at the moment that the contract is signed, plus a payment per unit of production, ε, which is paid every time a unit is produced using the licensed technology. A contract is a pair (F, ε). If the monopolist buys the patent and then produces a quantity Q, his total costs will be $F + (c + \varepsilon)\, Q$. Call $\Pi^m(x)$ the monopolist's profits when the average cost is x (and there are no fixed costs). That is to say:

$$\Pi^m(x) = [p^m(x) - x]\, D(p^m(x))$$

where $p^m(x)$ is the monopoly price with costs x:

$$p^m(x) \in \arg\max_{p} \, [p - x]\, D(p).$$

Let $D^m(x) = D(p^m(x))$ be the monopolist's demand at the price $p^m(x)$. The monopolist compares the profits that he can get without the licence, $\Pi^m(c^0)$, with those available if he buys the licence, $\Pi^m(c + \varepsilon) - F$.

The seller's (the principal) problem is to maximize the profits from the licence, taking into account that the buyer must be prepared to accept the contract, with $F \geq 0, \varepsilon \geq 0$. The problem is:

$$\begin{aligned} \underset{(F, e)}{\text{Max}} \quad & F + \varepsilon\, D^m(c + \varepsilon) \\ \text{s.t.} \quad & F \leq \Pi^m(c + \varepsilon) - \Pi^m(c^0) \\ & \varepsilon \geq 0 \\ & F \geq 0. \end{aligned}$$

It is easy to see that the participation constraint binds, and that the solution to the problem, (F^*, ε^*) is given by:

$$\varepsilon^* = 0 \quad \text{and} \quad F^* = \Pi^m(c) - \Pi^m(c^0).$$

Hence the optimal licensing contract only includes a fixed payment. This is true if the buyer and the seller share symmetric information.

Now consider what would happen if the buyer has more information than the seller, in other words, there is an adverse selection problem. The private information could be with respect to any one of several variables; for example, the buyer may be better informed as to the market demand function, or the buyer may possess more information as to how the innovation can be best applied to his particular production process. We shall model the second of these ideas. Assume that the innovation may take one of two possible types, good (G) or bad (B). A good innovation allows average costs to be reduced down to some level c^G, while if the innovation is bad, the average costs will be c^B, where $c^G < c^B < c^0$. The monopolist knows the value of the innovation but the seller is uninformed. Under symmetric information the optimal contracts would be:

$$\varepsilon^{G*} = 0 \qquad F^{G*} = \Pi^m(c^G) - \Pi^m(c^0)$$

and

$$\varepsilon^{B*} = 0 \qquad F^{B*} = \Pi^m(c^B) - \Pi^m(c^0).$$

However, given the adverse selection problem, the proposed contracts must be altered. The following result tells us what form the optimal asymmetric information contract will take.

Result. The optimal contract menu proposed by the seller is separating and has the following characteristics:

$$\varepsilon^G = \varepsilon^{G*} = 0 \qquad \varepsilon^B > 0 \qquad F^G < F^{G*} \qquad F^B < F^G.$$

Proof. In order to prove this result, let q be the initial probability that the innovation is good. The seller's problem is to maximize expected profits under the self-selection and participation conditions (the Lagrange multipliers for the first are μ and λ, while those of the second are ρ, δ), as well as the conditions that give non-negative parameter values. For simplicity, we label the equations according to the associated multiplier.

$$\max_{(F^G, \varepsilon^G, F^B, \varepsilon^B)} \{q\,[F^G + \varepsilon^G D^m(c^G + \varepsilon^G)] + (1-q)\,[F^B + \varepsilon^B D^m(c^B + \varepsilon^B)]\}$$

$$\Pi^m(c^G + \varepsilon^G) - F^G - \Pi^m(c^G + \varepsilon^B) + F^B \geq 0 \qquad (\mu)$$

$$\Pi^m(c^B + \varepsilon^B) - F^B - \Pi^m(c^B + \varepsilon^G) + F^G \geq 0 \qquad (\lambda)$$

$$\Pi^m(c^G + \varepsilon^G) - F^G - \Pi^m(c^0) \geq 0 \qquad (\rho)$$

$$\Pi^m(c^B + \varepsilon^B) - F^B - \Pi^m(c^0) \geq 0 \qquad (\delta)$$

$$F^G \geq 0 \qquad (\alpha^G)$$

$$F^B \geq 0 \qquad (\alpha^B)$$

$$\varepsilon^G \geq 0 \qquad (\beta^G)$$

$$\varepsilon^B \geq 0 \qquad (\beta^B)$$

It is easy to see that the participation constraint of a buyer with a high valuation of the innovation (ρ) will always hold if the bad types' participation and incentive constraints ((δ) and (μ) respectively) hold. Therefore we can eliminate ρ. We have, first:

$$\frac{\partial L}{\partial F^G} = q - \mu + \lambda + \alpha^G = 0 \Leftrightarrow \mu = q + \lambda + \alpha^G > 0$$

from which:

$$F^G = \Pi^m(c^G + \varepsilon^G) - \Pi^m(c^G + \varepsilon^B) + F^B.$$

Second: $$\frac{\partial L}{\partial F^B} = (1-q) + \mu - \lambda - \delta + \alpha^B = 0 \Leftrightarrow 1 + \alpha^G + \alpha^B = \delta > 0.$$

Hence it is true that:

$$F^B = \Pi^m(c^B + \varepsilon^B) - \Pi^m(c^0) \geq 0$$

$$F^G = \Pi^m(c^G + \varepsilon^G) - \Pi^m(c^G + \varepsilon^B) + \Pi^m(c^B + \varepsilon^B) - \Pi^m(c^0).$$

Third: $$\frac{\partial L}{\partial \varepsilon^G} = q\, D^m(c^G + \varepsilon^G) + q\varepsilon^G D^{m\prime}(c^G + \varepsilon^G) - \mu\, D^m(c^G + \varepsilon^G) + \lambda\, D^m(c^B + \varepsilon^G) + \beta^G = 0$$

$$\Leftrightarrow -q\varepsilon^G D^{m\prime}(c^G + \varepsilon^G) + \lambda\,[D^m(c^G + \varepsilon^G) - D^m(c^B + \varepsilon^G)] + \alpha^G D^m(c^G + \varepsilon^G) = \beta^G.$$

This last equation implies $\varepsilon^G = 0$. This is true since, on the one hand, if $\beta^G > 0$, then the corresponding restriction must bind, from which $\varepsilon^G = 0$. On the other hand, if $\beta^G = 0$, then the three summed terms of the previous equation must cancel out, from which in particular, ε^G must be zero (as well as $\lambda = 0$ and $\alpha^G = 0$).

Fourth: $$\frac{\partial L}{\partial \varepsilon^B} = (1-q)\, D^m(c^B + \varepsilon^B) + (1-q)\,\varepsilon^B D^{m\prime}(c^B + \varepsilon^B) + \mu\, D^m(c^G + \varepsilon^B) - \lambda\, D^m(c^B + \varepsilon^B) - \delta\, D^m(c^B + \varepsilon^B) + \beta^B = 0$$

$$\Leftrightarrow \mu\,[D^m(c^G + \varepsilon^B) - D^m(c^B + \varepsilon^B)] - \alpha^B D^m(c^B + \varepsilon^B) + (1-q)\,\varepsilon^B D^{m\prime}(c^B + \varepsilon^B) + \beta^B = 0.$$

This last equation implies that $\varepsilon^B > 0$. In order to see this, assume that ε^B is equal to zero. Since $\delta > 0$, we have

$$F^B = \Pi^m(c^B) - \Pi^m(c^0) > 0,$$

from which $\alpha^B = 0$. However, this requires that

$$\mu\,[D^m(c^G) - D^m(c^B)] + \beta^B = 0,$$

which is not possible since $\mu > 0$ and $\beta^B \geq 0$. *Q.E.D.*

We have proved that, when the buyer has private information with respect to the value of the innovation, piecewise payments allow us to separate the low-quality innovations, while the buyers that value the innovation highly will be offered a contract based entirely on a fixed payment. This fixed payment is, however, less than that corresponding to symmetric information since the buyers that value the innovation highly obtain an informational income. Hence the casual observation of piecewise payments may be due to the existence of buyer-specific private information. These contracts arise in order to separate the bad applications of an innovation. By deforming the optimal contract of a type-B firm, the principal can demand a higher fixed premium from the firm that most highly values the innovation. Graphically, the relative location of the two contracts is shown in Figure 4.21.

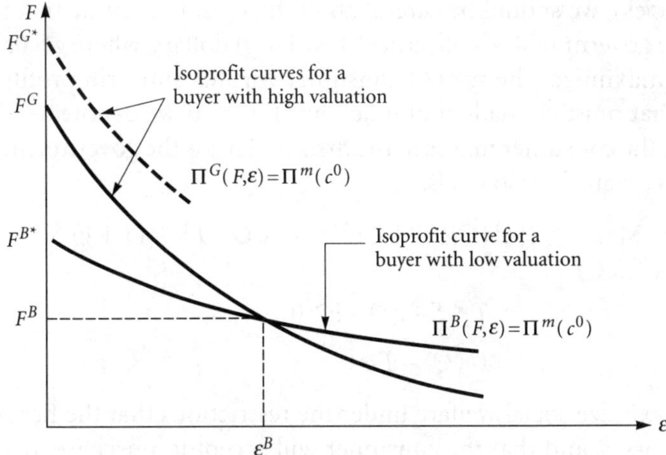

Fig. 4.21

4B.3 Regulation in asymmetric information contexts

Over the past few decades important work has been done on regulated industries. There has been, and there continue to be, many complaints by consumers concerning the prices, the quality, or the efficiency of regulated firms. Given this scenario, the proposed solutions have differed according to the particular industry, the country, or budgetary problems. We have witnessed both an important deregulation process and numerous attempts to design the adequate incentives for regulated firms, or the managers of these firms. The objective of this application is the consider the importance of the informational considerations in the regulation context, and to study the consequences of these considerations on the way in which regulation should be implemented.

We shall consider the simplest possible situation. A government wants to regulate a monopoly industry. Let the firm's production level be Q, and let $C(Q) = F + cQ$ be the cost of producing Q units of the good, i.e. the marginal cost of production is c and the fixed cost is F. There is only one representative consumer, with utility function $U(Q)$.

How can the government optimally regulate the monopolist? The optimal situation requires that the monopolist set price equal to marginal cost, that is, that the marginal utility of the agent coincides with this marginal cost: $U'(Q) = c$. Therefore, the *optimal regulation* calls for the monopolist to set price equal to marginal cost. Since the government may have to subsidize the firm, and since it is generally accepted that subsidies to firms create distortions over the rest of the economy, and hence are not desirable (since collecting money is costly to the state, and besides, the required taxes generate certain inefficiencies), we should be careful about this result. Assume that the social cost to the government of collecting \$1 is $(1 + g)$ dollars, where $g > 0$. The government maximizes the sum of consumer surplus and firm profits, less the transfer that must be made multiplied by $(1 + g)$. If we denote by T the payment that the consumer makes to the firm, and if S is the government transfer, then the regulator's problem is:

$$\begin{aligned} \underset{(T,S,Q)}{\text{Max}} \quad & \{[U(Q) - T] + [T + S - cQ - F] - [(1+g)\,S]\} \\ \text{s.t.} \quad & T + S - cQ - F \geq 0 \\ & U(Q) - T \geq 0\,, \end{aligned}$$

that is, maximize social welfare under the restrictions that the firm does not generate losses, and that the consumer will accept to purchase. If we let the Lagrange multipliers to the restrictions be respectively λ and μ, it is not difficult to see that the first-order condition of the problem leads directly to:

$$\lambda = \mu = g > 0$$

$$U'(Q) = c\,,$$

which indicate that the restrictions bind, and that the quantity decision is optimal: the marginal price, represented by the marginal willingness to pay for the good, is equal to the marginal cost.

Now that we have seen the optimal way in which the government can regulate a monopolist, we must consider the possibility of implementing this regulation policy. In order to do this it is necessary that nothing exists that would make carrying out the proposed rule unfeasible. For example, there may exist political or administrative restrictions. In this application, however, we will concentrate on another type of restriction: informational restrictions.

The amount of information that the government requires to be able to carry out an optimal regulation is, even in the simplified framework used here, somewhat unrealistic. Basically, the government must posses reliable information regarding two aspects. The government needs to know, on the one hand, the firm's cost function, and, on the other hand, information on the demand function is also required. We shall analyse here the first of these two problems, relegating the second to Exercise 7.

When the regulated monopoly has private information, the most efficient solution for the government is to offer a menu of different regulation contracts, each designed with a particular type of firm in mind, in which the monetary price that the firm can charge consumers, the quantity that it can sell, and the subsidy that it will receive from the government are all set out. Let's assume that there are two possible types of firm according to marginal costs. Specifically, let the marginal costs of the first type be c^G, while those of the second type are c^B, with $c^G < c^B$. The government offers a menu of contracts $\{(T^G, S^G, Q^G),(T^B, S^B, Q^B)\}$, in order that the firm chooses that which it most prefers. But in order for this contract menu to make sense, it must be such that each type of firm has incentives to elect the contract that the government designed for it.

Let q be the government's subjective probability that the firm is efficient ($c = c^G$). The government must solve the following problem:

$$\max_{\{(T^G, S^G, Q^G),(T^B, S^B, Q^B)\}} \{[q\,(U(Q^G) - T^G) + (1-q)\,(U(Q^B) - T^B)]$$

$$+ [q\,(T^G + S^G - c^G Q^G - F) + (1-q)\,(T^B + S^B - c^B Q^B - F)]$$

$$- (1+g)\,[q\,S^G + (1-q)\,S^B]\}$$

$$\text{s.t.}\quad T^G + S^G - c^G Q^G - F \geq 0$$

$$T^B + S^B - c^B Q^B - F \geq 0 \qquad (\lambda)$$

$$T^G + S^G - c^G Q^G - F \geq T^B + S^B - c^G Q^B - F \qquad (\mu)$$

$$T^B + S^B - c^B Q^B - F \geq T^G + S^G - c^B Q^G - F \qquad (\gamma)$$

$$U(Q^G) - T^G \geq 0 \qquad (\alpha)$$

$$U(Q^B) - T^B \geq 0 \qquad (\beta)$$

The first two restrictions are the participation constraints of the firms, and the last two are the participation constraints of the consumer (one for each possible situation), while (μ) and (γ) represent the incentive compatibility constraints: no firm wants to pass itself off as some type that is not its own. We have not included a multiplier for the first participation restriction since, as always, it is implied by (λ) and (μ).

In spite of the fact that we have many restrictions and many variables to determine, the problem is not difficult to solve. The first-order conditions of the Lagrangean with respect to T^G, T^B, S^G, S^B, Q^G, Q^B are:

$$-q+q+\mu-\gamma-\alpha=0 \Leftrightarrow \alpha=\mu-\gamma \tag{4.A1}$$

$$-(1-q)+(1-q)+\lambda-\mu+\gamma-\beta=0 \Leftrightarrow \beta=\lambda-\mu+\gamma \tag{4.A2}$$

$$q-q(1+g)+\mu-\gamma=0 \tag{4.A3}$$

$$(1-q)-(1-q)(1+g)+\lambda-\mu+\gamma=0 \tag{4.A4}$$

$$q\,U'(Q^G)-q\,c^G-\mu\,c^G+\gamma\,c^B+\alpha\,U'(Q^G)=0 \tag{4.A5}$$

$$(1-q)\,U'(Q^B)-(1-q)\,c^B-\lambda\,c^B+\mu\,c^G-\gamma\,c^B+\beta\,U'(Q^B)=0. \tag{4.A6}$$

Equations (4.A3) and (4.A4) imply that $\lambda = g > 0, \mu = q\,g+\gamma > 0$, from which, using (4.A1) and (4.A2), we also know that $\alpha = q\,g > 0$, $\beta = (1-q)\,g > 0$. We can now express equations (4.A5) and (4.A6) in function of the multiplier γ by substituting the corresponding values of λ, μ, α, and β. Simple calculations reveal that:

$$U'(Q^G)-c^G=-\gamma\frac{c^B-c^G}{q(1+g)}\leq 0 \tag{4.A7}$$

$$U'(Q^B)-c^B=(\gamma+q\,g)\frac{c^B-c^G}{(1-q)(1+g)}>0. \tag{4.A8}$$

We shall now prove that, as often occurs in adverse selection, the incentive compatibility constraint for the least efficient monopoly is not binding, that is to say, $\gamma=0$ (we already know that $\mu>0$). In order to do this, it must be pointed out that if both multipliers were positive, $\mu>0$ and $\gamma>0$, then the incentive compatibility restrictions (μ) and (γ) would bind, which is only possible if $Q^G = Q^B$. However, in this case $c^G < c^B$ implies that $U'(Q^G)-c^G > U'(Q^B)-c^B$, which is impossible, since according to (4.A7) and (4.A8) $U'(Q^G)-c^G \leq 0$ and $U'(Q^B)-c^B>0$. Hence we have shown that it is impossible that $\gamma>0$, leaving us with $\gamma=0$. Given this, the above equations reduce to:

$$U'(Q^G)=c^G \quad \text{and} \quad U'(Q^B)=c^B+q\,g\frac{c^B-c^G}{(1-q)(1+g)}>c^B.$$

Note that, when marginal costs are low, the quantity sold is optimal, but when marginal costs are high, the quantity is strictly less than the optimal amount. Aside from this, the efficient firm obtains strictly positive profits: informational income. It is interesting to note that this income does not correspond to the government wanting to reward efficiency, but rather that the efficient firm can 'camouflage' itself as inefficient, and this forces the government to provide it with income. On the other hand, since the government would like that the informational income accruing to the efficient firm to be as low as possible, the contract of the least efficient firm is distorted in order that this contract is less attractive to the efficient firm, thereby reducing its informational income.

The existence of asymmetric information makes it impossible to arrive at an optimal allocation. Hence, there is a cost to regulation that should be compared with the advantages that regulation creates for certain activities. It is important to look closely at exactly how easy it is for regulated firms to hide relevant information. The analysis shows that it may well be rational for a regulator to dedicate resources to controlling and auditing regulated firms. Even though this activity implies a wasteful cost, it may make the relevant information less important, thus permitting savings in other resources.

4B.4 Decision of monopoly product quality[17]

It is frequently found that, in certain markets, some consumers are willing to pay more than others to get high-quality goods. In other words, consumers are different according to their preferences for quality. Firms take decisions as to what type of products to sell, and at the same time they decide the prices that each type of product will sell for. This, however, depends largely on the firm's ability to discriminate between (or distinguish) the different types of consumer. In this application we will study the consequences of the existence of an asymmetric information problem when willingness to pay is private information. We shall do so using an example.

Let q stand for the quality of the good, $p(q)$ the price that the market establishes for a good of quality q, and $c(q)$ the unitary cost of producing a good of quality q, where $c'(q) > 0$ and $c''(q) > 0$. There are two different types of consumer in this market, $k \in \{k^G, k^B\}$, where $k^G > k^B$. Each consumer buys one unit of the good. The utility of a type-k consumer that buys a unit of quality q is given by the utility function $U(x, q; k) = x + kq$, where x represents all other goods. The consumer's total wealth is W, and so the budget constraint is written as: $p + x \leq W$. The consumer prefers to buy a good of quality q at price p to not buying it if the purchase increases net utility, i.e. $W - p + kq \geq W$.

Consider the simple case when the industry is a monopoly. As always, the reference case is the situation with symmetric information. In this case, the quality that the monopolist offers to a type-k consumer and the price charged

[17] This application was developed by Mussa and Rosen (1978).

are the solution to the problem of profit maximization under the restriction that the consumer accepts, given his type.

$$\max_{(q,p)} \quad [p - c(q)]$$
$$\text{s.t.} \quad k\,q \geq p.$$

The solution to this problem is defined by $c'(q) = k$ and $p = q\,k$. That is, the qualities and prices that the discriminating monopolist offers to the consumers of types k^G and k^B are (respectively):

$$c'(q^{G*}) = k^G, p^{G*} = q^{G*}k^G \quad \text{and} \quad c'(q^{B*}) = k^B, p^{B*} = q^{B*}k^B.$$

Figure 4.22 shows graphically the points (p^{G*}, q^{G*}) and (p^{B*}, q^{B*}) (denoted in the graph as E and F respectively). The lines passing through the origin represent the points for which the two types of consumer are indifferent between buying the good and not buying it (when quality increases, the consumer is willing to pay more, and this willingness to pay is greater for consumers of type k^G than for consumers of type k^B).

What happens if the consumer's type is private information, in other words, if the monopolist cannot discriminate? The above contracts are no longer a good deal for the monopolist. A type-k^G consumer will pretend to be type k^B since by so doing he will obtain greater utility in this case. In order to see this, we only need to realize that the consumer surplus of a type k^G buying a unit of

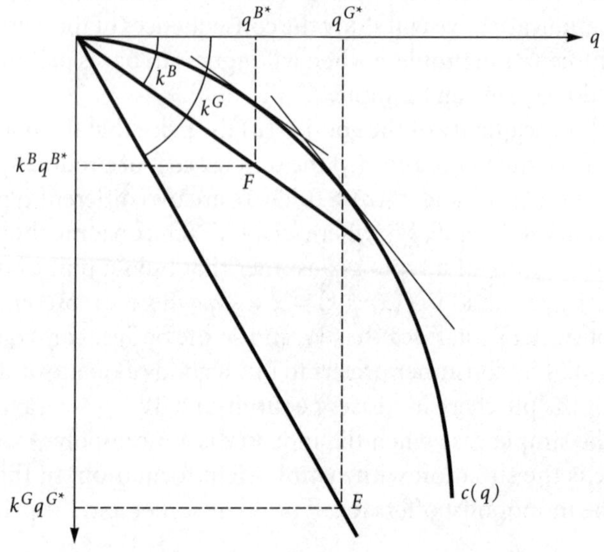

Fig. 4.22

quality q^{B*} at price p^{B*} is $q^{B*}\, k^G - p^{B*} = q^{B*}\,(k^G - k^B)$ (since $q^{B*}\, k^B - p^{B*} = 0$). Graphically, this can be seen by the fact that the agent (consumer) obtains greater utility the higher he is in the graph. Therefore his utility at *F* is greater than his utility at *E*.

Given this adverse selection situation, the monopolist designs the optimal contract menu, $\{(p^G, q^G), (p^B, q^B)\}$, that satisfies the participation and incentive compatibility constraints. As is usual in adverse selection, the product quality sold to the buyer who most values the good is not distorted, $q^G = q^{G*}$, while the quality offered to the consumer who least values the good is distorted, $q^B < q^{B*}$. Aside from this, a type-k^B consumer is indifferent between buying or not, and a type-k^G receives income in this market.[18] Points *G* and *H* in Figure 4.23 represent, respectively, (p^G, q^G) and (p^B, q^B).

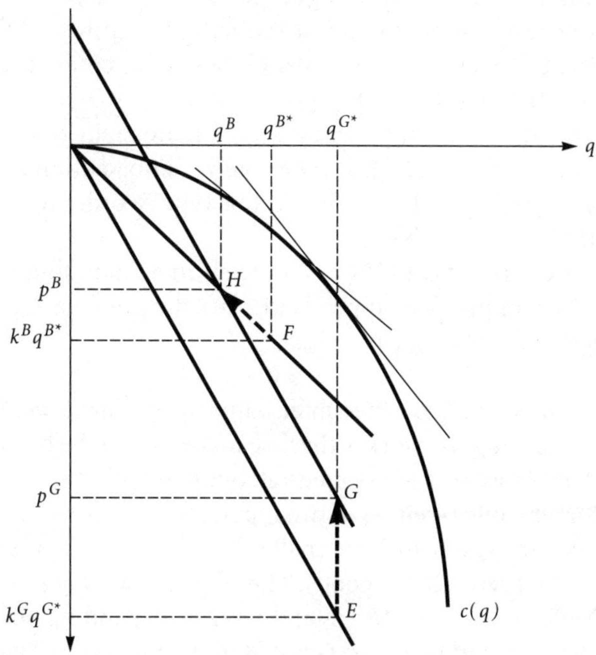

Fig. 4.23

The monopolist's interest in reducing the attractiveness of low quality for those consumers who are willing to pay more for high quality results in lower than efficient quality being sold. This has the effect that, under asymmetric information, the range of qualities on offer is greater than under symmetric information, since $q^G - q^B > q^{G*} - q^{B*}$.

18 See exercise 13 of this chapter.

Exercises

Exercise 1. In the adverse selection framework of Section 2 of this chapter, we assumed that a single principal wants to contract agents of two types. Type-G agents suffer a lower effort cost than type-B agents. When we observe the optimal contract menu offered by the principal:

(*a*) We know that one of the two types of agent is indifferent between accepting his contract or not, that is, he receives exactly his reservation utility. Which of the two types is this? Explain the intuition behind this result.

(*b*) We know that the contract designed for one of the types is efficient in the sense that we cannot alter it without reducing the utility of the principal and/or the agent. Which of the two agent types is this contract designed for? Explain the reasons for this result.

(*c*) One of the two agent types receives informational income. Which of the types is this? Given that this agent type receives informational income, why doesn't the other type pass himself off as this type in order to receive this income as well?

(*d*) Find an example (it could be a completely imaginary situation) in which an adverse selection problem appears, identify the possible agent types, and apply the results of parts (*a*), (*b*) and (*c*).

Exercise 2. Assume that a businessman wants to contract a worker, but there are aspects concerning the worker that are unknown to the businessman. He does know that the worker is risk-neutral, but that with respect to effort disutility, the worker could be either of two types. His disutility is either e^2, or $2\,e^2$. That is, the second type (which we shall call bad) suffers greater disutility to effort than the first type (called good). Therefore the worker's utility function is either $U^G(w, e) = w - e^2$, or $U^B(w, e) = w - 2\,e^2$, depending on his type. The probability that the worker is type G is q. Both worker types have reservation utility of $\underline{U} = 0$. The businessman, who is also risk-neutral, values worker effort at $\Pi(e) = k\,e$, where k is a sufficiently large constant for the foreman to be interested in contracting the agent, independent of his type. Hence, for each unit of effort supplied, the businessman receives k units of profit.

(*a*) Formulate, and solve, the businessman's problem if he had perfect information as to the worker's type. What effort levels are demanded, and what wages are paid?

(*b*) Formulate the problem when an adverse selection problem is present.

(*c*) Solve the problem calculating the optimal contract characteristics. (You may want to use the fact that some restrictions are not binding, but justify your reasons for doing this.)

(*d*) Compare the cases of symmetric and asymmetric information.

Exercise 3. For several months not a drop of rain has fallen in Bilbao, and daily water usage restrictions have had to be enforced. All classic methods of solving the problem have failed, and the mayor is searching for drastic and imaginative solutions. One of the mayor's aides tells him about a sorcerer from India who is able to make it rain. Naturally, the mayor is unconvinced that the sorcerer is for real, and is afraid that he will turn out to be a fake. Therefore, the mayor is trying to find a contract to offer the sorcerer such that he will accept only if he is for real.

Everybody knows that a phoney sorcerer has no power over the rain. If the mayor contracted a fake, the probability of rain would remain unchanged. It is currently estimated that the probability of rain in the next week (which is the time required to adequately test the powers of a sorcerer) is 2/100. On the other hand, an authentic sorcerer, in spite of having powers, is not infallible, and will increase the probability of rain within a week to 20/100.

Both authentic sorcerers and fakes are risk-averse, their utility function being of the form $u(w) = \sqrt{w}$. No authentic sorcerer will work unless the utility he receives from the contract is at least $\underline{U} = 10$. Fakes, on the other hand, are willing to charge less since their reservation utility is $\underline{U} = 1$. The mayor of Bilbao, who is risk-neutral, is concerned with designing a contract that would only be accepted by an authentic sorcerer, since the political cost of being publicly ridiculed should anyone somehow realize that a fake had been hired for the job, is prohibitively high.

(*a*) Formulate the problem that Bilbao's mayor must solve. (A word of warning; an optimal contract menu is not needed here, since the mayor is only interested in contracting an authentic sorcerer, and would like fakes to refuse the contract.)

(*b*) Calculate the optimal contract.

(*c*) Calculate the costs of this contract compared to symmetric information.

Exercise 4. Assume the same framework considered in Exercise 2, but in which the firm's profits are now $\Pi(e, w) = e - w$ (i.e. $k = 1$) and the initial probability that the worker is good is $q = 1/2$.

(*a*) Find the optimal solutions for the businessman in this case, for both symmetric and asymmetric information (when both types of worker may be hired). Calculate the profits from these contracts.

(*b*) Consider the other possibility that the businessman has: only contract the agent if he is good. Calculate the optimal contract in this case (we are still in asymmetric information). Calculate the firm's profits.

(*c*) Compare the situations in (*a*) and (*b*) under asymmetric information. Which is the optimal contract?

Exercise 5. A local college requires the services of an expert in semitic philology. However, there is only one graduate in Semitic philology in the entire country, and he works in the university. The college wants the expert to translate a part of a large manuscript written in a Semitic language that has fallen into their hands by chance. Since the translation is very complicated, the only person capable of doing it is the graduate, who can tackle it in his free time. The graduate could be one of two possible types: he is either a fast translator, capable of doing two pages per hour, or he is a slow translator, only capable of doing one page per hour. An hour of translating implies a disutility to the graduate (independent of his type) that must be compensated with $10.

(*a*) The college director has calculated how many pages of the manuscript he wants translated and how much to pay the translator. These calculations were done under the assumption that he is able to recognize whether the translator is fast or slow. His decision is to translate 50 pages of manuscript if the translator is slow, paying $500 for the job, and 80 pages if the translator is fast, paying only $400. Explain why this contract is reasonable.

(*b*) Once the translator arrives at the college, the director realizes that there is no way of knowing if he is fast or slow. Given the two contracts, the translator assures the director that he is slow, but the director does not believe him. Why not?

(*c*) The director decides to redo his calculations, and to offer a new contract menu to the translator. Explain the form that the menu will take. Will the director ask for more or less pages from each type? How will he calculate the payments?

(*d*) Verify your results of part (*c*) analytically, using the function $\Pi(n)$ for the value that the college places on a translation of n pages, with $\Pi'(n) > 0$ y $\Pi''(n) < 0$.

Exercise 6. Consider a risk-neutral principal who wants to contract a risk-averse agent to exert an effort. The agent may be one of two types, differentiated by their productivity; the first type's productivity of effort is given by the function $\Pi(e)$, and the productivity of effort of the second type is given by $k\Pi(e)$, with $k > 1$. Hence, the second type has greater productivity for any given effort. We shall refer to the first type as being bad (B) and the second type as being good (G), since for any given effort, the principal receives greater profits from the second type than from the first. We have $U^G(w, e) = U^B(w, e) = u(w) - v(e)$, which says that the agent's utility function is independent of his type. Both agent types have the same reservation utility. In order that the problem be concave, assume that $\Pi'(e) > 0$ and $\Pi''(e) < 0$.

(*a*) Write the system of equations that defines the optimal symmetric information contracts.

(*b*) Describe the situation graphically. What are the differences between the contracts of the two agent types?

(*c*) Analyse what happens if there is an adverse selection problem in that the principal cannot observe agent types.

Exercise 7. Consider a regulated monopoly that sells its product in an industry in which the consumers are of two different types (this exercise complements application 3). The firm's production costs are public information, and equal to $C(Q) = F + cQ$. The regulation establishes the amount of the payment that the consumer makes to the monopoly if a product is bought (T), the quantity that the monopoly can sell (Q), and the amount of the subsidy that the government transfers to the monopoly (S). The social cost to the government of collecting \$1 is $(1 + g)$ dollars, where $g > 0$. Therefore, the total cost to the government of the subsidy is $(1 + g)\,S$.

(*a*) Assume that there is only one representative consumer, whose utility function is known to be $U(Q)$. Formulate the problem that the government must solve, bearing in mind that the monopolist's profits could be negative and that the consumer may decide not to buy. Characterize the optimal regulation policy.

(*b*) Assume that there is asymmetric information with respect to the consumers. Let $U^G(Q)$ and $U^B(Q)$ be the utility of consumers of type 'G' and 'B' from the consumption of Q units of the good, where $U^G(Q) > U^B(Q)$ and $U^{G\prime}(Q) > U^{B\prime}(Q)$. Let q be the proportion of type-G consumers. Formulate the problem that the regulator must solve (maximize social welfare under the conditions of participation of the different consumer types, incentive compatibility to reveal the true characteristic, and participation for the firm for both possible consumer types).

(*c*) In the above problem, it is easy to calculate the optimal levels for the subsidy in function of the other parameters of the problem (from the first-order conditions with respect to the subsidy). Hence formulate the problem only in terms of $\{(T^G, Q^G), (T^B, Q^B)\}$.

(*d*) Using the first-order conditions, prove that the incentive compatibility constraint of the consumer who least values the good does not bind. Show that the optimal contract must satisfy: $U^{B\prime}(Q^B) = c$ and $U^{M\prime}(Q^M) > c$. Discuss these results.

Exercise 8. Mr. Jones decides to go to an insurance company in order to insure his car against accidents. From the insurance company's point of view, Mr Jones could be either a safe driver or a reckless driver. The probability that Jones is a safe driver is $t \in (0, 1)$. The probability that a safe driver will suffer an accident is $p_s = 1/3$, while the probability that a reckless driver will suffer an accident is $p_a = 1/2$. Assume that there are many insurance companies in the market, and that they are all risk-neutral. Jones's utility function is $u(x) = \ln(x)$, where x represents his wealth. Initially his wealth is $W = 64$, and an accident implies a cost of $C = 63$. All insurance companies offer contracts that include a premium ρ and a coverage amount q if an accident occurs. Jones will choose the contract (ρ, q) that he most prefers.

(*a*) Write Mr Jones's expected utility function when he signs a contract (ρ, q), according to whether he is a safe or a reckless driver. How is the participation constraint written (that is, the restriction that guarantees that Jones will really be interested in buying the policy (ρ, q))?

(*b*) Calculate the profits of an insurance company that doesn't insure Mr. Jones, if he is insured and he is a safe driver, if he is insured and he is a reckless driver, and finally, if he is insured (under contract (ρ, q)) without knowing for sure what type of driver he is.

(*c*) Calculate the contracts that will exist in this market if the information is symmetric, given that there are many insurance companies. Will Jones be fully insured?

(*d*) Why would these contracts not appear in the market if the insurance companies cannot observe whether Jones is safe or reckless?

(*e*) Using the results obtained in application 1 (they coincide with those of Section 3) of this chapter, calculate the contracts that could comprise a separating equilibrium in this market under asymmetric information.

(*f*)* Show that if the probability t that one is safe were 2/3, the previous contract menu is no longer an equilibrium. In order to do this, show that if the above contracts existed in the market, insurance companies could offer contracts designed for both types of driver, that fully insure and that give strictly positive profits.

Exercise 9. Consider a relationship between a principal and an agent, both risk-neutral. If the agent accepts the principal's contract, he will observe some characteristic in the market that will inform him of the current market conditions. If market conditions are good, then an effort of e will result in an outcome of $e + \theta^G$. If, on the other hand, the market conditions are bad, the same effort will give an outcome of $e + \theta^B$, where $\theta^B < \theta^G$. The principal does not observe either the market conditions, θ, or the effort, e, only the outcome, $e + \theta$, is a verifiable variable. The initial probability that the state will be good is q.

The principal maximizes the value of the result less the wage paid to the agent. On the other hand the agent maximizes his wage less the disutility of his effort, $v(e)$. Once the contract is signed, the agent can break the relationship if he wishes to. Hence, his utility must be greater than his reservation utility $\underline{U}$ under both possible market conditions (*ex post* participation constraint). Given this situation, the principal offers the agent a contract menu $\{(e^G, w^G), (e^B, w^B)\}$ such that the agent will prefer the first contract if the state turns out to be good, and the second it turns out to be bad.

(*a*) Formulate the problem that the principal must solve in order to design the optimal contract menu (there should be two participation constraints, and two incentive compatibility constraints). One of the two participation constraints is unimportant. Which one, and why?

(*b*) Write down the Kuhn–Tucker first-order conditions. Call λ the multiplier of the participation constraint which must be binding, and μ and γ the multipliers for the incentive compatibility constraints for not lying when the state is good and bad respectively. Show that $\lambda = 1$ and $\mu = \gamma + q$.

(*c*)* The multiplier γ cannot be strictly positive. Show why. (You could use a trick similar to that of part (iii) of complementary material 2 in this chapter.)

(*d*) Describe and comment on the characteristics of the optimal contract.

Exercise 10. Consider a situation of moral hazard with private information, in which the agent takes his participation decision *ex ante*. The framework will be the same as that developed in complementary material 2, but we will assume now that both principal and agent are risk-neutral. Show that in this case it is possible to arrive at the efficient situation. In particular, the contract menu $\{(e^G, w^G), (e^B, w^B)\}$ with $e^G = e^B = e^*$, defined by $v'(e^*) = 1$, and $w^G = \underline{U} + (2-q)\, v(e^*) - (1-q)\, v(e^* + \theta^B - \theta^G)$, $w^B = \underline{U} + (1-q)\, v(e^*) + q\, v(e^* + \theta^B - \theta^G)$, is efficient. Why is it that in this case there is no efficiency loss due to the moral hazard problem?

Exercise 11. Recently, a friend of ours mentioned that he had gone to insure his car and he had been offered several different policies. He could choose between an expensive contract with full insurance, or a contract with a voluntary excess of \$500 (a voluntary excess clause means that the company will pay all losses from accidents over and above the first \$500). The policy with the excess was significantly cheaper. Our friend argued that insurance companies offer contracts with excess clauses since that way they make the drivers who suffer many accidents pay \$500 each time. Is this a reasonable argument? Whether your answer is affirmative or not, you should argue in terms of an adverse selection situation (the insurance company cannot observe whether or not the driver is reckless).

Exercise 12. Formulate the problem of the principal in the framework analysed in Section 4, where there was symmetric information as to the agent's characteristic, k. Show that the solution to this problem will satisfy the equation:

$$v'(e(k)) = \frac{\Pi'(e(k))}{k}.$$

Are further hypothesis required? Interpret the condition.

Exercise 13. Formulate the problem that the monopolist of Application 4 of this chapter faces. Assume that the monopolist has a subjective probability α, for the consumer being of type k^G. Analyse the characteristics of the optimal contract.

Exercise 14. Consider a firm that works with a technology in which $x = e$, where e is the effort of the agent and x is the level of production. The cost function of the agent is not observable. Assume that there exist two types of agent (as in Section 2 of this chapter), differentiated by their disutility of effort. Let the utility function be represented by $U_i(w, e) = w - v_i(e)$, for $i = 1, 2$, where we assume that $v_1(.) < v_2(.)$, i.e. type-1 agents have less disutility of effort.

The firm can perfectly observe the production level, but does not know which type of agent is being contracted. Let q be the firm's subjective probability of the event that the worker is type 1.

Assume that $v'_1(.) < v'_2(.)$, for all effort levels.

(*a*) Interpret this condition, called unique intersection, which was implicitly included in section 2 of this chapter, and prove that this assumption can be deduced from the equation $v_2(e'') - v_2(e') > v_1(e'') - v_1(e')$, where e' and e'' are two effort levels such that $e'' > e'$.

(*b*) Calculate the payment mechanism that the principal must offer to each agent type and the effort demanded of each if the types were verifiable. Represent the situation graphically in the plane defined by production (or effort) and marginal cost.

(*c*) Prove that the optimal symmetric information scheme calculated above does not separate the agent types (in other words, one of the agent types prefers the contract designed for the other).

(*d*) How much must the principal pay to agent type 1, over and above reservation utility, in order that this type is not interested in signing the contract designed for type-2 agents? Is maintaining the contract designed for type-2 agents intact, and manipulating only the contract designed for type-1 agents the best strategy for the principal when agent types are not observable? Explain your answer.

(*e*) Calculate the contract menu that the principal will offer to the agents when their types are unknown.

Exercise 15. In this exercise we consider a risk-neutral government that wants to establish a policy of subsidies to firms that carry out efforts to decontaminate. Let e stand for the decontaminating effort. The cost to a firm of the decontaminating action is ce^2, where c is a parameter whose value depends on the type of firm at hand, $c \in [1, 2]$. The government's policy consists in a certain decontamination level e and a transfer t that the firm will receive if the decontamination has been carried out. The firm will not accept the subsidy scheme if it does not at least cover the costs. The firm is risk-neutral, and so the utility it earns from accepting the subsidy scheme is $t - ce^2$. The government bears in mind the social benefits of decontamination, valued at $2e$. On the other hand, the government prefers to pay out the lowest subsidy possible to the firm, and so a payment of t implies a disutility to the government of ρt, where $\rho \in (0, 1)$ (it costs the government $(1 + \rho)$ dollars to collect \$1, and hence the social utility of transferring t dollars to a firm is $t - (1 - \rho)\, t$). Given this, the government's objective function is $B(e, t) = 2e - \rho\, t$.

(*a*) Calculate the level of decontamination $e^*(c)$ and the transfer $t^*(c)$ that the government would propose to a firm whose decontamination cost is ce^2, when the government knows c.

(*b*) Now assume that the government does not know the parameter c. The government believes that c is uniformly distributed on the interval $[1, 2]$, i.e. $f(c) = 1$, $F(c) = c - 1$. Find the menu of possibilities $\{e(c), t(c) \mid c \in [1, 2]\}$, in order that the firm chooses the contract it most prefers. Formulate the problem that the government must solve. Identify the important participation restriction and calculate, using the incentive compatibility constraints, the informational income of the firm in function of the parameter c. Using this, rewrite the problem. (The analysis is parallel to that developed in Section 4 of this chapter.)

(*c*) Calculate the optimal subsidy policy for the government $\{e(c), t(c) \mid c \in [1, 2]\}$.

(*d*) The principal is not always interested in offering a subsidy that all firm types will accept, but rather sometimes it is preferable to leave out those firms with high decontamination costs. Hence, the government can design a menu $\{e(c), t(c) \mid c \in [1, c^\circ]\}$, where c° is a parameter between 1 and 2. Calculate the optimal menu, fixing c°. Prove that, in this example, it is optimal for the government to design a menu intended for all firm types (i.e. $c^\circ = 2$).

Exercise 16. Consider a situation in which the participants have the same utility functions as in Section 2. A principal's utility function is $\Pi(e) - w$, and the utility function of an agent is either $u(w) - v(e)$ or $u(w) - k\,v(e)$, depending on his type. However, assume that there are now many principals in the market, and that they must compete for the agents (as was the case in Section 3).

(*a*) Represent the optimal contract (e^G, w^G) graphically for the situation in which all agents are type *G*. Do the same for the optimal contract (e^B, w^B) when all agents are type *B*.

(*b*) What happens when the principals cannot distinguish agent types? What are the consequences of the asymmetric information?

4C Advanced Themes

We shall present here some extensions to the adverse selection model, pointing out the aspects that have been analysed and mentioning some relevant articles on each line of research.

4C.1 Relationships with several agents: Auctions

When the principal simultaneously contracts with several agents, the relationships between them, and between their information sets are important. Imagine that a principal contracts several agents to develop different phases of a certain productive process. It may be that the agents' types are independent (in which case any information obtained from one does not allow the principal to conclude anything with respect to the others), or perhaps they are correlated. In this second case, it is possible that the principal can, through the competition between the agents (comparing their messages), arrive at the same situation as if she had perfect information as to the agents' characteristics (see Maskin and Riley, 1980, and Crémer and McLean, 1985). Understanding this is easier if we assume perfect correlation between the agents' types. In this case each agent knows his own type and that of all other agents. If the principal does not receive the same message from each agent, she can impose fines that, if sufficiently severe, will induce the agents to behave honestly.

One of the most common mechanisms used to sell goods are *auctions*. Works of art in galleries, fish markets, public contracts, or financial assets are all transacted at auctions. However, not all auctions are the same. Art galleries generally use *English Auctions:* the agents bid 'upwards', or in other words, from an initial minimum price, each competing agent must better the previous bid (if you have seen Cary Grant in *Alone Against Danger* you will know that is bad form to bid less than the going price). On the other hand, fish markets are generally examples of *Dutch Auctions*: the seller reduces the price of the good until someone stops the auction by buying. There are other types of auctions as well. On some occasions all the agents must hand in a closed envelope containing their bid (this is how public contracts are generally awarded). Among these auctions we can distinguish between *first price* and *second price* auctions. In both types of auction the good is sold to the highest bidder, but only in the first case does the winner pay his own bid. In second price auctions, the person who bids the highest gets to buy the good at a price equal to the second highest bid.

Auctions exist since the seller of the good does not know how much the agents are willing to pay, that is, or in particular, which agent has the highest *reservation price.* Hence it is a situation of adverse selection. Were the information perfect, the seller would just set a price equal to the reservation price of the agent who most highly values the good. The literature has centred fundamentally on two questions.[19] First, which type of auction is better from the seller's point of view? And, secondly, do auctions introduce distortions in the allocation of goods in such a way that the good is not always sold, or it is not sold to the agent with the highest reservation price?

Vickrey (1961) compares English and Dutch auctions (which we can also consider to be, respectively, second price and first price auctions) when the participants are risk-neutral and the individual reservation prices (or personal valuations) are independent drawings from the same distribution (under these conditions the English and Dutch auctions are strategically identical to the second price and the first price auctions, respectively). He proved that both types of auction are equivalent, since in both cases the agent who wins is the one with the greatest reservation price, and the expected revenue of the seller is the same in both auction types since in both cases the expected winning bid is the expected value of the second highest reservation price. In this situation the existence of private information does not generate any distortions with respect to who ends up getting the good, but the revenue of the seller is less than under symmetric information.

What does an optimal auction look like? What mechanism maximizes the expected revenue of the seller? Myerson (1981) solves this general mechanism design problem when the bidders have independent types and all agents are risk-neutral.[20] Let v_i be the valuation of bidder *i* and v_0 be the seller's valuation. Myerson (1981) has shown that, because of the adverse selection problem and the need to give rents to the bidders, the expected payment that the seller can

19 McAfee and McMillan (1987*b*), Milgrom (1987*b*), and Bullow and Roberts (1989) present excellent surveys of papers on auctions.

20 The analysis in Myerson (1981) is very complex for the reader less familiar with this type of problems. However, Bullow and Roberts (1989) have shown that all the analysis can be done using the standard tools of models of pricing by a monopolist.

obtain from bidder i is equal to $J_i(v_i) = v_i - (1 - F_i(v_i))/f_i(v_i)$, which is known as bidder i's virtual valuation. For the case of most distributions the virtual valuations increase in the true valuations and the optimal auction is then easily constructed. First, the seller only sells to a bidder with a virtual valuation greater than the seller's valuation, i.e. bidder i may win the good only if $J_i(v_i) \geq v_0$. In a standard auction this rule can be implemented through a minimum bid policy. Second, the seller will want to sell to the bidder with the highest virtual valuation, which, in general, is not the highest valuation. Hence, in general, the optimal auction is different form the English (second price) or Dutch (first price) auction. This result should be no surprise and can be understood with the following example. Assume that there are only two bidders, whose valuations are independently and uniformly distributed with $v_L \in [0, 1]$ and $v_H \in [1, 2]$. If the good always goes to the highest bidder, agent H does not bid more than 1, and the seller's revenue is at most 1. However, if the two valuations are not too different, the seller may prefer to lose money and sell to agent L in order to provide incentives for agent H to bid more than 1, with a corresponding increase in the seller's revenue. As a specific case, if the valuation (which is private information) is drawn from the same distribution for both agents, the model is symmetric and the highest virtual valuation comes from the bidder with the highest valuation. In this case, the English (second price) and the Dutch (first price) auctions, with the appropriate minimum bids, are optimal. These auctions are still not efficient: the seller may not sell the good even if it would be efficient to sell it, because the minimum bids are higher that the seller's valuation.

The results of Myerson (1981) have been generalized by Branco (1992) to situations of common values (the value of the good is the same for all bidders but unknown at the time of the auction), as long as the agents' types are independent. If the true common value is $V(k)$, where k is the vector of private signals, which are independent and identically distributed, the model inherits the essential properties of the private values mode. Now the English, second price and first price auctions, with the appropriate minimum bids, are optimal mechanisms. However, the Dutch auction is no longer optimal. The new feature is that the minimum bid required from bidder i is endogenous and depends on the other bidders' information. The Dutch auction does not provide to the seller the information she needs to compute the minimum bids.

Most of the recent work has been directed at relaxing some of the assumptions of the model of Myerson (1981). The assumption of independence of the types is crucial for the previous results. Milgrom and Weber (1982) considered a situation in which the types are affiliated,[21] and analysed the performance of the standard auctions. The equivalence breaks down. The strategic

[21] Two variables are affiliated if they are not negatively correlated in any subset of their domain.

correspondence between English and second price auctions disappears: during the English auction the bidders reveal information to each other, which is now valuable. As a result in terms of revenue to the seller the best is the English auction, followed by the second price auctions and by the Dutch auction (which is still equivalent to the first price auction).[22] Neither one of these auctions maximizes the revenue of the seller. Crémer and McLean (1985, 1988) and McAfee, McMillan, and Reny (1989) have shown that in this case the seller may extract all (or almost all) the surplus from the bidders, as if there was no asymmetric information. To understand this result assume that the types are perfectly correlated. The principal may announce heavy fines if all agents do not reveal the same information; then, it is an equilibrium for agents to behave honestly. This kind of result can be achieved even if the correlation is low. But the principal may need to impose very high punishments to prevent deviation from truth-telling, i.e. the assumptions of risk-neutrality and unlimited liability are really stretched.

What happens if one drops the risk-neutrality? Auctions with risk-averse buyers were studied by Maskin and Riley (1984) and Matthews (1988). When bidders are risk-neutral, the second price auction has an equilibrium in dominant strategies: each agent is willing to bid exactly his reservation value. But this is still an equilibrium if the bidders are risk-averse. Hence the expected revenue raised by the English (second price) auction is the same regardless of the bidders' position relative to risk. By contrast, in the Dutch (first price) auction, the bidders will be more aggressive when they are risk-averse. The reason is very simple. Using the bidding function of a risk-neutral bidder, the agent will be faced with risk: his utility will be equal to 0 if he loses, and will be positive if he wins. A risk-averse bidder will care about this risk and will want to be exposed to less risk, which can be accomplished by raising his bid. In the limit, if the bid is equal to the agent's reservation value the agent's utility will be zero for sure: the risk will be eliminated. This is not in general the optimal solution. The optimal bid will be between the bidder's reservation value and the expected value of the second bidder's reservation value. Hence, the Dutch (first price) auction will raise more revenue. Still, these auctions put too much risk on the bidders and, in particular, the bidders with higher reservation values (so the ones that have greater probabilities of winning) are the ones that face more risk. Maskin and Riley (1984) showed that the interest of the seller will be better achieved if she designs a scheme in which the bidders that bid high face a low risk and the bidders that bid low face a high risk. These properties reduce the incentive for underbidding by the high-type bidders.

[22] For simplicity, the English auction is normally studied under the *Japanese* modification, in which all bidders who are willing to pay a particular price announce this fact, and the seller increases the price until only one bidder remains.

In recent years some attention has been given to auctions of multiple units. Maskin and Riley (1989) studied a model of a divisible good auction with private values. Branco (1996) generalized his previous model to the context of multiple indivisible units. The results point out to a complex structure of the optimal auctions. Unless the bidders only demand one unit, the discriminatory price (generalizes the first price, in the sense that the highest bidders win and pay their own bid) or the uniform price (generalizes the second price auction, in the sense that the highest bidders win and pay the highest rejected bid) are not optimal.

To conclude, we point out that there exist another group of models in which the principal contracts with several agents simultaneously, but does not attempt to maximize her own profits. This is the case of a benevolent regulator or planner, who attempts to maximize the sum of the utilities of the agents. In this case, which could be exemplified by the provision of a public good, a part of the problem is related to the fact that balancing the budget and efficiency are incompatible objectives. See, for example, Clarke (1971), Groves (1973), Laffont and Maskin (1979), and Myerson and Satterthwaite (1983).

4C.2 Organization design

Adverse selection models, as with moral hazard models, have attempted to explain such themes as task assignment, the advantages of delegation, or the optimal structure of the relationship.

One of the decisions that the principal must take in certain circumstances is which tasks to delegate to agent, and which ones to carry out personally. Riordan and Sappington (1987) analyse the advantages and inconveniences of delegation in a situation with two parameters that could be private information. They establish a model in which there are two tasks to be done. The first (in time) task (the task of development or choice of quality) is always done by the agent: the second task (the production or choice of quantity) could be done by either the principal or the agent. Both are identical with respect to their ability to carry out this second task, and both are risk-neutral. It is the principal who decides who will be responsible for the task. Given these conditions, under symmetric information, it wouldn't matter at all who took care of the production. However, if the person in charge of each task has private information as to the costs associated with the task, then the assignment of tasks within the organization is an important decision.

The results of the above-mentioned paper are associated with two effects. The first is the effect on the decision in the first phase. The agent's eventual control during the second task influences his incentives during the first. More concretely, control during the second task increases the agent's incentives to exaggerate the costs of the first period, in the hope of obtaining greater utility, when the costs of both periods are positively correlated. This leads the principal to prefer to take control of the production if there is a positive correlation. On the other hand, control during the second task reduces the agent's incentives to exaggerate the costs of the first period when the costs are negatively correlated. In this case, the principal will prefer to delegate the production to the agent. The second effect is related to the distortion of the optimal decision in the second period. If the principal takes charge of the task, she will learn all costs for that phase, while if she delegates the cost of production will be information private to the agent. Both have an incentive to manipulate the second phase if they are responsible for it: the agent in order to cover his announcement or his first period behaviour, and the principal in order to reduce the wage paid to the agent for his decision during the first period. For example, if the correlation is positive, when the agent takes charge of the second task, he has an incentive to produce low quantity (exaggerate the costs) in order to cover his overvaluation of the first period costs. For the same case, the principal will tend to produce an amount greater than the optimum in order to contradict the agent and reduce his payment. The combination of these two effects bring us to the following results:

(*a*) If the costs of the two tasks are independent, the principal is indifferent between delegating the second task to the agent or doing it personally. (This result is related to the assumption of risk-neutrality of the agent.)

(*b*) If both costs are positively correlated, then the principal will prefer to take charge of the second phase herself. This is due to the fact that this way she thwarts the adverse effect of delegating the task to the agent.

(*c*) If the costs are negatively correlated, but if this correlation is small, the principal will choose to assign the second task to the agent. In this case, the agent's incentives to manipulate the first period quality decision are weaker, since the production is unimportant as a signal of first period costs, and the principal's moral hazard problem is avoided.

(*d*) When the costs are negatively correlated, and when this correlation is large, it is not possible to give an unambiguous answer. There will be cases in which delegation of the second task is optimal, and cases in which it is not.

The optimal structure of an organization depends critically on the conditions under which it is established. Melumad and Reichelstein (1987) ask if the delegation of a certain decision is efficient or not in a framework in which the decision variable is verifiable (i.e. it can be included in the contract). First, they show that if communication between the principal and the agent is not possible (the principal cannot 'ask' the agent about his environment), then the delegation of decisions cannot be bad for the principal, and it is strictly better on many occasions. It is better to incite the agent, via a contract, to take the best decision given the environment, than for the principal to decide without observing this private information. Secondly, they show that when communication is possible, the principal is indifferent about delegating the decision or not. Either of the two contractual formats is able to incite acceptable behaviour from the agent.

One of the questions that the principal must decide is the design of the organization. For example, when the government regulates a productive sector in which several phases are required in order to obtain the final product (think of electricity, which must be produced and distributed), one of the possible measures that can be taken is to separate the different productive phases, or, contrarily, concentrate them in a single firm. Baron and Besanko (1992), Dana (1993), and Da-Rocha-Alvarez (1994) analyse the optimal hierarchical structure in industries with several productive phases, when the firms have private information relating to their costs. One could imagine that it concerns a problem of joint production, or a problem in which both phases are needed to get a single unit of production. The costs of the phases can vary within a predetermined interval, and the only one who really knows the exact value is the agent in charge of carrying out that particular phase. The structure chosen determines the type of game established between the regulator and the firm(s). If the principal decides to merge the firms together, it only needs one to transmit all the information on costs. The firm, since it controls all productive phases, has a greater '*marge de manoeuvre*'. This is the negative aspect of the integration of activities. However, there is also a positive aspect. The fact that information signals are co-ordinated avoids the negative external effects of separate firms stepping on each others' toes. The above-mentioned studies show that structures that concentrate all tasks to a single agent are superior. The advantage of centralization is due to an efficiency argument: when the tasks are all carried out by a single agent, the incentives to dishonestly reveal the costs of each of the phases is less since the fact that each announcement affects the decision of the other phase is taken into account. This result is robust to the introduction of competition between the agents that carry out any one of the phases. What is more, the introduction of competition in the first phase of production (the generation of electricity in the case of our example) is not only good from the principal's point of view, as is expected, but it also may be good from the point of view of the agents. This allows us to explain why, in the recent process of reform of the electricity sector in Spain, the established firms have preferred to maintain all their activities even though competition has been introduced in some of the productive phases.

The advantage of centralizing production, even though it may extend over many different frameworks, depends on the assumption that the cost support is the same for both phases of production. When they are different, for example due to specific particularities in each phase, Da-Rocha-Alvarez and De-Frutos (1999) show that the absolute advantage of the centralized hierarchy is not maintained. If the differences in costs between the different phases are sufficiently important, it is advantageous to decentralize them, contracting a different firm for each one. To the efficiency advantage of centralization (the elimination of external effects between the agents), we must now add an effect that is favourable to decentralized structures (that before was zero). This new effect is linked to the fact that information concentration in one single agent gives him, in this case, enough power for it to become a cost on the relationship.

Another important aspect are the advantages and inconveniences of the decentralization of contracts, that is, the comparison between an organization in which all contracts are proposed by the principal, and one in which the principal contracts an agent who is then responsible for contracting the rest. Myerson (1982) shows that in an adverse selection framework, any result that can be obtained as a non-co-operative equilibrium in a decentralized organization can also be obtained in a centralized structure. In other words, the set of obtainable results of centralized organizations contains that of decentralized organizations. The consequence of this is that centralization cannot be worse than decentralization, since it is always possible to replicate a decentralized contract with a centralized one. This result is really a generalization of the revelation principle. The principal maximizes her utility through a mechanism of revelation in which each agent is asked to announce to the principal the private information at his disposal. In an unlimited and costless communication framework, the decision on contracts should be delegated.

Now that we have seen that centralization is capable of reproducing any decentralization result, we should ask if the opposite is ever true. In a study by Melumad, Mookherjee, and Reichelstein (1995), this idea is explored. In a relationship that involves a principal and two agents, these authors show that if, in a decentralized organization, the principal can establish a 'sufficiently attractive' intermediate contract with the agent (if the principal can make the payments of this agent depend on the contract that he signs with the second agent), then the two organizational structures are equivalent (a similar result is proved by Baron and Besanko (1992)). If, on the other hand, the contract between the principal and the intermediate agent can depend only on the results obtained from the actions of both agents, then a centralized organization is strictly superior. Given an adverse selection problem, the disadvantage of decentralization is associated with the fact that, in order to obtain similar results to centralized structures, the contracts to be established must include more variables.

One of the fundamental hypotheses for the validity of the result of the superiority of centralized organizations is that the agents can costlessly (without omission or misinterpretation) communicate all their information to the principal. We can relate this assumption to that of unbounded rationality. As Melumad, Mookherjee, and Reichelstein (1995) show, a decentralized organization can be more efficient when it is not possible (or it is very costly) for the agents to transmit information to the principal. The delegation of an agent's contract to another agent has the advantage that the contracting agent can use all relevant information that cannot be adequately communicated to the principal in the design of the contract.

4C.3 Repeated adverse selection

Given an adverse selection problem, the principal's aim is to extract private information from the agent via the contract, introducing the least amount of inefficiencies and costs possible. When the relationship is repeated during several periods, one must consider whether the repetition can help the principal in this search for information, and what will be the form of the optimal contracts. Recall that in a relationship under moral hazard, repetition of the relationship does help to reduce the problem since it allows the incentives to be better distributed over time. We could think that, under adverse selection, the information revealed by the agent at the beginning of the relationship can be used in successive periods to reduce the informational advantage of the agent. In this way, the contractual design in each period would depend on the information revealed by the agent in the past, which should improve the static allocations. However, as we shall see, this does not occur.[23]

To start off, consider the simple case of a repeated relationship in which the agent's information is modified in each period. Assume that the agent has private information at the start of each period, having learnt this information immediately before signing the contract (different contracts are signed each period) and there is no relationship between this information over periods. This is equivalent to a change in the agent's type over time, when there is no intertemporal correlation between these types. In this case, any current information revealed does not affect the future, and hence the repeated problem is equivalent to simple repetition of the initial relationship. The optimal intertemporal contract will be the sequence of optimal single-period contracts.

What happens in repeated relationships in which an agent with relevant private information before signing learns new private information that

[23] Baron (1989) and Arnaudin-Fagart (1991) present a substantial part of the results that will be discussed in this section.

corresponds to other periods, before taking decisions in these other periods, and when the contract covers the entire relationship? If both the principal and the agent are risk-neutral, and if the private information is independent over periods, then Besanko (1985) shows that there are only inefficiencies in the first period, and that these are identical to those of the static model. The reason for this result lies in the fact that the adverse selection problem really only appears in the first period, since the others are better understood as problems of moral hazard with hidden information. As in Exercise 10 of this chapter, these problems do not generate inefficiencies if acceptance is *ex ante*, and if both participants are risk-neutral. Hence only the first-period private information can induce inefficiencies.

When the information of an agent at any particular point in time affects not only the result of the current period, but also those of the future, then the situation is rather different. To see why, consider the opposite of the previous case, the agent's type being constant over time. If the principal offers the optimal first-period contract, and if the agent decides to reveal truthfully, then the principal is in a situation of symmetric information during the rest of the periods, and so can design efficient contracts that extract all surpluses from the agent. The agent will anticipate this behaviour, and so will have even more incentives to misrepresent than in a single-period game. The incentives of the principal to search for information are transformed into incentives for the agent to lie. In order to characterize the optimal contract, we must distinguish between the situation in which the principal can establish a multi-period contract (i.e. there is an ability to commit) and the situation in which the contract of any period is signed only once the previous periods are over.[24]

Baron and Besanko (1984) show that if the principal can commit herself with a contract that covers all the periods, then the optimal contract is the repetition of the optimal static contract. This is as if the principal were to lose her memory at the end of the first period (since, during this period the agents have revealed their characteristic). In the optimal contract, this information will not be used to design the contracts of subsequent periods. This characterization implies that the optimal long-term contract is not sequentially rational: the principal will be interested in offering the optimal static contract as of the second period, since the agents have announced their types in the first period. Not only is the contract not sequentially rational, but it is also not robust to renegotiation. Given that the optimal symmetric information

[24] As in repeated moral hazard, in long-term agreements, sometimes principal and agent cannot commit not to renegotiate a contract later. In other words, although, sometimes a long-term contract can be enforced if one of the parties wants it to be enforced, principal and agent can agree to replace the initial contract with a new one if they both benefit from doing so. This renegotiation can be prevented only if one of the parties has the means to commit not to do it. For more details on renegotiation problems see, e.g. Hart and Tirole (1988) and Laffont and Tirole (1990).

contract is not efficient, there is room for Pareto improvements if the principal and the agent renegotiate the contract.

Therefore there are many reasons that back up the possibility that it is often not possible for the principal to commit to a long-term contract, or at least commit to not renegotiating it. In the first case, when the principal cannot commit to the long-term arrangement, it may be impossible to find a mechanism that induces the agent to reveal his type in the first periods. In particular, Laffont and Tirole (1988) show that if the parameter that is private information of the agent can take continuous values (as in the model of Section 4.4), then it is impossible to propose perfect revelation contracts in the first periods. This is known as the *ratchet effect.* When the agent's type can only take two different values, then it is possible to offer a contract that induces the agent to announce his type honestly from the start.[25] However, as Freixas, Guesnerie, and Tirole (1985), and Laffont and Tirole (1987) have pointed out, information revelation may be so costly that it is not always desirable. Given that the cost of obtaining information increases with the number of periods remaining (since the agent's incentives to lie increase), we should expect that information be revealed progressively over time.

Baron and Besanko (1987) and Laffont and Tirole (1990) establish frameworks in which it is possible to propose perfect revelation contracts, even though it is not profitable to do so. On the one hand, this is the case when the agent can commit to participation in the relationship and the principal can commit to respecting the individual rationality of the agent (a reasonable hypothesis, for example, in a situation of regulation). On the other hand, the conclusions are true when the principal can commit to a long-term contract, but cannot commit to not renegotiating it.

The ability to commit oneself is therefore profitable for the principal. The absence of this feature will introduce the 'ratchet effect', in which a single contract is offered to several different agent types, since separating them is simply impossible, or too costly.

Finally, we would like to note that the above conclusions were obtained in frameworks in which the agent is interested in hiding his characteristics. When this is not the case, for example, when competition between principals allows the agent to extract all the surplus from the relationship, then the repetition of the relationship allows the agent to better reveal his private information, since he is interested in doing so. Haneda (1986) shows that, in a similar framework to Rothschild and Stiglitz (1976) studied in application 1, using multi-period contracts can result in the accumulation of information on agent type over time, and the premium charged to the agent will depend on the accumulated

[25] This statement does not generalize to a large number of types.

information. In this way, the repetition of the relationship can reduce the inefficiencies associated with the problem of adverse selection.

4C.4 Models of moral hazard and adverse selection

Standard models of moral hazard (in which the agent's behaviour is not observable) and of adverse selection (in which the informational advantage of the agent is with respect to his characteristics) have been extensively analysed. However, within the theory of agency, one of the most costly developments is that of situations in which there are simultaneously elements of moral hazard and adverse selection.

The focus adopted by most of the models that consider that the agent may simultaneously possess private information on some characteristic of the relationship, and on his decision within the relationship, has been to simplify the models in order to make them more easily handled. In particular, many studies have considered that all participants be risk-neutral. The introduction of risk-aversion makes the models more difficult to solve (even though we know the existence conditions, see Page, 1992), except when the agents have utility functions with constant risk-aversion and the contracts are linear (see McAfee and McMillan (1986, 1987*a*). Since, from the moral hazard literature we know that when the agent is risk-neutral, the trade-off between the objectives of insurance and incentives are not in conflict, this hypothesis deserves to be discussed. A contract with a deductible (voluntary excess) in which the principal sells the firm to the agent for a fixed payment allows efficient allocation to be achieved in a pure moral hazard framework. Under the hypothesis of agent risk-neutrality, if there were only moral hazard, then the problem is not very interesting. However, this does not mean that the problem to be solved, when both types of asymmetric information problems are present in contexts in which the participants are risk-neutral, are trivial. The reason is that, under adverse selection, the deductible contract solution is totally inefficient.[26]

One very common class of model that considers simultaneous moral hazard and adverse selection is that in which it is assumed that both variables determine the production level. Therefore the principal cannot distinguish the part due to effort from the part due to the agent's efficiency parameter. In general, both the agent's effort and his characteristic will only affect the average result observed at the end of the relationship. This result depends on a

[26] As can be seen from the previous discussion, restricting ourselves to situations in which all the participants are risk-neutral is associated with the adverse selection component, even though it is not a necessary hypothesis in pure adverse selection models.

random variable as well: the observation error. Generally it is assumed that the participants have the same initial distribution over this random variable (see Picard, 1987, and Guesnerie, Picard, and Rey, 1989). These papers show that, if the effort demanded of the different agents is not decreasing in the characteristic (if a higher value of this parameter implies greater efficiency), then the optimal contract is a menu of distortionary deductibles designed to separate the agents. The principal sells the firm to the most efficient agents, while the least efficient agents pay a lower price, since they only keep a part of the production. On the other hand, when the adverse selection component is such that the most efficient agents prefer to sign the deductible contracts of the least efficient agents, 'fines' for unexpected deviations are needed so that the agents honestly reveal their characteristic. In this case a linear contract menu is not optimal, but quadratic contracts are. In fact these contract menus are optimal for the case of pure adverse selection.

This fact has meant that sometimes it appears that, under risk-neutrality, the principle message of this literature is that the optimal solution for problems that mix adverse selection and moral hazard does not imply efficiency losses with respect to the pure adverse selection solution when the agent's effort is observable. Even though this is true for some cases (for example, in the model of Guesnerie, Picard, and Rey, 1989), in other frameworks (like that of Laffont and Tirole, 1986, and Picard, 1987), it is only when both problems are mixed when a true problem of asymmetric information appears, and efficiency losses are evident. Therefore, the same solution cannot be achieved as when only the agent's characteristic is private information.

Until now we have only discussed models in which both sources of asymmetric information appear simultaneously. It could be that, in multi-period models, they appear sequentially. That is, it could be that in the first period there is a moral hazard problem that generates an adverse selection situation in the second period, since the agent is the only one who knows his exact behaviour (see, for example, the situations analysed by Fudenberg and Tirole, 1990, Ma, 1991, Chiappori, Macho-Stadler, Rey, and Salanié, 1994). This would be the case of the manager of a firm that chooses the investment that will determine the production costs in the future.

4C.5 Several principals

In some situations, an agent with private information is contracted by several principals, none of which knows the agent's characteristic. If the principals group themselves, we are in a framework that is very similar to that of adverse selection with only one principal. However, when they don't group together, but rather act separately, the first problem that appears is the difficulty of extending the principle of revelation to this type of situation. This is due to the fact that now there is not a single contract but rather an entire set of contracts, each proposed by different principals, which are interrelated. This difficulty has been pointed out by Stole (1990) and Martimort (1992). With respect to the relationship, we need to distinguish two cases: the first is when the agents' activities or efforts carried out on behalf of the different principals are complementary, and the second case is when they are substitutes. An example of the first type of situation is a firm that produces a final good, and requires two complementary intermediate goods in the production process. The industries that sell these intermediate goods do not know the technology of the firm. In this case the firm that produces the final good is the agent, and the industries that produce the intermediate goods are the principals.

An example in which the activities are substitutes are multinationals that have private information as to their cost structure and that produce substitute goods in different countries. These firms are in general subject to taxes in these countries according to the production in national territory. Here the multinational is playing the part of the agent and the countries in which it has firms are the principals.

Hence we consider two principals that are in a relationship with a single agent whose characteristic is unknown to them. This agent works for both, or in other words he sends messages that determines his effort to each principal. The relationship between these efforts is central to the conclusions obtained. If we accept that agent's messages are restricted to the set of characteristics, we can point out the following results. If the activities or efforts that the agent carries out for the two principals are substitutes, then the symmetric equilibrium effort levels are such that, when the solution to this game is compared with the solution in which both principals group together, we obtain the usual result on the distortion of the efficient solution. The most efficient agent will have to supply his optimal effort, and only the effort demanded of the least efficient agent is distorted. This means that when the efforts are substitutes, there are no distortions in the effort demanded in the contract designed for the most efficient agents. Even though the principals compete, each one prefers that the agent honestly reveals to the other principal. Hence each principal is really internalizing the preferences of the other.

However, the lack of co-operation between the principals introduces an additional distortion on the adverse selection problem. The distortion appears in the contracts designed for the least efficient agent. As is usual, each principal would like to reduce the effort demanded of the least efficient agent in order to reduce the informational income of the most efficient one. But she does not control the agent's behaviour completely. In particular the efficient agent could use high efforts in his relationship with the other principal. This would induce each principal not to reduce too much (less than what they would have done in the case of co-operating together) the effort demanded of the inefficient agent, from which the distortion is reduced.

If the activities that the agent carries out for the principals are complementary, then the comparison of the results under co-operation and no co-operation between the principals reveals that, in the second case, if a principal reduces the effort demanded of the agent, this will imply that it is also profitable for the other principal to do the same. Therefore, the distortion in the decisions is greater to that produced in the case in which the principals co-operate.

5

SIGNALLING

Summary

In many contractual relationships, one of the parties has more information than the other as to some relevant variables. When it is beneficial to do so, the informed party will try to *signal* the information to the other party via some action or decision. In this chapter we study, on the one hand, the possibility that the participants signal their characteristic through actions previous to the contractual relationship. On the other hand, we study the value of the very contract as a means of indirect transmission of information when the principal has information that she would like the agent to know.

As was shown in Chapter 4, when the principals compete for agents, the best agents (the most efficient ones) get less utility if their efficiency is unknown to the principals. Carrying out some action whose cost decreases with the agent's efficiency, previous to the signing of the contract, can be a signal that allows the principal to ascertain if the agent is efficient or not. This action is adequate as a signal if its cost is sufficiently high so that the low efficiency agents won't carry it out, and yet sufficiently low so that the high efficiency agents will. For example, the level of education is often considered to be a signal of the intellectual and work ability of the candidates for certain job openings.

On other occasions, the agent has less information than the principal as to the true conditions surrounding the relationship, should it be initiated. However, these conditions influence the agent's decision to accept the contract or not. The agent knows that if the conditions are unfavourable, the principal will attempt to make the agent believe the contrary. Doing so would negatively affect the profits of a principal who is offering favourable conditions. Hence, in this case, the principal may be interested in offering a contract that is different from that which would be offered under symmetric information, if by doing so she can clearly show that she is offering favourable conditions, as she would never have offered the contract had the conditions been adverse.

5.1 Introduction

It is quite normal to open the job vacancies section of the newspaper and find an advertisement like the following: 'Firm seeks to hire recent graduate', without specifying the exact studies required. However, when a student chooses his university study programme, his own personal preferences aside, the choice is usually the degree that the student believes will be useful as a knowledge base for some future job, hence allowing him to earn higher wages than workers without university qualifications. What is the sense of an advertisement in which having a university degree is important, but the content of the degree is not?

It was Spence (1973) who answered this question: education acts as a *signal*. The fact that someone has a university degree, independent of its content, can be interpreted as a signal that the person is 'capable of learning'. Hence, if a firm is seeking a person who is 'capable of learning', it is perfectly rational to offer work to graduates of any type. This is true even if the fact that the worker 'has a degree' is of no real value to the firm, and so the signalling system is wasteful in the sense that the individual who ends up getting the job would, in principle, have the same capacity had he not bothered to become a graduate. However, the only way in which his aptitude can be reliably tested is to have finished a degree of some sort. Even if this argument may seem somewhat strange, it is in fact very close to the truth.

In this chapter we will analyse situations in which one of the parties to a contract is interested in signalling some characteristic before the contract is signed. As we shall see, via examples and applications, such situations are rather numerous. Before continuing, however, it is worth while to clarify just what we mean by a signal, and who may be interested in sending a particular signal.

5.2 The Value of Private Information and of Signalling

We have seen in previous chapters how the existence of private information influences a contract's format. We always set out under the assumption that if someone has private information, he will try to use it in his own personal interests. For example, given a moral hazard situation, the agent chooses an effort that maximizes his own expected utility, not the surplus of the relationship. In the same way, when the problem facing the principal is adverse selection, the conflict arises since the agent chooses the contract that maximizes his utility, passing himself off as some other type of agent if by so doing his own well-being is improved. *Private information distorts contracts since the agent attempts to take advantage of it.*

However, since the principal designs the optimal contract taking into account the asymmetry in information, the agent cannot always use private information to enhance his utility. Think about what happens under moral hazard. Because the agent prefers to slack rather than to work hard, and since effort cannot be allowed for in a contract, the principal offers a contract contingent upon the results. But it is a contract that gives the agent, in expected value, exactly his reservation utility, and so, in this case, the private information is clearly detrimental to the principal without being beneficial to the agent.

Situations in which the agent holds back private information before the contract is signed do not have the same properties as the preceding case. Take, for example, the classic agency relationship between a principal and an agent, as set out in Section 2 of Chapter 4 (the following arguments are equally valid if there is a continuum of possible agent types, as in section 4 of Chapter 4). In the contract menu offered by the principal, not all agent types receive, in expected value, their reservation utility, but rather some obtain informational income. The need to give incentives in order that no agent is interested in misrepresenting his type requires that the contract improves the average utility of those agents who are most likely to take advantage of the relationship. Therefore, the possibility of hiding information would, in this case, benefit the agents (or at least, some types of agent). The principal is undoubtedly worse off in this situation than if the information had been symmetric for two reasons: she must guarantee some agents greater expected utility than their reservation level, and in addition, the contracts must be distorted in order that the agents do not 'camouflage' themselves.

The agents are not always made better off by having more information than the principals. Sometimes they would prefer that this information be public. This occurs when, thanks to the principals competing intensely for agents, they manage to get all the surplus of the relationship (as occurred in the framework of Section 3, Chapter 4). Comparing the results under symmetric and asymmetric information, we concluded that while one type of agent is indifferent between both situations, the other type is strictly worse off since he cannot prove what type he is. Hence possessing private information, but being unable to make it public, in this case is harmful to the interests of the agents.[1]

[1] The conclusion is similar to that attained in a model with moral hazard in which the principals compete for the agent. In this case, given that the agent obtains all the surplus of the relationship, he gets greater utility when effort is a verifiable variable, and so having private information is to his detriment.

Summing up, asymmetric information always generates inefficiencies, because of the leeway that it gives to one of the contracting parts (the agent). However, having this leeway is not always interesting to the agent. We have seen circumstances in which the agent obtains the same expected utility with and without private information, circumstances in which having more information generated greater utility from the relationship, and cases in which the fact that the information is not public is harmful to the agent.

These arguments should allow us to understand better when and why an agent may be interested in signalling his characteristic (when and why a worker will want to study in order to prove his ability to learn). *An agent is never interested in revealing private information if he obtains greater utility by keeping it secret.* In the same way, he will also not want to signal the information if the signal is costly, and if the signalling act does not end up covering this cost. On the other hand, the agent will be interested in signalling his characteristic when making this information public makes him better off. Of all the frameworks studied up to now, we can only study the phenomenon of signalling in that in which the principals compete for agents.

Before continuing, we should clarify what a signal is, and what we understand by signalling. Consider the following situation. Once upon a time there was a kingdom ruled by a king who had a daughter but no sons. The king wanted his only daughter to marry a brave knight in order that the kingdom be properly defended once he left the throne. Of course, all the knights in the kingdom declared themselves to be brave, since they all wanted to become princes. Therefore the wise old king proposed a test: the knight that spent a night in a local haunted castle, occupied by evil ghosts and awful demons, would have the hand of the princess. The castle was so frightening that only one of the knights, Bruce the Bold, dared to sleep the night there. Hence he passed the king's test and was married to the princess, and they all lived happily ever after.

The fact that Bruce the Bold slept a night in the haunted castle is a signal of undoubted bravery. Why is it a signal? Because the 'cost' of the test to all non-brave knights is so high that they are not prepared to undertake it, even though they would get the prize if they did. However, the 'cost' to courageous knights, that is those who are not afraid of evil demons, is low, and so these knights are prepared to spend the night in the castle in order to win the prize. It is worth while to point out that the test does not make the knight that passes it any braver (this is not its objective). That is, Bruce the Bold is just as bold after having passed the test as he was before. Hence sleeping the night in the castle can be thought of as being unproductive or inefficient in the sense that had the king known that Bruce the Bold was the bravest knight in the kingdom, he would have selected him as son-in-law without requiring him to confront the haunted castle. However, since information as to Bruce's bravery was not public, the king had to devise the test in order that real brave knight signals himself as such.

The analysis developed by Spence has the same structure as the story of Bruce the Bold. Firms search for workers with an ability to learn, and in order to signal this ability, some potential workers spontaneously pass a test: they invest a few years studying, even if the courses taken are of no use at all to the firms.

Therefore a signal is some activity, or some decision, that proves that the agent concerned has a certain ability or characteristic, or possesses certain information, or in other words that the agent concerned belongs to a certain subset of the entire population. In order for the signal to be informative, only the agents that really are of the implied population group should be interested in carrying out the signalling activity (those that can really earn something by revealing their type).

Given the definition of a signal, it is easy to see that agents will only signal private information if their utility is greater when their characteristic is public information than when it is private information. Of the three frameworks analysed in Chapter 4, only that in which principals compete for agents can admit the possibility of signalling, and so in the following sections of this chapter this will be the framework used.

Our description of a signal as an activity intended only to transmit information, is in actual fact somewhat narrow. More correctly, in any relationship it is the case that, *whenever a participant who has private information takes a decision, this decision may reveal all or part of the information.* In order to see what we mean by this, we shall use a framework that is slightly different from those of the previous chapters. Take the following set-up.

Many relationships are characterized by the fact that the party that offers the contract, rather than the party contracted, is the owner of private information. In some cases, this informational problem is irrelevant. For example, if a firm has more information than a worker as to the value of final production, the worker's behaviour need not be affected. Therefore, the optimal contracts will not be distorted by this informational asymmetry. On the other hand, there are situations in which an informed principal can pose a serious problem. Think of a firm that has private information as to what the job will really cost the worker in effort terms. The worker will not accept the contract with a low wage if he is afraid that the job will be very arduous. The contract will eventually try to signal ('convince') the worker that the job is in fact easy, and so a low wage is justified.

Any contract offered by an informed party can be considered, in the broadest sense of the term, to be a signal. A firm that produces consumer goods will try to pass on information as to the quality of its products via its prices, or the guarantee included. The owner of a patent that offers licensing contracts signals the value of the patent through the terms of the technology transmission contract. In Section 5 we shall consider a model of this type of signal.

5.3 Education as a Signal

In this section we will develop an introductory example based on Spence (1973), in which education is used as a means of signalling good worker characteristics among candidates for some job.[2] We will do it briefly, as the following section will elaborate on the same arguments.

Assume that in the labour market there are two types of worker, those with 'good' productivity (equal to 2), and those with 'bad' productivity (equal to 1). When a firm contracts an agent, paying a wage of w, its profits will be either $2 - w$ or $1 - w$, depending on the type of agent hired. The problem is that the firms cannot distinguish the agent's type. If they could, given that they are competing intensely in the market, they would pay wages of either $w = 2$ or $w = 1$, according to the type of agent.

Before entering the labour market, all agents have the possibility of obtaining education (studying). We shall denote by y the time dedicated to education. Studying implies a cost to an agent, and this cost depends on the agent's type. In particular, the cost of y units of education is y for type-B agents, and $y/2$ for the type Gs. However, we assume that education has no effect on productivity.

To find an equilibrium in this signalling game, we will assume that the firms have certain initial beliefs as to the value of a worker's productivity, given educational level, and we shall see under what conditions these beliefs are self-confirmed by the different types of agents' behaviour. Let us suppose that the firms believe that a candidate is good if he has an education level $y \geq y^*$, and bad otherwise ($y < y^*$) for a certain y^*. With these beliefs, they are willing to offer the wage $w = 2$ if $y \geq y^*$, and $w = 1$ if $y < y^*$.

Given the wages on offer in the labour market, each type of agent will choose that level of education that maximizes his surplus. In any case, all agents will choose either $y = 0$ or $y = y^*$, since the signalling value of any $y \in (0, y^*)$ is the same as $y = 0$, but the cost is greater, and similarly for $y > y^*$ with respect to $y = y^*$. The firms' beliefs will be self-confirming in this market if type-G agents choose $y = y^*$, and type-B agents choose $y = 0$. The conditions that reflect these choices are:

[2] See also Riley (1979).

$$2-\frac{y^\star}{2}\geq 1-0 \quad \text{for } G$$

$$1-0\geq 2-y^\star \quad \text{for } B$$

that is:

$$1\leq y^\star \leq 2.$$

Hence so long as some education level between 1 and 2 is possible, there will exist an equilibrium under which each type of agent will choose different signalling behaviour. If a firm observes that a certain agent has education, it will believe that he is type-G, since only type-G agents have an incentive to become educated. On the contrary, a non-educated agent will be considered as a type-B agent, that is, as an agent whose cost of education is high. As is readily seen in the above condition, the signaling equilibrium education level is not unique. Any $y \in [1, 2]$ is fine as a signal of productivity. Hence there exist multiple equilibria. It is, however, more 'reasonable' that the cost of the signal be as low as possible, that is, $y^\star = 1$, since education has no other associated value. This equilibrium is called the *least-cost separating* equilibrium.

In the following section we will go further into the arguments that allow us to select this equilibrium as being the most reasonable. The same model that we have been using throughout the book will be used here as well.

5.4 The Agents Signal their Characteristic

We will consider the same situation as in Section 3, Chapter 4, that is, the agents (or at least, some of them) would like their private information to be public. Remember that we are assuming that there are two types of agent, good ones (G) whose probability of success is p^G, and bad ones (B) with probability $p^B < p^G$. The principal values the result at either Π_S or Π_F, depending on whether it was a success or a failure. There are many principals competing for the agents, and so they get zero expected profits while the agents are able to obtain all surplus from the relationship. In order for the situation to be reasonably simple, we shall assume that the probability that an agent be of type B is sufficiently high for there to exist a separating equilibrium under asymmetric information (i.e. we are always in the situation described by Figure 4.10).

Under symmetric information the agents get:

$$U^{G\star} = u\,(p^G\Pi_S + (1-p^G)\,\Pi_F)$$

and

$$U^{B\star} = u\,(p^B \Pi_S + (1 - p^B)\,\Pi_F)\,.$$

Denote $w^{G\star} = p^G \Pi_S + (1 - p^G)\,\Pi_F$ and $w^{B\star} = p^B \Pi_S + (1 - p^B)\,\Pi_F$, that is, $w^{G\star}$ and $w^{B\star}$ are the wages that the principals offer to the agents under symmetric information. On the other hand, if the information is not public, the agents' expected utilities are (as we saw in Chapter 4, Section 3)

$$\mathrm{E}U^G = p^G u\,(w_S^G) + (1 - p^G)\,u\,(w_F^G) < U^{G\star}$$

and

$$U^B = U^{B\star},$$

where the contract (w_S^G, w_F^G) is the optimal contract designed for agent G in an adverse selection situation, and the principal offers agent B the salary $w^B = w^{B\star}$.

Assume that the principals cannot distinguish agent types, and q is the probability that an agent is type G. However, in this model, before going to the market to contract with the principals, we assume that the agents can carry out another activity. In order not to introduce too many complications, we shall assume that it is an activity that is not beneficial to anyone, or in other words, neither principals nor agents derive utility directly from this activity (no one is really better off from Bruce the Bold having spent the night in the haunted castle). Following the idea of Spence (1973), we can interpret this activity as being education: before going to the job market, workers have the opportunity of attending a process of education (here understood as a waste).

More formally, let the agent decide how much time, t, he will spend at university before going to the job market. This t is observable by the principals.[3] The disutility of this education is given by $v^G\,(t)$ if the agent is type G, and $v^B\,(t)$ if he is type B. For simplification, assume that t can take two values, $t \in \{0, t'\}$, with $v^G\,(t') > v^G\,(0)$ and $v^B\,(t') > v^B\,(0)$. Furthermore, we lose no generality by normalizing so that $v^B\,(0) = v^G\,(0) = 0$ and from now on we use $v^G \equiv v^G\,(t')$, $v^B \equiv v^B\,(t')$.

Before describing the timing of the game, note that the decision taken with respect to t can eventually influence the principal's beliefs as to the type of agent with whom she is contracting. The principal's prior belief on the probability that an agent is type G is q, but once t has been observed, this probability belief may be revised. Call $q\,(t)$ the probability belief of the principal for the event that the agent is type G after observing the decision t. The timing of the game is summarized in Figure 5.1.

[3] Note that when the information arrives before the signing of the contract, a principal does not care if it is verifiable or only observable. She will offer a different contract to the agent, according to what is observed, even if she can't prove it.

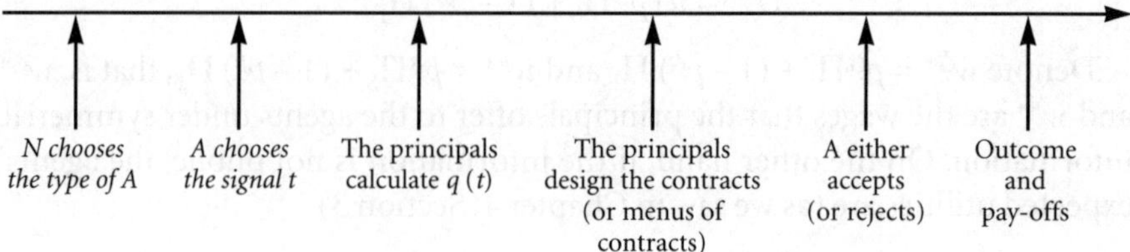

Fig. 5.1

To calculate $q(t)$, the principals apply Bayes's rule, bearing in mind the prior probability q and the agents' behaviour in equilibrium. This can be understood by considering the following two cases. First, assume that the agent always chooses the same value of t, independent of whether he is type G or B. In this case, observing t sheds no further light on an agent's type, since all types behave in the same way, and so $q(t) = q$. In this case the signal is not informative. Now consider the opposite case, when type-G agents choose $t = t'$, and type-B agents choose $t = 0$. Now when the principal observes t', she knows that the signal could not come from a type B agent, and so sets $q(t') = 1$. In the same way, $q(0) = 0$. In this case the signal is informative. The first case is known as a *pooling equilibrium* (since both agent types are pooled at the same decision), while the second case is known as a *separating equilibrium.*

In order to even speak about equilibrium, we must ensure ourselves that the agents are taking the best decision for themselves. In particular, if we are in a pooling equilibrium, no agent can be interested in deviating from this equilibrium, whatever his type. If we are in a separating equilibrium, no B agent can be interested in taking a type-G decision, and vice versa. And in order to know when an agent would be interested in deviating, we need to know what the principals will think of any particular message, that is, we need to identify $q(t)$ for any possible t (even if some t is not an equilibrium). We are using the logic of *perfect Bayesian equilibrium*, and this is the equilibrium idea that we will apply. This notion implies, first, that each participant is taking the optimal decision for him at any time in which he may play, and second, that the probabilities (the 'beliefs') $q(t)$ must be calculated using the Bayes's rule given the agent's strategy.

One frequent problem is that there are several possible equilibria. However, some of them are not very reasonable, and will be eliminated. We shall concentrate on two equilibrium possibilities, a separating and a pooling equilibrium, and we shall see when these are 'reasonable'. As will become increasingly clear, the difficulty of the analysis is in the construction of the beliefs $q(t)$ that a principal forms as to agent type, once the message t has been sent.

5.4.1 Separating equilibria

The idea that a signal can be informative as to an agent's type depends on the fact that the principal will form different beliefs with regard to the agent according to which signal is sent. Spence proposed the following logic: assume that the principals think that an agent is type G if they observe $t = t'$, and type B if $t = 0$. That is,

$$q(t') = 1, \quad q(0) = 0.$$

If this is correct, then the principals will offer wages of (they are equal to the perfect information wages since given t they are certain of the agent's type):

$$w(t) = \begin{cases} w^{G*} & \text{if } t = t' \\ w^{B*} & \text{if } t = 0. \end{cases}$$

The utility that the agents get in this market is therefore equal to,

$$U^{G*} \quad \text{if } t = t'$$

$$U^{B*} \quad \text{if } t = 0,$$

independent of type (since wages do not depend on the result). For this to be an equilibrium situation, the agent's behaviour must confirm the principal's expectations, or in other words, no type-G agent is ever interested in sending a signal $t = 0$, and no type B is interested in sending a signal $t = t'$. Hence the conditions for this reasoning to lead to an equilibrium are:

$$U^{G*} - v^G \geq U^{B*} \quad \text{for the type } G,$$

and

$$U^{B*} \geq U^{G*} - v^B \quad \text{for the type } B.$$

These conditions can be rewritten as:

$$v^G \leq U^{G*} - U^{B*}, \tag{5.1}$$

$$v^B \geq U^{G*} - U^{B*}. \tag{5.2}$$

Result 5.1. A necessary condition for the beliefs $\{q(t') = 1, q(0) = 0\}$ to form an equilibrium is $v^G \leq v^B$.[4]

[4] The fact that the cost of the signal decreases with the agent's productivity (his type) is the Spence–Mirrlees condition. In signalling games, the single-crossing condition plays the same role as in Adverse Selection models. For more details, see Sect. 4 and complement 1 in Ch. 3.

The proof follows immediately from equations (5.1) and (5.2).

Result 5.1 tells us that $v^G \leq v^B$ is a necessary condition for a situation in which type-G agents choosing $t = t'$ and type-B agents choosing $t = 0$, to be an equilibrium. The condition is that the signal must be less costly the better is the agent. However, this condition is not sufficient. It is not enough that the signal t' be more costly to agents of type-B than to agents of type G. It must be sufficiently costly to type Bs for them not to send the message t', but it must be sufficiently cheap for type Gs for the cost of the signal to be less than the utility gain from sending it. Hence the conditions (5.1) and (5.2) that we obtained above are sufficient, as is shown in result 5.2.

Result 5.2. If the signal t' satisfies conditions (5.1) and (5.2), then there exists a perfect Bayesian equilibrium in which:

(i) the agent chooses $t = t'$ if he is type G and the agent chooses $t = 0$ if he is type B;

(ii) the principals have beliefs $q(t') = 1, q(0) = 0$;

(iii) the wages offered are $w(t') = w^{G*}$ and $w(0) = w^{B*}$.

Proof. The proof of this result is not difficult, but we must take care in that we do it 'backwards', and taking into account the participants' believes. We then apply the concept of perfect Bayesian equilibrium, analysing first (iii), then (ii), and finally (i). In other words, the later an action happens (see Figure 5.1 for the time line of the game), the earlier we should analyse it.

If the principals' beliefs are $q(t') = 1, q(0) = 0$, then when they observe t' they are sure that the agent is type G, and when they observe $t = 0$ they are sure he is type B. Therefore, the situation is similar to one of symmetric information. In a symmetric information situation, Section 3 of Chapter 4 showed that the equilibrium wages are precisely $w(t') = w^{G*}$ and $w(0) = w^{B*}$. Hence (iii) is an equilibrium since it is an optimal decision.

We now analyse how these beliefs are formed, that is, (ii). Clearly, if the agent chooses $t = t'$ so long as he is type G, and $t = 0$ so long as he is type B, then the principals' beliefs must be $q(t') = 1$ and $q(0) = 0$.

Lastly, we have seen that when the contracts are the same as under symmetric information, the conditions for a type-G agent not to send the signal $t = 0$, and for a type-B agent not to send the signal $t = t'$, are precisely (5.1) and (5.2). Hence when these two conditions are satisfied, and the wages offered are those defined in (iii), then the best that type-G agents can do is $t = t'$, while the best strategy for the type-Bs is $t = 0$. We have now proven that (i) forms a part of the perfect Bayesian equilibrium. *Q.E.D.*

Result 5.2 shows that it can be perfectly rational for an agent to spend resources on an activity that is apparently uninteresting both to him and to the principal (as destroying money, or burning his vessels). The fact that the activity has a different cost for different agents is what makes doing it useful.

Note that we have analysed the possibility of the separating equilibrium in which good agents signal their characteristic, that is, $q(t') = 1$ and $q(0) = 0$. It is easy to see that the other possibility, in which bad agents get educated while good agents do not, cannot constitute an equilibrium. Bad agents would have no interest in paying the cost of education in order to be identified as being bad! We do not enter into details now. Result 5.6 will properly prove this statement for a similar model.

5.4.2 Pooling equilibria

We now go on to consider when we may find ourselves in an equilibrium situation in which both agent types send the same signal (and hence the signal is not informative at all). This type of situation is known as a pooling equilibrium.

The first thing to note is that in a pooling equilibrium, since the signal is not informative, the principals find themselves in exactly the same situation as classic adverse selection (as discussed in Section 3, Chapter 4), and so $q(t) = q$ for the signal that all the agents send. Hence in a pooling equilibrium, the principals will offer the agents a contract menu that gives them utilities $(\mathrm{E}U^G, U^{B*})$ respectively.

A first conclusion of the analysis is the following: if the agent sends the same signal independent of his type, the signal must be $t = 0$. A situation in which both types of agent send the signal $t = t'$ cannot be optimal for the type-B agent. Effectively, if $q(t') = q$, a type-B agent will always decide to deviate and send the signal $t = 0$: he loses nothing by doing so, since the least he can get by deviating is U^{B*}, which is the same that he receives in the pooling equilibrium, and he will save v^B. Given this, we shall only study pooling equilibria with $t = 0$.

As before, in order to analyse the agents' behaviour, we need to describe the principals' beliefs according to the different signals that can be sent. It is always possible that the principals form beliefs that lead to a pooling equilibrium. Result 5.3 describes a simple pooling equilibrium, although other pooling equilibria exist.

Result 5.3. The following strategies form a perfect Bayesian (pooling) equilibrium:

(i) the agent chooses $t = 0$, independent of his type;
(ii) the principals' beliefs are $q(0) = q$, $q(t') = 0$;
(iii) the wages offered are:

$$\text{the menu } \{ (w_S^G, w_F^G), w^{B\star} \} \qquad \text{if } t = 0,$$

$$\text{the wage } w^{B\star} \qquad \text{if } t = t'.$$

Proof. Given subgame perfection, we will firstly analyse stage (iii), then (ii), and finally (i). We have seen that if the signal $t = 0$ does not change the principals' beliefs, i.e. if $q(0) = q$, then the final equilibrium must include the menu $\{(w_S^G, w_F^G), w^{B\star}\}$ when the signal $t = 0$ is received. On the other hand, if the signal t' is observed, and if this leads the principals to conclude that the agent is type B, i.e. $q(t') = 0$, then the equilibrium will lead them to offer the symmetric information optimal contract for type-B agents: $w = w^{B\star}$.

We shall now see that the beliefs defined in point (ii) are Bayesian. First, if both agent types choose $t = 0$, the signal is uninformative and so it must be that $q(0) = q$. Secondly, since in equilibrium, no agent will choose t' there is no restriction on what the principals can think if t' is observed. Any belief is possible, since in equilibrium, t' never happens. In particular, $q(t') = 0$ is Bayesian.

Finally, given the contracts that the principals will offer according to the signal, neither type of agent is interested in choosing $t = t'$. To send the signal $t = t'$, the signalling cost must be paid, and this is strictly positive for both types of agent, but the signal $t = t'$ will lead to a lower (for type G) or equal (type B) wage as would be received by choosing the signal $t = 0$. *Q.E.D.*

Therefore, a pooling equilibrium always exists. However, it is important to note that this equilibrium is upheld by the principals' beliefs. In particular, the principals believe that if some agent chooses $t = t'$ (deviation from equilibrium), then he must be type B (since we have assumed that $q(t') = 0$). Are these beliefs with respect to which agent type deviates with $t = t'$ reasonable? In some circumstances these beliefs are not too reasonable, or we could say they are not '*intuitive*'. In order to explain this statement, think about what are the incentives of the agents to deviate from the proposed equilibrium. Let's start with the type-B agents.

Imagine the most optimistic agent possible: he believes that if he deviates he will trick the principals into thinking he is type G, and he will be guaranteed an expected utility of $U^{G\star}$ (no principal will pay more than $w^{G\star}$ to any agent, and so $U^{G\star}$ is the true maximum that an agent can earn). For this optimistic type-B agent, deviation by choosing t' is interesting if:

$$U^{G\star} - v^B > U^{B\star}.$$

We can be sure that no type-B agent will deviate if

$$v^B \geq U^{G\star} - U^{B\star}. \tag{5.2}$$

On the other hand, an optimistic type-G agent (that is one who thinks that by deviating he will identify himself as a good agent, and so will receive $U^{G\star}$) is interested in choosing t' if:

$$U^{G*} - v^G > \text{E}U^G,$$

that is if:

$$v^G < U^{G*} - \text{E}U^G. \tag{5.3}$$

Let's assume now that conditions (5.2) and (5.3) are satisfied. Given (5.2), the principals know that no type-B agent is interested in deviating, independently of the principals' beliefs, $q\,(t')$. On the other hand, type-G agents will change their signal if they can expect to receive U^{G*}, which is to say, $q\,(t') = 1$. What will the principals make of a signal of $t = t'$? Probably that it is a type-G agent. Hence $q\,(t') = 1$ and offering the wage w^{G*} if $t = t'$ would appear 'reasonable'. However, in this case the type-G agents will indeed want to choose the signal t'.

What we have explained is that, if (5.2) and (5.3) are satisfied, no beliefs apart from $q\,(t') = 1$ seem to be reasonable. In particular, the beliefs of result 5.3 would appear to be unreasonable if (5.2) and (5.3) are satisfied. The criterion that we have used to eliminate unreasonable beliefs is known as the '*intuitive criterion*' as defined by Cho and Kreps (1987). In complement 1 we will give a more formal definition of this criterion.

Result 5.4. The equilibria described in result 5.3 overcome the intuitive criterion if either (5.2) or (5.3) is not satisfied.

Result 5.4 identifies the condition under which a pooling equilibrium exists, and the intuitive criterion is satisfied in which no agent type is interested in sending a costly signal before entering into a contractual relationship with the principal. If (5.2) and (5.3) are both satisfied, then no pooling equilibrium exists such that the intuitive criterion is satisfied in this market.[5]

5.4.3 Conclusion

We shall conclude this section by considering which equilibria should be found in the framework that we are considering. In particular, we shall be concerned with equilibria that satisfy the intuitive criterion, since they seem to be more 'reasonable' than those that do not satisfy the criteria. On the other hand, this does not present any important problem since there will always exist an equilibrium that satisfies the intuitive criterion.

[5] Note that when either (5.2) or (5.3) is not satisfied (that is, when we are in the framework of result 5.4), we can find pooling equilibria that satisfy the intuitive criterion in which the principals' beliefs are different to $q\,(t') = 0$; e.g., we could think of beliefs such that $q\,(t') = 1$. For this to occur, more stringent conditions must be satisfied. We will limit ourselves to saying that the situation is more favourable to the existence of pooling equilibria if $q\,(t') = 0$, and we shall not study in any greater detail the conditions of the other cases.

Before establishing result 5.5, which is the summary of results 5.2 and 5.4, we should note that equation (5.3) is stronger than (5.1). Since $U^{B*} < \mathrm{E}U^G$, we have:

$$U^{G*} - \mathrm{E}U^G < U^{G*} - U^{B*}.$$

Hence if v^G satisfies condition (5.3), then it will also satisfy (5.1).

Result 5.5. In the proposed market, there will always exist an equilibrium that satisfies the intuitive criterion:

(*a*) Consider the situation in which both (5.2) and (5.3) are satisfied, that is, $v^B \geq U^{G*} - U^{B*}$ and $v^G < U^{G*} - \mathrm{E}U^G$. Then a separating equilibrium exists, but no pooling equilibrium exists.

(*b*) If the parameters satisfy (5.1) and (5.2), but not (5.3), that is, $v^B \geq U^{G*} - U^{B*}$ and $v^G \in [U^{G*} - \mathrm{E}U^G, U^{G*} - U^{B*}]$, then both separating and pooling equilibria exist.

(*c*) Finally, in a situation in which either (5.2) or (5.1) is not satisfied, that is, either $v^B < U^{G*} - U^{B*}$, or $v^G \geq U^{G*} - U^{B*}$, then a pooling equilibrium exists, but no separating equilibrium exists.

We can interpret result 5.5 in the following manner. First, case (*a*), if the cost of sending the signal is low for agents of type *G*, but high for agents of type *B*, then only the best agents (*G*) will be interested in sending the signal, and so the principals will conclude that an agent who sends the signal is type *G*. Hence the equilibrium is separating. Secondly, case (*c*), when the cost of the signal is low for bad agents, the principals will not know if a signal has come from a good or a bad agent, and so they may decide to pay a low wage, so that no one is interested in sending the signal (it is not logical that the king, in order to find a future prince, proposes a test that all could pass). The equilibrium in this case will be pooling, in the same way that it will always be pooling when the cost of the signal is so high that even the good agents are not interested in sending it (if, in the test to marry the princess, the candidate had a 90 per cent chance of heart attack, even if he were brave, no one would be interested in passing the test). Finally, case (*b*), there is both separating and pooling equilibria when the cost of the signal is high for type-*B* agents and not too high for the type *G*s (sufficiently high for them not to want to deviate from a pooling equilibrium, but sufficiently low for them to send the signal in a separating equilibrium).

A pooling equilibrium is a situation in which the agents have the possibility to send signals, but they don't do it. In this sense, it is as if the signalling activity did not exist. In the end, the result obtained is exactly the same as that of pure adverse selection. On the other hand, *when a separating equilibrium emerges, then skilled agents have to pay a signalling cost for the problem to be transformed from one of adverse selection to one of symmetric information.* The fact that final contracts are the same as in the symmetric information situation is good from the point of view of efficiency, and so it is also good for the agents (since in this framework, they receive all the surplus from the relationship). However, in order to obtain this gain, they have had to pay the cost of the signal. In equilibrium, the good agents must pay v^G, which is a payment that benefits no one. In a separating equilibrium, it is worth while for good agents to signal their characteristics because the benefits of information diffusion are greater for them than the cost of the signal. The trade-off between the optimality of the contract and the signalling cost makes the welfare effect of signalling ambiguous. One can find situations where pooling is better for all types of agents than separation.

5.5 The Informational Power of Contracts

In Section 2 of this chapter we argued that whenever a participant with private information takes a decision, this decision may signal his private information. For example, if a seller has more information than a buyer as to the quality of the good she is transacting, the seller's decisions as to price, advertising, guarantees, etc. can signal to the buyer that the good is of high or shoddy quality. In the same way, the financial decisions of the managers of a firm can transmit to the market, or to banks, information relevant to the true value of the firm.

In the model that we have been using throughout this book, the simplest way of introducing the signalling effect of contracts is the following. Assume that the principal is risk-neutral, while the agent may be risk-averse or neutral. The principal has private information relevant to the type of job being offered to the agent. There are two possibilities that the agent cannot distinguish: either the job is easy and productivity is low, or the job is arduous although productivity is higher. In the first case, the profit and utility functions are written as:

$$B^1(w, e) = \Pi(e) - w$$

$$U^1(w, e) = u(w) - v(e),$$

while in the second possible situation we have:

$$B^k(w, e) = k\Pi(e) - w$$

$$U^k(w, e) = u(w) - k\,v(e),$$

where $k > 1$. The agent's reservation utility is $\underline{U}$.

A contract is a pair (w, e).[6] This means that effort is an observable variable, although the implied disutility is not. A businessman, for example, may establish a contract with an agent for a fixed number of hours, without specifying whether the job is arduous or not. When the difficulty of the job is information private to the businessman, an important problem arises in that the worker values both the hours worked (represented by the variable e) and the difficulty of the job (which is greater if the disutility of effort is multiplied by the parameter k).

In order to analyse the distortion produced by the informational asymmetry, and given that this model is somewhat different from those seen up to now, we will first consider what would happen if the information were symmetric.

5.5.1 Symmetric information

Call $C^{1*} \equiv (w^{1*}, e^{1*})$ and $C^{k*} \equiv (w^{k*}, e^{k*})$ the optimal symmetric information contracts. They are the respective solutions to the following constrained maximization problems:

$$\max_{(w,e)} \quad \Pi(e) - w$$
$$\text{s.t.} \quad u(w) - v(e) \geq \underline{U},$$

and

$$\max_{(w,e)} \quad k\Pi(e) - w$$
$$\text{s.t.} \quad u(w) - kv(e) \geq \underline{U}.$$

These two problems are similar to others that we have seen in this book. The equations that characterize the optimal contracts are:[7]

$$u(w^1) - v(e^1) = \underline{U} \tag{5.4}$$

$$\frac{\Pi'(e^1)}{v'(e^1)} = \frac{1}{u'(w^1)} \tag{5.5}$$

and

[6] See advanced theme 5C.3 of this chapter for a more complete analysis of the optimal contract format for this framework.

[7] Equation (5.5) is common to both contracts since we have assumed that the increase in the job's 'difficulty' in effort terms translates into an equivalent increase in productivity. If the effect on $v(e)$ were different to the effect on $\Pi(e)$, the conclusions would be similar, but the analysis would be more complicated.

$$u(w^k) - k\,v(e^k) = \underline{U} \qquad (5.6)$$

$$\frac{\Pi'(e^k)}{v'(e^k)} = \frac{1}{u'(w^k)}.$$

Graphically, the location of the contracts is shown in Figure 5.2. Note that the iso-profit curves of a type-*k* principal are more horizontal than those of a type-1 principal: type-*k* principals are willing to increase wages more in order to obtain a given increase in effort. Note also that the iso-utility curves of the agent are geometrically lower, and flatter the greater is *k*.

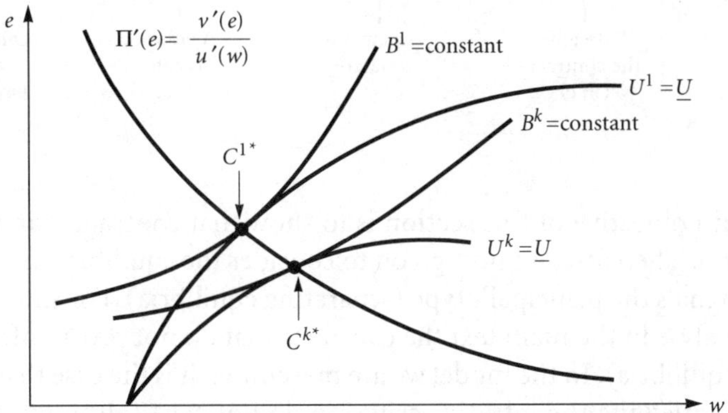

Fig. 5.2

Although an increase in effort is more beneficial to a type-*k* principal, the fact that she must pay a greater wage ($k\,v(e) > v(e)$) implies that the optimal contracts C^{1*} and C^{k*} satisfy the following relationship:

$$e^{k*} < e^{1*} \quad \text{and} \quad w^{k*} > w^{1*}.$$

5.5.2 The agent is uninformed as to the difficulty of the job

The contracts $C^{1*}$and C^{k*} are no longer a valid offer if there is no way in which the agent can acquire the information relating to his disutility of effort before signing the contract. For both types of principal, C^{1*} is strictly preferred to C^{k*}: they get greater effort at a lower wage. A type-*k* principal is therefore interested in passing herself off as type 1, in order to pay less for greater effort. If an agent receives the offer C^{1*}, he knows that it may have come from either type of principal, and so he will not accept it.

In the same way as in the model analysed in the previous section, the beliefs that the uninformed party has over the informed party's type become very important in this model, once the informed party has carried out an action. For the case at hand, the action of the informed party is the contract offered. This action, as we shall see, can reveal information. To make this even clearer, we will describe the time-line of the game. Let q stand for the agent's prior probability that the principal is type 1, so that $(1 - q)$ is the prior for the principal being type k. Denote by $q\,(w, e)$ the agent's posterior probability that the principal is type 1 once the contract (w, e) has been offered. Figure 5.3 summarizes the timing of the relationship.

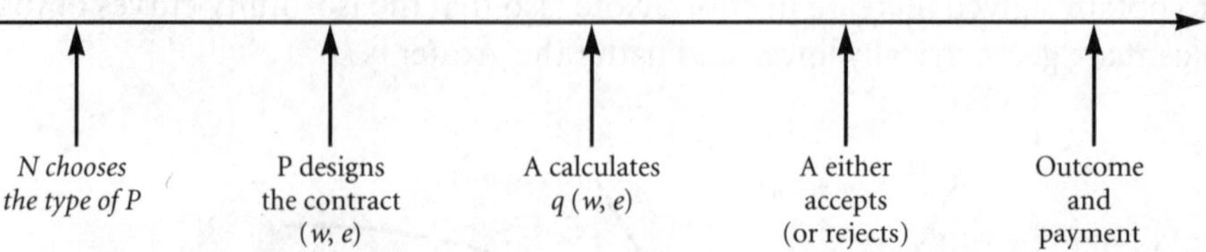

Fig. 5.3

The main objective of this section is to show that contracts can transmit information. Therefore, we now go on to consider the equilibria in which the contract signals the principal's type (separating equilibria). For simplicity, we will not analyse in the main text the contracts that do not reveal information (pooling equilibria). In the model we are presenting, it is the case that pooling equilibria satisfying the intuitive criterion do not exist (although there are models in which there are pooling equilibria satisfying this criterion). Exercise 10 asks the reader to prove this point graphically.

5.5.3 Separating equilibria

A separating equilibrium is one in which the contract offered perfectly identifies the principal's type. This means that, in equilibrium, the agent can receive two offers, denoted by $C^1 \equiv (w^1, e^1)$ and $C^k \equiv (w^k, e^k)$, according to the principal being of type 1 or type k respectively. The agent has beliefs $q\,(C^1) = 1$, $q\,(C^k) = 0$, since when he is offered C^1 he is sure that the offer is for an easy job, while an offer of C^k is taken to be for an arduous job. Therefore, in order for these contracts to form an equilibrium, each type of principal must be interested in offering only that contract that the equilibrium assigns her, rather that attempting to pass herself of as the other type.

In the present model, the only type of principal that is interested in 'disguising' herself is the type k (since she induces greater disutility of effort). Therefore, the principal who needs to signal herself is the type 1, in order that the agent does not confuse her with a type k (since this would require a higher wage). Besides, the type-1 principal's need to signal that she is offering the easy job does not distort the contract offered in equilibrium by the principal with the arduous job. This is the message of result 5.6.

Result 5.6. In a perfect Bayesian separating equilibrium $\{C^1, C^k\} \equiv \{(w^1, e^1), (w^k, e^k)\}$, it must always be true that $C^k = C^{k*}$, that is to say,

$$(w^k, e^k) = (w^{k*}, e^{k*}).$$

Proof. To prove this result we will show that there cannot exist a perfect separating equilibrium $\{C^1, C^k\}$ with $C^k \neq C^{k*}$. If such an equilibrium did exist, it would have to be true that $q\,(C^k) = 0$ since, in this equilibrium, a type-1 principal never offers C^k (the equilibrium separates the two principal types). This means that, in order for the agent to accept the contract, knowing that the job is arduous, he must receive his reservation utility. Hence the following condition must be satisfied:

$$u\,(w^k) - k\,v\,(e^k) \geq \underline{U}.$$

Now, any contract that satisfies this condition and that is not C^{k*} will give the principal profits strictly lower than those of C^{k*} (bear in mind that C^{k*} is the only contract that maximizes the principal's profits, under the agent's participation condition). The principal has incentives to deviate from (w^k, e^k) by choosing C^{k*} whenever she can be sure that the agent will accept C^{k*}. This will depend, in principle, on the agent's beliefs $q\,(C^{k*})$, or in other words, what the agent thinks when he is offered C^{k*}. We shall prove that independent of $q\,(C^{k*})$, the agent is interested in accepting the contract. Note that the greater is $q\,(C^{k*})$, the greater is the agent's expected utility, since the probability that disutility is $v\,(e)$ instead of $k\,v\,(e)$ is greater. Hence the worst of all possibilities is $q\,(C^{k*}) = 0$. However, even in this case the agent is interested in accepting the contract since his utility, given that he is sure that his principal is type k is:

$$u\,(w^{k*}) - k\,v\,(e^{k*}) = \underline{U}.$$

Therefore if the principal deviates from C^k by choosing C^{k*} she obtains greater profits, and can be sure that the agent will accept the contract. In this way $C^k \neq C^{k*}$ cannot form a part of a perfect separating equilibrium (since the principal would be interested in deviating if she is type k). *Q.E.D.*

(The fact that, in a separating equilibrium, the contract offered by the party who is interested in disguising himself coincides with his symmetric information contract is a common characteristic of this type of model. As an example of this result, see application 2 of this chapter.)

Once the type-k principal's contract has been identified, we are interested in the restrictions that must satisfy $C^1 \equiv (w^1, e^1)$ in order to form a part of the separating equilibrium. First, it must be a contract that the agent wants to accept when $q\,(C^1) = 1$, which is to say:

$$u(w^1) - v(e^1) \geq \underline{U}. \tag{5.7}$$

Secondly, it cannot be a contract that appeals to a type-k principal. The profits of this type of principal must be at least as great from offering the contract that the equilibrium demands of her. This condition can be written as:

$$k\Pi(e^{k*}) - w^{k*} \geq k\Pi(e^1) - w^1. \tag{5.8}$$

In words, condition (5.8) says that a type-k principal earns more from offering C^{k*} than from offering C^1.

Finally, the type-1 principal must prefer this contract to C^{k*}. In other words, she cannot be interested in passing herself off as a type-k principal:

$$\Pi(e^1) - w^1 \geq \Pi(e^{k*}) - w^{k*}. \tag{5.9}$$

Graphically, the set of admissible contracts corresponds to the shaded zone Z in Figure 5.4. Note that geometrically higher iso-profit curves correspond to greater profit levels, while the opposite is true of the iso-utility curves. In order to satisfy (5.7), the contract must be located below the curve $U^1 = \underline{U}$. On the other hand, condition (5.8) requires that C^1 be below the type-k principal's iso-profit curve that passes through C^{k*}, B^k = constant. Lastly, the contract is above B^1 = constant when (5.9) is satisfied.

We now go on to characterize the contracts $C^1 \equiv (w^1, e^1)$ that can form a part of a perfect Bayesian equilibrium. Besides the participation condition, (5.7), and the incentive compatibility conditions, (5.8) and (5.9), we also require that all participants are maximizing, and we must describe the agents' beliefs. There are really many contracts that can form a part of an equilibrium. However, not all the contracts situated in zone Z of Figure 5.4 are candidates to be a separating equilibrium. Note that a part of Z is below the curve $U^k = \underline{U}$, which means that they are contracts that give the agent greater utility than $\underline{U}$, even if the job

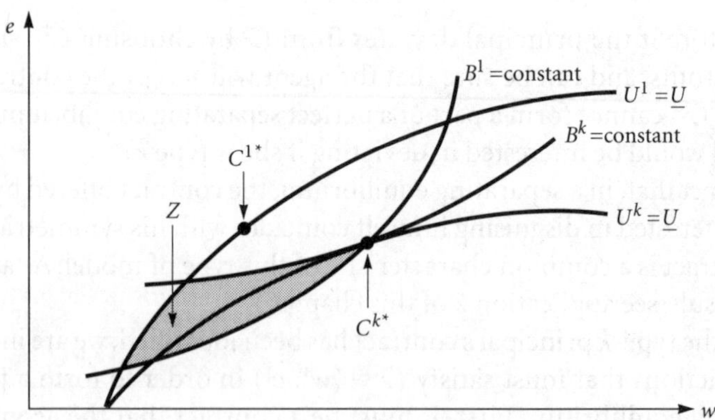

Fig. 5.4

is arduous. These contracts will be accepted by the agent in all cases (i.e. for any belief). The principal will choose that contract among these that gives her the greatest profit, from which the rest are never optimal. The upshot of this is that there is a part of Z that is irrelevant.

Result 5.7 describes the possible perfect Bayesian equilibria, while the shaded zone of Figure 5.5 shows the set of contracts C^1 that are candidates to form a part of such an equilibrium. In order to introduce the result and the figure, we shall formalize the above argument on the irrelevant part of Z. Denote by B' the maximum profits that a type-1 principal can achieve when the agent believes that she is type k. That is, B' is the profit of a pessimistic type-1 principal, since the agent is more reluctant to accept the contract the greater is the probability assigned to the principal being type k. In this case, we are thinking of the worst situation for the principal.

$$\mathrm{B}' = \underset{(w,e)}{\mathrm{Max}} \;\; \Pi(e) - w$$
$$\text{s.t.} \;\; u(w) - kv(e) \geq \underline{U}.$$

Consider the class of contracts (w^1, e^1) that guarantee a type-1 principal profits of at least B':

$$\Pi(e^1) - w^1 \geq B'. \tag{5.10}$$

Since, in particular, (e^{k*}, w^{k*}) satisfies $u(w^{k*}) - k\,v(e^{k*}) \geq \underline{U}$, we know that $B' \geq \Pi(e^{k*}) - w^{k*}$, and so equation (5.10) implies (5.9).

Recall that, since we want equilibrium to be Bayesian, we require that Bayes's rule be applied to update beliefs referring to contracts that are signed in equilibrium. (Bayes's rule says nothing about out of equilibrium beliefs.)

Result 5.7. Consider a contract $C^1 \equiv (w^1, e^1)$ that satisfies equations (5.7), (5.8), and (5.10). Then the following strategies and beliefs are a perfect Bayesian equilibrium:

(i) The principal chooses C^1 if she is type 1
The principal chooses C^{k*} if she is type k.

(ii) $q(C^1) = 1$
$q(C^{k*}) = 0$
$q(w, e) = 0$ if $(w, e) \neq C^1$ and $(w, e) \neq C^{k*}$.

(iii) The agent accepts both contracts C^1 and C^{k*}. He also accepts any other (w, e) such that $u(w) - k\,v(e) \geq \underline{U}$. He rejects all other contracts.

(The first two conditions of (ii) are to fulfil the requirement that beliefs be Bayesian, given the principal's behaviour in (i), while (iii) ensures that the agent will accept those contracts that guarantee him more than U, given his beliefs (ii)).

Proof. Since we are analysing perfect equilibria, we shall begin with the last stage. For those contracts (w, e) for which $q(w, e) = 0$, the agent is interested in accepting if he gets utility greater than $\underline{U}$ (or in other words, when $u(w) - k\,v(e) \geq U$). It is also optimal to accept C^{k*}, which gives utility equal to $\underline{U}$. finally, if $q(C^1) = 1$ then he gets at least $\underline{U}$ with C^1, since it is below the curve $U^1 = \underline{U}$ (by (5.7)).

With respect to (ii), we must show that the beliefs are Bayesian. This is trivial, since Bayes requires that if only type-1 principals choose C^1 then $q(C^1) = 1$; and if only type k principals offer C^{k*}, then $q(C^{k*}) = 0$. For all other contracts, Bayes does not impose any restrictions. In particular, $q(w, e) = 0$ is possible.

Finally, we will analyse (i). First, a type-1 principal will prefer C^1 to C^{k*}, since it gives greater profits (since C^1 satisfies (5.9)). Aside from this, she prefers C^1 to all other contracts that the agent would accept, since the agent only accepts contracts for which $u(w) - k\,v(e) \geq \underline{U}$, and the maximum that the principal can get from these is B', while (5.10) assures us that C^1 guarantees at least B'. On the other hand, a type-k principal prefers C^{k*} to C^1, given (5.8). In the same way as above, among all the contracts that satisfy $u(w) - k\,v(e) \geq \underline{U}$ (which are all the contracts that the agent will accept in (iii)), the type-k principal maximizes with C^{k*}. *Q.E.D.*

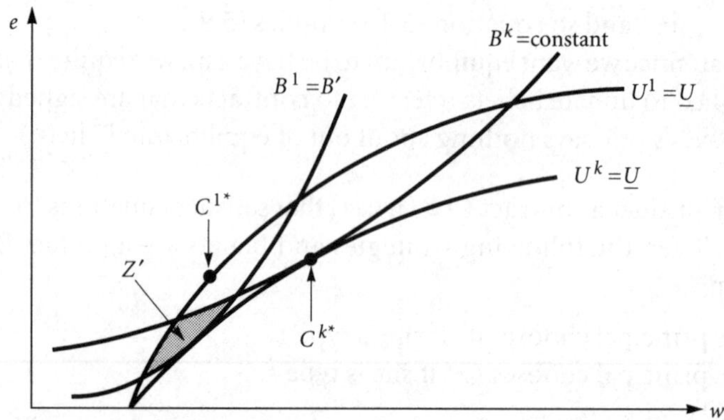

Fig. 5.5

Hence there are many contracts (w^1, e^1) that could form a part of a perfect Bayesian equilibrium (all the contracts in the zone Z' in Figure 5.5). However, they all share certain common characteristics:

$$w^1 < w^{k*} \text{ and } e^1 < e^{k*}.$$

That is, the only way in which a type-1 principal can convince the agent that she really is type 1 consists in making him see that she is less interested in effort than a type-k principal. Hence she demands less effort than e^{k*} and pays a wage lower than w^{k*}. The wage difference is sufficiently small for a type-k principal to prefer e^{k*} to e^1, but it is sufficiently large for a type-1 principal to prefer e^1 (recall that the agent's effort is more productive for a type-k principal).

What of the agent's utility? Does he get greater utility thanks to the asymmetric information? In the zone Z', there are contracts for which the agent gets exactly $\underline{U}$ (those that satisfy equation (5.7), or in other words, those that are on the curve $U^1 = \underline{U}$), but there are others for which he gets greater utility (those that are strictly below the curve $U^1 = \underline{U}$). However, if we refine a little more by eliminating some of the possible equilibria for being based on 'unreasonable' beliefs for the deviation case, then we arrive at a clearer conclusion. In particular, if we apply the intuitive criterion of Cho and Kreps as in the previous section, only one separating equilibrium remains. The following result identifies this equilibrium and proposes a proof, not altogether rigorous, but at least intuitive, of the reasons for which this contract is the most 'reasonable'.

Result 5.8. Let $C^{1**} \equiv (w^1, e^1)$ be the contract defined by the following two equations:

$$u(w^1) - v(e^1) = \underline{U} \qquad (5.7')$$

$$k\Pi(e^{k*}) - w^{k*} = k\Pi(e^1) - w^1. \qquad (5.8')$$

The contract thus defined is the only one for which the beliefs defined in part (ii) of result 5.7 satisfy the intuitive criterion.

Proof. The reason why C^{1**} is the only contract that satisfies the intuitive criterion is linked to the fact that C^{1**} is the contract in Z' that maximizes the profits of a type-1 principal (graphically, this is true since the slope of the iso-profit curves $B^1 =$ constant is greater than that of $B^k =$ constant, while it is less than the slope of the iso-utility curve $U^1 = \underline{U}$ up to the point C^{1*}). Given that C^{1**} maximizes B^1 in Z', why do other equilibria (w, e) exist? The answer is that at these other equilibria we are assuming that $q(C^{1**}) = 0$, from which if the principal chooses C^{1**} the agent will not accept the contract since he believes that the principal offering it is type k. Is it reasonable that $q(C^{1**}) = 0$ in an equilibrium in which a type-k principal chooses C^{k*}? The intuitive criterion says that this is not reasonable. The reason why is that a type-k principal is not interested in offering C^{1**} instead of C^{k*}, independent of the agent's beliefs. On the other hand, a type-1 principal gets greater profits from C^{1**} than from any other contract in Z'. If the agent observes that someone has deviated from the equilibrium contract, it is 'reasonable' that he thinks it was a type-1 principal, from which $q(C^{1**})$ must equal 1, and it is not 'intuitive' that $q(C^{1**})= 0$.

Q.E.D.

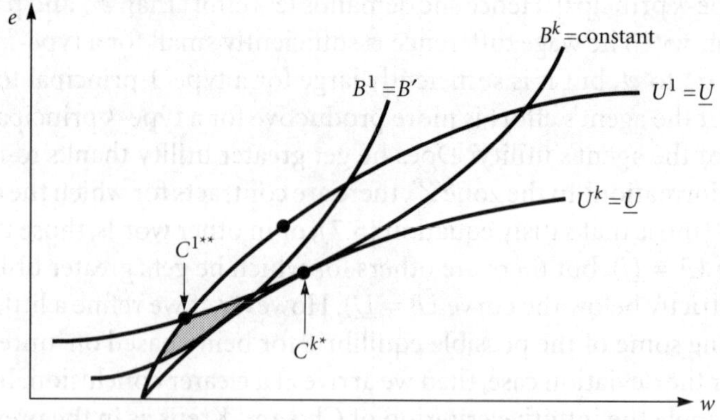

Fig. 5.6

In order to interpret result 5.8 (shown in Figure 5.6), imagine that the principal is a businessman who contracts a worker (the agent). The contract specifies the number of hours that the worker must be on the job (the effort e) and the wage w to be paid. The worker does not know if the job is arduous (k is high) or easy ($k = 1$), but he does know that the more arduous is the job, the greater will be the businessman's profits. How can the businessman signal that the job he is offering is easy? The answer is by demanding only a few hours work (and paying a correspondingly low wage). The worker knows that if the job were arduous and so very profitable to the businessman, the contract would specify many hours work, even though this means paying a higher wage. Therefore, the offer of only a few hours is a signal, in this model, of an easy, but not very profitable, job. The worker will accept the contract with the low wage, both because the number of hours is low, and because he can be sure the job is easy.

In the only equilibrium that satisfies the intuitive criterion (see Figure 5.6), we have the result that the agent's utility is equal to his reservation utility. This is a characteristic of the model we have analysed. On other occasions, the principal will signal her type by offering contracts in which the agent obtains some of the surplus of the relationship, since if she tried to extract any more surplus, the contract would no longer be a clear indication of the principal's type (see, for example, application 1).

The main message of this section is the following. On many occasions, the party who offers a contract (or, more generally, the party who initiates the relationship) has more information than the accepting party. When this information is relevant to the contract's acceptance (to the conditions under which the agent accepts it), the terms of the contract can indirectly transmit all or a part of this information. Therefore, on occasions apparently inefficient contracts are offered (or, more correctly, they would be inefficient if the information were symmetric). The objective is to clearly indicate the offering principal's 'type', thereby distinguishing her from other types that would never have proposed the same contract.

5.6 Comments

In the last decade, many economists have applied the ideas of signalling models to diverse economic situations. Fields such as industrial organization, financial economics, economic policy, and public economics, among others, have found explanations to certain phenomena in signalling activity. Some examples will help to understand the explanatory power of the theory.

Consider a businessman who knows the value of the company he manages and who wants to signal this value to the market (for example, because he wants to increase capital and receive a fair price for the new shares). In order that a decision of the businessman be considered by the market as proof that the company is healthy, it must be a decision that would never have been taken had the company been in a bad situation. We shall use the framework analysed by Ross (1977), in which the wage of the businessman is an average of the market value of the company before and after the expansion, but where the businessman pays a fine if the company goes bankrupt. In this situation, a high debt level can be interpreted as a signal that the company is working on good projects, since a high debt level would mean a high probability of bankruptcy for a bad company, and hence a high probability of the fine for the businessman. The debt level of the company is a signal of its profitability since it is more costly for a businessman to maintain the worse is the company's true situation.

A very clear example of economic agents that need to give believable information are the producers of new consumer goods. How can a consumer be induced to buy a product so that the consumer will learn that it is high quality (given that this is the case)? Low initial prices, or initial advertising spending are methods often used to introduce new goods, whose consumption is continued (soft-drinks, food products, monthly series of books, etc.). These strategies are a signal of quality since they are more profitable the better is the product; the percentage of consumers that will continue to buy the good once it has been tried increases with the quality of the good. On the other hand, a long guarantee period, or a money-back guarantee for unsatisfied clients are strategies often used by sellers of durable consumer goods, since the cost of these strategies is higher if the product is of shoddy quality, and lower for high-quality goods.

However, we should not think that signalling is a phenomenon that appears in very particular economic situations. Governments like to signal their future political actions to voters (sometimes successfully, sometimes not) or to the institutions related to them.[8] Countries need to signal themselves as attractive to foreign investors, or for the celebration of international events. We all try to signal that we are suitable for the job when being interviewed for work, or that we are nice people when we want to make friends. However, these attempts are only useful if they are believable. In the words of J. Saramago[9]: 'In spite of the words of the ingenuous (which is all of us at one time or another), it is not enough to speak the truth. It is worthless in human relationships if it is not believable, and perhaps this should even be its main characteristic. The truth is only half of what is needed, the other half is called believability.'

5A Complementary Material

5A.1 The intuitive criterion[10]

In this annexe we shall give a more precise definition of the intuitive criterion. It is a criterion which eliminates those perfect Bayesian equilibria that are not very 'intuitive' or that are 'unreasonable'. To do so, a condition on out-of-equilibrium beliefs is imposed (in equilibrium, the beliefs are given by Bayes's law).

Since we have seen both signalling games in which the party who signals is the agent and games in which it is the principal who signals via the contract, in this annexe we will use a slightly different notation that covers both cases. We will also change the names of the participants for the same reason.

Call the signalling party the *leader*, and the other party the *follower* (in Section 4 the agent was the leader, while in Section 5 the leader was the principal). The leader is the party who possesses private information. The leader may be any one of several types, which we shall denote by $k \in K$, where $K = \{1, 2, \ldots, n\}$ is a finite set. The set of signals, or messages, that the leader can send is M, and we shall denote a particular message by $m \in M$ (a message is the time spent in education in the Spence model, a price in the model of a seller who offers a product whose quality only he knows, a licensing contract for the owner of a technology whose profitability is unknown to the buyer,

[8] Banks (1991) presents a monograph on the application of signalling models to political economy.

[9] *A bagagem do viajante*, 1986, ed. Caminho, S.A..

[10] See Cho and Kreps (1987).

etc.).[11] Call $q(m)$ the follower's beliefs as to the leader's type if the signal m has been sent. Now, since there are more than two possible types of leader, $q(m)$ will be a vector $q \equiv (q^1(m), \ldots, q^n(m))$, with $\Sigma_{i=1}^{n} q^i(m) = 1$.

Consider a subset of K, $H \subset K$, and let a message $m \in M$. Denote by $BR(H, m)$ the set of all pure-strategy best responses of the follower when the message m has been sent and the beliefs are defined on H (that is, $\Sigma_{k \in H} q^k(m) = 1$).[12] $BR(H, m)$ therefore, includes all the strategies that could be optimal when the follower knows that the leader is of some type in H, but he doesn't know exactly which. The strategies that do not belong to $BR(H, m)$ are not optimal for any beliefs q in which $q^k(m) = 0$ when $k \notin H$.

Denote by $U(k, m, r)$ the utility of a type-k leader when message m is sent and when the follower's action is r. Consider an equilibrium in which the messages that are sent are $m^*(k)$, and the reactions are $r^*(m)$, and denote by $U^*(k)$ the equilibrium utility of a type-k leader.

$$U^*(k) = U\big(k, m^*(k), r^*(m^*(k))\big).$$

For a message m that is never sent in equilibrium, define $S(m)$ as the set of leader types k such that

$$U^*(k) > \max\{U(k, m, r) \mid r \in BR(K, m)\},$$

or in other words, $S(m)$ is the set of leaders who are not interested in sending message m independently of what the follower may believe: optimal follower strategies, for any q, leave the leaders in $S(m)$ worse off than what they were in equilibrium.

We say that an equilibrium does not survive the application of the *intuitive criterion* if there exists a leader type $k' \in K$ such that:

$$U^*(k') < \min\{U(k', m, r) \mid r \in BR(K - S(m), m)\},$$

which says that a leader of type k' earns less in equilibrium than she can earn by deviating, if the only possible follower best responses are those that are optimal for the beliefs under which zero probability is assigned to the types of leader that are not interested in deviating. In an equilibrium that does not satisfy the intuitive criterion we would find a leader type k', that is using a message $m^*(k')$ and that would prefer to send some other message m. If he doesn't send m instead of $m^*(k')$ it is because the follower's beliefs are not very 'intuitive':

[11] The definition can be easily generalized to the case in which there exist messages that some types of leader can send and others cannot. In order not to complicate any further our notation, we assume that the possible messages are the same for all leaders.

[12] When the utility of the follower does not depend directly on the message, as is the case of Spence, $BR(H, m)$ will also not depend on m. In the examples of signalling of the quality of a product or of a patent, the utility of the buyer depends directly on the price of the good, or on the transference contract, and so $BR(H, m)$ depends on m.

they assign a positive probability to the leader who sends message m being in $S(m)$, the set of leaders who are never interested in sending such a message.

5B Applications

5B.1 Prices that signal quality[13]

Consider a monopolist that produces some good. The quality of the good is known by the firm, but not by the consumers. The consumers think that the quality could be either good or bad, and that the probability that it is good is q. If the quality is G, the consumers receive a surplus of X, while quality B gives zero surplus. If the price paid for the good is p, the utility of the consumers is either $X - p$, or $- p$, according to whether the quality is good or not. The unitary production cost is c^G if the good is of quality G, and c^B in the other case, where $c^G > c^B$.

There are two periods, and the consumers can buy one unit of the good in each period. If a consumer buys the good in period $t = 1$ then he learns the good's quality, and so can buy in period $t = 2$ with symmetric information. In order to simplify, we shall assume that if a consumer does not buy in $t = 1$, then he cannot buy in $t = 2$ either.

Since we are assuming the firm to be a monopolist, it is easy to see what will be the optimal decision in period $t = 2$, since the consumers now know the quality and are willing to pay any $p_2 \leq X$ if the quality is good, and they will not buy if quality is B. Hence the price will be $p_2 = X$ for G, and there will be no market for B. The consumers pay in period $t = 2$ exactly what the good is worth.

We shall assume that $q X < c^B$. In this case there cannot exist a pooling equilibrium. The reason for this is that if the consumer buys without knowing quality, the expected value of the surplus is $q X$, and so the maximum they are willing to pay is $p_1 = q X$. However, at this price a bad-quality-producing monopolist will not sell, since the first period profits would be $\Pi_1 = q X - c^B < 0$, and the second period profits are zero.

Consider the cases in which the monopolist can signal (separate) good quality. The characteristics of an equilibrium must be the following:

(i) In a separating equilibrium the consumers 'know' that the quality is bad when the monopolist is type B, and so they would not buy at any price.

13 Milgrom and Roberts (1986) showed how the price that a firm charges can give information on the quality of the good sold. We shall consider a simpler model here, based on Tirole (1988*b*).

Therefore, in a separating equilibrium a type B will not sell in the market and hence will get zero profits.

(ii) The profits for good quality with a period $t = 1$ price of p_1, are:

$$\Pi^G = (p_1 - c^G) + \delta\,(X - c^G)$$

where $\delta \in (0, 1)$ is the discount rate for future earnings. Clearly if $\Pi^G \geq 0$, then the good-quality-producing monopolist will not want to deviate. In order that he doesn't have incentives to camouflage himself as low quality either, we need that $p_1 \leq c^B$. Setting $p_1 = c^B$ is therefore a sufficiently informative signal.[14] The profits of a type-G monopolist in the proposed separating equilibrium are:

$$\Pi^G = (c^B - c^G) + \delta\,(X - c^G).$$

Now we must distinguish two possibilities:

(*a*) When $\delta\,(X - c^G) < c^G - c^B$, then the profits Π^G in the candidate equilibrium are negative and so it is not an equilibrium. Given that we have seen that, with positive prices there is no pooling equilibrium either, no market will exist in this industry. The possibility that the good is bad quality implies that it is not sold, even if it is really of good quality, since the consumers cannot test the quality of the good if they do not buy it even once.

(*b*) When $\delta\,(X - c^G) \geq c^G - c^B$, then an equilibrium with revelation (separation) exists in which the monopolist charges a price $p_1 = c^B$ if the good is of good quality, below his production cost c^G, while the monopolist does not enter the market if his quality is B. This equilibrium could be the explanation of why initial selling prices are low, only to rise once the consumers know the quality of the good. Many consumer goods present this price sequence. For example, foodstuffs are often sold at low prices when they first appear on the market.

5B.2 Optimal licensing contracts when the seller has private information

The objective of this application of signalling problems is to analyse the optimal way in which a technology-licensing contract can be established when it is the seller who has private information as to the value of the patent. We have

14 Other separating equilibria exist. At these equilibria, $p_1 < c^B$ and the consumers have beliefs such that any deviation $p \neq p_1$ can come from a monopolist of quality B, that is to say $q\,(p) \neq 1$. However, none of these equilibria survives the application of the intuitive criterion. The reason is the following. Let $p' \in (p_1, c^M)$. A low-quality monopolist will never have incentives to set price p', since this would give negative profits. However, if his quality were high, he would earn greater profits with p' than with p_1 so long as the consumers buy. Hence a 'deviation' to p' can only ('intuitively') come from G, from which $q\,(p') = 1$. Hence the beliefs that support $p_1 < c^M$ as an equilibrium are not 'intuitive'.

already seen (in application 2, Chapter 4) how the contract is deformed when it is the buyer who has private information as to the utility of the patent. In this application, we shall use the same analytical framework as was used in application 2, Chapter 4.

We maintain the assumption that the seller of the patent is an investigation laboratory and that the buyer is a monopolist in the industry. The demand function is $D(p)$. The initial marginal production costs are c^O, and the innovation allows these costs to be reduced to either c^G or c^B, where $c^G < c^B < c^O$. In the current framework, it is the inventor who knows what the final cost will be, while the buyer is unable to distinguish one type of innovation from the other. A licensing contract specifies the fixed payment F and the royalty, ε, that the buyer must pay. As we saw in Chapter 4, the symmetric information contracts are:

$$\varepsilon^{G*} = 0 \qquad F^{G*} = \Pi^m(c^G) - \Pi^m(c^O)$$

$$\varepsilon^{B*} = 0 \qquad F^{B*} = \Pi^m(c^B) - \Pi^m(c^O).$$

If the buyer does not have information regarding the quality of the patent, these contracts are not a valid offer since the owner will want to propose $(F^{G*}, 0)$ independently of the true value of the patent. The buyers, in anticipation of this behaviour, will not accept the contract. The owners of a high-quality innovation need to signal this fact by offering a contract that would never be offered if the innovation were low quality.

We first show that there always exists a separating equilibrium in which each type of innovator offers a different contract. We begin by finding the contracts $\{(F^G, \varepsilon^G), (F^B, \varepsilon^B)\}$ that are candidates to form a separating equilibrium. This can be done by determining the contract offered by low-quality innovators, and then analysing the conditions that must be satisfied by the contract of the owner of a high-quality innovation. The following result characterizes the only contract (F^B, ε^B) that can form a part of a separating equilibrium.

Result. If a sequential separating equilibrium $\{(F^G, \varepsilon^G), (F^B, \varepsilon^B)\}$ exists, then:

$$F^B = F^{B*} = \Pi^m(c^B) - \Pi^m(c^O) \qquad \text{and} \qquad \varepsilon^B = \varepsilon^{B*} = 0.$$

Proof. In a separating equilibrium, $\{(F^G, \varepsilon^G), (F^B, \varepsilon^B)\}$, the buyer 'knows' that if he is offered the contract (F^B, ε^B) then the innovation is of low quality (if we use a similar notation to that of the main body of the chapter, the beliefs of the buyer once (F^B, ε^B) has been observed are: $q(F^B, \varepsilon^B) = 0$). If the contract is accepted, it is because the buyer gets at least $\Pi^m(c^O)$ from the contract, or in other words, (F^B, ε^B) must satisfy the participation constraint of the buyer. Therefore, any contract (F^B, ε^B) different from $(F^{B*}, 0)$ guarantees the owner a pay-off strictly less than $\Pi^m(c^B) - \Pi^m(c^O)$, since $(F^{B*}, 0)$ is the optimal participation constraint satisfying contract. Hence the owner is interested in deviating from any different contract. On top of this, since the participation constraint is satisfied, the contract will be accepted if the seller offers it (independently of the beliefs q, since if q were strictly positive, the agent is even more interested in accepting), and so $(F^{B*}, 0)$ is the only possible separating equilibrium contract. *Q.E.D.*

The conditions that the contract (F^G, ε^G) must satisfy in order to form a part of a separating equilibrium are the following. First, the participation condition (when $q = 1$):

$$\Pi^m(c^G + \varepsilon^G) - F^G \geq \Pi^m(c^O). \tag{5.A1}$$

Secondly, in order that $\{(F^G, \varepsilon^G), (F^{B*}, 0)\}$ be a separating equilibrium, it is necessary that the bad-quality innovator is not interested in passing himself off as a good-quality innovator:

$$F^G + \varepsilon^G D^m(c^B + \varepsilon^G) \leq F^{B*}. \tag{5.A2}$$

Finally, in order that the owner of a good-quality innovation is not interested in offering the contract $(F^{B*}, 0)$, it is necessary that:

$$F^G + \varepsilon^G D^m(c^G + \varepsilon^G) \geq F^{B*}. \tag{5.A3}$$

There are many contracts (F^G, ε^G) that satisfy the system of equations (5.A1)-(5.A3). This means that there are many contracts that signal good quality. As always, we shall only consider the best of these contracts: the seller will choose that contract that maximizes his profits. This is the same as applying the intuitive criterion (the logic is the following: in order for some other contract, different from the C that maximizes profits under (5.A1)-(5.A3), to form a part of a separating equilibrium, it must be that the buyer has beliefs such that $q(C) < 1$ once C is observed; but this is not 'reasonable' since C is a contract that the seller would only be interested in offering if he is type G). Hence the candidate contract (F^G, ε^G) must be the solution to the following problem $[P^M]$:

$$[P^M] \qquad \max_{(F,\varepsilon)} \{F + \varepsilon D^m(c^G + \varepsilon)\}$$

$$\text{s.t.} \quad F \leq \Pi^m(c^G + \varepsilon) - \Pi^m(c^O) \tag{5.A1}$$

$$F \leq F^{B*} - \varepsilon D^m(c^B + \varepsilon) \tag{5.A2}$$

$$0 \leq \varepsilon \leq c^O - c^G.$$

(we can forget about condition (5.A3) since we are maximizing along the left-hand side of the expression; since in particular a contract in which $F^G = F^{B*}$

and $\varepsilon^G = 0$ satisfies all the restrictions, including (5.A3), which binds, we can be sure that the solution to the problem $[P^M]$ also satisfies (5.A3)). The following result shows that the seller of good quality will always be interested in signalling, and he will do so by offering a contract that includes a greater royalty payment than the optimal symmetric information contract.

Result. There exists a separating equilibrium in licensing contracts $\{(F^G, \varepsilon^G), (F^B, \varepsilon^B)\}$ such that the intuitive criterion is satisfied. This contract will take the following form:

$$F^G < F^B = F^{B\star} \quad \text{and} \quad \varepsilon^G > \varepsilon^B = \varepsilon^{B\star} = 0.$$

Proof. For sufficiently small values of ε, the active restriction of problem $[P^M]$ is (5.A2). In fact (5.A2) implies (5.A1) close to $\varepsilon = 0$. In order to prove the result, all that is needed is to show that the solution to the problem:

$$\begin{aligned} &\underset{(F,\varepsilon)}{\text{Max}} \quad \{F + \varepsilon\, D^m(c^G + \varepsilon)\} \\ &\text{s.t.} \quad F \leq \Pi^m(c^B) - \varepsilon\, D^m(c^B + \varepsilon) - \Pi^m(c^O) \end{aligned}$$

is some $\varepsilon > 0$. This is easy to see since the restriction will bind, and simply substituting F into the objective function gives the result. *Q.E.D.*

Figure 5.7 shows the intuition behind the proof of the above result. At the point $(F^{B\star}, 0)$, the slopes to the iso-profit curves of the two seller types are such that any deviation to a contract situated in the shaded zone will signal that the innovation is of good quality. All the contracts in this zone are based on royalty payments and they give the owner of a good innovation a profit greater than $F^{B\star}$. On top of this, these contracts will be accepted by the monopolist when the buyer is sure that he is buying a good-quality innovation.

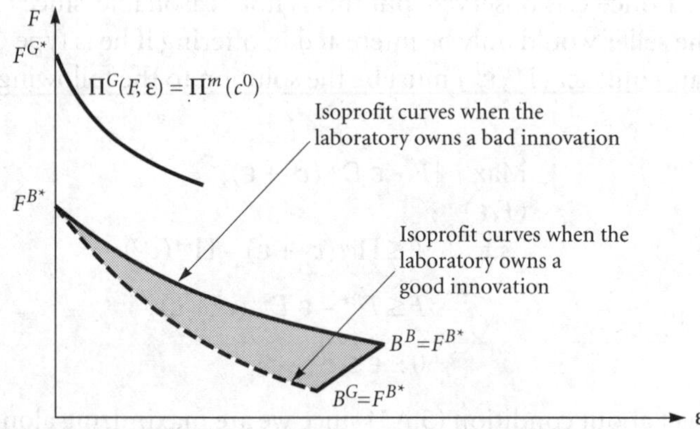

Fig. 5.7

The explication of the result is the following. The quantity sold in the market is greater if production is based on good innovations. Therefore, their owners receive greater profits through royalty payments than if the innovation were of bad quality, while the fixed payment does not distinguish between the two types of innovations. In order to signal quality, royalty payments must be used.

The analysis of pooling contracts in this framework is rather more complicated, and does not add anything interesting to the analysis. In general, pooling equilibria that satisfy the intuitive criterion do not exist, or in other words it is not possible that the two sellers choose, in equilibrium, the same contract. In Macho-Stadler and Pérez-Castrillo (1991*c*) it is shown that a sufficient condition for this is $D^{m''}(c) < 0$.

5B.3 Debt level as a signal of the value of a firm[15]

Modigliani and Miller (1958) proved a classic theorem in finance: a firm's choice of financial structure does not alter its value. This theorem, however, is untrue under asymmetric information. We will consider a simple model that allows us to explain the fact that the value of a firm is directly related to the debt level contracted.

The manager of the firm knows the true value of the earnings distribution, but investors do not have this information. Assume that the earnings x of a type-k firm in period $t = 1$ (when these earnings are realized) are uniformly distributed in the interval $[0, k]$, or in other words, $f(x) = 1/k$ and $F(x) = x/k$ for $x \in [0, k]$. Only the manager knows the value of k. The manager chooses a debt level D that maximizes the weighted sum of the market value of the firm in the periods $t = 0$ and $t = 1$, but a fine of L must be paid if the firm goes bankrupt (when the final value of the firm is less than the debt level D). Let $V_0(D)$ be the value of the shares at time $t = 0$ if the debt level is D. At $t = 1$, the true value of the firm becomes known (for simplicity). The manager's objective function is:

$$U(D) = (1-\gamma)\, V_0(D) + \gamma \left(\int_D^k x \frac{1}{k}\, dx + \int_0^D (x-L) \frac{1}{k}\, dx \right),$$

[15] As we have seen in application 3, Ch. 3, in financial markets information is fundamental. For this reason, the effects of asymmetric information have been well studied in these markets. Harris and Raviv (1991) present a good literature review of models that study this type of problem. The application that we present is based on Ross (1977). Exercise 7, inspired by Myers and Majluf (1984), is an illustration of the consequences of the difficulty of firms to signal their true situation.

where the parameter γ is the relative weight of the value of the firm in the second period. Solving the integrals gives:

$$U(D) = (1-\gamma)\, V_0(D) + \gamma\left(\frac{k}{2} - \frac{LD}{k}\right).$$

If the information were symmetric, the manager would choose $D = 0$. To see this, note that the expected value of the firm in period $t = 0$ is $V_0(D) = k/2$, which is a constant known by the investors (that is, the debt level says nothing new about the value of the firm). To maximize $U(D)$ is to minimize D, since it is subtracted in the second term.

If the investors do not have information on k, and if they observe the optimal symmetric information debt level of $D = 0$, then they do not know if the firm is a good type or a bad type, from which the value $V_0(0)$ will be less than the true value for firms with a high k. These firms would like to be able to somehow signal their type. The debt level is one way to do this. To see why, note that in the expression for $U(D)$, the cost of issuing debt is lower the greater is k, which is a necessary condition for debt to signal k. Does a separating equilibrium, in which the debt level signals the firm's value in period $t = 0$, exist? We shall study the situation in which only two types of firm are possible, with values k^G and k^B, $k^G > k^B$.

We already know that in a separating equilibrium the bad type of firm, that is, that type which no one wants to admit to being, will behave in the same way as in symmetric information. In the case at hand, this property assures that the debt level that a type-B firm chooses is $D^B = 0$. The utility of the managers of a firm with value k^B is:

$$U(D=0) = (1-\gamma)\,\frac{k^B}{2} + \gamma\frac{k^B}{2} = \frac{k^B}{2},$$

since by observing $D = 0$ in the first period, the investors correctly deduce that the value of the firm is k^B. In order for a debt level of D^G to be a signal of the value of a type-G firm, it must be some level that would never be chosen by the manager of a firm whose value is k^B, since this manager would earn more using D^B, and yet it must be the preferred choice for the manager of a firm whose value is k^G. In other words, the following two conditions must be satisfied:

$$(1-\gamma)\,\frac{k^G}{2} + \gamma\left(\frac{k^B}{2} - \frac{LD^G}{k^B}\right) \leq \frac{k^B}{2},$$

$$(1-\gamma)\,\frac{k^G}{2} + \gamma\left(\frac{k^G}{2} - \frac{LD^G}{k^G}\right) \geq (1-\gamma)\,\frac{k^B}{2} + \gamma\,\frac{k^G}{2}.$$

These equations can be written as:

$$D^G \in \left[\frac{(1-\gamma)}{\gamma} \frac{(k^G - k^B)}{2L} k^B, \frac{(1-\gamma)}{\gamma} \frac{(k^G - k^B)}{2L} k^G \right].$$

The preceding equation says that if the debt level is high, it can be interpreted by the investors as a signal that the firm has a high value. The reason why is that only in the case of a firm with a high value would the managers risk being fined in the next period, since the probability of the fine is small. The expected cost for the managers is greater the worse is the firm. Finally, we note that the minimum debt level needed to signal increases with the difference between the possible values of the firms, $k^G - k^B$, and it decreases with the fine L included in the manager's contract in case of bankruptcy.

Exercises

Exercise 1. Assume that in the market there exist two types of worker, differentiated by their productivity. Type-k^G workers have productivity $k = 2$, while the productivity of the type-k^B workers is $k = 1$. The cost of achieving a given level of education is greater for type-k^B workers than for type k^G workers. In particular, the cost of e units of education for a type-k worker is $c(e; k) = e/k$. The utility function of a type-k individual is $U(w, e; k) = w - c(e; k)$.

(*a*) Does a worker's education level influence his productivity? What would be the optimal education level if firms had the same information as workers as to the value of k?

Now assume that a worker's productivity is not observable by firms, but that the education level is. Furthermore, assume that firms believe that education greater than or equal to a certain level e^O is a signal of high productivity, while education less than this level signals low productivity. Hence firms offer wages according to $w(e) = 2$ if $e \geq e^O$ and $w(e) = 1$ if $e < e^O$.

(*b*) Given these wages, calculate the level of education that each type of agent will choose.

(*c*) Find the necessary condition on e^O so that education is an effective signal of productivity.

(*d*) Prove that, for the values of e^O found in (*c*), the beliefs of the firms in equilibrium are coherent.

(*e*) Discuss your results.

Exercise 2.[16] Consider a market in which a homogeneous good is sold, and in which the demand function is $p = 18 - Q$, where Q is the quantity offered by the firm(s). The market exists during two periods. In the first period, there is only one established firm, firm 1, and so it is in a monopoly position. Firm 1's production costs are either $C^G(q) = 0$, or $C^B(q) = 6\,q$. In the second period there is a second competitor, firm 2, that must decide whether or not to enter the market. Firm 2's production costs are $C^e(q) = 3\,q$, but this firm must also pay a fixed cost of 20 if it decides to enter the market. If the decision is to enter, then the two firms compete in the second period in Cournot fashion. The discount rate is 1, or in other words, firm 1 maximizes the sum of profits from the two periods.

(*a*) Assume that everyone knows the costs of the established firm. Calculate the quantity decisions of firm 1, q_1^{Gm}, q_1^{Bm} (in function of marginal cost) when this firm is in a monopoly position, and the decisions q_1^{Gd}, q_1^{Bd}, q_2^{Gd} and q_2^{Bd} of firms 1 and 2 respectively when they are in a duopoly situation. Also, calculate the profits Π_1^{Gd}, Π_1^{Bd}, Π_2^{Gd} and Π_2^{Bd}. Will firm 2 enter in the second period?

(*b*) If the costs of firm 1 are unknown to firm 2, show that the above decisions are no longer reasonable, since firm 1 has incentives to make firm 2 believe that it is type G independently if this is true or not (that is, no separating equilibrium exists in which each type behaves as if the information were symmetric).

(*c*) Show that a situation in which the production decisions in the first period for each type of firm are $q_1^G = 12$ and $q_1^B = 6$ is a separating equilibrium. Determine the beliefs of the entrant as to firm 1's type when firm 1's decision is $q = 7$, $q = 8$, $q = 9$, $q = 10$, or $q = 11$.

(*d*) Assume that the probability that firm 1 is type G is 1/2. Would a situation in which both types of firm decide $q_1 = 9$ be a pooling equilibrium?

(*e*) Would the situation of (*d*) be a pooling equilibrium if the probability that firm 1 is type G were 9/10?

Exercise 3. The soft drinks firm Lemonade wants to place a new refreshment on the market. The quality of this refreshment may be good or bad. There will be either many or few consumers who will drink the new refreshment frequently (thus making the new product either a success or a failure), depending on whether it is of good or bad quality, something that can be tested with one initial consumption. Lemonade can advertise its product (not informative advertising, but rather brand advertising not related to the product). Of course advertising implies a cost to the firm. Discuss carefully (and formally if you

[16] This exercise presents a numerical example that shows how prices can reveal information as to the production costs of existing firms to the potential entrants. It is a study, developed by Milgrom and Roberts (1982), pioneered in the signalling literature.

can) the value of advertising as a signal of good quality, even though it does not have a direct influence on the product's quality. What condition would have to hold for the advertising to effectively identify a good-quality drink?

Exercise 4. Once upon a time, King Solomon was visited by two women each claiming to be the mother of a certain child. It was very difficult to prove who was the real mother. King Solomon told the women that the child would be cut in half in order to give half to each woman. Given this possibility, one of the two women agreed while the other did not, preferring that the child be cared for by the other rather than being killed. The wise King Solomon recognized that the second woman was the real mother, and gave her custody of the child.

(*a*) In the above situation, one of the participants did not act in a rational manner. Who?

(*b*) Even though the final result was satisfactory, this does not seem to be a very convincing way of judging motherhood. In fact, if it were a good method, it would be used today in custody trials. Why is it not used?

Exercise 5. Consider the relationship between the producer of a good and the retailer who sells it. The producer has constant marginal cost c. The demand is $q = D - p$, where q is the quantity sold, p is the price, and D is the demand volume, which can take two values, $D \in \{D^G, D^B\}$, with $D^G > D^B$. Denote by $T(q) = a + b\,q$ the franchise contract that the producer offers the retailer.

(*a*) Calculate the optimal production decision q, the price and the retailer's profits Π given the contract $T(q)$.

(*b*) If both the producer and the retailer know the demand situation, what is the optimal franchise contract for the producer to offer?

(*c*) Sometimes the producer has more information than the retailer as to the true demand conditions. Assume, for example, that the producer knows the demand parameter D, $D \in \{D^G, D^B\}$, while the retailer will not know this parameter until after the contract has been signed (although before the production decision is taken). Show that, in this case, the producer has incentives to make out that the demand is good, whether this is true or not.

(*d*) What type of behaviour by the producer could 'convince' (signal) to the retailer that the demand is good when this is in fact true.

(*e*) Let's search for a separating equilibrium $\{(a^G, b^G), (a^B, b^B)\}$ in this framework. Write down the incentive compatibility constraints for each type of producer to effectively be interested in offering only that contract that corresponds to his type. Summing these restrictions, show which type of producer would ask for a greater variable payment b, and which type would ask for a greater fixed payment a.

(*f*) Argue (or prove analytically) why it must be true that $(a^B, b^B) = (a^{B*}, b^{B*})$ in a separating equilibrium.

(*g*)* We know that in order for (a^G, b^G) to form a part of a separating equilibrium it must be true that the retailer does not earn negative profits when he believes that the demand is good, and that the producer does not have incentives to offer this contract when the demand is bad. Show that the contract pair $\{(a^G, b^G), (a^{B*}, b^{B*})\}$, in which (a^G, b^G) saturates the above two conditions, is a separating equilibrium. Give the intuition as to why this contract pair is the only separating equilibrium that satisfies the intuitive criterion.

Exercise 6. When, in 1992, the International Olympic Committee chose Sydney as the host city for the Olympic games of the year 2000, a large part of the investments required for the games had already been carried out. This is a common practice among cities that are candidates to host the Olympic Games (although on a somewhat smaller scale, a similar phenomenon occurred in Barcelona). In principle, there is no economic reason why a city should carry out such investments before being chosen as the host city, since there is enough time for construction after being chosen, while these investments constitute a large loss if the city is not chosen because a large part of the work carried out is only useful should the city be chosen. Think about this phenomenon in the context of the intuition developed in this chapter, and find an explanation for it.

Exercise 7. (*a*) Consider a firm whose shares are worth $G = 160$. The firm has the chance to carry out a project valued at 120 (net) by issuing new shares, the objective of which is to collect 100 (the liquidity required to carry out the project). The managers maximize the profits of the (current) shareholders of the firm. Therefore, they will sell the shares at a fair price. Show that in order to get 100, the managers will have to give a fraction $\beta^G = 5/14$ of the firm to the new shareholders. Calculate the final value of the shares of the original shareholders.

(*b*) Now assume that the value of the firm is $B = 80$. What fraction β^B of the firm must be sold to the new investors so that they agree to invest 100? Why is $\beta^B > \beta^G$? What is the final value of the shares of the original shareholders?

(*c*) What would be the value of the shares of the original shareholders after the sale of a fraction β^B of the firm in exchange for an investment of 100 when the shares were really worth $G = 160$?

(*d*) In actual fact, in this market the only ones who really know the value of the shares of the firm are the managers. Only they know whether the firm is worth 160 or 80. Assume that, after investing in the project, everyone knows the final value of the firm. The managers take the decision to invest in the project or not with the objective of maximizing the value of the original shares (since the managers have a responsibility to the original shareholders). Show that a situation in which a fraction β^G of the firm is sold when the managers declare the value to be 160, and a fraction β^B is sold when the managers declare the value to be 80 cannot be an equilibrium.

(*e*) Show that a separating equilibrium exists in which the firm carries out the investment when it is type *B*, offering a fraction β^B of the shares, while if the value of the firm is $g = 160$, the managers prefer not to invest in the new project.

Exercise 8. A seller and a buyer enter into a relationship to transact a good. The good may or may not break. If it doesn't break, its monetary value to the buyer is b_1, while if it breaks, it is only worth b_2 to the buyer. The probability that the good will break depends on its quality. If it is of good quality, the probability of breakage is q^G, while if it is of bad quality the breakage probability is $q^B > q^G$. Assume that the seller is risk-neutral and that the buyer is risk-averse. The seller proposes a contract that includes the price p at which the good is to be sold and a guarantee g, which is the amount that the seller must pay the buyer should the good break. The utility of the buyer is $u\,(b_1 - p)$ if the good does not break, and $u\,(b_2 - p + g)$ if it does, where $u'' < 0$. The buyer will buy so long as his expected utility is greater than or equal to $u\,(0)$.

(*a*) Calculate the optimal contract for each quality for the case of symmetric information on quality.

(*b*) Calculate the optimal contracts if the seller knows the quality but the buyer doesn't. Does the contract signal quality? Explain why, or why not.

Exercise 9. Consider the same framework as Exercise 8, but now the buyer is risk-neutral, with utility function $u\,(x) = x$, while the seller is risk-averse, with von Neumann-Morgenstern utility function $B\,(.)$, with $B'' < 0$.

(*a*) Calculate the optimal contract according to quality if the information is symmetric.

(*b*) Are the symmetric information contracts adequate when only the seller knows the quality of the good? Explain why, or why not.

(*c*) Provide an intuitive description of what a seller could do to signal that the good he is selling has low breakdown probability. Is it useful to offer a guarantee?

(*d*) When a seller offers a guarantee, he needs to increase the price of the good in order to compensate the possible indemnity should the good break. Show analytically that the price rise required for an increase in guarantee on a low-quality good (such that the seller's utility is constant) is greater than that required for a high-quality good. Given this observation, consider the existence of a separating equilibrium and describe its characteristics.

Exercise 10. Consider the framework analysed in Section 5 of this chapter. The principal has private information relevant to the type of job being offered to the agent. Either the job is easy and productivity is low, or the job is arduous although productivity is high. Let q stand for the agent's prior probability that the job is easy.

(*a*) In the wage/effort space (see, for example, Figure 5.4), depict the participation constraint when the agent knows the type of the principal, and when he does not know it. Identify a point (w, e) candidate to be a pooling equilibrium, in the sense that it satisfies the agent's participation constraint given the probability q that the job is easy.

(*b*) Depict the isoprofit curves that pass through (w, e) for a type-1 principal and for a type-k principal. Identify the contracts that a type-1 principal prefers to (w, e), while they give less profits to a type-k principal.

(*c*) Explain why (w, e) cannot constitute a pooling equilibrium satisfying the intuitive criterion.

5C Advanced Themes

5C.1 Equilibrium refinements

As we have seen, both in the main body of the chapter and in the applications and exercises, in signalling problems there are often many equilibria. Even if we apply classic refinement techniques like subgame perfection, sequential equilibrium, or Bayesian equilibrium, there are still many equilibria. The main reason behind the many equilibria is that the signal space is normally larger than the type space (we have seen examples with two types of agent and a continuum of possible messages). This means that there are many signals that will never be sent. Neither Nash equilibrium nor the above refinements impose any restrictions on the beliefs of the players for these messages.

Could some of the equilibria be preferred? This is the objective of the different refinements that have been proposed, which can, in general, be related to the concept of *stability* of Kohlberg and Mertens (1986).[17] Throughout the chapter we have been using the intuitive criterion idea (Cho and Kreps, 1987) to choose the most 'reasonable' equilibrium from those possible. The idea behind the intuitive criterion is the following. Consider an equilibrium. If a type-t' leader[18] obtains less utility by sending a message m than by sending the

[17] See Van Damme (1991) for a detailed and careful revision of several refinements.

[18] As for complementary material 1, we call the player who moves first (the player with private information) the leader.

equilibrium message $m^*(t')$ for any optimal follower response, and if there is some other leader type t for which the message m is more profitable than $m^*(t)$, then the follower's beliefs should attach zero probability to the event of the leader being type t' if message m is observed.

Within the same idea, Cho and Kreps (1987) and Banks and Sobel (1987) propose other, somewhat more demanding criteria, that the equilibrium should satisfy. We shall briefly comment on two of these: the 'D1' criterion and the 'universal divinity' or 'D2' criteria. The D1 criteria demands the following. If, for all possible follower (mixed-strategy) best responses for which a type-t' leader weakly prefers to send message m instead of message $m^*(t')$, it turns out that a type-t leader strictly prefers message m to $m^*(t)$, then the follower should attach zero probability to the event that the leader is type t' when message m is observed. The intuition behind this refinement is that, since a type-t leader always finds message m to be strictly more profitable in all instances when a type-t' leader finds this message to be weakly more profitable, it is more 'normal' to think that if someone has deviated from equilibrium it was a type-t leader, and so the probability that it was a type t' should be zero.

The *universal divinity* criterion imposes basically the same as the D1 criterion, but it is rather more restrictive. It requires that zero probability be attached to the event that the person sending message m out of equilibrium be type t' if, for any (mixed-strategy) best response for which this type has greater or equal utility than that corresponding to $m^*(t')$, we can find some other type t (not necessarily the same one for all responses) that strictly prefers m to $m^*(t)$. We should point out that the above criteria select the same equilibria for a wide set of problems. In particular, whenever the intuitive criterion selects a unique equilibrium, the other criteria will give the same answer, since they are more demanding, and there always exists an equilibrium that satisfies them.

In most of the cases we have studied, we achieve uniqueness by applying the intuitive criterion. This is related to the assumption that in our models there are only two types of agents. However, in general there may still be many equilibria after applying this refinement. This is the case when applied to more than two types. Consider for example that there are three types of agents (Cho and Kreps, 1987). In this situation, in addition to full pooling equilibria and full separating equilibria, there can also exist semi-pooling equilibria. Consider the equilibrium outcome in which types 1 and 2 pool at a certain education level (say e^P) and type 3 is screened at educational level $e_3 > e^P$. To break the pool, type 2 needs to offer an educational level e so that type 1 would never do so in preference to the equilibrium. But since the principals could respond as if this out-of-equilibrium signal came from type 3, they could offer a salary of $3e$ (this salary is a best response if the principals believe that it is indeed a type-3 agent who deviates). The educational level needed to be sure that a type-1 agent does not deviate is quite high (there are beliefs for which the deviation is very profitable). At this high level of effort, a type-2 agent that deviates can be sure to get a wage of $2e$ or more. But this will not guarantee that he gets more from the defection than what he gets from the equilibrium. Therefore, the equilibrium satisfies the intuitive criterion. However, it fails to satisfy other criteria, such as the D1 criterion. The reason is that, in order to satisfy the D1 criterion, the beliefs associated with any deviation $e > e^P$ should attach zero probability to the event that the agent is of type 1, because for any response (wage) that a type-1 agent would prefer to the equilibrium, the type-2 agent would strictly prefer. Therefore, the type-2 agent does not need to offer a very high effort in order to be assured of a wage appropriate to his type.

Also more restrictive than the intuitive criterion is the *perfect sequential equilibrium*, suggested by Grossman and Perry (1986) (a very similar idea was proposed by Farrell, 1984). Its objective is to extend the idea of backward induction to games with asymmetric information. To do this, they define a 'meta-strategy' to be a function that assigns, to each information-set and each belief possible, the action that the player will carry out. Imagine an equilibrium supported by certain beliefs in which each type of leader sends a message. Consider what would happen if the follower observes an out-of-equilibrium message m, or in other words, a message that is not compatible with the beliefs that support an equilibrium in which no leader type is interested in sending the message m. When m is observed, the follower carries out the following logic. First, he throws out his equilibrium beliefs, and for any belief μ possible, he calculates his best response (that indicated by the meta-strategy) associated with m and μ. He then considers the types of leader that earn more with this response than in equilibrium. In order for the initial equilibrium to be sequentially perfect, it cannot occur that the set of leaders that find the deviation profitable be a support of the new beliefs μ (that is, these are the types for which μ attaches positive probability). If this were the case, the original equilibrium beliefs given m would not be '*consistent*'. Therefore, the consistency (which is the base of the definition of perfect sequential equilibrium) is, fundamentally, a fixed-point argument. The problem with this refinement is that it does not always exist. For this reason, the authors recommend that it be used to refine the set of equilibria that satisfy the intuitive criterion, when this set has several elements.

5C.2 Cheap-talk games

In Section 2 of this chapter, we noted that in order for a decision to be a signal, it must involve some cost. Moreover, there are games with signalling possibilities, but in which the signals have no associated cost. These types of game are known as *cheap-talk games* (see Crawford and Sobel, 1982), and they have the following characteristics: (1) the signals have no associated cost, (2) the signals are not binding, that is, the player who sends the signal has no obligation to fulfil what he announces, and (3) the content of the signal is not verifiable.

In order to understand the type of situation in which cheap-talk can be useful, reconsider the situation analysed by Spence. There, cheap-talk would consist of, for example, all candidates for a job announcing that they are 'high productivity'. But this message will not be believed by the firms, and hence will not change the result of the game. Why is cheap-talk useless in Spence's game? The reason why is that all types of worker have the same preferences with respect to wages.

In situations in which the preferences of the informed player with respect to the uninformed player's action depend on his characteristic, initial cheap-talk may be valuable. The conditions that must be satisfied for this to occur are, first, that different types of agent have different preferences over the decisions of the uninformed player, and, second, that the preferences of the uninformed player are not completely opposed to those of the informed player, i.e. there is not total conflict of interests. These characteristics guarantee us that sharing information makes available better potential agreements, but it also has strategic effects, so revealing all the information is not the most advantageous behaviour.

The time-line of a game with simple cheap-talk is similar to that of a signalling game. Therefore, the solution concept that is applied is also that of perfect Bayesian equilibrium, One important difference with the signalling games that we have studied is that in cheap-talk games we can always get pooling equilibria in which the uninformed player ignores all messages and the best response of the player with private information is to pool (since the messages do not have a direct effect on the utility function of the player who sends them). However, these are not the only equilibria of the game.

Crawford and Sobel (1982) show that the set of equilibria of these games is rather peculiar. Although the sender's choice is not restricted a priori, in equilibrium he partitions the support of the probability distribution of the variable that represents his private information, and reports which element of the partition his observation actually lies in. Even though several equilibria exist, these authors argue that the most reasonable one is that with the greatest number of elements in the partition, since this equilibrium is Pareto–superior to the rest. The more similar are the preferences of the players, the more informative is the signal sent in equilibrium.

An application of cheap-talk games that allows us to explain the value of certain announcements of the monetary authorities is given in Stein (1989).

5C.3 Optimal design of mechanisms in signalling models

In this chapter we have studied signalling models in which, either an agent with private information chooses an action before entering into a relationship with a principal, or a principal with private information proposes a contract knowing that the terms of the contract can signal the information. This framework seems to be valid for certain contexts. For example, in the model of Milgrom and Roberts (1986) that we studied in application 1, the firm chooses a price for the product, and this 'contract' with the consumer is the only message that can be sent, since the product is singular. In the same way, the debt level chosen by the managers of a firm is a message that is 'judged' by the market (Ross, 1977, or application 3 of this chapter). However, there are many other frameworks in which the mechanisms that the principal may use are richer that what we have allowed.[19]

The principal can pose a game in the following way: first, she proposes a *mechanism* that determines the final offer to the agent according to the actions chosen by both; secondly, the agent accepts or rejects the proposed mechanism; thirdly, if the agent has accepted the mechanism, both participants play out the game. We first note that, as for the information revealing mechanisms designed by the uninformed party, it is possible to show that those designed by the informed party can be restricted to the space of the true characteristics. In other words, they are *direct revealing mechanisms.* If only the principal has private information, the mechanism consists in offering a menu of contracts. If the agent accepts the menu, the principal will then choose which will be used for the relationship by announcing her true characteristic. In the model that we have used in Section 5 of this chapter, this amounted to the following game: first, the principal chooses a menu $\{(w^1, e^1), (w^k, e^k)\}$; secondly, the agent accepts or rejects the contract menu; and, finally, if the agent has accepted, the principal announces her type by signing the contract (w^1, e^1) if she declares herself to by type 1, or (w^k, e^k) if she is type k.

In order to see the new possibilities that are opened when an informed principal offers a contract menu (one contract for each type of principal) instead of one single contract, it is useful to refer to Maskin and Tirole (1990). These authors studied the case in which the expected utility of the agent depends only on the principal's behaviour, and not on her information. It is a situation of *private values,* in which if we consider the principal's behaviour to be fixed,

[19] Maskin and Tirole (1990, 1992) studied the optimal *mechanisms* for the principal when she has private information, (Myerson (1983) analyses information revelation through the contracts using techniques of co-operative and non-cooperative game theory).

her private information is not an argument of the agent's utility function, nor of the probabilities that the agent assigns to the variables in his utility function. To this signalling problem, Maskin and Tirole add a problem of adverse selection, since the agent also has private information. The menu will lead to self-selection of both principal and agent in the third stage. The mechanism proposed by the principal will be a 'matrix' of contracts, from which the principal selects a row when she declares her type, and the agent selects a column, thereby obtaining the contract that will be used in the relationship. In this case, the principal can, in general, obtain strictly greater profits than those obtained under symmetric information as to her type (that is, in pure adverse selection). The reason for this result is that, given that the agent accepts the expected contract (without knowing the type of principal that is offering it), the participation and incentive compatibility conditions are only satisfied in expected value terms, which gives the principal greater room for movement. For example, if for a type-k principal the participation constraint is very costly (the associated Lagrange multiplier is very high) while the incentive compatibility constraint is not so costly, and if the opposite occurs for a type-k' principal, then these two types can agree to the following 'exchange'; the type k principal can relax the participation constraint a bit in exchange for restricting the incentive compatibility constraint a bit more, in order that the type k'-principal can relax the incentive compatibility condition in exchange for not binding the participation condition.

Maskin and Tirole (1992) also studied the revelation mechanisms for signalling problems with *common values,* which is to say, problems in which the principal's private information is an argument that appears in the agent's objective function. In order to see what changes when a revealing contract menu is offered in a signalling game, following Spence's (1973) education model, we can think of the agent choosing both his educational level and the contract offered by the firm. In the framework of this chapter we assumed that each worker, given his education, is offered a different contract. However, a mechanism now includes an educational level and a wage for each type of worker. The worker makes clear in the mechanism, not only the contract that he will finally accept, but also that which he would accept were he of some other type, thereby assuring the firm of sufficient profits independent of the worker's type. The firm does not need to maintain beliefs over the contracts that are not offered, but only needs to calculate which contract from the menu will be chosen by each worker type. This guarantees that, in equilibrium, the decision of a good type will be the minimum separating level of education (without turning to refinements). Maskin and Tirole (1992) show that the optimal mechanisms are those allocations that satisfy the incentive compatibility condition of the principals, and that Pareto-dominate the RSW allocations (Rothschild–Stiglitz–Wilson) with respect to reservation utility (a RSW allocation with respect to reservation utility maximizes the pay-off to each type of principal within the class of allocations that satisfy the incentive compatibility conditions and that guarantee the agent his reservation utility).

Mathematical Appendix
CONCAVITY AND OPTIMIZATION

This appendix is to very briefly cover the necessary and sufficient conditions of a constrained optimization problem. There are several texts that study the theory of concavity and optimization in detail. The book by Madden (1986) is clear and intuitive, while those by Luenberger (1984) and Sydsaeter and Hammond (1995) are also useful.

Definition A.1. A set $D \subset \mathbb{R}^n$ is *convex* if:

$$\lambda x + (1-\lambda) y \in D \quad \text{for all } \lambda \in [0,1], x, y \in D.$$

Definition A.2. Let $D \subset \mathbb{R}^n$ be a convex set.

(1) The function $f: D \longrightarrow \mathbb{R}$ is *concave* if:

$$f(\lambda x + (1-\lambda) y) \geq \lambda f(x) + (1-\lambda) f(y) \quad \text{for all } \lambda \in [0,1], x, y \in D.$$

(2) f is *strictly concave* if:

$$f(\lambda x + (1-\lambda) y) > \lambda f(x) + (1-\lambda) f(y) \quad \text{for all } \lambda \in (0,1), x, y \in D, x \neq y.$$

Proposition A.1. Let $D \subset \mathbb{R}^n$ be a convex set and $f: D \longrightarrow \mathbb{R}$.

(*a*) If f is concave, then f is continuous.

(b1) Assume that f is C^1.[1] Then, f is concave if and only if:

$$f(x^*) + (x - x^*) f'(x^*) \geq f(x) \quad \text{for all } x, x^* \in D.$$

(b2) Assume that f is C^1. Then, f is strictly concave if and only if:

$$f(x^*) + (x - x^*) f'(x^*) > f(x) \quad \text{for all } x, x^* \in D, x \neq x^*.$$

(c1) Assume that f is C^2. Then, f is concave if and only if $f''(x)$ is negative semi-definite for all $x \in D$.[2]

(c2) Assume that f is C^2. Then, if $f''(x)$ is negative definite for all $x \in D$, it is also true that f is strictly concave.

[1] A function $f: D \longrightarrow \mathbb{R}$ is C^i if it is continuous and differentiable i times, and these i derivatives are continuous.

[2] A matrix M of dimension $n \times n$ is negative semi-definite if $z^T A z \leq 0$, for all $z \in \mathbb{R}^n$. M is negative semi-definite if and only if the kth order principal minors, $k = 1, \ldots, n$, have sign $(-1)^k$ or are zero.

A matrix M of dimension $n \times n$ is negative definite if $z^T A z < 0$, for all $z \in \mathbb{R}^n$, $z \neq 0$. If all the kth order principal minors, $k = 1, \ldots, n$, are of sign $(-1)^k$, then M is negative definite.

Call [P$^{A.1}$] the following unrestricted optimization problem:

[P$^{A.1}$] $$\max_{x \in D} f(x).$$

Definition A.3. A *global maximum* of f on D is a point $x^* \in D$ such that $f(x^*) \geq f(x)$, for all $x \in D$.

Proposition A.2. Let D be an open convex set, and assume that f is a concave C^1 *function.* Then, $x^* \in D$ is a global maximum of f on D if and only if $f'(x^*) = 0$.

Denote by [P$^{A.2}$] the following problem:

[P$^{A.2}$] $$\max_{x \in D} f(x) \text{ subject to } g^i(x) \geq 0, \text{ for } i = 1, \ldots, m.$$

The property of *restriction qualification* (RQ) is:

(RQ) There exists an $x \in D$ for which $g^i(x) > 0$, for all $i = 1, \ldots, m$.

Finally, denote by $L(x, \lambda)$ the *Lagrangean function* corresponding to problem [P$^{A.2}$], that depends on the problem variables (x) and a new set of variables $\lambda \equiv (\lambda^1, \ldots, \lambda^m)$, one for each constraint, called *Lagrange multipliers*:

$$L(x, \lambda) = f(x) + \sum_{i=1}^{m} \lambda^i g^i(x).$$

Proposition A.3. Let D be an open convex set, and assume that f and g^i, $i = 1, \ldots, m$, are concave functions and that (RQ) is satisfied. Then, $x^* \in D$ is the solution to [P$^{A.2}$] if and only if there exists a vector λ^* such that the following *Kuhn–Tucker conditions* are satisfied:

(*a*) $L(x^*, \lambda^*) \geq L(x, \lambda^*)$ for all $x \in D$,

(*b*) $\lambda^{i*} \geq 0$ for $i = 1, \ldots, m$,

(*c*) for $i = 1, \ldots, m$, $\lambda^{i*} g^i(x^*) = 0$,

(*d*) for $i = 1, \ldots, m$, $g^i(x^*) \geq 0$.

Comments. (i) If the functions f, g^i, $i = 1, \ldots, m$, are C^1, then condition (a) can be replaced (given proposition A.2) by the first-order conditions of the Lagrangean with respect to the variables x_k, $k = 1, \ldots, n$:

$$\frac{\partial L}{\partial x_k}(x^*, \lambda^*) = \frac{\partial f}{\partial x_k}(x^*) + \sum_{i=1}^{m} \lambda^{i*} \frac{\partial g^i}{\partial x_k}(x^*) = 0 \quad \text{for } k = 1, \ldots, n.$$

(ii) To solve a minimization problem, we need only note that Min $f(x)$ is equivalent to Max $\{-f(x)\}$. On the other hand, if we decide to do it directly, including f in the Lagrangean function instead of $-f$, then we can still use the Kuhn–Tucker conditions, but condition (b) must be transformed into (b') $\lambda^{i*} \leq 0$ for $i = 1, \ldots, m$.

(iii) There will always be a solution to [P$^{A.2}$] in any of the following cases:

(iii1) f is strictly concave

(iii2) f is not stationary[3] and g^i is strictly concave for all $i = 1, \ldots, m$.

(iv) There exist conditions in terms of the *quasi-concavity* of the functions f and g^i such that a proposition similar to A.3 is satisfied.[4]

(v) If the set D on which we are maximizing is convex but not open, then theorem A.2 ensures that if the maximum is located at an interior point of D, in which case the Kuhn–Tucker conditions (a)–(d) must be satisfied. However, the maximum may lie on the boundary of D (or it may not exist). If D is compact (closed and bounded), then there is a maximum in D that either satisfies the Kuhn–Tucker conditions or is on the boundary of D.

(vi) Define the problem:

$$[\text{P}^{A.3}] \qquad \underset{x \in D}{\text{Max}} \quad f(x) \text{ subject to } g^i(x) = 0, \text{ for } i = 1, \ldots, m.$$

Let D be open and convex, f concave, (RQ) satisfied, and let $x^* \in D$, λ^* be such that x^* satisfies (a) and $g^i(x^*) = 0$, for $i = 1, \ldots, m$. Then, if g^i is concave when $\lambda^{i*} \geq 0$, and g^i is convex when $\lambda^{i*} \leq 0$, then it is still true that x^* is the solution to [P$^{A.3}$]. (If g^i is linear, we need not worry about the sign of λ^i.)

Definition A.4. A *local maximum* of f on D is a point $x^* \in D$ such that $f(x^*) \geq f(x)$, for all x sufficiently close to x^*.

Proposition A.4. Let D be an open set, and $f: D \longrightarrow \mathbb{R}$ a C^2 function. (a) If, at the point $x^* \in D$, we have $f'(x^*) = 0$ and if $f''(x^*)$ is negative definite, then x^* is a local maximum of f on D.

(b) If $x^* \in D$ is a local maximum of f on D, then it is true that $f'(x^*) = 0$ and $f''(x^*)$ is negative semi-definite.

Finally, let's look at a necessary condition and a sufficient condition for the local maximums of problems with equality constraints (the constraints are defined as equalities rather than inequalities).

[3] f is not stationary is there does not exist $x \in D$ such that $f'(x) = 0$.

[4] We will not explain these conditions, since we do not use quasi-concavity in this book. Interested readers should consult Madden (1986), in particular theorems 14.3 and 20.1.

Definition A.5. Let x^* be such that $g^1(x^*) = 0, \ldots, g^m(x^*) = 0$. We say that x^* is a *regular point* if the gradients of the functions $g^1, \ldots, g^m$, are linearly independent:

$$\begin{pmatrix} \frac{\partial g^1}{\partial x_1}(x^*) & \ldots & \frac{\partial g^1}{\partial x_n}(x^*) \\ \ldots & & \ldots \\ \frac{\partial g^m}{\partial x_1}(x^*) & \ldots & \frac{\partial g^m}{\partial x_n}(x^*) \end{pmatrix} \text{ has rank } m.$$

Proposition A.5 (necessary condition). Assume that f and $g^1, \ldots, g^m$ are C^1 functions on the convex set D. Let x^* be a local maximum for problem [PA.3]. Assume also that x^* is a regular point. Then there exists one (and only one) vector λ^* such that

$$\frac{\partial L}{\partial x^i}(x^*, \lambda^*) = 0, \text{ for } i = 1, \ldots, n$$

(that is, x^* locally satisfies condition (a) of proposition A.4).

Proposition A.6 (sufficient condition). Assume that f and $g^1, \ldots, g^m$ are C^2 functions on the convex set D. Let x^* be a point such that $g^1(x^*) = 0, \ldots, g^m(x^*) = 0$ and that satisfies:

$$\frac{\partial L}{\partial x^i}(x^*, \lambda^*) = 0, \text{ for } i = 1, \ldots, n$$

for a some λ^*. If the Hessian of $L(x^*, \lambda^*)$ with respect to the variables x is negative definite, then x^* is a local maximum of problem [PA.3].

Comment. If the point x^* satisfies the Kuhn–Tucker conditions (b)–(d), then the conditions of proposition A.6 are also sufficient for x^* to be a local maximum of [PA.2].

Let us consider the following class of maximization problems:

[PA.4] $\max_{x \in D} \; f(x; \alpha)$ subject to $g^i(x; \alpha) \geq 0$, for $i = 1, \ldots, m$, $\alpha \in A$

We denote $x^*(\alpha)$ and $\lambda^*(\alpha)$ the solution and the multipliers of [PA.4] (depending on α, which is a constant in each problem), and $V(\alpha) = f(x^*(\alpha); \alpha)$ the value function which associates to α the maximum value of f on D.

Proposition A.7 (Envelop theorem). Let D and A be two sets, convex and open. Assume that for all $\alpha \in A$ it is true that f and g^i are concave and C^2

functions, and that [RQ] is verified. Assume also that for any $\alpha \in A$ there is unique solution to [PA.4], $x^*(\alpha)$ and $\lambda^*(\alpha)$ are C^1, and $V(\alpha)$ is C^2 on α. Then,

$$\frac{\partial V}{\partial \alpha^i}(\alpha) = \frac{\partial L}{\partial \alpha^i}(x, \lambda; \alpha), \text{ for } i = 1, \ldots, m$$

where the Lagrangean is evaluated at $x = x^*(\alpha)$ and $\lambda = \lambda^*(\alpha)$.

REFERENCES

Akerlof, G., 1970, 'The Market for 'Lemons': Qualitative Uncertainty and the Market Mechanism', *Quarterly Journal of Economics* 89, 488–500.

Alchian, A., and Demsetz, H., 1972, 'Production, Information Costs, and Economic Organization', *American Economic Review* 62, 777–95.

Arnaudin-Fagart, M. C., 1991, 'Concurrence, Asymétrie d'Information et Théory des Incitations: Quelques Developpements du Modèle Principal-Agent', Ph.D. diss., Université de Paris I Panthéon-Sorbonne.

Aron, D. J., Olivella, P., 1994, 'Bonuses and Penalties as Equilibrium Incentive Devices, with Application to Manufacturing Systems', *Journal of Law, Economics, and Organization* 10 (1), 1–34.

Banks, J. S., 1991, *Signaling Games in Political Science*, Harwood Academic Publishers, New York.

—— and Sobel, J., 1987, 'Equilibrium Selection in Signalling Games', *Econometrica* 55, 647–63.

Baron, D., 1989, 'Design of Regulatory Mechanisms and Institutions', in the *Handbook of Industrial Organizations* 2, R. Schmalensee, and R. Willig (eds.), North-Holland, Amsterdam.

—— and Besanko, D., 1984, 'Regulation and Information in a Continuing Relationship', *Information Economics and Policy* 1, 267–302.

—— —— 1987, 'Commitment and Fairness in a Dynamic Regulatory Relationship', *Review of Economic Studies* 54, 413–36.

—— —— 1992, 'Information, Control and Organizational Structure', *Journal of Economics and Management Strategy* 1 (2), 237–75.

—— Myerson, R., 1982, 'Regulating a Monopoly with Unknown Costs', *Econometrica* 50, 911–30.

Bernheim, B. D., and Whinston, M. D., 1986, 'Common Agency', *Econometrica* 54 (4), 923–42.

Besanko, D., 1985, 'Multi-period Contracts between Principal and Agent with Adverse Selection', *Economics Letters* 17, 33–7.

Bester, H., and Helwig, M., 1987, 'Moral Hazard and Equilibrium Credit Rationing: An Overview of the Issues', discussion paper A-125, Bonn.

Bhattacharya, S., 1979, 'Imperfect Information, Dividend Policy, and the Bird in the Hand Fallacy', *Bell Journal of Economics* 95 (1), 1–24.

Branco, F., 1992, 'Essays on Optimal Auctions', Ph.D. diss., MIT.

—— 1996, 'Multiple Unit Auctions of an Indivisible Good', in *Economic Theory* 8(1), 77–101.

Bullow, J., and Roberts, J., 1989, 'The Simple Economics of Optimal Auctions', *Journal of Political Economy*, 97 (5), 1060–90.

Chiappori, P. A., and Macho-Stadler, I., 1990, 'Contrats de Travail Répétés: Le Rôle de la Mémoire', *Annales d'Economie et de Statistique* 17 (1), 47–70.

—— Macho-Stadler, I., Rey, P., and Salanié, B., 1994, 'Repeated Moral Hazard: The Role of Memory, Commitment and Acces to Credit Markets', *European Economic Review* 38, 1527–53.

Cho, I. K., and Kreps, D., 1987, 'Signaling Games and Stable Equilibria', *Quarterly Journal of Economics* 102, 179–221.

Clarke, E., 1971, 'Multipart Pricing of Public Goods', *Public Choice* 8, 19–33.

Crawford, V., and Sobel, J., 1982, 'Strategic Information Transmission', *Econometrica* 50 (6), 1431–51.

Crémer, J., and McLean, R., 1985, 'Optimal Selling Strategies under Uncertainty for a Discriminating Monopolist when Demands are Interdependent', *Econometrica* 53, 345–61.

—— 'Full Extractions of the Surplus in Bayesian and Dominant Strategy Auctions', *Econometrica* 56 (6), 1247–57.

Da-Rocha-Alvarez, J. M., and De-Frutos, M. A., 1999, 'A Note on the Optimal Structure of Production', *Journal of Economic Theory* 89(2), 234–46.

—— 1994, 'Horizontal competition in a regulated market with joint production and adverse selection', Working Paper 258.94 UAB.

Dana Jr., J. D., 1993, 'The Organization and Scope of Agents: Regulating Multiproduct Industries', *Journal of Economic Theory* 59, 288–310.

De-Bijl, P. W. J., 1995, 'Delegation of Responsibility in Organizations', CentER Discussion Paper, Tilburg University.

Demski, J. S., and Sappington, D., 1986, 'Line-item Reporting, Factor Acquisition and Subcontracting', *Journal of Accounting Research* 24, 250–69.

Dewatripont, M., 1989, Renegotiation and Information Revelation over Time: The Case of Optimal Labour Contracts', *Quarterly Journal of Economics* 104, 589–619.

Farrell, J., 1984, 'Credible Neologisms in Games of Communication', Working Paper 386, MIT.

Faulí, R., 1995, 'Competition and Cooperation within a Multidivisional Firm', *Journal of Industrial Economics* 43 (1), 77–99.

Freixas, X., Guesnerie, R., and Tirole, J., 1985, 'Planning under Information and the Rachet Effect', *Review of Economic Studies* 52, 173–92.

Fudenberg, D., Holmström, B., and Milgrom, B., 1990, 'Short-term Contracts and Long-term Agency Relationships', *Journal of Economic Theory* 51, 1–31.

—— and Tirole, J., 1990, 'Moral Hazard and Renegotiation in Agency', *Econometrica* 58, 1279–320.

—— 1991, *Game Theory*, MIT Press, Cambridge, Mass.

Gallastegui, M. C., Iñarra, E., and Macho-Stadler, I., 1993, 'Contratos de Pesca desde la Perspectiva de la Teoría de la Agencia', *Estudios de Economía* 20 (2), 329–54.

Gibbard, A., 1973, 'Manipulation for Voting Schemes', *Econometrica* 41, 587–601.

Gibbons, R., 1992, *A Primer in Game Theory*, Harvester Wheatsheaf Hemel Hempstead.

Green, J. L., and Laffont, J.-J., 1977, 'Characterization of Satisfactory Mechanisms for the Revelation of Preferences for Public Goods', *Econometrica* 45, 427–38.

Green, J. R., and Stokey, N. L., 1983, 'A Comparison of Tournaments and Contracts', *Journal of Political Economy* 91, 349–64.

Grossman, S. J., 1981, 'The Informational Role of Guarranties and Private Disclosure about Product Quality', *Journal of Law and Economics* 24, 461–83.

—— and Hart, O. D., 1983, 'An Analysis of the Principal-Agent Problem', *Econometrica* 51, 7–45.

—— and Perry, M., 1986, 'Perfect Sequential Equilibrium', *Journal of Economic Theory* 39, 97–119.

Groves, T., 1973, 'Incentives in Teams', *Econometrica* 41, 617–31.

Guesnerie, R., and Laffont, J.-J., 1984, 'A Complete Solution to a Class of Principal-Agent Problems with Application to the Control of a Self-Managed Firm', *Journal of Public Economics* 25, 329–69.

—— Picard, P., and Rey, P., 1989, 'Adverse Selection and Moral Hazard with Risk Neutral Agents', *European Economic Review* 33, 807–23.

Haneda, T., 1986, 'Multiperiod Insurance Contracts under Asymmetric Information', *Keio Economic Studies* 23 (2), 61–76.

Harris, M., and Raviv, A., 1978, 'Some Results on Incentive Contracts with Applications to Education and Employment, Health Insurance and Law Enforcement', *American Economic Review* 68 (1), 20–30.

—— —— 1979, 'Optimal Incentive Contracts with Imperfect Information', *Journal of Economic Theory* 2 (3), 231–59.

—— —— 1991, 'The Theory of Capital Structure', *Journal of Finance* 46, 297–355.

Hart, O., and Holmström, B., 1987, 'The Theory of Contracts', in T. Bewley (ed.), *Advances in Economic Theory, Fifth World Congress*, Cambridge University Press, Cambridge.

—— and Tirole, J., 1988, 'Contract Renegotiation and Coasian Dynamics', *Review of Economic Studies* 55, 509–40.

Holmström, B., 1979, 'Moral Hazard and Observability', *Bell Journal of Economics* 10 (1), 74–91.

—— 1982, 'Moral Hazard in Teams', *Bell Journal of Economics* 13 (2), 324–40.

—— and Milgrom, P., 1990, 'Regulating Trade among Agents', *Journal of Institutional and Theoretical Economics* 146 (1), 85–105.

—— —— 1991, 'Multitask Principal-Agent Analysis: Incentive Contracts, Assets Ownership, and Job Design', *Journal of Law, Economics, and Organization* 7 (Suppl.), 24–52.

Itoh, H., 1990, 'Incentives to Help in Multi-Agent Situations', *Econometrica* 59, 611–36.

—— 1993, 'Collusion, Incentives and Risk Sharing', *Journal of Economic Theory* 60, 410–27.

Kofman, A. M., and Lawarrée, J., 1993, 'Collusion in Hierarchical Agency', *Econometrica* 61 (3), 629–56.

Kohlberg, E., and Mertens, J. F., 1986, 'On the Strategic Stability of Equilibria', *Econometrica* 54, 1003–39.

Kreps, D., 1990, *A Course in Microeconomic Theory*, Harvester Wheatsheaf, New York.
—— and Sobel, J., 1994, 'Signalling', in R. Aumann and S. Hart (eds.), *Handbook of Game Theory*. Amsterdam, Elsevier/North Holland.
—— and Wilson, R., 1982, 'Sequential Equilibria', *Econometrica* 50, 863–94.
Laffont, J.-J., 1988, 'Hidden Games in Hierarchies: Facts and Models', *The Economic Record* 295–306.
—— 1989, *The Economics of Uncertainty and Information*, MIT Press, Cambridge, Mass.
—— 1990, 'Analysis of Hidden Gaming in a Three Levels Hierarchy', *Journal of Law, Economics, and Organization* 6, 301–24.
—— and Maskin, E., 1979, 'A Differentiable Approach to Expected Utility Maximizing Mechanisms', in J.J. Laffont, (ed.), *Aggregation and Revelation of Preferences*, North-Holland, Amsterdam.
—— —— and Rochet, J.-C., 1987, 'Optimal Non-linear Pricing with two Dimensional Characteristics', in T. Groves, R. Radner, and S. Reiter (eds.), *Information, Incentives and Economic Mechanisms*, Univ. of Minnesota Press, Minneapolis.
—— and Tirole, J., 1986, 'Using Cost Observation to Regulate Firms', *Journal of Political Economy* 94, 614–41.
—— —— 1987, 'Comparative Statics of the Optimal Dynamic Incentive Contract', *European Economic Review* 31, 901–26.
—— —— 1988, 'The Dynamics of Incentive Contracts', *Econometrica* 56, 1153–176.
—— —— 1990, 'Adverse Selection and Renegociation in Procurement', *Review of Economic Studies* 57, 597–626.
—— —— 1993, *A Theory of Incentives in Procurement and Regulation*, Cambridge, Mass. MIT Press, Cambridge, Mass.
Lambert, R., 1983, 'Long Term Contrats and Moral Hazard', *Bell Journal of Economics* 14, 441–52.
Lazear, E. P., and Rosen, S., 1981, 'Rank-order Tournaments as Optimum Labor Contracts', *Journal of Political Economy* 89, 841–64.
Lewis, T. R., and Sappington, D. E. M., 1993, 'Ignorance in Agency Problems', *Journal of Economic Theory* 61, 169–83.
Luenberger, D. G., 1984, *Linear and Non-linear Programming*, 2nd edn., Addison-Wesley, Reading, Mass.
Ma, C., 1991, 'Adverse Selection in Dynamic Moral Hazard', *Quarterly Journal of Economics*, 255–75.
McAfee, P., and McMillan, J., 1986 'Bidding for Contracts: A Principal-Agent Analysis', *Rand Journal of Economics* 17, 326–38.
—— —— 1987*a*, 'Competition for Agency Contracts', *Rand Journal of Economics* 18, 296–307.
—— —— 1987*b*, 'Auctions and Bidding', *Journal of Economic Literature* 25, 699–738.
—— —— 1988, 'Multidimensional Incentive Compatibility and Mechanism Design', *Journal of Economic Theory* 46, 335–54.
—— —— Reny, P., 1989, 'Extracting the Surplus in the Common Value Auction', *Econometrica* 5 (6), 1451–9.

Macho-Stadler, I., Martinez-Giralt, X., and Pérez-Castrillo, J. D., 1996, 'The Role of Information in Licensing Contract Design', *Research Policy* 25 (1), 25–41.

—— and Pérez-Castrillo, J. D., 1991*a*, 'Moral Hazard and Cooperation', *Economics Letters* 35 (1), 17–20.

—— —— 1991*b*, 'Double Risque Moral et Délégation', *Recherches Economiques de Louvain*, 57, 277–96.

—— —— 1991*c*, 'Contrats de Licence et Asymétrie d'Information', *Annales d'Economie et de Statistique* 24, 189–208.

—— —— 1993, 'Moral Hazard with Several Agents: the Gains from Cooperation', *International Journal of Industrial Organization* 11, 73–100.

—— —— 1998, 'Centralized and Decentralized Contracts in a Moral Hazard Environment', *Journal of Industrial Èconomics* 46(4), 489–510.

Madden, P., 1986, *Concavity and Optimization in Microeconomics*, Blackwell, Oxford.

Malcomson, J. M., 1984, 'Work Incentives, Hierarchies and Internal Labor Markets', *Journal of Political Economy* 92, 486–507.

—— 1986, 'Rank-order Contracts for a Principal with Many Agents', *Review of Economic Studies* 53, 807–17.

—— and Spinnewyn, F., 1988, 'The Multiperiod Principal-Agent Problem', *Review of Economic Studies* 55, 391–408.

Malinvaud, E., 1968, *Leçons de Théorie Microéconomique*, Dunod, Paris.

Martimort, D., 1992, 'Multiprincipaux en Economie de l'Information', Ph. D. diss., EHESS, Toulouse.

Maskin, E., and Riley, J., 1980, 'Auction Design with Correlated Values', Working Paper, University of California, Los Angeles.

—— —— 1984, 'Optimal Auctions with Risk Averse Buyers', *Econometrica* 52 (6), 1473–518.

—— —— 1989, 'Optimal Multi-Unit Auctions', in F. Hahn (ed.), *The Economics of Missing Markets, Information, and Games*, Ch. 14, 312–35, Oxford University Press, Oxford.

—— and Tirole, J., 1990, 'The Principal-Agent Relationship with an Informed Principal, I: Private Values', *Econometrica* 58 (2), 379–410.

—— —— 1992, 'The Principal-Agent Relationship with an Informed Principal, II: Common Value', *Econometrica* 60 (1), 1–42.

Mass-Colell, A., Whinston, M. D., and Green, J. R., 1995, '*Microeconomic Theory*', Oxford University Press, Oxford.

Matthews, S. A., 1983, 'Selling the Risk Averse Buyers with Unobservable Tastes', *Journal of Economic Theory* 30 (2), 370–400.

Melumad, N., Mookherjee, D., and Reichelstein, S., 1995, 'Hierarchical Decentralization of Incentive Contracts', *Rand Journal of Economics* 26(4), 654–72.

—— and Reichelstein, S., 1987, 'Centralization vs Delegation and the Value of Communication', *Journal of Accounting Research* 25, 1–18.

Milgrom, P., 1981, 'Good News and Bad News: Representation Theorems and Applications', *Bell Journal of Economics* 13, 380–91.

Milgrom, P., 1987*a*, 'Adverse Selection without Hidden Information', Working Paper, 8742 UC-Berkeley.
—— 1987*b*, 'Auction Theory', in *Advances in Economic Theory: Fifth World Congress*, F. Bewley (ed.), Cambridge University Press, Cambridge.
—— 1988, 'Employment Contracts, Influence Activities and Efficient Organization Design', *Journal of Political Economy* 96, 42–60.
—— Roberts, J., 1982, 'Limit Pricing and Entry under Incomplete Information: An Equilibrium Analysis', *Econometrica* 50 (2), 443–60.
—— —— 1986, 'Prices and Advertising Signals of Product Quality', *Journal of Political Economy* 94, 796–821.
—— —— 1992, *Economics, Organization and Management*, Prentice-Hall, Englewood Cliffs.
—— Weber, R. J., 1982, 'A Theory of Auctions and Competitive Bidding', *Econometrica* 50, 1089–122.
Mirrlees, J., 1971, 'An Exploration in the Theory of Optimum Income Taxation', *Review of Economic Studies* 38, 175–208.
—— 1974, 'Notes on Welfare Economics, Information and Uncertainty', in M. Balch, D. McFadden and S. Wu (eds.), *Essays in Economic Behavior in Uncertainty*, North-Holland, Amsterdam.
—— 1975, 'The Theory of Moral Hazard and Unobservable Behavior, Part I', Working Paper, Nuffield College, Oxford.
—— 1976, 'The Optimal Structure of Incentives and Autority within an Organization', *Bell Journal of Economics* 7, 105–31.
Modigliani, F., and Miller, M. H., 1958, 'Cost of Capital, Corporation Finance, and the Theory of Investment', *American Economic Review* 48 (3), 261–97.
Mookherjee, D., 1984, 'Optimal Incentive Schemes with Many Agents', *Review of Economic Studies* 51, 433–46.
Mussa, M., and Rosen, S., 1978, 'Monopoly and Product Quality', *Journal of Economic Theory* 18, 301–17.
Myers, S. C., and Majluf, N. S., 1984, 'The Capital Structure Puzzle', *Journal of Finance* 39, 575–92.
Myerson, R., 1979, 'Incentive Compatibility and the Bargaining Problem', *Econometrica* 47, 61–73.
—— 1981, 'Optimal Auction Design', *Mathematics of Operations Research* 6, 58–73.
—— 1982, 'Optimal Coordination Mechanisms in Generalized Principal-Agent Problems', *Journal of Mathematical Economics* 10, 67–81.
—— 1983, 'Mechanism Design by an Informed Principal', *Econometrica* 51, 1767–98.
—— and Satterthwaite, M., 1983, 'Efficient Mechanisms for Bilateral Trading', *Journal of Economic Theory* 28, 265–81.
Nalebuff, B. J., and Stiglitz, J. E., 1983, 'Prizes and Incentives: Towards a General Theory of Compensation and Competition', *Bell Journal of Economics* 14, 21–43.
Olivella, P., 1995, 'Information Structures and the Delegation of Monitoring', *Annales d'Economie et de Statistique* 39, 1–32.

Ortuño, I., 1992, 'Inspection in Models of Adverse Selection', Working Paper, -A.D. 92–01, IVIE.

Page, F. H. Jr., 1992, 'Optimal Contract Mechanisms for Principal-Agent Problems with Moral Hazard and Adverse Selection', *Economic Theory* 1, 323–38.

Picard, P., 1987, 'On the Design of Incentive Schemes under Moral Hazard and Adverse Selection', *Journal of Public Economics* 33, 305–31.

Radner, R., 1981, 'Monitoring Cooperative Agreements in a Repeated Principal-Agent Relationship', *Econometrica* 49, 1127–48.

Ramakrishnan, R., and Thakor, A., 1991, 'Cooperation versus Competition in Agency', *Journal of Law, Economics, and Organization* 7, 248–83.

Rasmusen, B., 1987, *Games and Information: An Introduction to Game Theory*, Blackwell, Oxford, and Cambridge, Mass.

Rees, R., 1987, 'The Theory of Principal and Agent', in *Surveys in the Economics of Uncertainty*, J. Hey and P. Lambert (eds.), Basil Blackwell, 46–90.

Rey, P., and Salanié, B., 1990, 'Long term, Short term and Renegotiation', *Econometrica* 58, 597–619.

Ricketts, M., 1986, 'The Geometry of Principal and Agent: Yet Another Use for the Edgeworth Box', *Scottish Journal of Political Economy*, 228–247.

Riley, J. G., 1979, 'Informational Equilibrium', *Econometrica* 47, 331–359.

—— and Samuelson, W., 1981, 'Optimal Auctions', *American Economic Review* 71, 381–92.

Riordan, M. H., and Sappington, D. E., 1987, 'Information, Incentives, and the Organizational Mode', *Quarterly Journal of Economics* 102 (2), 243–63.

Rogerson, W., 1985*a*, 'The First Order Approach to Principal-Agent Problems', *Econometrica* 53 (6), 1357–67.

—— 1985*b*, 'Repeated Moral Hazard', *Econometrica* 53, 69–76.

Ross, S. A., 1973, 'The Economic Theory of Agency: The Principal's Problem', *American Economic Review* 63, 134–9.

—— 1977, 'The Determination of the Financial Structure: The Incentive Signaling Approach', *Bell Journal of Economics* 8 (1), 23–40.

Rothschild, M., and Stiglitz, J., 1976, 'Equilibrium in Competitive Insurance Markets: An Essay in the Economics of Imperfect Information', *Quarterly Journal of Economics* 90, 629–50.

Rubinstein, A., and Yaari, M. E., 1983, 'Repeated Insurance Contrats and Moral Hazard', *Journal of Economic Theory* 30, 74–97.

Salas-Fumás, V., 1992, 'Relative Performance Evaluation of Management: The Effects on Industrial Competition and Risk Sharing', *International Journal of Industrial Organization* 10, 473–89.

Schmidt, K. M., and Schnitzer, M., 1995, 'The Interaction of Explicit and Implicit Contracts', *Economics Letters* 48, 193–9.

Shavell, S., 1979, 'Risk Sharing and Incentives in the Principal and Agent Relationship', *Bell Journal of Economics* 10, 55–73.

Sinclair-Desgagné, B., 1994, 'The First-Order Approach to Multi-Signal Principal-Agent Problems', *Econometrica* 62 (2), 459–65.

Spence, M., 1973, 'Job Market Signaling', *Quarterly Journal of Economics* 87, 355–74.
—— 1974, *Market Signaling*, Harvard University Press, Cambridge, Mass.

Spiller, P. T., and Urbiztondo, S., 1991, 'Interest Groups and the Control of the Bureaucracy: An Agency Perspective on the Administrative Procedure Act', *Anales de la Asociación Argentina de Economía Política.*

Stein, J., 1989, 'Cheap Talk and the Fed: A Theory of Imprecise Policy Announcements', *American Economic Review* 79, 32–42.

Stiglitz, J. E., and Weiss, A., 1981, 'Credit Rationing in Markets with Imperfect Information', *American Economic Review* 71 (3), 393–410.

Stole, L., 1990, 'Mechanism Design under Common Agency', Working Paper, MIT.

Sydsaeter, K., and Hammond, P. J., 1995, *Mathematics for Economic Analysis*, Prentice-Hall (International Edns.), Englewood-Cliffs, NJ.

Tirole, J., 1986, 'Hierarchies and Bureaucracies: On the Role of Collusion in Organizations', *Journal of Law, Economics and Organization* 2 (2), 181–214.
—— 1988*a*, 'The Multicontract Organization', *Canadian Journal of Economics / Revue Canadienne d'Economie*, 21 (3), 459–66.
—— 1988*b*, *The Theory of Industrial Organization*, MIT Press, Cambridge, Mass.
—— 1992, 'Collusion and the Theory of Organizations', in J.-J. Laffont (ed.,), *Advances in Economic Theory*, Sixth World Congress of the Econometric Society, Cambridge.

Van Damme, E. E. C., 1991, *Stability and Perfection of Nash Equilibria*, 2nd edn., Springer-Verlag, Berlin.

Varian, H., 1992, *Microeconomic Analysis*, 3rd edn., W. W. Norton & Co., New York.

Vickers, J., 1985, 'Delegation and the Theory of the Firm', *Economic Journal* (Suppl.) 75, 138–47.

Vickrey, W., 1961, 'Counterspeculation, Auctions and Competitive Sealed Tenders', *Journal of Finance* 16, 8–37.

SOLUTIONS TO THE EXERCISES

Chapter 2

Solution to Exercise 1. (a) $$\max_{\{e,\, w(x)\}} \int_{\underline{x}}^{\overline{x}} B(x - w(x))\, f(x; e)\, dx$$

$$\text{s.t.} \int_{\underline{x}}^{\overline{x}} u(w(x))\, f(x; e)\, dx - v(e) \geq \underline{U}.$$

The first-order conditions with respect to the optimal contract are:

$$\frac{\partial H}{\partial w(x)}(w^o(x)) = -f(x; e)\, B'(x - w^o(x)) + \lambda^o f(x; e)\, u'(w(x)) = 0,$$

from which $\lambda^o = B'(x - w^o(x))/u'(w(x))$, for all $x \in X$. The discussion on the form of the function $w^o(x)$, according to the degree of risk-aversion of the principal and the agent, is similar to that considered in the text of this chapter.

(*b*) If the principal is risk-neutral, then we have: $w^o(x) = w^o =$ constant, for all $x \in X$. Using the participation condition, we arrive at $w^o = u^{-1}(\underline{U} + v(e))$.

(*c*) Once the wage that must be paid to the agent in order that he exerts an effort of *e* is known, the problem that the principal must solve to calculate the optimal effort is:

$$\max_{e} \int_{\underline{x}}^{\overline{x}} (x - w^o)\, f(x; e)\, dx \Leftrightarrow \max_{e} \int_{\underline{x}}^{\overline{x}} x f(x; e)\, dx - u^{-1}(\underline{U} + v(e)).$$

From the first-order condition we have:

$$\int_{\underline{x}}^{\overline{x}} x f_e'(x; e)\, dx = v'(e)\, (u^{-1})'(\underline{U} + v(e)),$$

which is the familiar equality between marginal revenue and marginal cost. It may be that the problem is not concave in effort; the sufficient condition that ensures a local maximum is:

$$\int_{\underline{x}}^{\overline{x}} x f_{ee}''(x; e)\, dx - v''(e)\, (u^{-1})'(\underline{U} + v(e)) - [v'(e)]^2 (u^{-1})''(\underline{U} + v(e)) < 0.$$

We know that $v'' > 0$, $(u^{-1})' > 0$, and $(u^{-1})'' > 0$. [The reader can check that $(u^{-1})''(\underline{U} + v(e)) = -u''(w^o)/[u'(w^o)]^3$, where $w^o = u^{-1}(\underline{U} + v(e))$. To do so, use the fact that $(u^{-1})'\,(\underline{U}+v\,(e)\,) = 1/u'\,(u^{-1}\,(\underline{U}+v\,(e)\,)\,)]$. Therefore, a sufficient condition for the above inequality to be satisfied is:

$$\int_{\underline{x}}^{\overline{x}} x f''_{ee}\,(x; e)\,dx \leq 0.$$

The function f must be concave in the efforts for the highest results. For the distribution $f(x; e) = 1 + e\,[x-(1/2)]$, the sufficient condition is satisfied trivially, since $f''_{ee}\,(x; e) = 0$ (it is also a global condition, i.e. it is satisfied at all points, not just the maximum). Therefore, the first-order condition gives us the maximum point, so long as it is interior. The effort $e \in (0, 1)$ is a maximum when:

$$\int_0^1 x\left[x-\frac{1}{2}\right]dx = \frac{v'\,(e)}{u'\,(u^{-1}(\underline{U}+v\,(e)\,)\,)}.$$

(When the level of e that satisfies this equation is less than zero or greater than one, there cannot be an interior solution, and we have a corner solution, either $e=0$ or $e=1$.)

Solution to Exercise 2. (*a*) Without insurance, an individual gets $\underline{U} = (1-p)\,u\,(w+L) + p\,u\,(w)$.

(*b*) An insurance contract will include a price and a coverage: (ρ, q).

(*c*)
$$\max_{\rho,\,q}\ \{\rho - p\,q\}$$
$$\text{s.t. } (1-p)\,u\,(w+L-\rho) + p\,u\,(w-\rho+q) \geq \underline{U}.$$

From the first-order conditions of this problem we can deduce that the participation constraint binds and

$$\frac{1}{p} = \frac{(1-p)\,u'\,(w+L-\rho) + p\,u'\,(w-\rho+q)}{p\,u'\,(w-\rho+q)} \Leftrightarrow \frac{1-p}{p} = \frac{(1-p)\,u'\,(w+L-\rho)}{p\,u'\,(w-\rho+q)},$$

from which $u'\,(w+L-\rho) = u'\,(w-\rho+q)$ and therefore $L = q$ since $u'' \neq 0$ (i.e. the individual completely insures). The price is determined by the participation constraint: $u\,(w+L-\rho) = \underline{U} = (1-p)\,u\,(w+L) + p\,u\,(w)$, from which $\rho = w + L - u^{-1}\,(\underline{U})$. The insurance company's profits are strictly positive, since $\rho - p\,L = w + L - u^{-1}\,(\underline{U}) - p\,L > 0 \Leftrightarrow u\,(w+(1-p)\,L) > \underline{U} = (1-p)\,u\,(w+L) + p\,u\,(w)$, which is true whenever the individual is risk-averse.

(*d*) If the agent were risk-neutral, his participation constraint is $w - \rho + (1-p)\,L + pq \geq w + (1-p)\,L \Leftrightarrow p\,q - \rho \geq 0$. Since the company will only insure if $\rho \geq p\,q$, we have that $\rho = p\,q$ in this case. Both the company and the individual are indifferent to the amount of coverage. The company will earn zero profits: there is no way to earn money by insuring risk-neutral individuals.

(e) The payment ρ must be compatible with the zero profit condition, that is written $\rho = p\,L$, since it is always optimal that $q = L$.

(f)
$$\max_{\rho,\,q} \; \{(1-p)\,B(\rho) + p\,B(\rho - q)\}$$
$$\text{s.t. } (1-p)\,u\,(w+L-\rho) + p\,u\,(w-\rho+q) \geq \underline{U}.$$

Solving this gives us the expression that indicates an optimal risk distribution:

$$\frac{B'\,(\rho)}{B'\,(\rho - q)} = \frac{u'\,(w+L-\rho)}{u'\,(w-\rho+q)}.$$

In order to see that full insurance is not optimal, note that if we take $q = L$, the above formula would become: $B'\,(\rho)/B'\,(\rho - L) = 1$, which is impossible if $B'' < 0$ and $L > 0$.

Solution to Exercise 3. (a) When the principal is risk-neutral and the agent is risk-averse, the wage is independent of the result and is given by equation (2.5), while equation (2.8) is written as $p_S'\,(e^O)\,[x_S - x_F] = (u^{-1})'\,(\underline{U} + v\,(e^O)\,)\;v'\,(e^O)$. If the principal is risk-averse and the agent is risk-neutral, then equation (2.6) gives the optimal contract, and the necessary condition for optimal effort (2.11) is written: $p_S'\,(e^O)\,[x_S - x_F] = v'\,(e^O)$.

(b) The sufficient condition for this effort to be a local maximum, (2.10), is: $p_S''\,(e^O)\,[x_S - x_F] < x_F$, which means that $p_S''\,(e^O) < 0$. Besides this, in this case a sufficient condition for the problem to be concave in effort is $p_S''\,(e) \leq 0$ for all e. This is a classic condition of decreasing returns to scale. The condition has a simple interpretation since we have only two possible results, success and failure.

Solution to Exercise 4.
$$\max_{\{w_i(n)\}_{i=1,\ldots,k}} \; \sum_{i=1}^{k} p_i(n)\,[x_i - w_i(n)]$$
$$\text{s.t.} \quad \sum_{i=1}^{k} p_i(n)\,u\,(w_i(n)\,) - c \geq \underline{U},$$

where n is the number of workers that the firm contracts. From the first-order conditions, we get that $w_1\,(n) = w_2\,(n) = \ldots = w_k\,(n)$. From the participation constraint, which binds, the wage can be calculated as $w = u^{-1}\,(u\,(s) + c)$.

(b) In the above contract, the employed workers receive the same wage whichever result occurs, independently of the number of workers contracted, and they even receive the same utility whether they are employed or not. The firm not only buys their labour, but it also insures them (completely) against the randomness of the result.

(c) $$\underset{n}{\text{Max}} \quad \sum_{i=1}^{k} p_i(n)\, x_i - n\, u^{-1}(u(s) + c).$$

From the first-order condition we get $\Sigma_{i=1}^{k}\, p_i'(n)\, x_i = u^{-1}(u(s) + c)$. The second-order condition is $\Sigma_{i=1}^{k}\, p_i''(n)\, x_i < 0$.

Differentiating the first-order condition with respect to n and s we get that the employment level decreases with the unemployment benefit:

$$\sum_{i=1}^{k} p_i''(n)\, x_i\, dn - (u^{-1})'(u(s) + c)\, u'(s)\, ds = 0 \Leftrightarrow \frac{dn}{ds} = \frac{(u^{-1})\,(u(s) + c)\, u'(s)}{\sum_{i=1}^{k} p_i''(n)\, x_i} < 0.$$

Chapter 3

Solution to Exercise 1. It gives an incentive to improve the record many times, one centimetre at a time, but not to achieve the best possible performance. Whoever offers this prize must be interested in Bubka appearing many times on the winner's podium rather than getting the best possible performance.

Solution to Exercise 2. If the principal demands low effort she will pay a constant wage of $w = 1/10$ to the agent (this is true both under symmetric and asymmetric information). The principal's profit is $U_P = (1/4)\,20 - 1/10 = 49/10$. If the principal demands high effort, and if this effort is contractual, she will offer a constant wage of $w = 10/98$. The principal's profit in this case is $U_P = (3/4)\,20 - 10/98 = 14.988$. When there is asymmetric information on effort, the principal should offer a contract (w^S, w^F) that depends on success or failure. The contract should satisfy both the participation and incentive compatibility constraints when the effort exerted is high. It is easy to see that the two constraints must bind. The system of two equations in two unknowns can be rewritten as:

$$\frac{3}{w^S} + \frac{1}{w^F} = \frac{392}{10} \quad \text{and} \quad \frac{1}{w^F} - \frac{1}{w^S} = \frac{4}{10}.$$

The solution is $w^S = 10/97$ and $w^F = 10/101$. The expected profit of the principal is $U_P = 3/4\,[20 - 10/97] - 1/4\,(10/101)$, which is greater than that obtained with low effort.

Solution to Exercise 3. (a) The principal is risk-neutral and the agent is risk-averse.

(*b*) The optimal contracts are derived from (i) the principal accepts all the risk, and (ii) the participation constraint binds. If $e = 6$, then w is such that $w^{1/2} - 6^2 = 114$, which is $w = 22{,}500$. In this case, $U_P = 50{,}000 - 22{,}500 = 27{,}500$. If $e = 4$, then $w = 16{,}900$ and $U_P = 23{,}100$. The symmetric information solution is: $e^* = 6$, $w^* = 22{,}500$. If the principal was not risk-neutral, then both participants would share the risk inherent in the relationship.

(*c*) The optimal contract if $e = 4$ is the same as before: $w = 16{,}900$, since given a constant wage the agent will always choose the lowest effort level. In order to achieve $e = 6$, the principal must offer a contract that is contingent on the result. She will pay $w\,(60)$ if the result is 60,000 and $w\,(30)$ if the result is 30,000. The contract must simultaneously satisfy the participation and the incentive constraints:

$$\frac{2}{3}\,[w\,(60)]^{1/2} + \frac{1}{3}\,[w\,(30)]^{1/2} - 36 \geq 114$$

$$\frac{2}{3}\,[w\,(60)]^{1/2} + \frac{1}{3}\,[w\,(30)]^{1/2} - 36 \geq \frac{2}{3}\,[w\,(30)]^{1/2} + \frac{1}{3}\,[w\,(60)]^{1/2} - 16.$$

Both restrictions will bind in the solution to the principal's problem of 'spending the least possible amount'. We have two equations in two unknowns that lead to the solution $w\,(60) = 28{,}900$ and $w\,(30) = 12{,}100$. The principal's expected utility is $U_P = 26{,}700$. Under asymmetric information the principal also chooses $e = 6$, since $26{,}700 > 23{,}100$, but with an efficiency loss measured by the reduction in the expected profits of the principal (the agent always obtains his reservation utility).

Solution to Exercise 4. (*a*) The government is unable to verifiably determine the exact amount of resources that the firm dedicates to R&D.

(*b*) This fixed subsidy does not give incentives. The firm will exert the same investment effort as if there were no subsidy. Hence such a subsidy is useless and a waste of public resources.

(*c*) This policy does inspire greater investment in research activities. Therefore it is useful since if the government wants the firm to invest more in R&D, this is one way to achieve the goal.

(*d*) When the government can effectively control the firm's spending on the project (and only in this case!), subsidizing a part of the cost of R&D is a good technological policy, since reducing the costs will incite the firm to carry out more R&D.

Solution to Exercise 5. (*a*) Let q be the probability that an individual is alcohol tested, and let f be the fine if he has drunk too much. The expected utility of an individual who has chosen not to drink (e^N) is, if the test is perfect, $u\,(e^N)$, since he will never be fined even though he is tested. If the individual chooses to drink (e^B), his expected utility is $(1-q)\,u(e^B) + q\,[u(e^B) - v(f)] = u(e^B) - q\,v(f)$. We can safely assume that $u(e^B) > u(e^N)$, since otherwise no one would ever drink alcohol. Given the testing policy, in order for someone to prefer e^N to e^B it must be true that: $u(e^N) \geq u(e^B) - q\,v(f) \Leftrightarrow u(e^B) - u(e^N) \leq q\,v(f)$. Or in other words, the combination of testing and fines (the expected 'punishment') must have greater expected value than the utility difference between choosing to drink and choosing not to drink (the sure thing).

(*b*) Let $P(e^B)$ be the probability of accident for e^B. The individual will decide not to drink if $u(e^B) - u(e^N) \leq P(e^B)\,v(f)$. Therefore this method will only be effective if $P(e^B) > q$. Otherwise it would be necessary to set greater fines in the case of accident and alcohol than those that are needed in the case of alcohol testing. (Note that in order to compare the two policies, we must also compare the control cost for both cases.)

(*c*) The fact that there are injuries or not has nothing to do with the driver's intoxication. Therefore it is never useful to distinguish between accidents with injuries and those without. All that is important is the average fine.

(*d*) Fining drivers that are not drunk and that have an accident only makes not drinking less attractive, thus providing a motive to drink.

(*e*) If the objective of the mechanisms proposed is to incite someone to take a given action, then only the informative part of any available signal should be taken into account.

Solution to Exercise 6. (*a*) Under symmetric information the agent receives a fixed pay-off, determined by the participation constraint. i) For e^1, the wage is $w = 25{,}600$ and the principal's profits are $U_P = 18{,}150$. ii) For e^2, $w = 19{,}600$ and $U_P = 17{,}900$. iii) For e^3, $w = 15{,}625$ and $U_P = 15{,}625$. Hence, under symmetric information the principal chooses e^1.

(*b*) If a moral hazard problem exists, then: (*i*) When the principal demands the effort e^1, she must use the pay-off mechanism contingent on the result $(w(25), w(50))$ that solves the following problem:

$$\underset{w(25),\, w(50)}{\text{Min}} \quad \frac{1}{4} w(25) + \frac{3}{4} w(50)$$

$$\text{s.t.} \quad \frac{1}{4} w(25)^{1/2} + \frac{3}{4} w(50)^{1/2} - 40 \geq 120$$

$$\frac{1}{4} w(25)^{1/2} + \frac{3}{4} w(50)^{1/2} - 40 \geq \frac{1}{2} w(25)^{1/2} + \frac{1}{2} w(50)^{1/2} - 20$$

$$\frac{1}{4} w(25)^{1/2} + \frac{3}{4} w(50)^{1/2} - 40 \geq \frac{3}{4} w(25)^{1/2} + \frac{1}{4} w(50)^{1/2} - 5.$$

The solution is $w(25) = 10{,}000$, $w(50) = 32{,}400$, and $U_P = 16{,}950$.

(ii) If the principal wants the agent to exert effort e^2, then the pay-off mechanism is $w(25) = 12{,}100$, $w(50) = 28{,}900$, and $U_P = 17{,}000$ (see Annexe).

(iii) The optimal contract to incite effort of e^3 is the same as under symmetric information, i.e. $w(25) = w(50) = 15{,}625$ and $U_P = 15{,}625$. Under symmetric information the principal chooses effort level e^2. The asymmetric information not only results in lower profits for e^2 ($17{,}000 < 17{,}900$), but also the effort chosen is different ($e^2 < e^1$).

Annexe: Here we shall rigorously solve the problem of case (ii). We will use the following substitutions: $s(25) = w(25)^{1/2}$ and $s(50) = w(50)^{1/2}$.

$$\max_{s(25),\, s(50)} \quad -s(25)^2 - s(50)^2$$

$$\text{s.t.} \quad s(25) + s(50) \geq 280, \quad s(25) - s(50) \leq 80, \text{ and } s(50) - s(25) \geq 60.$$

Denote by λ, μ, and δ the multipliers of the three constraints. The first-order conditions of the Lagrangean are written: $-2s(25) + \lambda + \mu - \delta = 0$ and $-2s(50) + \lambda - \mu + \delta = 0$, which implies that $\lambda = s(50) + s(25)$. The first constraint binds. Since the second and third constraints both cannot bind, one of them will not bind, and so either $\mu = 0$, or $\delta = 0$. If $\delta = 0$ then, from the first-order conditions of the Lagrangean and the expression for λ, we have that $\mu = s(25) - s(50)$, which is impossible since $s(50) - s(25) \geq 60 \geq 0$. Hence $\mu = 0$, from which $\delta = s(50) - s(25) > 0$. This implies that the third restriction binds. $s(25)$ and $s(50)$ are calculated from the system of equations formed by the first and third restrictions written with strict equality.

Solution to Exercise 7. (*a*) Under symmetric information, $\sqrt{w} - e^2 = 21$. Therefore, for $e = 0$: $w = 441$ and $\Pi(e = 0) = 459$; for $e = 3$: $w = 900$ and $\Pi(e = 3) = 500$. The principal will choose $e = 3$.

(*b*) The contract is the same as under symmetric information.

(*c*) $\text{Min } 0.2\, w(0) + 0.4\, w(1) + 0.4\, w(2)$

$$\text{s.t.} \quad 0.2\sqrt{w(0)} + 0.4\sqrt{w(1)} + 0.4\sqrt{w(2)} - 9 \geq 21$$

$$0.2\sqrt{w(0)} + 0.4\sqrt{w(1)} + 0.4\sqrt{w(2)} - 9 \geq 0.4\sqrt{w(0)} + 0.4\sqrt{w(1)} + 0.2\sqrt{w(2)}.$$

The solution is $w(0) = 0$, $w(1) = 900$ and $w(2) = 2{,}025$. $\Pi(e = 3) = 230$.

(*d*) The principal demands effort $e = 0$.

(*e*) If the agent is risk-neutral, the optimal contract would be to sell him the firm.

Solution to Exercise 8. (*a*) Paying Fred all the profits from the case makes him the residual claimant, and so he receives an expected payment of $4,000, the certainty equivalent of which is less than $4,000 if Fred is risk-averse.

(*b*) If Fred prefers $3,000 for sure, if his effort is verifiable and if the law firm is risk-neutral, then it is Pareto-superior for the firm to pay him $3,000 for his work (the firm earns an expected $1,000).

(*c*) From the point of view of incentives (*a*) is better than (*b*).

Solution to Exercise 9. (*a*)

$$\underset{[w_2, w_1, e]}{\text{Max}} \quad e\,B(x_2 - w_2) + (1 - e)\,B(x_1 - w_1)$$

$$\text{s.t.} \quad e\,u(w_2) + (1 - e)\,u(w_1) - v(e) \geq \underline{U}.$$

From the first-order conditions: $B'(x_2 - w_2)/B'(x_1 - w_1) = u'(w_2)/u'(w_1)$.

(*b*) The incentive compatibility constraint is:

$$e \in \arg\max_{\hat{e}} \hat{e}u(w_2) + (1 - \hat{e})\,u(w_1) - v(\hat{e}),$$

and the corresponding first-order condition is $u(w_2) - u(w_1) - v'(e) = 0$. Since the agent's utility function is concave in e, since $v(e)$ is convex, so the first-order condition is necessary and sufficient for a maximum. The first-order approach is valid. The problem of the principal is:

$$\underset{[w_2, w_1, e]}{\text{Max}} \quad e\,B(x_2 - w_2) + (1 - e)\,B(x_1 - w_1)$$

$$\text{s.t.} \quad e\,u(w_2) + (1 - e)\,u(w_1) - v(e) \geq \underline{U}$$

$$u(w_2) - u(w_1) - v'(e) = 0.$$

From this problem we get:

$$\frac{B'(x_2 - w_2)}{B'(x_1 - w_1)} = \frac{\lambda + \dfrac{\mu}{e}}{\lambda - \dfrac{\mu}{1 - e}} \; \frac{u'(w_2)}{u'(w_1)},$$

from which $B'(x_2 - w_2)/B'(x_1 - w_1) > u'(w_2)/u'(w_1)$ if the multipliers are positive. This implies that the principal makes the agent carry more than the efficient level of risk. That is, the moral hazard problem's solution contract makes the agent more interested in the result than what is really optimal. Hence this is a generalization of what we have studied for a risk-neutral principal. Note also that $B(x_2 - w_2) - B(x_1 - w_1) = \mu\, v''(e)$.

Solution to Exercise 10. In this case the optimal contract consists of asking the firm for an amount $p_a X_a$ whether the project is successful or not. Under this contract, the firm is interested in carrying out project (a), since this is the one that gives greatest profits. A zero surplus is obtained, and so there is no credit rationing. This result is reasonable since if we do not restrict the type of contract and if both parties are risk-neutral, the efficient allocation is obtained.

Solution to Exercise 11. (a) The principal maximizes expected profits under the participation and incentive compatibility constraints (we denote $w_i \equiv w(x_i)$):

$$\underset{[w_1, w_2, w_3]}{\text{Max}} \quad \frac{1}{4}(x_1 - w_1) + \frac{1}{4}(x_2 - w_2) + \frac{1}{2}(x_3 - w_3)$$

$$\text{s.t.} \quad \frac{1}{4}u(w_1) + \frac{1}{4}u(w_2) + \frac{1}{2}u(w_3) - v(e^H) \geq \underline{U}$$

$$\frac{1}{4}u(w_1) + \frac{1}{4}u(w_2) + \frac{1}{2}u(w_3) - v(e^H) \geq \frac{1}{4}u(w_1) + \frac{1}{2}u(w_2) + \frac{1}{4}u(w_3) - v(e^L).$$

Using λ and μ respectively for the multipliers of the restrictions, we get that $\lambda = 1/u'(w_1)$ and $\lambda - \mu = 1/u'(w_2)$, from which $w_1 \geq w_2$. However, μ must be strictly positive, and so $w_1 > w_2$.

(b) The result x_1 is 100 per cent proof that the agent has exerted low effort. If we impose a very harsh punishment (a fine) if x_1 occurs, then the worker will always exert high effort. Therefore, we could pay wages equal to the symmetric information wages for x_2 and x_3 (so that $w_2 = w_3$) and use some large negative number for w_1.

Solution to Exercise 12. (a) Under symmetric information, the pay-off is constant and is determined by the participation constraint: $w^L = \underline{w}$ and $w^H = (\sqrt{\underline{w}} + v)^2$. The owner demands the high effort if $p(\pi_2 - \pi_1) \geq (\sqrt{\underline{w}} + v)^2 - \underline{w}$.

(b) With the same wage $\underline{w}$ the manager would spontaneously exert low effort. The optimal contract that achieves high effort is $w_2 = \underline{w}$ and $w_1 = (v/p + \sqrt{\underline{w}})^2$.

(c) The owner will demand effort e^H if $\pi_1 - \pi_2 \geq (v/p + \sqrt{\underline{w}})^2 - \underline{w}$.

(d) Given these parameters, the conditions for the owner to prefer high effort under symmetric and asymmetric information are, respectively, $\pi_1 - \pi_2 \geq 28$ and $\pi_1 - \pi_2 \geq 34$. Therefore, in case ($d1$) the owner always prefers high effort; in case ($d2$) high effort would only be preferred under symmetric information; and in the situation of ($d3$) low effort is always preferred. The asymmetric information not only affects the optimal contract, but also the choice of effort.

Solution to Exercise 13. (*a*) The risk derived from the examination system is due to two factors. First, each student suffers individual risk, since even if he studies all the material, there is always one part that he learns better than others (this is known as idiosyncratic noise). On the other hand, there is a risk that is suffered in the same way by all the students: the exam may be in general easy or more difficult, and it is often difficult for a professor to know the exact degree of difficulty of the exam (this is known as common noise). The advantage of an exam format under which a specific passing grade is required to pass is that only each particular student's luck and the common noise are important, but the luck of the other students does not influence each student's grade. The advantage of tournaments, in which half of the students pass, is that passing or not does not depend on the amount of common noise, since the grade achieved is unimportant, but only a student's ranking is important. Therefore, when there is a lot of common noise (there is a lot of uncertainty as to whether the exam will be easy or difficult) the best system is that in which half of the students pass. On the other hand, when there is a lot of idiosyncratic noise, it is best that each student's grade does not depend on the luck of the others, and so the best system is that which has a set passing grade.

(*b*) Under a tournament system, no one is willing to help classmates, and so this system does not motivate cooperation.

(*c*) Tournaments also provide an incentive to not let anyone copy you, and so they have this positive aspect.

Solution to Exercise 14. The agent's utility function is a monotonic transformation of the expected utility of an exponential function with constant absolute risk-aversion, $U(w, e) = -\exp[-rw - v(e)]$, where r represents the degree of absolute risk-aversion. If w is a normally distributed random variable then the expected utility of the agent is

$$EU = -\int \exp[-rw - v(e)]\, f(w)\, dw = -\exp\left[-E(w) + r\frac{\sigma w^2}{2} - v(e)\right].$$

Taking a monotonic transformation, we obtain the utility function given for this problem, which is equivalent to using the mean-variance criterion for choice under uncertainty rather than the expected utility criterion.

(*a*) The utility of the agent given the system of incentives $w(x) = A + Bx$ is given by $A + Be - rB^2\sigma^2/2 - v(e)$. If the principal observes the agent's effort, she would propose the sure contract $A > 0$, $B = 0$, such that $A = \underline{U} + v(e)$.

(*b*) The first-order condition that defines the effort incentives is $B = v'(e)$ in the non-verifiable case. The first-order condition with respect to effort of the principal's problem is: $1 - r v'(e) v''(e) \sigma^2 - v'(e) = 0$. Using the condition $v'(e) = B$, we have $B = 1/(1 + r v''(e) \sigma^2)$.

Solution to Exercise 15. (*a*) Under symmetric information the agent receives a constant wage: $w(e_i) = [\underline{U} + v_i]^n$. For each e_i we can calculate the principal's expected profits: $U_P(e_i) = p_i X - [\underline{U} + v_i]^n$. She chooses the effort that gives her the greatest profits.

(*b*) We first calculate the least cost, i.e. the optimal pay-off mechanism that allows the principal to get each effort level e_i in a moral hazard situation. (i) If the principal demands the lowest effort, e_1, she offers the first best contract: $\overline{w}_1 = \underline{w}_1 = [\underline{U} + v_1]^n$. (ii) If she demands e_2, the optimal contract must satisfy:

$$p_2\, \overline{w}_2^{1/n} + (1-p_2)\, \underline{w}_2^{1/n} - v_2 \geq \underline{U}$$

$$p_2\, \overline{w}_2^{1/n} + (1-p_2)\, \underline{w}_2^{1/n} - v_2 \geq p_1\, \overline{w}_2^{1/n} + (1-p_1)\, \underline{w}_2^{1/n} - v_1$$

$$p_2\, \overline{w}_2^{1/n} + (1-p_2)\, \underline{w}_2^{1/n} - v_2 \geq p_3\, \overline{w}_2^{1/n} + (1-p_3)\, \underline{w}_2^{1/n} - v_3$$

$$p_2\, \overline{w}_2^{1/n} + (1-p_2)\, \underline{w}_2^{1/n} - v_2 \geq p_4\, \overline{w}_2^{1/n} + (1-p_4)\, \underline{w}_2^{1/n} - v_4.$$

From which the contract $[\underline{w}_2, \overline{w}_2]$ is:

$$\underline{w}_2 = \left[\underline{U} + v_2 - p_2 \frac{v_2 - v_1}{p_2 - p_1}\right]^n \quad \text{and} \quad \overline{w}_2 = \left[\underline{U} + v_2 + (1-p_2) \frac{v_2 - v_1}{p_2 - p_1}\right]^n.$$

(iii) $$\overline{w}_3 = \left[\underline{U} + v_3 + (1-p_3) \max\left\{\frac{v_3 - v_1}{p_3 - p_1}, \frac{v_3 - v_2}{p_3 - p_2}\right\}\right]^n$$

$$\underline{w}_3 = \left[\underline{U} + v_3 - p_3 \max\left\{\frac{v_3 - v_1}{p_3 - p_1}, \frac{v_3 - v_2}{p_3 - p_2}\right\}\right]^n.$$

(iv) $$\overline{w}_4 = \left[\underline{U} + v_4 + (1-p_4) \max\left\{\frac{v_4 - v_1}{p_4 - p_1}, \frac{v_4 - v_2}{p_4 - p_2}, \frac{v_4 - v_3}{p_4 - p_3}\right\}\right]^n$$

$$\underline{w}_4 = \left[\underline{U} + v_4 - p_4 \max\left\{\frac{v_4 - v_1}{p_4 - p_1}, \frac{v_4 - v_2}{p_4 - p_2}, \frac{v_4 - v_3}{p_4 - p_3}\right\}\right]^n.$$

(v) The profits associated with each effort level are:

$$U_P(e_1) = p_1 X - [\underline{U} + v_1]^n, \qquad U_P(e_2) = p_2 X - p_2\, \overline{w}_2 - (1-p_2)\, \underline{w}_2,$$

$$U_P(e_3) = p_3 X - p_3\, \overline{w}_3 - (1-p_3)\, \underline{w}_3, \qquad U_P(e_4) = p_4 X - p_4\, \overline{w}_4 - (1-p_4)\, \underline{w}_4.$$

The principal chooses the effort level that, under conditions of moral hazard, guarantee her the greatest profit.

Chapter 4

Solution to Exercise 1. (*a*) Type *B*, the one that suffers the greatest effort cost. If his constraint was not binding and the principal lowered the wage, *B* would still participate, *G* would have less incentive to pass himself off as *B*, and the principal would earn greater profits.

(*b*) Type *G*. Since *B* is not interested in passing himself off as *G*, there is no need to distort the contract offered to *G* in incentive terms.

(*c*) Type *G* receives the informational income. Type *B* does not camouflage himself since the cost of the effort demanded of *G* is greater for *B*, and so he obtains less utility and does not earn informational income.

(*d*)[1] A dictator, whose main interest is to repress, contracts a prime minister. The contracted person may be either of two possible types: either repression has a low cost for him (he is 'evil') or it has a high cost (he is 'kind'). If the dictator knew the prime minister's type, he would demand less repression from the 'kind' minister than from the 'evil' one. When the two types cannot be distinguished, under the optimal asymmetric information contracts, the 'evil' minister will have less incentives to pass himself off as being 'kind', and so he will repress less and will obtain greater utility (since repression also implies a cost to an evil minister). In order to avoid one type disguising himself as the other, the optimal contract for adverse selection is such that the 'kind' minister must offer a degree of repression which is less than under symmetric information, he will be paid less, the repression demanded from the 'evil' minister will be the same as under symmetric information, and his wage will supply him with an informational income.

Solution to Exercise 2. (*a*) For *B*, w^B and e^B, are the solution to:

$$\max_{[w,\,e]} \quad k\,e - w, \quad \text{subject to the restriction } w - 2\,e^2 \geq 0,$$

from which $e^B = k/4$ and $w^B = 2\,e^{B2} = k^2/8$. In the same way, given a good worker, the optimal contract is $e^G = k/2$ and $w^G = e^{G2} = k^2/4$.

(*b*) The participation constraint for the most efficient agents and the incentive compatibility constraint of the least efficient agent do not bind. Hence the problem is:

$$\max_{[w^G,\, e^G,\, w^B,\, e^B]} \quad q\,[k\,e^G - w^G] + (1-q)\,[k\,e^B - w^B]$$

$$\text{s.t.} \quad w^G - e^{G2} - w^B + e^{B2} \geq 0$$

$$w^B - 2\,e^{B2} \geq 0.$$

[1] This example was proposed by Aleix Calveras during a course.

(c) Denoting by λ, μ the multipliers of the problem, the derivatives of the Lagrangean with respect to w^G, w^B, e^G, and e^B are, respectfully:

$$\lambda = q > 0$$

$$\mu = 1 - q + \lambda \Leftrightarrow \mu = 1 > 0$$

$$q\,k - 2\,\lambda\, e^G = 0 \Leftrightarrow e^G = k/2$$

$$(1-q)\,k + 2\,\lambda\, e^B - 4\,\mu\, e^B = 0 \Leftrightarrow e^B = (1-q)\,k/(4-2\,q)$$

and the first two equations imply that $w^B = 2\, e^{B2}$ and $w^G = e^{G2} + w^B - e^{B2} = e^{G2} + e^{B2}$. As expected, at the solution the participation constraint for G and the incentive compatibility constraint for B both bind.

(*d*) The effort demanded of the most efficient worker is the same as under symmetric information, while the type-B worker will exert less effort. Also, the type B receives exactly his reservation utility, while the type G gets an informational income.

Solution to Exercise 3. (*a*) The mayor of Bilbao maximizes his utility (or, what amounts to the same thing, minimizes his payments) under the constraints that the sorcerer accepts the contract, but the fake does not. The only way in which the mayor can separate the two types is by paying differently according to whether it rains or not. Call w_R the wage if it rains and w_N the wage if there is no rain. The problem is written as:

$$\max_{[w_R,\, w_N]} \quad -0.2\, w_R - 0.8\, w_N$$

$$\text{s.t.} \quad 0.2\,\sqrt{w_R} + 0.8\,\sqrt{w_N} \geq \underline{U} = 10$$

$$0.02\,\sqrt{w_R} + 0{,}98\,\sqrt{w_N} \leq \underline{\underline{U}} = 1.$$

(*b*) Let λ and μ be the multipliers of the above constraints. We shall show that they are both strictly positive. From the first-order conditions of the Lagrangean we get:

$$-1 + \frac{\lambda}{2\,\sqrt{w_R}} - \frac{\mu}{2\,\sqrt{w_R}} = 0 \qquad \text{and} \qquad -4 + \frac{4\,\lambda}{2\,\sqrt{w_N}} - \frac{49\,\mu}{2\,\sqrt{w_N}} = 0,$$

which imply: $\mu = (8/45)\,(\sqrt{w_R} - \sqrt{w_N})$ and $\lambda = \mu + 2\,\sqrt{w_R}$. This means that both μ and λ are strictly positive, since if $\sqrt{w_R}$ were less than $\sqrt{w_N}$, it would be impossible for the two constraints to be simultaneously satisfied. $w_R = 2{,}500$ and $w_N = 0$.

(*c*) If a sorcerer is contracted, the contract implies an expected cost for the local government of Bilbao of $C(w_R = 2{,}500\,,\, w_N = 0) = 500$. If the mayor had been sure that the person with which he was dealing was a real sorcerer then he would have paid him the fixed amount 100. The cost of the asymmetric information is 400.

Solution to Exercise 4. (a) Under symmetric information the optimal contracts are: $e^G = 1/2$, $w^G = 1/4$, $e^B = 1/4$, and $w^B = 1/8$. The principal's profits are: $\Pi = 3/16$. When there is an adverse selection problem, the optimal contracts are: $e^G = 1/2$, $w^G = 5/18$, $e^B = 1/6$, and $w^B = 1/18$. In this case the principal's profits are: $\Pi = 1/6$.

(*b*) $e^G = 1/2$, $w^G = 1/4$. The principal's profits are: $\Pi = 1/8$.

(*c*) The principal decides to contract the worker independently of his type if and only if $1/8 < 1/6$, which is always true. $e^G = 1/2$, $w^G = 5/18$, $e^B = 1/6$ y $w^B = 1/18$.

Solution to Exercise 5. (*a*) It is normal to demand more pages from the fast translator than from the slow one, since the cost per page is lower for the fast translator. It is also optimal to pay each translator the minimum wage necessary so that he will accept the job, that is, \$10 per page for the slow translator and \$5 for the fast one.

(*b*) The fast translator gets a surplus of 250 if he accepts the contract designed for the slow translator. Hence he is interested in lying. The slow translator is not interested in passing himself off as being fast.

(*c*) We know that the contract for the fast translator will be efficient, and so the number of pages demanded of him will be $n^f = 80$. We also know that the slow translator's contract will be distorted so that it is less attractive for the fast translator. If we call n^s the number of pages demanded of the slow one, $n^s < 50$. The wage of the slow translator will just cover his disutility of effort, i.e. $w^s = 10\, n^s$. Finally, the wage of the fast translator will be such that he is not interested in saying he is slow, $w^f = 5\, n^f + w^s - 5\, n^s$, which guarantees him an excess of $5n^s$.

(*d*) Under symmetric information, $\Pi'(n^{s*}) = 10$, $w^{s*} = 10\, n^{s*}$ and $\Pi'(n^{f*}) = 5$, $w^{f*} = 5\, n^{f*}$. Since $\Pi'' < 0$, the above contracts imply in particular that $n^{s*} < n^{f*}$. When the director cannot observe the translator's type, the problem is:

$$\max_{(w^f, n^f, w^s, n^s)} \quad q\,[\Pi(n^f) - w^f] + (1-q)\,[\Pi(n^s) - w^s]$$

$$\text{s.t.} \quad w^f - 5\, n^f \geq 0$$

$$w^s - 10\, n^s \geq 0 \qquad (\lambda)$$

$$w^f - 5\, n^f \geq w^s - 5\, n^s \qquad (\mu)$$

$$w^s - 10\, n^s \geq w^f - 10\, n^f \qquad (\gamma)$$

(as always, (λ) and (μ) imply that the first constraint holds). The Kuhn–Tucker conditions lead to: $\lambda = 1, \mu = q, \gamma = 0, \Pi'(n^f) = 5, \Pi'(n^s) = 10 - 5\,q/(1-q)$. This, in particular, implies that $n^f = n^{f*}$ and $n^s < n^{s*}$. On top of this, the wages will be such that the participation constraint for the slow translator and the incentive compatibility constraint for the fast translator both bind, (or, respectively, $\lambda > 0$ and $\mu > 0$).

Solution to Exercise 6. (*a*) The optimal contract (e^{B*}, w^{B*}) is characterized by:

$$u(w^{B*}) - v(e^{B*}) = \underline{U} \text{ and } \Pi'(e^{B*}) = \frac{v'(e^{B*})}{u'(w^{B*})}$$

and the contract (e^{G*}, w^{G*}) is given by:

$$u(w^{G*}) - v(e^{G*}) = \underline{U} \text{ and } k\Pi'(e^{G*}) = \frac{v'(e^{G*})}{u'(w^{G*})}.$$

(*b*) In Figure E1 it is easy to see that $e^{G*} > e^{B*}$, and that $w^{G*} > w^{B*}$. The principal demands greater effort of G, since he is the more productive agent, and he is compensated for the greater disutility of effort by a greater wage. Figure E2 shows another graphical representation of how the optimal contracts can be calculated. In this figure are drawn the principal's iso-profit curves that intersect with the curves that mark out the points at which the agent gets his reservation utility.

(*c*) If there is an asymmetric information problem in which the agent knows his type but the principal doesn't, the contracts ((e^{G*}, w^{G*}), (e^{B*}, w^{B*})) are still a good deal for the principal: since both contracts ensure that the agent receives exactly $\underline{U}$, the agent is indifferent between signing either of the two contracts, and we can safely assume that he will sign that contract designed for him.

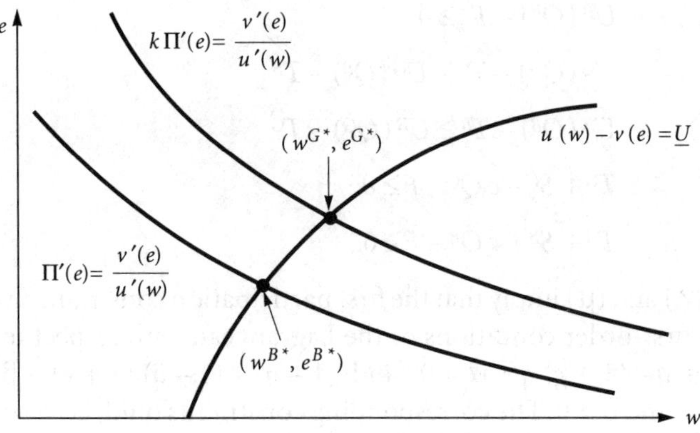

Fig. E1

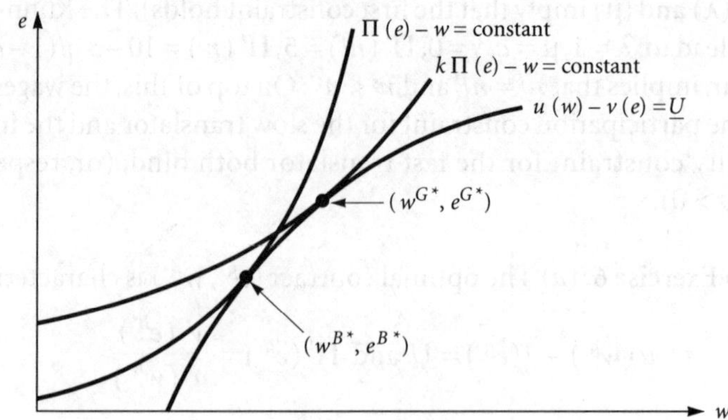

Fig. E2

Solution to Exercise 7.

(*a*)

$$\max_{(T,S,Q)} \{[U(Q) - T] + [T + S - cQ - F] - [(1+g)\,S]\}$$

$$\text{s.t.} \quad T + S - cQ - F \geq 0$$

$$U(Q) - T \geq 0.$$

From which $\lambda = \mu = g > 0$ and $U'(Q) = c$.

(*b*) The government will offer a contract menu $\{(T^G, S^G, Q^G), (T^B, S^B, Q^B)\}$ such that:

$$\text{Max } \{[q\,(U^G(Q^G) - T^G) + (1-q)\,(U^B(Q^B) - T^B)] + q\,(T^G + S^G - c\,Q^G - F) + (1-q)\,(T^B + S^B - c\,Q^B - F)] - (1+g)\,[q\,S^G + (1-q)\,S^B]\}$$

$$\text{s.t.} \quad U^G(Q^G) - T^G \geq 0$$

$$U^B(Q^B) - T^B \geq 0 \quad (\lambda)$$

$$U^G(Q^G) - T^G \geq U^G(Q^B) - T^B \quad (\mu)$$

$$U^B(Q^B) - T^B \geq U^B(Q^G) - T^G \quad (\gamma)$$

$$T^G + S^G - c\,Q^G - F \geq 0 \quad (\alpha)$$

$$T^B + S^B - c\,Q^B - F \geq 0. \quad (\beta)$$

Together, (λ) and (μ) imply that the first participation constraint always holds.

(*c*) The first-order conditions of the Lagrangean with respect to S^G and S^B are written: $q - (1+g)\,q + \alpha = 0$, and $(1-q) - (1-q)\,(1+g) + \beta = 0$, from which $\alpha > 0$ and $\beta > 0$. The corresponding constraints bind, i.e. $S^G = c\,Q^G + F - T^G$ and $S^B = c\,Q^B + F - T^B$ and the problem can now be rewritten as:

$$\max_{\{(T_G, Q_G), (T_B, Q_B)\}} \{[q(U^G(Q^G) - T^G) + (1-q)(U^B(Q^B) - T^B)]$$

$$- (1+g)[q(cQ^G + F - T^G) + (1-q)(cQ^B + F - T^B)]\}$$

$$\text{s.t.} \quad U^B(Q^B) - T^B \geq 0 \qquad (\lambda)$$

$$U^G(Q^G) - T^G \geq U^G(Q^B) - T^B \qquad (\mu)$$

$$U^B(Q^B) - T^B \geq U^B(Q^G) - T^G. \qquad (\gamma)$$

(*d*) From the first-order conditions of the above problem with respect to (T^G, T^B, Q^G, Q^B) and making use of the facts that $\lambda = g$, and $\mu = qg + \gamma$, we arrive at:

$$U^{G\prime}(Q^G) - c = -\gamma \frac{U^{G\prime}(Q^G) - U^{B\prime}(Q^G)}{q(1+g)} \leq 0$$

$$U^{B\prime}(Q^B) - c = (\gamma + qg)\frac{U^{G\prime}(Q^B) - U^{B\prime}(Q^B)}{(1-q)(1+g)} > 0.$$

The logic showing that $\gamma = 0$ is similar to that of application 3. If $\gamma > 0$, then the two incentive compatibility constraints bind: $U^G(Q^G) - T^G = U^G(Q^B) - T^B$ and $U^B(Q^B) - T^B = U^B(Q^G) - T^G$. This implies that $U^G(Q^G) - U^B(Q^G) = U^G(Q^B) - U^B(Q^B)$. Since the function $U^G(Q) - U^B(Q)$ strictly increases in Q, or $U^{G\prime}(Q) > U^{B\prime}(Q)$, the only way in which the equality can be satisfied is if $Q^G = Q^B$. Hence $U^{G\prime}(Q^G) - c > U^{B\prime}(Q^B) - c$ is impossible since $U^{G\prime}(Q^G) - c \leq 0$, and $U^{B\prime}(Q^B) - c > 0$. Therefore, $\gamma = 0$. The optimal contract satisfies:

$$U^{G\prime}(Q^G) - c = 0 \quad \text{and} \quad U^{B\prime}(Q^B) - c = qg\frac{U^{G\prime}(Q^B) - U^{B\prime}(Q^B)}{(1-q)(1+g)} > 0.$$

Solution to Exercise 8. (*a*) If he is safe, $EU_s(\rho, q) = 2/3 \ln(64 - \rho) + 1/3 \ln(1 + q - \rho)$. He will insure himself if $EU_s(\rho, q) \geq 2/3 \ln(64) + 1/3 \ln(1)$, that is, if $(64 - \rho)^{2/3}(1 + q - \rho)^{1/3} \geq 16$. If he is reckless, $EU_r(\rho, q) = 1/2 \ln(64 - \rho) + 1/2 \ln(1 + q - \rho)$ and he will insure himself if $EU_r(\rho, q) \geq 1/3 \ln(64) + 1/2 \ln(1)$, that is, if $(64 - \rho)^{1/2}(1 + q - \rho)^{1/2} \geq 8$.

(*b*) If the insurance company does not establish a contract, $\Pi = 0$. If the company insures, knowing that it is a safe driver, $\Pi_s(\rho, q) = \rho - 1/3\, q$, and if the company insures knowing that it is a reckless driver $\Pi_r(\rho, q) = \rho - 1/2\, q$. When the company insures without knowing the driver's type, expected profits are $E\Pi = \rho - (1/3\, t + 1/2\,(1 - t))\, q$.

(*c*) The symmetric information contract always has $q = 63$. Competition between insurance companies implies that profits will be zero, and so the premium that a safe driver must pay is $\rho_s = 21$, while a reckless driver's premium is $\rho_r = 63/2$.

(*d*) Because both will announce themselves to be safe in order to pay $\rho = 21$ instead of $\rho = 63/2$.

(*e*) $q_r = 63$ and $\rho_r = 63/2$. The equilibrium contract intended for safe drivers, (ρ_s, q_s), is determined by the zero profit condition and the condition that reckless drivers must not be interested in this contract when (ρ_r, q_r) is available. In other words, (ρ_s, q_s) must satisfy $\rho_s = 1/3\ q_s$ and $1/2 \ln(64 - \rho_s) + 1/2 \ln(1 + q_s - \rho_s) \geq \ln(64 - (63/2))$. The solution ρ_s to this system of equations is given by the positive root of the equation $8\rho_s^2 - 508\rho_s + 3969 = 0$ (ρ_s is approximately equal to 73/8), while $q_s = 3\rho_s$.

(*f*)* If $t = 2/3$, then the expected profits of a contract intended for both types of driver are $E\Pi = \rho - (7/18)\ q$. Consider a contract that completely insures the drivers and that gives zero profits to so long as both types of driver accept, i.e. $\rho = (7/18)\ q = 49/2$. A reckless driver prefers (ρ, q) to (ρ_r, q_r) since the coverage is the same while the premium is less, $49/2 < 63/2$. On the other hand, in order for a safe driver to also prefer (ρ, q) over (ρ_s, q_s), the following equation must be satisfied: $\ln(64 - 49/2) > 2/3 \ln(64 - \rho_s) + 1/3 \ln(1 + q_s - \rho_s)$. From the equation that defines ρ_s in (*e*) above, we have $\rho_s > 9$, and so $64 - \rho_s < 55$. Since $79^3/2^3 > (4225/4)\ 55$, it will always be true that a safe driver prefers (ρ, q) to (ρ_s, q_s). Since both types of driver strictly prefer the new contract, the menu $\{(\rho_s, q_s), (\rho_r, q_r)\}$ cannot be an equilibrium. A firm could always offer a pooling contract (with full insurance and a premium slightly greater than 49/2, that both types of driver are willing to pay) that will give strictly positive profits.

Solution to Exercise 9.

(*a*)

$$\max_{(e^G, w^G, e^B, w^B)} \{q(\theta^G + e^G - w^G) + (1-q)(\theta^B + e^B - w^B)\}$$

s.t.

$$w^G - v(e^G) \geq \underline{U}$$

$$w^B - v(e^B) \geq \underline{U} \qquad (\lambda)$$

$$w^G - v(e^G) \geq w^B - v(e^B + \theta^B - \theta^G) \qquad (\mu)$$

$$w^B - v(e^B) \geq w^G - v(e^G + \theta^G - \theta^B). \qquad (\gamma)$$

Equations (μ) and (λ) imply that the first constraint always holds.

(*b*) This is done using the first-order conditions with respect to w^G and w^B.

(*c*) When $\gamma > 0$ then given the form of the multipliers of the first-order conditions with respect to e^G and e^B, and since $v'(e^G + \theta^G - \theta^B) - v'(e^G) > 0$ and $v'(e^B) - v'(e^B + \theta^B - \theta^G) > 0$, it must be true that $v'(e^G) > 1$, while $v'(e^B) < 1$.

This implies that $e^G > e^B$. Also, since $\mu > 0$, if $\gamma > 0$ too, then equations (μ) and (γ) would both bind. Then $v(e^G + \theta^G - \theta^B) - v(e^G) = v(e^B) - v(e^B + \theta^B - \theta^G)$ and, for the reason explained in the complementary material, it would be true that $e^G + \theta^G - \theta^B = e^B$, which is incompatible with $e^G > e^B$.

(*d*) At the optimal contract, $\gamma = 0$ and $\mu > 0$. Efficient effort is chosen if θ^G: $v'(e^G) = 1$; inefficient effort is chosen if θ^B: $v'(e^B) < 1$; the agent gets reservation utility if θ^B ($\lambda > 0$); and he gets informational rent if θ^G: $w^G - v(e^G) = \underline{U} + [v(e^B) - v(e^B + \theta^B - \theta^G)]$.

Solution to Exercise 10. It is enough to check that the proposed contract satisfies the incentive compatibility constraints (μ) and (γ) and the participation constraint (λ) of the problem described in complementary material 2. Also, since the efforts are efficient and the agent is risk-neutral, he gets an expected utility exactly equal to his reservation utility. The contract is optimal (it satisfies (4.C1)–(4.C4) when the multipliers are $\lambda = 1, \mu = \gamma = 0$). There is no efficiency loss here because the agent being risk-neutral means that separating the wages to incite him to take the adequate decision does not introduce efficiency losses. Since acceptance is *ex ante*, the utility that is guaranteed to the agent in expected value is the same as under symmetric information.

Solution to Exercise 11. The reasoning is illogical. The more reckless is the driver, that is, the greater is the probability that he will have an accident, the less he likes franchise contracts. This means that if someone prefers a franchise contract, then it will be a rather safe client, and those clients with the greatest probability of accident will never pay a franchise, preferring to be fully insured. The argument here can be related to that established in application 1: in the equilibrium, the bad risks are fully insured, while the good risks get only partial coverage (they pay a franchise).

Solution to Exercise 12.

$$\max_{\{(e(k), w(k))\}} \int_K [\Pi(e(k)) - w(k)] f(k)\, dk$$

$$\text{s.t.} \quad u(w(k)) - k\, v(e(k)) \geq \underline{U} \qquad \text{for all } k \in K.$$

From the necessary first-order conditions we can deduce that $\Pi'(e^*(k)) = k\, v'(e^*(k))/u'(w(k))$. Hence under the hypothesis of risk-neutrality, $v'(e^*(k)) = \Pi'(e^*(k))/k$. This condition requires a type k agent's marginal cost of a unit of effort, $k\, v'(e^*(k))$, to be equal to his marginal revenue, $\Pi'(e^*(k))$.

Solution to Exercise 13.

$$\max_{(q^G, p^G, q^B, p^B)} \{\alpha\,[p^G - c\,(q^G)] + (1-\alpha)\,[p^B - c\,(q^B)]\}$$

$$\text{s.t.} \quad q^G k^G - p^G \geq 0$$

$$q^B k^B - p^B \geq 0 \qquad (\lambda)$$

$$q^G k^G - p^G \geq q^B k^G - p^B \qquad (\mu)$$

$$q^B k^B - p^B \geq q^G k^B - p^G \qquad (\gamma)$$

We get: $c'\,(q^G) \geq k^G$ and $c'\,(q^B) < k^B$. Since, by assumption, we have $k^G > k^B$ and $c''\,(q) > 0$, it must be true that $q^G > q^B$. It is easy to see that (γ) binds. The optimal contract is characterized by:

$$c'\,(q^G) = k^G \qquad p^G = q^G k^G - q^B\,(k^B - k^G),$$

$$c'\,(q^B) = k^B - \frac{\alpha}{1-\alpha}\,(k^G - k^B), \qquad p^B = q^B k^B.$$

Solution to Exercise 14. (*a*) This condition implies that the least cost agent also has lower marginal costs. Geometrically, any indifference curve of agent 1 will only cut an indifference curve of agent 2 once. It is a technical condition that eases the analysis. The proof that $e'' > e'$ implies $v_2\,(e'') - v_2\,(e') > v_1\,(e'') - v_1\,(e')$, is immediate since,

$$v_i\,(e'') - v_i\,(e') = \int_{e'}^{e''} v'_i\,(e)\,de.$$

(*b*)

$$\max_{(w_1, w_2)} \quad q\,(x_1 - w_1\,(x_1)\,) + (1-q)\ (x_2 - w_2\,(x_2)\,)$$

$$\text{s.t.} \quad w_i - v_i\,(e_i) = 0 \quad \text{and} \quad e_i = x_i \qquad \text{for } i = 1, 2.$$

The solution to this problem implies $v'_i\,(e^*_i) = 1$, for $i = 1, 2$, and $w_i = v_i\,(e_i)$. Consequently, $e^*_1 > e^*_2$ and we know nothing about the relationship between the wages (see Figure E3).

(*c*) 1 prefers the contract designed for 2, since under this contract he obtains an informational income of $w^*_2 - v_1\,(e^*_2)$.

(*d*) The principal should pay agent 1 the income that he would obtain by hiding himself, that is, $w^*_1 + w^*_2 - v_1\,(e^*_2)$ if he is to exert effort e^*_1. This strategy is not optimal from the principal's point of view. Agent 2's contract is agent 1's temptation, and reducing the effort demanded of the former can reduce the informational income of the latter. Reducing the effort demanded implies a second-order profit loss (since at e^*_2 the derivative of the principal's profit function with respect to agent 2's effort is zero). However, the reduction in agent 1's income is of first order.

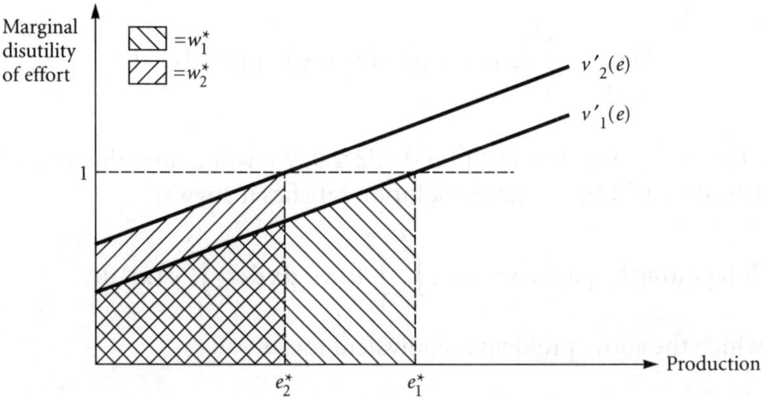

Fig. E3

(*e*) The solution to the principal's problem in which we should introduce the self-selection restriction leads to the fact that only the participation constraint of type 2 and the incentive constraint of the type 1 bind (this is possible thanks to the single-crossing condition). The solution is $w_1 = v_1(e_1) + w_2 - v_1(e_2)$ and $w_2 = v_2(e_2)$. The effort levels are such that $v'_1(e_1) = 1$, and $v_2(e_2) = 1 + (q/(1-q))\,(v'_1(e_2) - v'_2(e_2))$.

Solution to Exercise 15. (*a*)

$$\underset{(e,t)}{\text{Max}} \quad 2e - gt$$

$$\text{s.t.} \quad t - ce^2 \geq 0$$

whose solution is $e^*(c) = 1/gc$ and $t^*(c) = 1/g^2 c$.

(*b*)

$$\underset{\{e(c),\,t(c)\}}{\text{Max}} \quad \int_1^2 [2e(c) - g\,t(c)]\,\mathrm{d}c$$

$$\text{s.t.} \quad t(c) - c\,e(c)^2 \geq 0 \qquad \text{for all } c \in [1,2]$$

$$t(c) - c\,e(c)^2 \geq t(c') - c\,e(c')^2 \qquad \text{for all } c, c' \in [1,2]$$

The only important participation constraint is that corresponding to the least efficient firm, and this constraint will bind, that is, $t(2) = 2\,e(2)^2$. As equation (4.14) shows, the transfer that the government must make to the firm in order that it implement a given decontamination policy $\{e(c)\}$ is:

$$t(c) = c\,e(c)^2 + \int_c^2 e(x)\,\mathrm{d}x,$$

where the integral measures the informational income. The problem can be rewritten as:

$$\underset{\{e(c)\}}{\text{Max}} \int_1^2 \left(2\, e(c) - g\, c\, e(c)^2 - g \int_c^2 e(x)^2\, dx\right) dc$$

under the monotonicity condition $de/dc \leq 0$. We will ignore this restriction and instead we will show that the solution satisfies it anyway.

(*c*) Integrating by parts, we have: $\int_1^2 \int_c^2 e(x)^2\, dx\, dc = \int_1^2 e(x)^2\, dc,$

from which the above problem is equivalent to:

$$\underset{\{e(c)\}}{\text{Max}} \int_1^2 [2\, e(c) - g(2\, c - 1)\, e(c)^2]\, dc.$$

From the first order condition we get $e(c) = 1/g(2\, c - 1)$ and the transfer is:

$$t(c) = \frac{c}{g^2(2c-1)^2} + \int_c^2 \frac{1}{g^2(2\, x - 1)^2}\, dx = \frac{c}{g^2(2\, c - 1)^2} + \frac{1}{2\, g^2(2\, c - 1)} - \frac{1}{6\, g^2}.$$

(*d*) In this case the government must solve the following problem:

$$\underset{\{e(c)\}}{\text{Max}} \int_1^{c^o} [2\, e(c) - g(2\, c - 1)\, e(c)^2]\, dc$$

whose solution is:

$$e(c) = \frac{1}{g(2\, c - 1)} \quad \text{and} \quad t(c) = \frac{c}{g^2(2\, c - 1)^2} + \frac{1}{2\, g^2(2\, c - 1)} - \frac{1}{2\, g^2(2\, c^O - 1)}.$$

When the government subsidizes up to c^O, social welfare is:

$$B(c^O) = \int_1^{c^o} \left(\frac{2}{g(2\, c - 1)} - \frac{c}{g(2\, c - 1)^2} - \frac{1}{2\, g(2\, c - 1)} + \frac{1}{2\, g(2\, c^O - 1)}\right) dc.$$

The derivative of the function $B(c^O)$ is negative, and so the optimum is at $c^O = 2$.

Solution to Exercise 16. Contracts $\{(e^G, w^G), (e^B, w^B)\}$ constitute a self-selecting menu of contracts. In this case, the asymmetry of information has no effect on the contracts offered.

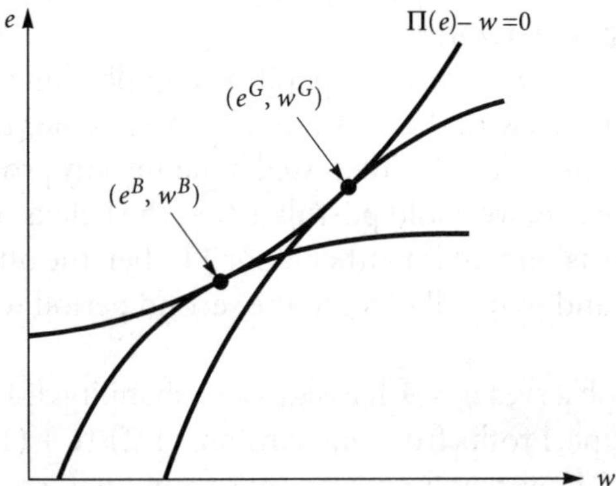

Fig. E4

Chapter 5

Solution to Exercise 1. (*a*) The level of education does not influence the agent's productivity. Therefore, the optimal symmetric information education level is zero.

(*b*) If he is type *G*, the worker will choose e^o if $2 - e^o/2 > 1$, that is, if $e^o < 2$. In the same way, if his productivity is k^B, the worker will strictly prefer $e = e^o$ to $e = 0$ if $e^o < 1$.

(*c*) $e^o \in [1, 2]$.

(*d*) If $e^o \in [1, 2]$, then the good-productivity workers are interested in choosing this education level, given the wage structure offered, while the bad quality workers prefer $e = 0$. Hence the firm's beliefs are coherent with the worker's choices.

(*e*) The argument follows exactly as that developed in the chapter.

Solution to Exercise 2. (*a*) A monopoly with marginal costs of *c* produces $q = (18 - c)/2$ and gets profits of $\Pi = (18 - c)^2/4$, hence $q_1^{Gm} = 9$, $q_1^{Bm} = 6$, $\Pi_1^{Gm} = 81$ and $\Pi_1^{Bm} = 36$. On the other hand, a duopoly firm with marginal cost *c* and with a rival whose marginal cost is c' will decide to produce $q = (18 - 2c + c')/3$ and will obtain profits (without taking into account the potential fixed cost) of $\Pi = (18 - 2c + c')^2/9$. Hence $q_1^{Gd} = 7$, $q_1^{Bd} = 3$, $q_2^{Gd} = 4$, $q_2^{Bd} = 6$, $\Pi_1^{Gd} = 49$, $\Pi_1^{Bd} = 9$, $\Pi_2^{Gd} = 16$ and $\Pi_2^{Bd} = 36$. The entrant covers the fixed entry costs of 20 only when the costs of firm 1 are high (when it is type *B*). Hence it will only enter if this is the case.

(*b*) In a separating equilibrium in which the decisions of each type of firm are q_1^{Gm} and q_1^{Bm}, if the firm is type *B* and produces the quantity q_1^{Bm}, then its profits are $\Pi_1^{Bm} + \Pi_1^{Bd} = 45$, while if it produces q_1^{Gm} then its profits are (18 – 9

$-6)\,9+36=63$. Hence the decisions (q_1^{Gm}, q_1^{Bm}) do not form a separating equilibrium, as both types prefer q_1^{Gm}.

(*c*) $(q_1^G = 12, q_1^B = 6)$ does form a separating equilibrium since each type of firm earns greater profits with the decision that corresponds to its own type. In order that neither type of firm be interested in taking any production decision different from these two, we could postulate that the beliefs of firm 2 are such that, observing a decision that is neither 6 nor 11, then the other firm is type B with probability 1, and so it will enter in the second period whatever the decision.

(*d*) No. If firm 2 observes $q_1 = 9$, it assigns a probability of 1/2 to the fact that firm 1 is of either type. Profits from entering are $(1/2)\,16 + (1/2)\,36 = 26 > 20$, and so it will enter. However, knowing that firm 2 will enter if first period production is 9, a type-B firm 1 would prefer to produce its optimal level of $q_1 = 6$.

(*e*) Yes, because firm 2 will decide not to enter if $q_1 = 9$ is observed, since its expected profits are $(9/10)\,16 + (1/10)\,36 = 18 < 20$, and a type-$B$ firm 1 would prefer to produce 9 in the first period and then be a monopolist in the second, to producing 6 in the first period and then having firm 2 enter.

Solution to Exercise 3. Advertising can be a signal of the quality of a consumer product that is bought repeatedly, in the same way as a low initial price can signal quality (application 1). The greater is the quality of Lemonade, the greater will be its profits once it has got the potential customers to try the drink. Call Π^G (Π^B) the present value of the profits obtained if the quality is good (bad), with $\Pi^G > \Pi^B$. Assume that the consumers are not interested in trying the drink unless they think that it is of good quality, and they observe advertising spending to the amount of $G \geq \Pi^B$. What will they think? Of course that the quality is good, since Lemonade would never spend G in order to obtain profits of Π^B. Therefore, (apparently useless) advertising spending can signal in this case the product's quality. Note that since the cost of the signal is the same for both types of drink, in order for this to work as a signal, we require that one type earns more than the other after having sent it. Therefore, the above logic is valid for products that are consumed regularly, but is not valid for products that are consumed only once.

Solution to Exercise 4. (*a*) The woman who was not the mother should not have said that she agreed to cut the child in half. She gained nothing with half of the child, and she clearly signaled that she was the false mother.

(*b*) Because all the women who go to court would declare that they would rather the other have the child instead of having it cut in two. No one has an incentive to declare otherwise.

Solution to Exercise 5. (*a*) $T(q) = a + b\,q$ represents the retailer's cost. If he decides to produce, the optimal production decision will be: $q = (D - b)/2, p = (D + b)/2, \Pi = (D - b)^2/4 - a$.

(*b*)
$$\underset{(a,b)}{\text{Max}} \quad \{a + (b - c)\,\frac{D - b}{2}\}$$
$$\text{s.t} \quad \frac{(D - b)^2}{4} - a \geq 0.$$

The solution is $b = c$ and $a = (D - c)^2/4$.

(*c*) The optimal symmetric information contracts are: $b^{G*} = c$, $a^{G*} = (D^G - c)^2/4$, $b^{B*} = c$ and $a^{B*} = (D^B - c)^2/4$. Since $b^{B*} = b^{G*}$ and $a^{B*} < a^{G*}$, the manufacturer is interested in making the retailer believe that demand is high, whether this is true or not.

(*d*) Offer a contract that would never be offered if demand were low.

(*e*) The incentive constraints are written:

$$a^G + (b^G - c)\,\frac{D^G - b^G}{2} \geq a^B + (b^B - c)\,\frac{D^G - b^B}{2}$$
$$a^B + (b^B - c)\,\frac{D^B - b^B}{2} \geq a^G + (b^G - c)\,\frac{D^B - b^G}{2}.$$

If we add these two equations together and then simplify, we get $(b^G - b^B)\,(D^G - D^B) \geq 0$. Since $D^G - D^B > 0$, it must be true that $b^G - b^B \geq 0$. On top of this, in order that the contract (a^G, b^G) is not always preferred to (a^B, b^B), it must be that $a^G \leq a^B$. The variable pay-off must be greater when demand is high, in exchange for a lower fixed pay-off.

(*f*) The intuition is the same as that set out in result 5.6 or in application 2 of this chapter. First, in a separating equilibrium the retailer believes that if he receives an offer of (a^B, b^B), it is because the demand is bad. Secondly, any other contract that the retailer accepts believing that the demand is low gives the manufacturer profits lower than those associated with (a^{B*}, b^{B*}), since this is his best contract. Finally, the retailer accepts (a^{B*}, b^{B*}) independent of his beliefs.

(*g*)* The method is similar to the analysis of result 5.6 or of application 3. The contract (a^G, b^G) is the solution to the problem:

$$\underset{(a,b)}{\text{Max}} \quad \{a + (b - c)\,\frac{D^G - b}{2}\}$$
$$\text{s.t.} \quad \frac{(D^G - b)^2}{4} - a \geq 0$$
$$a^{B*} + (b^{B*} - c)\,\frac{D^B - b^{B*}}{2} \geq a + (b - c)\,\frac{D^B - b}{2}.$$

In order to see this, we must show that the Lagrange multipliers of both constraints are strictly positive (and hence the solution must satisfy the constraints with strict equality). If only the first constraint were active, the contract would be $(a^G, b^G) = (a^{G*}, b^{G*})$, which we already know does not satisfy the second constraint, and so is not possible. If only the second constraint were active, it is easy to see that it would be optimal to pay a unitary amount b, as high as was needed, which also cannot solve the problem. Hence both constraints must bind at the optimal contract.

Since the contract (a^G, b^G) solves the above problem, we know: (i) the manufacturer prefers (a^{B*}, b^{B*}) to (a^G, b^G) if demand is low; (ii) the manufacturer prefers (a^G, b^G) to (a^{B*}, b^{B*}) if demand is high ((a^{B*}, b^{B*}) satisfies the constraints of the above problem, and so the optimum must be better, or at least it is never worse); (iii) a retailer accepts (a^{B*}, b^{B*}) if demand is low; and (iv) a retailer accepts (a^G, b^G) if demand is high. Hence $\{(a^G, b^G), (a^{B*}, b^{B*})\}$ is a separating equilibrium.

Any pair of contracts that satisfy the above conditions (i)–(iv) is a separating equilibrium. However, only (a^G, b^G), that maximizes the profits of a manufacturer who knows that demand is high, satisfies the intuitive criterion. When will this manufacturer offer another contract that guarantees him lower profits? Only when the retailer is not willing to accept the first contract. But this only happens when the retailer is not sure that the person offering the contract really knows that demand is high. Such beliefs do not satisfy the intuitive criterion since the manufacturer is only interested in offering the contract when demand really is high.

Solution to Exercise 6. In order to hold the Olympic Games, interested cities need heavy political and economic backing, both from their own local institutions and from the national government and citizens etc. All potential host cities announce that they have this backing when they present their candidature. A clear signal that this is true is precisely the investment of resources before being elected as host city, spending that would be useless, or at least inefficient, should the city not be chosen, since this is direct proof that the required backing has been found even before being chosen to host the games. Therefore, investing before being nominated as official host increases the probability that a given city is finally chosen (there are other political and sporting factors that influence the decision of the International Olympic Committee, and so we can only speak of 'the probability of being chosen').

Solution to Exercise 7. (*a*) After floating the new shares, the value of the firm is 280. In order that the new shareholders recover exactly the value of their investment, they must own 5/14 of the firm. The value of the shares of the old shareholders goes from 160 to 180.

(*b*) $\beta^B = 1/2$. $\beta^B > \beta^G$ since the relative value of 100 is greater if the firm is worth B than if it is worth G. The value of the shares of the old shareholders is 100.

(*c*) $[1 - (1/2)]\ 280 = 140$.

(*d*) Independently of whether the firm is worth 160 or 80, the managers are interested in offering the smallest possible fraction, that is β^G. The potential investors, given the uncertainty, have no interest in investing.

(*e*) In order to see that it is an equilibrium, we must make clear what are the beliefs of the potential new shareholders when a given fraction, β, of the shares of the company are offered in the market in exchange for an investment of 100. Assume that the investors believed that if the company decided to invest then it is worth only 80. These beliefs are Bayesian, since in the equilibrium only type-B firms invest. Under these beliefs, the potential new shareholders only invest in the firm if the fraction of shares that is obtained is at least β^B. Given this behaviour, the best strategy of a type-B firm is to invest in exchange for a fraction β^B of the shares. On the other hand, a firm that is worth 160 will prefer not to invest, since its worth after the investment will be 140, less than its current value. We should point out that the firm cannot offer a fraction β^G in exchange for the investment, since the investors will believe that it is a firm that is only worth 80, and so will not invest. (Besides, we cannot rule these beliefs out using the intuitive criterion, since the both the low-valued firms and the high-valued ones are interested in offering a fraction β^G in exchange for the investment.)

Solution to Exercise 8. (*a*) The optimal contract fully insures the buyer: $g = b_1 - b_2$, and the price demanded of the consumer is the highest that he is willing to pay: $p = b_1 - u^{-1}(u(0))$.

(*b*) Since the optimal symmetric information contract does not depend on q, it will continue to be optimal under asymmetric information. No signal needs to be sent.

Solution to Exercise 9. (*a*) The optimal contract never includes a guarantee, $g = 0$. The price that the buyer is willing to pay for the product depends on his valuation: $p^G = b_1 - q^G(b_1 - b_2)$ and $p^B = b_1 - q^B(b_1 - b_2)$.

(*b*) They are not adequate since both types of seller want to set a price of p^G. But the buyer is only willing to pay p^G if he is sure to get a good quality product.

(*c*) A guarantee $g > 0$ could be offered, since this guarantee is more costly to the seller of a product when the probability of breakage is high.

(*d*) The expected utility of a seller with breakage probability q is:

$$\mathrm{E}U(p, g) = q\,B(p - g) + (1 - q)\,B(p).$$

Differentiating, we get that in order for EU to remain constant:

$$[q\,B'(p-g)+(1-q)\,B'(p)]\,\mathrm{d}p - q\,B'(p-g)\,\mathrm{d}g = 0,$$

that is,

$$\left.\frac{\mathrm{d}p}{\mathrm{d}g}\right|_{EU=\text{ constant}} = \frac{q\,B'(p-g)}{q\,B'(p-g)+(1-q)\,B'(p)}$$

$$= \frac{1}{1+\dfrac{(1-q)}{q}\dfrac{B'(p)}{B'(p-g)}}.$$

Since $q^G < q^B$, it is easy to show that

$$\left.\frac{\mathrm{d}p}{\mathrm{d}g}\right|_{EU^B=\text{ constant}} > \left.\frac{\mathrm{d}p}{\mathrm{d}g}\right|_{EU^G=\text{ constant}},$$

from which a seller of low quality should increase his price more than a seller of high quality in order to compensate a greater guarantee. Hence we find a separating equilibrium in that the seller with breakage probability q^B sells using his efficient contract: $g^B = 0$ and $p^B = b_1 - q^B(b_1 - b_2)$ (this is a characteristic of separating equilibria: the type of principal which no one is interested in passing himself of as, offers the same contract as under symmetric information). On the other hand, the contract offered by the seller with breakage probability q^G includes $g^G > 0$. He will set the highest price such that the other type of seller is not interested in changing his own contract (that is, that it is an effective signal of a good-quality product) and that the buyer is interested in accepting (knowing that he is receiving good quality).

Solution to Exercise 10.

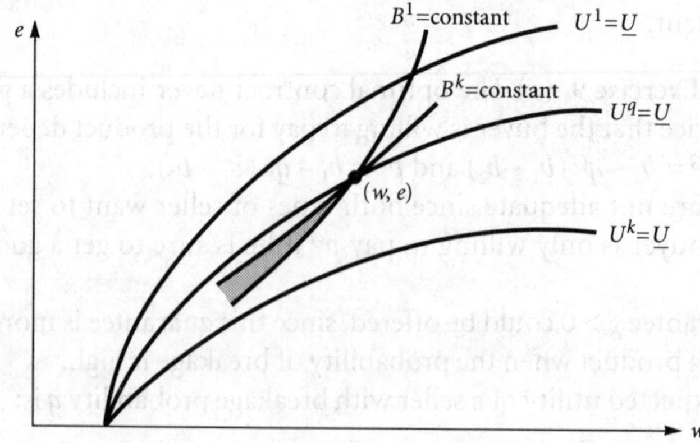

Fig. E5

We argue that the contract (w, e) cannot constitute a pooling equilibrium satisfying the intuitive criterion. The contracts in the shadow area are preferred by a type-1 principal to (w, e), while they give less profits to a type-k principal. Any contract in the shadow region can only 'intuitively' come from a type-1 principal. Therefore, if the agent sees a contract in this area (i.e., if he sees a deviation from the pooling equilibrium), he 'must' (according to the intuitive criterion) assign probability 1 to the fact that the deviating principal is of type 1. But under this belief he is ready to accept the contract, as it lies above his $\underline{U}$-indifference curve. Hence (w, e) is not an equilibrium satisfying the intuitive criterion since there is a profitable deviation to it.

INDEX

Index

ADDITIONAL EXERCISES

Exercise for Chapter 1

Exercise 1. Classify the situations presented in the following table as moral hazard (with hidden action), moral hazard (with hidden information), adverse selection, or a signalling problem. If you consider that some of the situations can be classified under more than one category argue why.

	Principal	Agent	Situation
1.	insurance company	policy holder	health precautions
2.	shareholders	managers	investment decisions
3.	insurance company	policy holder	care to avoid accidents
4.	society	criminal	refraining from crime
5.	bank	firm	firm project risk
6.	landlord	tenant	farming effort
7.	government	regulated firm	efficiency of the firm
8.	central bank	bank	safety of loans
9.	government	public project	cost of the project
10.	seller	buyer	quality / warranty
11.	employer	worker	skill / education
12.	investor	stock-issuer	stock value / percentage retained
13.	auctioneer	potential buyers	value of the item
14.	tax authority	taxpayer	true income
15.	insurance company	policy holder	health status
16.	licensor	licensee	quality of the technology
17.	individual	contractor	cost and quality of a house

Exercises for Chapter 3

Exercise 1. Comment on the incentive content of the wage systems of executives in the following figure (*The Economist*, 16 November 1996), where the fixed payment is the base wage they receive and the variable compensation, which includes bonus payments and shares in the company, is related with the management performance (at least in theory).

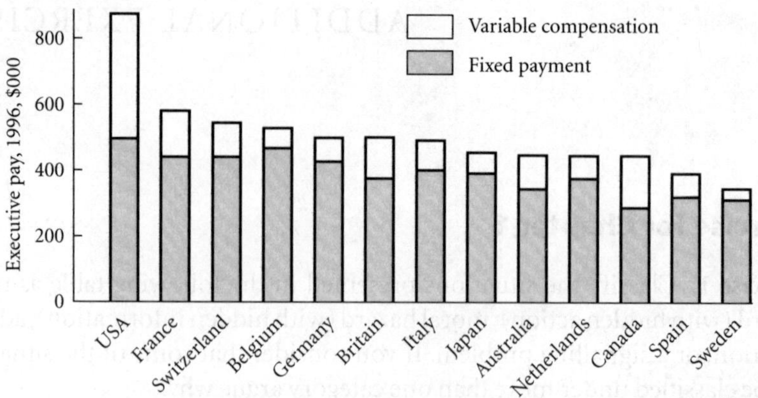

Exercise 2. Consider the moral hazard model in which effort can only take two levels (High or Low) and with a finite number of states of the world where the agent is a tenant and the principal a landlord. Assume the landlord observes two signals: (1) the outcome x_i, and (2) another variable, the weather, that can take two values, good weather (G) and bad weather (B). Let $p_i^{H,G}$ represent the probability that outcome x_i occurs if the tenant chooses the High level of effort and the weather is good and define $p_i^{H,B}$, $p_i^{L,G}$ and $p_i^{L,B}$ similarly. Under what condition on the probabilities $p_i^{m,n}$ (for $m = H, L$ and $n = G, B$) does the landlord use the weather in the contract, that is, under what condition is $w_{i,G}$ different from $w_{i,B}$?

Exercise 3. Many insurance contracts include a deductible clause, under which the client must pay the first part of any claim up to a pre-established deductible, and the insurance company only pays claims in excess of the deductible. A similar clause, often used in health policies, is a co-insurance clause such that the insurer only pays a fraction of the loss.

(*a*) Discuss the economic function of these types of clauses.

(*b*) It has been argued that deductible clauses can lead the insured firms to withhold information about defective products. Take the example of a car manufacturer that discovers that its cars have a defective part that will cause very bad accidents to a fraction of them. The car manufacturer can repair the cars at a cost that is below its deductible, so the car manufacturer will fully pay this cost should the cars be repaired. It can also not repair the cars and face some big payments in law suits, but the insurer will pay everything except the deductible. The fact that the car manufacturer has deductible insurance coverage can make it more prone to choose the second option. Do you agree with the argument? Do you think that replacing deductibles by co-payments can help to cope with this problem?

Exercise 4. Consider the two-effort-level moral hazard model with n states of the world. The probability that each state occurs is strictly positive for the two possible effort levels: $p^H_i > 0$ and $p^L_i > 0$ for $i = 1, \ldots, n$. Assume an infinitely risk averse agent, that is, $U(x_1, \ldots, x_n) = \text{Min}_{i=1,\ldots,n}\{x_i\}$. Can the principal induce the highest effort? Why? Interpret.

Exercise 5. Comment upon the depicted incentive system designed to avoid over-parking (called 'the automatic Court of Law for parking infringements').

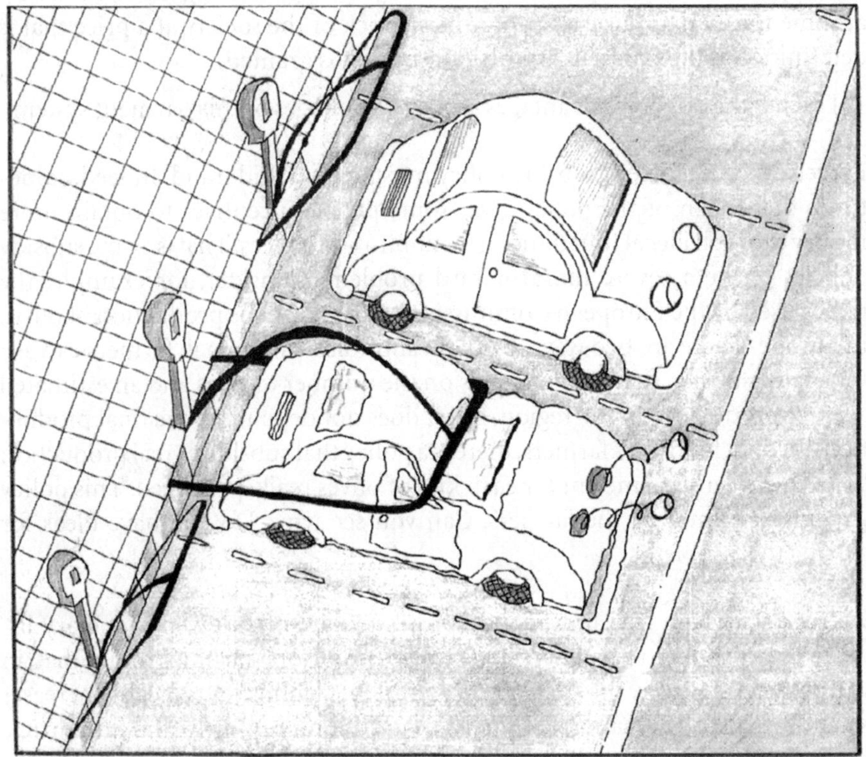

Exercise 6. Discuss the following situations with care:

(*a*) In Japan, doctors not only prescribe pharmaceuticals but they also sell them to their patients, thereby obtaining an important part of their income. Comment on the advantages and disadvantages of this arrangement.

(*b*) A medical centre is searching for measures that will reduce the waiting list for surgical operations. Currently the situation is the following: the doctors only work in the mornings and they operate strictly according to the waiting list. In return, they earn a constant wage. A proposal to reduce the waiting list has been initialized, and involves adding the following possibility to the normal morning session. Those doctors that so desire may also operate in the afternoons, and they may choose the patients they operate on. The doctors are paid a fixed amount for each operation performed in the afternoons. Comment on the advantages and disadvantages of this incentive system. Will it reduce the waiting list?

Exercise 7. One of the most popular ways to pay firm managers is through stock options. A stock option consists in the manager having the right to buy, at some future date, a certain amount of stock of the society at a price that is determined at the moment at which the option is granted.

Discuss the possible advantages and disadvantages of this payment system.

Exercise 8. An efficient subsidy policy must try to avoid fraud. Indeed, sometimes the design of the policy gives some people incentives to obtain more money through illegal (but difficult to monitor) practices. That is, some subsidy policies create a severe moral hazard problem. Consider, for example, the policy used by the European Commission to subsidize the production of olives in Europe. There are two ways to obtain subsidies. First, small farmers can ask for a fixed subsidy that only depends on the number of trees and an estimated average production in the region, but it does not depend on the final production. Second, for bigger farmers, there is a policy that subsidizes real production by paying a certain amount for each kilo of olives really produced. This policy gave rise to fraud by the farmers. Can you see why? Do you have ideas for solving this problem?

Exercise 9. In modern universities, professors are often given monetary incentives to produce research. A study of US professors' earnings found that, in the physical sciences, the first article a professor publishes typically increases salary by 6.0%. Thereafter, the increases accrue more slowly: the fifth article results on average in 1.3% more pay and the fiftieth in 0.5%.

(*a*) Discuss the role of monetary incentives in the research made by the professors.

(*b*) Discuss the reasons that you think can induce the payment scheme to give bonuses that decrease with the number of published articles.

Exercise 10. R. Crusoe and Friday live on an island and share the tasks in order to exploit the advantages of specialization. R. Crusoe is in charge of fishing and Friday of collecting coconuts.

(*a*) If instead of each consuming his own production, they share all production equally, will the total fishing and coconut collection increase or decrease? (or on what variables will the answer depend?)

(*b*) Find a model that represents the situation and that allows you to illustrate that in some cases (and paradoxically), it can be optimal from an efficiency point of view not to exploit the advantages of specialization.

Exercise 11. Corruption in government is a common problem in many countries. It is a serious problem because corruption can deter investment and retard growth. According to some studies, it appears that there is less corruption in countries where public servants are paid relatively well compared with other workers. Do you have some explanation for this finding?

Exercises for Chapter 4

Exercise 1. A company offers the only flight service between two cities. The cost per passenger is 400. Assume that the airline's potential clients can be divided into two groups: executives who travel for business reasons, and tourists who travel for vacations. For this particular service, if the meeting that an executive wants to attend takes place, then he is willing to pay a price of 1,000. On the other hand, tourists are willing to pay 600 for the same trip.

(*a*) What price will the airline charge if it can perfectly observe whether an individual is an executive or a tourist? What are the profits of the airline in this case?

Now assume that the airline cannot distinguish between tourists and executives.

(*b*) What price (or prices) will the company charge for a ticket? What are the profits of the airline now?

Assume that tourists are perfectly informed as to when they have their vacations, and the probability that they must cancel their trip is zero. On the other hand, executives believe that there is a 50% chance that their meeting will be cancelled or will be changed to another date. Assume now that the company can fix not only the price of the ticket but also the refund conditions when a ticket is cancelled.

(*c*) What contracts (or tickets) will the airline offer? Discuss.

Exercise 2. Jon Moynihan (*The Economist*, 28 August 1998), the executive chairman of PA Consulting, a management and technology consultancy firm based in Britain, cited the result of a survey that PA conducted of 400 large British firms that claimed that the firms that did worst were those that relied less on variable pay (that is, pay related to performance) and more on high fixed salaries. According to Moynihan, the main reason is that fixed salaries attract 'mediocrity disguised as talent'. In other words, more money attracts the best people only if it depends on performance.

Do you agree with the argument? Discuss it.

Exercise 3. Everybody likes red Corvettes (testimony to this is the famous song by Prince 'My Little Red Corvette'). Assume that there exist two types of potential Corvette purchasers. On one hand, 'snobs' are willing to pay 25,000 for a red Corvette but only 20,000 for a Corvette of another colour. On the other hand, 'less snobbish' purchasers are willing to pay 22,000 for a red Corvette and 20,000 if it is any other colour. The percentage of 'snob' purchasers is α, so that $(1 - \alpha)$% of purchasers are 'less snobbish'. The production cost of a Corvette is independent of its colour. Why are Corvettes of all colours seen on the streets? What parameters does your answer depend on?

Exercise 4. Genesis, the insurance company of the Bank of Santander and Metropolitan Life, uses a comic strip as an advertisement. In the strip, Charlie Brown asks Snoopy: 'Why is it that Genesis only accepts good drivers?' To which Snoopy answers: 'So that you don't pay for those who are not.' The advertisement is explicitly aimed at 'good' drivers, defined as being less than 30 years old, having at least ten years of driving experience (with a licence), and currently having a no-claims bonus.

Comment on this strategy and on the dialogue in the comic.

Exercise 5. The Spanish Consumers' Organization OCU has carried out some experiments to check the behaviour of repair technicians. The experiment that we describe here was published in *OCU-Compra Maestra* in October 1997. They went to 55 different technicians, some official and others not official, in several cities, in order for them to repair a video that had been damaged by a specialized laboratory and then they checked the repair work. The video was damaged in a very simple way; it was a mechanical rather than an electronic fault, that was simple to detect and that could be easily corrected. Specifically, the belt that moves the video tape was broken. All parts of the video were marked with a paint that was only visible under a special light in order to check if they had really been replaced or not. The only part that required replacing was the damaged belt. The amount of time required for the repair was estimated at 45 minutes.

The number of hours that were charged ranged from 45 minutes to two-and-a-half hours. As far as the replacement parts were concerned:

25 technicians did not return any old parts (almost all of them had 'thrown the old parts out'), in spite of the fact that some technicians charged for the replacement of (non-existent) parts.

15 technicians returned the damaged belt (and of these, 3 charged for other parts that they had replaced but had 'thrown away')

12 technicians returned, and charged for, parts that they said they had changed (when they had not), apart from the belt.

3 technicians said that they had not replaced any parts.

Of the parts that were returned (except for the belts), none were from the same model of video that was used for the experiment, and in some cases they were not even from a video. The average price charged for parts that were said to have been replaced but were not by the 28 technicians who did this was 4,195 pesetas, higher even than the cost of repairing the video.

Comment on this experiment.

Exercise 6. The relationship between the tax enforcement agency and taxpayers can be understood as an adverse selection problem. Each taxpayer holds private information concerning his true income over a given period, and the tax authority only observes the declaration, unless the taxpayer is audited. Some models that study the optimal audit policy conclude that low-income declarations should be more frequently audited than high-income declarations. This type of policy is often criticized as being a strategy that punishes, above all, low-income taxpayers. Discuss the rationality of this audit strategy.

Exercise 7. In short, the 'Peter principle' states that a worker should be promoted to the level at which his inefficiency is maximized. Can you find an argument that rationalizes this principle? (It may be necessary to bear in mind different elements of asymmetric information.)

Exercise 8. 'Cost-overrun contracts' are the most frequently used contracts for the realization of public works in many countries or for the development of specific projects, like NASA programs (if you have curiosity about the types of contract used by NASA, you can have a look at www.hq.nasa.gov/office/procurement). Under a cost-overrun contract, the government first pays a fixed price and then covers any cost overruns (i.e. the extra-contractual costs). Two different types of contracts are 'fixed-priced contracts', that involve only a fixed payment independent of the final cost, and 'cost-sharing contracts', which are an intermediate form since the government only pays a fraction of the cost overruns.

Discuss the advantages and disadvantages of the different contract forms. Think about the different informational problems that can arise in the relationship between the government and the contract and the type of contract that is better suited to deal with each problem.

Exercises for Chapter 5

Exercise 1. During a particular campaign, some German travel agencies offered 'sun insurance' on trips to the 'Costa Blanca' in Spain. These policies promised that a set percentage, x, of the amount paid would be returned if it rained more than y litres per square metre during the trip. Discuss the interest of this type of strategy, and why they are used for this type of trip only (what is the traveller searching for in these cases?) rather than for other trips (for example, to Scotland).

Exercise 2. In France, students must choose two foreign languages. The majority choose to study English as the first of the two. The choice of the second language is more varied, with the greatest demand being for German and Spanish. Although German is more difficult for a native French speaker to learn than is another Latin-based language, and in spite of the greater utility of Spanish as a means of communication, the best students choose German.

Can you think of a reason to explain this behaviour? Can you think of examples of other subjects that produce a similar phenomenon in your country?

Exercise 3. Discuss the following situation. An individual who wants to purchase a car goes to the outlet of the brand XX. The car salesman gives him information on the characteristics and performance features of several models. The potential buyer inquires about the average quality of the cars of brand XX, and he is told that the cars are all made of top quality materials. In fact, the brand only offers a guarantee on parts of one year, since, contrary to other brands, there is no need to guarantee the parts for any longer as they never break down.

Exercise 4. Discuss the following quotation: 'I have yet to find a swindler with a ragged coat. You only need to read the police reports to note that nineteen out of twenty cases begin with "Elegantly dressed youth . . ." . . .' (*Handbook of Swindling*, cited in Paul Keers (1989), *The Wardrobe of the Perfect Gentleman*).

Exercise 5. In an advertisement for GEVALIA coffee that appeared in some magazines in the USA, you can read: 'You will try this coffee because of the coffee maker that you will be given, but you will continue to purchase it because of the coffee.' The company in question sends a coffee maker (automatic for ten cups of coffee, with a choice of colour) free of charge to whoever wants to try GEVALIA coffee by purchasing two packets of 250 g. Comment.

Exercise 6. Bill Gates, president of Microsoft, says that he prefers to hire people who have made mistakes at some point of time: 'People who make mistakes are people who take risks, and these are the people who push firms forward.'

(*a*) Comment.

(*b*) Relate this to the problem of moral hazard. In particular, discuss whether the payment that must be offered to an agent to give him the correct incentives must always be increasing in accordance with the result obtained or not.

Exercise 7. Comment on the following episode:

In the *Chronicle of the Conquest of Granada*, Washington Irving described the following episode that took place during the long Christian siege of Baza, an important castle in Andalucia, Spain. At some point, Mohamed ben Hacén continued to give encouragement to his colleagues with the hope that the Christian army would soon abandon the siege. However, one day he heard shouts of jubilation from the Christian camp. When the soldiers came closer, they noticed a magnificently garbed royal dame, who they soon discovered to be Queen Isabel, the powerful queen of the Christian kingdom of Castilla and León. When old Mohamed was convinced that indeed it was Queen Isabel in person, who had come to the camp to establish her residence there, his heart did not fool him, and turning his head sadly to his captains he said, 'Sirs, the destiny of Baza has been decided!'.

Exercise 8. Managers act as devoted advocates of their companies. They try to convince the financial markets that their company is a good buy by providing information (typically, backward-looking financial measures) that reflect the 'good health' of the company. On the other hand, investors would also want managers to be specific about their firms' future prospects and obtain some non-financial information to help them complete the picture. However, managers are reluctant to disclose detailed information about future projects or strategy both because this information can help competitors and because making their goals public exposes the managers to more scrutiny.

Discuss the previous situation as a signalling situation and try to obtain conclusions about the level of disclosure of information by firms.